D0742501

Issues in the
Economics
of Aging

A National Bureau
of Economic Research
Project Report

Issues in the Economics of Aging

Edited by   David A. Wise

The University of Chicago Press

Chicago and London

DAVID A. WISE is the John F. Stambaugh Professor of Political
Economy at the John F. Kennedy School of Government, Harvard
University.

The University of Chicago Press, Chicago 60637
The University of Chicago Press, Ltd., London

© 1990 by the National Bureau of Economic Research
All rights reserved. Published 1990
Printed in the United States of America
99 98 97 96 95 94 93 92 91 90   5 4 3 2 1

Library of Congress Cataloging-in-Publication Data

Issues in the economics of aging / edited by David A. Wise.
     p.   cm. — (A National Bureau of Economic Research project
report)
  Includes bibliographical references.
  Includes index.
  ISBN 0-226-90297-8
  1. Old age—Economic aspects—United States—Congresses.
  2. Retirement—Economic aspects—United States—Congresses.
  3. Aged—Housing—United States—Congresses. I. Wise, David A.
  II. Series.
HQ1064.U5I89   1990
305.26—dc20   90-11035
                                               CIP

Relation of the Directors to the
Work and Publications of the
National Bureau of Economic Research

1. The object of the National Bureau of Economic Research is to ascertain and to present to the public important economic facts and their interpretation in a scientific and impartial manner. The Board of Directors is charged with the responsibility of ensuring that the work of the National Bureau is carried on in strict conformity with this object.

2. The President of the National Bureau shall submit to the Board of Directors, or to its Executive Committee, for their formal adoption all specific proposals for research to be instituted.

3. No research report shall be published by the National Bureau until the President has sent each member of the Board a notice that a manuscript is recommended for publication and that in the President's opinion it is suitable for publication in accordance with the principles of the National Bureau. Such notification will include an abstract or summary of the manuscript's content and a response form for use by those Directors who desire a copy of the manuscript for review. Each manuscript shall contain a summary drawing attention to the nature and treatment of the problem studied, the character of the data and their utilization in the report, and the main conclusions reached.

4. For each manuscript so submitted, a special committee of the Directors (including Directors Emeriti) shall be appointed by majority agreement of the President and Vice Presidents (or by the Executive Committee in case of inability to decide on the part of the President and Vice Presidents), consisting of three Directors selected as nearly as may be one from each general division of the Board. The names of the special manuscript committee shall be stated to each Director when notice of the proposed publication is submitted to him. It shall be the duty of each member of the special manuscript committee to read the manuscript. If each member of the manuscript committee signifies his approval within thirty days of the transmittal of the manuscript, the report may be published. If at the end of that period any member of the manuscript committee withholds his approval, the President shall then notify each member of the Board, requesting approval or disapproval of publication, and thirty days additional shall be granted for this purpose. The manuscript shall then not be published unless at least a majority of the entire Board who shall have voted on the proposal within the time fixed for the receipt of votes shall have approved.

5. No manuscript may be published, though approved by each member of the special manuscript committee, until forty-five days have elapsed from the transmittal of the report in manuscript form. The interval is allowed for the receipt of any memorandum of dissent or reservation, together with a brief statement of his reasons, that any member may wish to express; and such memorandum of dissent or reservation shall be published with the manuscript if he so desires. Publication does not, however, imply that each member of the Board has read the manuscript, or that either members of the Board in general or the special committee have passed on its validity in every detail.

6. Publications of the National Bureau issued for informational purposes concerning the work of the Bureau and its staff, or issued to inform the public of activities of Bureau staff, and volumes issued as a result of various conferences involving the National Bureau shall contain a specific disclaimer noting that such publication has not passed through the normal review procedures required in this resolution. The Executive Committee of the Board is charged with review of all such publications from time to time to ensure that they do not take on the character of formal research reports of the National Bureau, requiring formal Board approval.

7. Unless otherwise determined by the Board or exempted by the terms of paragraph 6, a copy of this resolution shall be printed in each National Bureau publication.

(Resolution adopted October 25, 1926, as revised through September 30, 1974)

Contents

Acknowledgments

This volume consists of papers presented at a conference held at the Boulders Resort in Carefree, Arizona, May 19–21, 1988. It is part of the National Bureau of Economic Research ongoing Project on the Economics of Aging. The majority of the work reported here was sponsored by the United States Department of Health and Human Services, National Institute on Aging Grant Numbers P01-AG05842 and R37-AG08146. Additional support was provided by the National Science Foundation, the Robert Wood Johnson Foundation, the Social Security Administration, and the Veteran's Administration.

Any opinions expressed in this volume are those of the respective authors and do not necessarily reflect the views of the National Bureau of Economic Research or any of the sponsoring organizations.

Overview

This volume contains papers presented at a National Bureau of Economic Research Conference on the Economics of Aging, in Carefree, Arizona, in May 1988. The conference was the second in a series of conferences associated with the NBER's ongoing Project on the Economics of Aging. The first conference was held in New Orleans in March 1987. The papers presented at that conference are contained in a volume entitled *The Economics of Aging* (Wise 1989). The goal of the Economics of Aging Project is to further our understanding of the consequences for older people and for the population at large of an aging population. The papers in this volume are divided into two broad categories: (1) housing and living arrangements and (2) labor market behavior and retirement.

Housing and Living Arrangements

The majority of the wealth of most older people is in the form of housing equity. This housing wealth is a potential source of support during retirement. It is claimed that many older people would choose to decrease their housing wealth to finance current consumption expenditures, were it not for the large transaction costs associated with moving. Indeed, the rationale for a market in reverse annuity mortgages has been that older people would like to withdraw wealth from housing without moving and without incurring the large transaction costs of moving. "But They Don't Want to Reduce Housing Equity," Steven Venti and David Wise conclude. Venti and Wise address two related questions: (1) Would the typical elderly family like to withdraw wealth from housing? (2) Do the transaction costs of moving constrain adjustments in the housing wealth of older people as they age?

In answer to the first question, the authors conclude that, were all elderly homeowners to choose their most preferred levels of housing wealth, given their existing financial and other circumstances, there would be little change in housing wealth on average. Although some elderly would make substantial changes in housing equity were they to choose new housing, some would choose to add to housing wealth and others to reduce it. On balance, were all elderly to move and choose optimal levels of housing equity, the amount of housing equity would be increased slightly. Thus, the results reinforce the earlier findings of Venti and Wise, and those of Feinstein and McFadden, both studies found in *The Economics of Aging*. Most elderly are not liquidity constrained. And, contrary to standard formulations of the life-cycle hypothesis, the typical elderly family has no desire to reduce housing equity. This is true even among families with low total wealth, for whom housing equity is a large fraction of total wealth. The desired reduction of housing equity is largest among families with low income and high housing wealth. Even in this case, however, the desired reductions are rather small and are more than offset by the desired increases of other families, especially those with high income and low housing wealth.

In answer to the second question, the authors conclude that the transaction costs of moving, including the psychic costs of changing neighborhoods and losing contact with old friends and the like, are very large. Because of these large transaction costs, the gain in utility from reallocating wealth from housing equity to more liquid financial assets has to be large in order to justify moving. The gain from moving, however, is very small for most older people. These results help explain the low rates of housing mobility. Based on the data in the Retirement History Survey, approximately 8 percent of homeowners move during a two-year period. Mobility rates increase to about 15 percent at the time of precipitating shocks like a change in marital status or retirement. The reluctance of most older people to move is reflected in the large transaction costs associated with moving.

The evidence of high moving transaction costs suggests that some families may be prevented from moving, even though they would like to reduce their housing equity. It is for these families that reverse annuity mortgages would apparently be most beneficial. Limited demand, though, may explain the absence of an active market for such financial instruments—most older people do not want to reduce their housing equity. Even families who overcome the moving transaction costs to move from one house to another are as likely to increase as to decrease the money that they tie up in housing. Moreover, the potential gain from reallocating wealth (either increasing or decreasing housing equity) is very small for most older people.

The paper by Chunrong Ai, Jonathan Feinstein, Daniel McFadden, and Henry Pollakowski, "The Dynamics of Housing Demand by the Elderly: User Cost Effects," is the second in a series of papers on the economic environment in which older people must make housing decisions, on the housing choices that they make, and on the consequences of these choices. The paper in this volume concentrates on the construction of a comprehensive measure of housing price and on the user costs of housing for older people.

The user cost of housing described in the paper includes several components. Because of the high transaction costs of moving (once a housing decision is made), the authors argue that housing choices should be based on an inclusive measure of housing cost that includes both the current costs and the expected future costs of any given housing choice. Thus, the first component of the authors' user cost is the expected present value of the future stream of out-of-pocket costs that will be incurred as long as the current dwelling is occupied. For renters, the out-of-pocket costs include only rent and utilities. For homeowners, out-of-pocket costs include mortgage payments, real estate taxes, utilities, maintenance, and insurance. The deductibility of home mortgage interest offsets a part of these direct costs. The second component of user cost is the transaction costs associated with moves, purchases, or sales. The third component of user cost applies only to homeowners and reflects the capital gains on the housing asset. The typically increasing market value of a home (the capital gain) offsets the direct cost of home ownership and thus lowers the net user cost of housing.

The approach taken in the paper is to calculate an annualized expected present value of user cost, taking account of all these factors, in a fashion that mimics the calculations of a representative household. A particularly novel component of the authors' calculations is a "Ricardian equivalence" assumption. To incorporate the value of bequests, it is assumed that a unit of consumption by descendants in the future has the same marginal utility for the nonsurviving household (who leaves the bequest) as it does for the surviving descendants (who receive the bequest).

The primary conclusion of this paper is that carefully constructed user costs for housing, which adjust for income tax offsets and capital gains, show *declining* annualized housing costs after age 60. While the income of older people declines even more rapidly, so that the housing share of consumption expenditures rises with age, this increase is not dramatic. The ratio of housing costs to income appears to level off for the very elderly. The authors also find that the user costs of housing increase sharply with dwelling size. The user cost of owner housing generally exceeds that of rental housing for middle-aged and elderly households. The persistence of ownership in the face of this differential suggests the presence of substantial quality differences in owned and rental housing, the authors conclude. They find little evidence in the relatively small Panel Study of Income Dynamics (PSID) data set that, at the margin, households are modifying choices to avoid relatively high-priced housing. The findings of Ai et al. are consistent with the finding of Venti and Wise that the typical elderly family does not want to reduce housing consumption as it ages.

Axel Börsch-Supan presents "A Dynamic Analysis of Household Dissolution and Living Arrangement Transitions by Elderly Americans," using data from the PSID. The stability of living arrangements over time is the most striking finding. Transitions to an institution or to the home of children are atypical. Even after the death of a spouse or the onset of disability or during the last five years before death, few older people change their living arrangements. While living arrangement transitions are infrequent overall, they are most common after the loss of a spouse. Almost all transitions take place in the same year as the spouse's death. Börsch-Supan also finds that older men are more likely to live in institutions or shared living arrangements and that nonwhite elderly are more likely than white elderly to live with family members or in other shared living arrangements.

Although living in an institution is inferior to other living arrangements from the point of view of most older people, the likelihood of institutionalization rose substantially between 1968 and 1984. During the same period, the likelihood of being "taken in" by relatives or friends fell dramatically. The author concludes, "this disturbing tendency toward isolation of the elderly— particularly pronounced among the very old, who are also the most vulnerable—is the most important message of this paper." The author suggests that the growing isolation of older people will affect the cost of health care and social support programs, which are largely assumed by a declining younger population. According to Börsch-Supan, if public policy stands any chance of improving the well-being of the elderly, the appropriate time for policy intervention is after the death of a spouse, when living arrangement transitions are most common.

In "The American Way of Aging: An Event History Analysis," David Ellwood and Thomas Kane also present a dynamic analysis of transitions in marital status, health and functional ability, living arrangements, and income. Like the Börsch-Supan analysis, their analysis is based on data in the PSID. The methodologies used in the two papers are different, however.

According to Ellwood and Kane, even though only 4 percent of the population aged 75–79 and 12 percent of the population aged 80 and over lived in institutions in 1980, a much larger percentage of older people enter institutions at some time during their lives. Their simulation analysis indicates that 12 percent of men and 38 percent of women will enter an institution at some time after age 65. Income was shown to be an important factor in both institutionalization and mortality. People with low incomes at age 65 lived four years fewer, on average, than people with high incomes and were much more likely to develop functional disabilities. People with low incomes were also much more likely to be in nursing homes or to be dependent on others in a shared living arrangement by age 80.

Comparing the previous characteristics of men who eventually entered institutions with the previous characteristics of men who did not enter institutions, the authors find no significant difference in previous functional ability but a substantial difference in previous income level. The men who eventually entered institutions were disproportionately from low-income backgrounds. By contrast, women who eventually entered institutions were virtually indistinguishable from women who did not. The authors argue that these findings result from differential mortality. Disabled men are more likely to enter institutions, but disabled men also die more quickly, which decreases the likelihood of entering an institution. Similarly, lower-income women are more likely to enter an institution, but they also die more quickly, which again decreases the likelihood of entering an institution.

Ellwood and Kane find that men and women entering institutions come from different prior living arrangements. Over one-third of the men who entered institutions were previously dependent on others in shared living arrangements. Only 18 percent of women entering institutions came from a shared living arrangement. Women who entered nursing homes were more likely to have been living independently and more likely to have been widows for some period of time. In addition, the authors find that unmarried women who were poor at age 80 were often relatively poor at age 65 as well. Over half of poor unmarried women at age 80 were not married at age 65. Widowhood led to a 20 percent drop in the standard of living of women, but widowers experienced only a 10 percent drop in their standard of living.

Perhaps no single statistic raises more concern about postwar changes in the U.S. family than the proportion of older people living alone. Since 1940, the proportion of unmarried noninstitutionalized older people living alone has risen from less than 25 percent to over 60 percent. For people over age 85, the proportion has increased from 13 percent to 57 percent. The proportion of those over 85 living in institutions has also increased dramatically. Since 1940, those proportion of people over age 85 living in institutions has increased from 7 percent to almost 25 percent. Part of the reason that older people are less likely to live with their children is simply that they have fewer children. In 1940, for each person age 80 and over, there were four people between ages 60 and 65; in 1985, for each person age 80 and over, there were fewer than two people between ages 60 and 65; and, when the baby boom population is in its 80s, there will be only one person between ages 60 and 65 for each baby boomer.

While age demographics appear to explain some of the living arrangement changes occurring over time, many believe that the rising income of older people is also an important factor. Laurence Kotlikoff and John Morris point out, however, that the analyses underlying this view have not considered the incomes and preferences of the children of older people. In "Why Don't the Elderly Live with their Children? A New Look," Kotlikoff and Morris present a model of the joint living arrangement choice of parents and children. They then use a new data set to analyze how the preferences and income levels of older people and their children influence living arrangement decisions. Their findings suggest that the preferences and income levels of children may be important factors in explaining why so many older people live alone. The analysis is based on new data collected through the 1986 Hebrew Rehabilitation Center for the Aged (HRCA) Elderly Survey and the 1986 HRC-NBER Child Survey.

The estimates reported by Kotlikoff and Morris suggest that many of the characteristics of adult children, such as income and marital status, are as important as parent characteristics in explaining living arrangement decisions. Their findings also indicate substantial differences in living arrangement preferences between elderly parents and their adult children. Almost half the parents appear to prefer shared living arrangements with their children. Only a quarter of the adult children appear to prefer shared living arrangements with their parents. This analysis suggests that a large number of elderly parents live alone, even though they would prefer to live with their children. The authors conclude that the intrinsic preferences of parent and child for shared living rather than the relative or absolute incomes of the two are most important in determining the probability of shared living. They also conclude that income differences are not as important as may previously have been thought in explaining living arrangements.

Alan Garber and Thomas MaCurdy concentrate on the determinants of "Predicting Nursing Home Utilization among the High-Risk Elderly." Their analysis is motivated by the needs of private insurers (particularly those developing and marketing private long-term care insurance products) and others for adequate information about expected future nursing home utilization. They consider the probability of nursing home admission, expected number of annual nursing home days, the distribution of lengths of stay in nursing homes, and how the aspects of utilization vary with other personal characteristics. They also explore some of the possible effects of moral hazard and adverse selection on future utilization. The analysis is based on data from the National Long Term Care Demonstration (Channeling), which has a sample population determined to have a high risk of nursing home utilization.

Garber and MaCurdy find that the factors that influence nursing home admissions are largely distinct from those that are generally expected to influence health and mortality. For example, functional limitations have very little effect on mortality but a very large effect on nursing home entry. Similarly, the factors that are associated with increased duration of nursing home stay are not necessarily the factors that indicate a strong risk of admission. The probability of nursing home entry is higher for nonhomeowners, people without living children, whites, Medicaid participants, older people, and functionally or mentally impaired people. Income does not appear to have a major independent association with nursing home entry. The probability of leaving a nursing home (shortening the duration of stay) is higher for married people and people with living children, confirming the important role of families in providing informal long-term care services. Homeownership and Medicaid coverage do not seem to matter once an individual is in a nursing home.

The authors point out that numerous previous studies have documented the association between socioeconomic factors and health status. The most important socioeconomic factors have been education and, to a lesser extent, income, wealth, occupation, and race. The authors found no evidence that these factors are closely tied to nursing home utilization, with two exceptions. Advanced education was associated with longer nursing home stays, and non-white race was associated with a lower probability of nursing home admission.

There were some differences in nursing home utilization between men and women. At any age, a woman is more likely to enter a nursing home than a comparable man. If she enters a nursing home, she will also tend to stay longer than her male counterpart. The authors emphasize, however, that elderly women are not comparable to elderly men. Women are more likely to be unmarried (because they usually live longer than their spouses) and to have functional impairment, so their nursing home utilization tends to be even higher, relative to men, than the authors' results suggest.

To show the effect of Medicaid coverage on nursing home utilization, the authors simulate the distribution of nursing home use for a very high risk individual—a severely impaired, unmarried 65-year-old male who does not own his home. Without Medicaid coverage, this person has a 54 percent probability of entering a nursing home by age 70 and will stay in the nursing home for an average of thirty-three weeks. An identically described person with Medicaid coverage has more than a 70 percent probability of entering a nursing home and will stay for an average of forty-six weeks. The same influence of Medicaid can be seen for women and for less-impaired persons with better social and economic supports. The authors find that, in every age category, both the likelihood of admission and the duration of stay in a nursing home are longer for men who have Medicaid coverage.

According to Garber and MaCurdy, forecasting future nursing home utilization involves distinguishing between the factors influencing survival and the factors influencing nursing home use. Disabled and sickly older people may not be the heaviest utilizers of nursing homes because they die early. In forecasting future nursing home utilization, life-prolonging technology might increase survival but have no effect on age-adjusted disability from chronic illness. As a result, life-prolonging technology could increase nursing home utilization dramatically. The different influence of dementia and functional impairment on survival and nursing home use is another example. Neither dementia nor functional impairment increase mortality (at least in this population), but both increase the likelihood of nursing home admission and the duration of stay in a nursing home. Both dementia and functional impairment are likely to be more common in the future as long as old-age survival continues to improve. Because there are no effective preventive measures or treatments for the most common causes of dementia or for most functional impairments, life-prolonging health interventions are likely to increase the demand for nursing home care.

Labor Market Behavior and Retirement

The labor force participation rates of older workers have declined dramatically in recent years. In 1971, for example, 74.1 percent of men aged 60–64 were in the labor force; in 1986, only 54.9 percent were in the labor force. A great deal of analysis has emphasized the role of Social Security provisions in encouraging earlier retirement. Particular attention has been directed to the large increases in Social Security benefits in the early 1970s. Largely ignored have been firm pension plans, which were introduced rapidly beginning in the late 1940s and 1950s and now cover about 50 percent of employees. About 75 percent of covered employees have defined benefit plans, under which the employer promises to pay the worker a specified retirement income. The amount of retirement income is typically determined by the final salary of the worker and the number of years of firm employment.

Previous work has demonstrated that defined benefit pension plans typically have substantial incentives for early retirement. The typical firm plan provides a very large reward for remaining with the firm until some age, often the early retirement age, and then a substantial inducement to leave the firm, often as early as age 55. Almost all plans incorporate a large penalty for working past age 65. The gain in wage earnings for working an additional year is often offset in large part by a loss in the present value of future pension benefits.

In "The Pension Inducement to Retire: An Option Value Analysis," James Stock and David Wise attempt to quantify the effects of pension plan provisions on departure rates from the firm and, in particular, to demonstrate the effect of potential changes in plan provisions. The analysis is based on the personnel records of a large *Fortune* 500 firm and applies the "option value" model described in the authors' earlier work. Comparing actual retirement rates with those predicted by the model, Stock and Wise have found that the model predicts very complicated retirement patterns with considerable precision.

A particularly important component of the analysis is to compare the effects of changes in Social Security provisions with changes in firm pension plan provisions. They find that the provisions of the firm's pension plan have a much greater effect than Social Security regulations on the retirement decisions of the firm's employees. Increasing the firm's early retirement age from 55 to 60, for example, would reduce by almost 40 percent, from .48 to .30, the fraction of employees that choose to retire by age 60. The effect of changes in Social Security rules, on the other hand, would be comparatively small. By raising the Social Security retirement ages by one year, for example, the proportion of workers retired by age 62 would decrease by only about 4 percent.

Stock and Wise suggest that changes in Social Security provisions that would otherwise encourage workers to continue working can easily be offset by countervailing changes in the provisions of the firm's pension plan. Firm responses, like delaying the Social Security offset to correspond to a later

Social Security retirement age, may simply be a logical revision of current firm plan provisions. The authors conclude that, in considering the effect of changes in Social Security rules, like the retirement age, it is important to understand the implications of private pension plan provisions. In particular, to predict the effect on retirement decisions of changes in Social Security rules accurately, the potential response of firms to the changes cannot be ignored.

Although their analysis is based on the retirement experience in a single large firm, Stock and Wise emphasize that the firm's pension plan is typical of defined benefit plans. Approximately 75 percent of the employees who are covered by a firm pension have defined benefit plans. Thus, the results suggest that pension plans in general have had a very substantial effect on the labor force participation rates of older workers.

Although the retirement behavior of men has been studied extensively, much less attention has been given to the retirement behavior of women and very little to the retirement behavior of couples. Studies of the labor supply decisions of couples typically find that the wife's labor supply is influenced by the husband's wage rate or by the husband's income. In "The Joint Retirement Decision of Husbands and Wives," Michael Hurd investigates the relation between the retirement decisions of husbands and wives.

Hurd's analysis, based on the New Beneficiary Survey, has two goals: (1) to study the correlation between the retirement dates of husbands and wives and (2) to determine whether observable economic variables contribute to any correlation in retirement dates. Hurd concludes that husbands and wives do indeed tend to retire at approximately the same time. For example, in a "male workers" sample, 6.1 percent of couples retired in the same month, 9.4 percent within one month of each other, 11 percent within two months of each other, and 24.6 percent in the same year.

A large fraction of the economic research on aging and retirement is motivated by—although possibly not constrained by—the assumption that individuals form rational and deliberate long-range plans. Implicit in these assumptions is the notion that individuals develop well-informed opinions about the economic factors that will affect their well-being in the future. But, in fact, very little is actually known about the manner in which individuals incorporate new information in arriving at expectations about future events. In "How Do the Elderly Form Expectations? An Analysis of Responses to New Information," Douglas Bernheim examines the evolution of self-reported expectations about Social Security benefits during the preretirement period and examines the effect of new information on these expectations. In particular, Bernheim considers whether changes, or "revisions," in expectations are "rational," in the sense that they closely resemble the effects of new information on actual measures of expected benefits.

This paper is the third in a series of papers by Bernheim on the accuracy and development of expectations. In a subsequent paper, he plans to study the relation between the self-reported expectations of individuals and the decisions of these individuals. Like the previous two papers, the analysis in this paper is based on data from the Retirement History Survey. Bernheim estimates how expectations change with new information and considers whether these changes in expectations are rational. He concludes that responses to new information during the period immediately preceding retirement appear to be highly rational. According to Bernheim, the data support the view that individuals form accurate assessments of the ultimate effect of new information on actual benefits.

Bernheim points out that these results contrast sharply with findings based on analyses of expected benefit levels, rather than changes in expected benefits. In prior work, Bernheim concluded that individuals did not make complete use of available information, especially current statutory Social Security benefit entitlements. Nevertheless, Bernheim finds that these same individuals are very good at using new information that they obtain just before retirement. Although people appear incompletely informed about the level of Social Security benefits associated with actual benefit formulas, they revise their benefit expectations as if they understand how new information affects the benefits prescribed by these formulas at the margin. The results suggest that individuals formulate expectations about the retirement period much more carefully as retirement approaches, substantiating the speculative conclusions made by Bernheim in earlier studies.

Firms are likely to adapt their behavior in response to the aging of the population. In "Adjusting to an Aging Labor Force," Edward Lazear speculates about how the demographic changes will affect labor force policies in the coming decades. Lazear begins his analysis by considering some of the labor force changes that might be expected. According to Lazear, the composition of the labor force is likely to include a larger proportion of older workers and a larger proportion of female workers. Aging will not be as pronounced for males as for females because the trend toward early retirement among males will offset the demographic changes. The size of the labor force will grow until about 2015 and then will decline. Given these predicted changes in the labor force, Lazear then explores how these changes might affect firm behavior.

Several of Lazear's conclusions are based on the assumption that older workers tend to be paid more than their marginal product. Since employing older workers then causes a firm deficit (defined as the difference between sales and labor costs), an aging labor force may mean an increase in the size of the firm deficit. Under these circumstances, Lazear argues, firms may do well to invest in assets that are highly correlated with the future uncertain nominal wage bill liability. An aging work force might also increase the desire of the firm to encourage retirement among its older workers. Lazear suggests that implicit buyouts, through strategically designed pension formulas, may be the most desirable way to reduce the size of the older work force. Because defined benefit pension plans offer implicit buyout features that are absent in defined contribution plans, firms may have a tendency to shift to defined benefit plans in the future. Lazear also speculates that an aging labor force is likely to affect firm productivity, but he acknowledges that the direction of the change is not clear.

John Rust's paper "Behavior of Male Workers at the End of the Life Cycle: An Empirical Analysis of States and Controls" is the second of a series of three papers on the retirement behavior of men. The first paper, "A Dynamic Programming Model of Retirement Behavior," presented a theoretical model based on the hypothesis that workers maximize expected discounted lifetime utility. The current paper explains how data from the Retirement History Survey were used to construct variables that will be used to implement the theoretical model. The third paper will use the constructed variables together with the theoretical model described in the first paper to estimate the unknown parameters and utility function that govern retirement behavior.

The success of the final stage depends critically on accurate measurement of the variables and on correct specification of workers' beliefs about the future. In the current paper, Rust discusses conceptual problems in measuring the variables in a way that closely approximates the theoretical underpinnings of his dynamic model. He presents solutions to the measurement problems and conducts an extensive comparative data analysis to assess the overall quality of the resulting variables.

This paper reports several interim findings. Although other authors have placed considerable emphasis on work after retirement, Rust finds that postretirement work is atypical. The typical male worker stays at a full-time job up until retirement (at age 62–65, e.g.), at which time he applies for Social Security and remains out of the labor force for the rest of his life. Rust finds that part-time work arrangements are also atypical. The distribution of total annual hours worked is highly bimodal, with most of its mass at either zero or two thousand, suggesting that workers do not treat annual hours of work as a continuous decision variable.

Rust finds that the distribution of real wealth changes is centered about zero, but with a large variance. On average, net worth is very small, about four times annual income, and 50–60 percent of this wealth is tied up in housing. These facts, he concludes, strongly support the view that the large swings in measured consumption implied by the changes in measured wealth are simply the result of response errors in measured wealth rather than erratic consumption-saving behavior. Thus, he concludes that implementation of his theoretical model will assume that workers choose labor force participation strategies to maximize the expected discounted value of future income, ignoring wealth and bequests and the theoretical possibility of smoothing consumption by borrowing and saving. Total income will be a good measure of actual annual consumption.

1   But They Don't Want to
Reduce Housing Equity

Steven F. Venti and David A. Wise

The majority of the wealth of most elderly people is in the form of housing equity. This housing wealth, it is claimed, is a potential source of support for the elderly as they age. It is further claimed that many elderly would choose to transfer wealth from housing to finance current consumption expenditure, were it not for the large transaction costs associated with changes in housing equity. In the past, it has typically been necessary for such families to move to withdraw wealth from housing. Indeed, the rationale for a market in reverse annuity mortgages has been that the elderly would like to withdraw wealth from housing were it possible to do so without incurring the large transaction costs associated with moving. This paper considers whether these claims are correct. Two related questions are addressed:

- Given the predetermined financial and other circumstances of families as they approach retirement ages, would the typical elderly family like to withdraw wealth from housing?
- Are the transaction costs of moving large, and do they constrain adjustments in the housing wealth of the elderly as they age?

The paper provides a clear answer to the first question. Were all elderly to choose optimal housing equity, given their existing circumstances, there would be little change in housing wealth on average. In particular, the typical elderly family would not choose to reduce housing equity. The answer to the second question is less evident. Assuming that the elderly could gain from a

Steven F. Venti is associate professor of economics at Dartmouth College and a research associate of the National Bureau of Economic Research. David A. Wise is John F. Stambaugh Professor of Political Economy at the John F. Kennedy School of Government, Harvard University, and a research associate of the National Bureau of Economic Research.

The authors wish to thank Alan Auerbach for his comments as the discussant, some of which are now incorporated in the paper. Financial support for this research was provided by National Institute on Aging grant P01-AG05842.

reallocation of wealth between housing equity and other assets, the relative gain, in these terms, necessary to justify moving is typically very large. Our evidence suggests a strong preference for remaining in existing housing as the elderly grow older. On the other hand, that the housing equity of the elderly is not typically reduced as they age is not explained by the high transaction costs of moving. The elderly like it that way.

In a predecessor to this paper (Venti and Wise 1989), we considered the change in housing equity when the elderly move. The primary conclusion of that analysis was that the elderly who move were about as likely to increase as to decrease housing equity. But families with low income relative to housing wealth were more likely to move and to reduce housing equity when they did. The latter finding raises the possibility that transaction costs constrained the choices of some elderly who otherwise would have chosen to transfer wealth out of housing.[1]

The current paper is a more formal treatment of moving and the choice of housing equity; the two are considered jointly. The method is analogous to the approach set forth in Venti and Wise (1984) and used to analyze the housing choices of low-income renters. The current paper considers the allocation of bequeathable wealth between housing and other assets, conditional on their predetermined levels and on the income and other circumstances of the elderly as they age. There are two key features of the model: one is that an elderly family moves if the gain from changing housing outweighs the transaction costs of moving. Transaction costs are understood to include, and are likely to be dominated by, the psychic costs associated with leaving friends, familiar surroundings, and the like. The other is that the housing equity chosen after a move represents the optimal level of housing equity, given current circumstances. Based on the second assumption, the model is used to simulate the changes in housing equity that the elderly would choose to make, were they to overcome the transaction costs of moving and choose optimal levels of housing equity. The analysis is based on the Retirement History Survey (RHS). Families are followed over the six RHS surveys, conducted every two years between 1969 and 1979.

The model is described in the first section. Parameter estimates are discussed in the second section and the results of simulations reported in the third. The fourth section contains concluding remarks.

1.1   The Model

The goal of the analysis is to estimate the housing equity that the elderly would prefer. With this goal in mind, we consider the allocation of bequeathable wealth between housing and other assets, conditional on current income and other circumstances. Suppose that the value of housing equity versus other wealth can be captured by the simple function

(1) $$V = H^\beta (W - H)^{1-\beta},$$

where H is housing equity, W is total bequeathable wealth, and β is a preference parameter depending on income and other individual characteristics. Then preferred housing equity is

(2) $$H = \beta W.$$

In fact, the precise functional form of (2), described below, was chosen to fit housing equity choices. Equation (1) was then chosen to be consistent with these empirically observable outcomes.[2] It essentially serves to compare existing housing equity with the preferred level and as a device to assure consistent treatment of moving and housing equity choices.

The family moves between two survey periods if

(3) $$\frac{V_*}{V_0 \cdot M} > 1,$$

where V_* is the value of the optimal allocation of wealth, V_0 is the value of the allocation at the beginning of the period, and M indicates the preference for current housing, presumably with a value greater than one. It reflects the transaction costs that must be overcome if the family is to move. If the gain from moving is G, the family will move if

(4) $$G = \ln V_* - \ln V_0 - \ln M > 0.$$

The transaction costs parameter M reflects everything that gives an advantage to current housing, after controlling for the equity value of housing and the wealth allocation that it represents.[3] For example, the value function in equation (1) could have been written with an additional multiplicative term E^α, where E represents attributes that accompany housing, in addition to its equity value. Then $\Delta \ln V$ would include a term $\alpha(\ln E_* - \ln E_0)$, which would be part of what $\ln M$ is presumed to capture.

Transaction costs M are parameterized as

(5) $$\ln M = m_0 + m(X) + e,$$

where m_0 is a constant term, $m(X)$ is a function of individual characteristics like change in marital status or retirement, and e is a random term. The random term is assumed to have the variance components form

(6) $$e_{it} = \lambda_i + \epsilon_{it}, \quad \mathrm{var}(\lambda) = \sigma_\lambda^2, \mathrm{var}(\epsilon) = \sigma_\epsilon^2 ,$$

where λ_i reflects variation among individuals in resistance to or preference for moving. It is clear that families could move for many reasons other than to change housing equity and that the value of the house to the family reflects much more than its asset value. It is also clear that many family attributes that may determine moving decisions are not included explicitly in our analysis.[4] Thus, the individual-specific term λ is assumed to persist over time. The ϵ_{it} component is assumed to be random across survey intervals and to be uncorrelated with λ. For any family, it captures the effect of changes in unmeasured variables from interval to interval. As will become clear below, it may also reflect the effect of the difference between actual alternative housing possibilities that exist in fact and the optimal choice that is assumed to exist.

If ϵ has a normal distribution with mean zero, the probability that the family will move between any two survey periods, conditional on λ, is

$$(7) \qquad \text{pr[move]} = \text{pr}[\epsilon < \Delta \ln V - m_0 - m(X) - \lambda]$$
$$= \Phi[(\Delta \ln V - m_0 - m(X) - \lambda)/\sigma_\epsilon],$$

where $\Delta \ln V = \ln V_* - \ln V_0$ and Φ is the cumulative normal distribution function.

The term $\Delta \ln V$ is a measure of disequilibrium; it is large if the optimal allocation of wealth between housing and other assets is very different from the existing allocation. The optimal allocation, however, is likely to vary among families. To capture potential differences among families in preferences for housing equity, β is parameterized as

$$(8) \qquad \beta_t = \beta_{t-1} + d(Z) + v, \quad E(v) = 0, \, \text{var}(v) = \sigma_v^2 .$$

That is, β is assumed to follow a random walk with drift $d(Z)$, where

$$(9) \qquad d(Z) = d_0 + d_1 A + d_2 A^2 + d_3 Y + d_4 W + d_5 Y \cdot W.$$

Here, the terms in age A capture the effect of age on the drift, reflecting the possibility that preferences change with age. The terms in income Y are to recognize that the amount of total wealth that the family prefers to have in housing equity is likely to depend on current income, which along with nonhousing bequeathable wealth can be used to finance current consumption. The disturbance v reflects random changes in preferences not captured by measured variables.

The allocation of wealth at the beginning of the period is taken as a base indication of preferences, and optimal choices are considered relative to that base. In period $t - 1$, we observe H_{t-1} and W_{t-1}; we set $\beta_{t-1} = H_{t-1}/W_{t-1}$. Desired housing in period t is then given by an estimate based on the proportion of total wealth allocated to housing in period $t - 1$, plus a deviation from that estimate. As the family ages, there may be an increasingly large difference between H_{t-1}/W_{t-1} and desired β_t, and the extent of disequilibrium may increase. The term $d(Z)$ reflects this possibility. In effect, the housing demand

equation predicts desired changes in housing equity. Based on equations
(8)–(9) and the definitions above, it is given by

(10) $H_t = (H_{t-1}/W_{t-1})W_t + [d(Z)]W_t + vW_t$.

The information to estimate this equation comes primarily from the changes
in housing equity for families who move during the survey period. In essence,
the model estimates the preferred change in housing equity as a function of age,
current income, and current total wealth.[5]

The random term v may be interpreted in two ways: one is as a maximization
error, reflecting, for example, an inability to find a house with precisely the
optimal value. The other is as a further indication of heterogeneity among
families, reflecting desired housing choices. The implications of both interpretations are considered below.

The data consist of five surveys conducted at two-year intervals. There are
two possible outcomes for each family: (1) the family does not move during
the entire ten-year survey period; (2) the family moves in period τ and chooses
a level of housing equity H_τ . The probability of the first outcome is given by

(11) $\text{pr[don't move]} = \int_\lambda \{[1 - \Phi_1] \ldots [1 - \Phi_5]\} f(\lambda)d\lambda$,

where Φ is defined in equation (7), the subscripts indicate intervals between
successive surveys, and $f(\lambda)$ is the density of λ. The probability of the second
outcome is given by

(12) $\text{pr[move between } \tau - 1 \text{ and } \tau \text{ and spend } H_\tau]$
            $= \{\int_\lambda \{[1 - \Phi_1] \ldots [1 - \Phi_{\tau-1}]\Phi_\tau\} f(\lambda)d\lambda\} \cdot g(H_\tau)$,

where $g(H\tau)$ is the density of desired housing equity in period τ. Given the
family-specific term λ_i, the probability of moving during the ten-year period
of the RHS is given by the product of univariate normal probabilities, each
representing the mobility decision for a two-year interval. Integrating over
possible values of λ_i is accomplished by Gaussian quadrature.[6] In calculating
the probability that the family moves, the terms $\ln V_{*t}$ and $\ln V_{0t}$ must be
evaluated. The first term represents the value of the optimal wealth allocation
and is given by $\ln V_{*t} = \beta_t \ln H_{*t} + (1 - \beta_t)\ln(W_t - H_{*t})$, where $H_{*t} =$
$\beta_t W_t$. The second term is the value of the wealth allocation inherited
from the previous period and is given by $\ln V_{0t} = \beta_t \ln H_{t-1} +$
$(1 - \beta_t)\ln(W_t - H_{t-1})$.[7]

In summary, families are followed until they move (or until 1979, when the
RHS panel survey ended). It is assumed that the optimal level of housing equity
H_{*t} is chosen when the family moves, up to an error component represented
by v. The family moves if the gain from moving outweighs the transaction
costs of moving. The predicted level of H_{*t} is used to determine the value of
preferred housing equity in period t; the value of current housing equity is

determined by the level of housing equity at the beginning of the interval, $V_{0,t}$. Heterogeneity in resistance to moving, or in attachment to current housing, is represented by a random term with a variance components decomposition. The family-specific component λ_i is assumed to be the same, for a given family, over the period of the analysis. The time-varying component is ϵ_{it}. The family moves between period $t - 1$ and t if $G_t = \ln V_{*t} - \ln V_{0t} - m_0 - m(X_t) > \lambda_i + \epsilon_{it}$. The disturbance terms v, λ_i, and ϵ_{it} are assumed to be mutually uncorrelated.

1.2   Parameter Estimates

Estimates are based on data from the RHS. The survey covered families headed by persons age 58–63 in 1969. The families were interviewed every two years between 1969 and 1979; there were six waves altogether. The final sample is composed of 3,423 families. Of these, 24 percent moved during the period 1969–79. Selection of the estimation sample is explained in an appendix. Estimates of the parameters in the model are shown in table 1.1. The estimated housing equity function is discussed first, then the probability of moving.

1.2.1   Housing Equity

The disturbance term in the housing equity function is heteroscedastic, with the specification $\sigma_v W$. The estimated σ_v is .2008; the mean of W is $74,465. Thus, given the ratio of housing wealth to total wealth in the last period, current income, current wealth, and age, the standard deviation of the desired change in housing equity is $14,953, evaluated at the mean of wealth. The mean difference between desired and actual equity is small, however, about $1,010, estimated over the whole sample. This means that on average the gain to be had by a reallocation of wealth between housing and other assets is small. The mean of the estimated values of $\Delta \ln V$ is only .041, indicating that the average potential gain, in utility terms, from a reallocation of wealth is only about 4 percent. It is substantially larger than that for some families, however. The standard deviation of the estimated $\Delta \ln V$ is .115.

The mean of the estimated values of β, the desired proportion of wealth in housing equity, is .53. The mean of the estimated values of d, the difference between the current and the desired proportions, is .0107. Thus, on average, the desired proportion of wealth in housing equity is very close to the existing proportion.

There is essentially no effect of age on desired housing equity. As the typical family ages one year, the desired proportion of wealth in housing is reduced by $-.0014$: $.0859 - 2(.000682)$age, evaluated at the mean age of 64.

The housing equity function fits the observed choices of movers very well, as shown in figure 1.1. The estimated values of β—the desired proportion of total wealth in housing equity—and the observed choices $H + W$ are graphed

Table 1.1   **Parameter Estimates**

	Parameter Estimate	Standard Error
Housing equity:		
Disturbance variance, σ_ν	.2008	.0077
Drift, $d(X)$:		
Constant	−2.6855	.1114
Age	.0859	.0037
Age squared (/100)	−.0682	.0031
Income	.0015	.0001
Wealth	−.0007	.0001
Income × wealth	.0001	.0000
Moving:		
Disturbance terms:		
σ_λ	.6197	.0826
σ_ϵ	.7710	.0837
Transaction costs, $\ln M$:		
Constant, m_0	2.0039	.1951
Retirement status:		
No → no	. . .	. . .
Yes → no	−.3034	.1010
No → yes	−.3810	.0580
Yes → yes	−.2700	.0558
Family status:		
Single → single	. . .	. . .
Married → married	−.2846	.0533
Change	−.5626	.0896
Health status:		
Same	. . .	. . .
Better	−.1728	.0496
Worse	.0508	.0407
Children:		
No	. . .	. . .
Yes	−.0269	.0554

Estimated values:	Mean	Standard Deviation
Mean $\Delta \ln v$	.0409	.1152
Mean $\ln M$	1.5578	.2180
Mean β	.5255	.2213
Mean d	.0107	.0108
Log-likelihood	−3,391.0	
Number of observations	3,423	

against total wealth percentile for movers. No systematic deviation of predicted from actual values is revealed.

1.2.2   Moving

Recall that the transaction costs parameter M reflects everything that gives an advantage to current housing, after controlling for the equity value of housing and the wealth allocation that it represents.

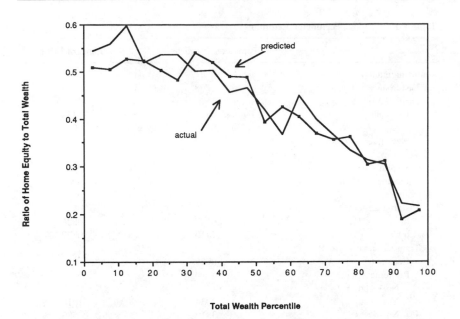

Fig. 1.1   Predicted vs. actual values of H/W by total wealth percentile

It is informative first to report the results from a two-stage estimation procedure: the housing equity equation (11) is estimated by nonlinear least squares in the first stage, using data for movers only. The prediction of desired housing equity from the first stage is used to calculate $\Delta \ln V$. A simple probit equation with $\Delta \ln V$ and other variables that are assumed to determine the probability of moving is estimated in the second stage. The relevant probabilities are of the form $\text{pr[move]} = \text{pr}[e < \Delta \ln V - \ln M]$, where e represents both the individual-specific and the period-specific random components of moving, $e = \lambda + \epsilon$. The larger $\Delta \ln V$, the greater the probability of moving, as expected.[8] But $\Delta \ln V$ explains only a small part of moving behavior. With no change in retirement, marital, or health status, the transaction costs parameter $\ln M$, which is the constant term in the probit equation, is large, say on the order of 1.5. Because $\Delta \ln V$ explains so little of moving behavior, the constant term must be large to yield the small probability of moving that the data exhibit. Thus, the results from this procedure indicate that the value associated with housing equity, and the wealth allocation that it represents, must be increased substantially—about 50 percent—for a family to move. Indeed, without a change in family status or retirement, the "transaction costs" of moving are apparently prohibitive for many families; the family is simply not going to move. This is consistent with the small moving probability in any two-year interval, about .08 on average.

Now consider the maximum likelihood estimates reported in table 1.1. Three key parameters determine the estimated transaction costs: m_0, estimated to be 2.00; σ_ϵ , estimated at .77; and σ_λ , with an estimated value of .62.[9] The mean of the estimated values of ln M is 1.56. Thus, the estimates suggest a mean transaction costs parameter of 1.56, with a standard deviation in any time interval of 1.39. For a few, then, the resistance to moving is very small if the estimates are taken literally; for many more the resistance is quite large. On average, the value associated with the allocation of total wealth would have to be increased by over 50 percent to induce the family to move.

Much more important than a potential reallocation of wealth—Δ ln V—in the decision to move are changes in retirement, marital, or health status. The probability of moving in the base case[10] is .075. If the family head retires during the interval, the probability is increased to .122. If there is a change in marital status—from married to divorced or from married to widowed, for example—the probability increases to .150.[11] A much larger proportion of families in these circumstances have very low transaction costs, by our definition, assuming the same disturbance variance. Families who otherwise would find moving extremely unattractive find that it is much less so at the time of these precipitating shocks.

1.3   Simulations

There are two distinct questions about the desired reallocation of wealth among housing equity and other assets: one is the magnitude of the desired changes; the other is whether they are positive or negative. The magnitude of the desired changes is shown in table 1.2. The entries in the table are the average (and median) of the absolute values of the difference between actual and desired housing equity. For a given family, the comparison is made for each survey year until the family moves; thus, a single family may contribute several observations. Actual housing equity is the value inherited from the previous period. To predict desired housing in the top half of table 1.2, the disturbance term in the housing equity equation (10) is not considered; it is assumed to reflect maximization error. The overall average, including both movers and stayers, is \$5,377. It is \$9,886 for movers but only \$5,117 for stayers. The medians show comparable differences, but the magnitudes are reduced; the overall median is \$2,315; it is \$5,159 for movers and \$2,195 for stayers. The difference apparently reflects the fact that, on average, families who move have more to gain from wealth reallocation than families who do not move. That is, to the extent that a reallocation of housing equity is a motivation for moving, the difference should be greater for those who have chosen to move than for those who have not. As emphasized above, however, it is clear that this is not the major reason for moving. The difference increases with both income and housing wealth quartile, especially the latter. The mean difference among movers with high incomes and high housing equity is \$20,069; the median is \$10,189. Among those with low income and low housing equity, the mean is only \$3,744, with a median of only \$2,233.

Table 1.2   **Mean (and Median) of Absolute Values of Preferred Minus Actual Housing Equity, by Move Status and by Housing Equity and Income Quartiles, Both Excluding and Including Disturbance Term**

Income	Housing Equity				
	Low	2d	3d	4th	Total
Excluding disturbance term:					
All:					
Low	1,734	3,415	4,590	8,243	3,555
	(660)	(1,685)	(2,244)	(5,384)	(1,360)
2d	2,569	3,663	4,918	7,844	4,503
	(1,162)	(2,176)	(2,617)	(4,270)	(2,187)
3d	2,888	3,742	5,155	8,285	5,054
	(1,324)	(2,125)	(2,806)	(4,420)	(2,496)
4th	4,052	4,317	6,409	12,394	8,396
	(1,705)	(2,101)	(3,367)	(6,016)	(3,717)
Total	2,435	3,737	5,343	9,980	5,377
	(963)	(2,020)	(2,815)	(4,996)	(2,315)
Movers:					
Low	3,744	8,899	8,352	11,060	7,473
	(2,233)	(6,205)	(7,861)	(11,272)	(4,932)
2d	4,526	6,716	8,328	16,509	9,062
	(2,584)	(3,598)	(5,340)	(9,264)	(4,865)
3d	6,883	6,156	5,707	13,064	8,099
	(3,552)	(3,966)	(4,243)	(8,286)	(4,587)
4th	8,635	8,247	10,829	20,069	14,211
	(3,187)	(6,314)	(6,008)	(10,189)	(7,171)
Total	5,699	7,432	8,257	16,407	9,886
	(2,707)	(4,662)	(5,337)	(9,707)	(5,159)
Stayers:					
Low	1,658	3,147	4,413	8,038	3,372
	(629)	(1,624)	(2,058)	(4,077)	(1,265)
2d	2,445	3,523	4,717	7,128	4,224
	(1,130)	(2,137)	(2,456)	(3,935)	(2,089)
3d	2,575	3,627	5,127	7,953	4,873
	(1,206)	(1,990)	(2,793)	(4,175)	(2,406)
4th	3,516	4,132	6,185	11,897	8,031
	(1,535)	(2,005)	(3,251)	(5,801)	(3,510)
Total	2,238	3,563	5,191	9,528	5,117
	(900)	(1,926)	(2,729)	(4,709)	(2,195)
Including disturbance term:					
All:					
Low	3,259	6,661	9,628	17,993	7,257
	(1,976)	(4,715)	(6,759)	(12,056)	(3,774)
2d	5,078	8,019	11,131	18,391	10,039
	(3,274)	(5,797)	(8,251)	(12,503)	(6,233)
3d	5,998	9,693	13,164	20,245	12,462
	(4,066)	(7,102)	(9,864)	(14,606)	(8,195)
4th	9,405	12,052	17,608	30,355	21,306
	(6,132)	(9,012)	(12,683)	(21,384)	(13,348)
Total	4,946	8,852	13,257	23,982	12,766
	(2,915)	(6,249)	(9,368)	(15,937)	(7,164)

Table 1.2 (continued)

Income	Housing Equity				
	Low	2d	3d	4th	Total
Movers:					
Low	5,395	11,430	12,065	16,727	10,546
	(3,071)	(7,371)	(10,255)	(13,238)	(6,969)
2d	7,118	9,368	14,742	26,544	14,546
	(5,107)	(6,276)	(11,029)	(16,448)	(8,465)
3d	10,234	13,601	15,903	21,743	15,539
	(6,542)	(10,102)	(12,349)	(16,605)	(10,621)
4th	14,578	18,375	21,636	36,847	26,698
	(7,856)	(13,333)	(17,182)	(23,704)	(16,643)
Total	8,877	12,736	16,504	28,251	17,283
	(5,301)	(8,264)	(12,593)	(17,795)	(10,242)
Stayers:					
Low	3,179	6,428	9,514	18,085	7,103
	(1,946)	(4,629)	(6,622)	(11,875)	(3,694)
2d	4,948	7,958	10,918	17,718	9,763
	(3,160)	(5,778)	(8,159)	(12,257)	(6,145)
3d	5,666	9,507	13,024	20,141	12,278
	(3,906)	(6,993)	(9,711)	(14,481)	(8,067)
4th	8,800	11,754	17,405	29,935	20,967
	(5,834)	(8,775)	(12,500)	(21,243)	(13,154)
Total	4,709	8,668	13,088	23,681	12,506
	(2,824)	(6,157)	(9,214)	(15,828)	(7,013)

The second half of table 1.2 is analogous to the first, but the disturbance term in the housing equation is assumed to reflect desired housing choice instead of a maximization error or deviation from the optimal level. To incorporate the disturbance term, a random draw is made from the estimated error distribution—normal with mean 0 and variance $.2008 \cdot W$—each time that desired housing is predicted. Although this does not affect the expected value of housing equity since the expected value of v is zero, it does affect the absolute values of the deviation. This can be seen by comparing the values in the second half of table 1.2 with those in the first. For example, the average of the absolute values of the desired change over all families is $5,377 when the disturbance term is not accounted for and $12,766 when it is.

The values in table 1.2 indicate the change in housing equity that would occur if transaction cost were zero. On average, the desired change in housing equity may be substantial.

But, also on average, the desire is not to reduce but rather to increase housing equity, as shown in table 1.3. This table shows the mean (and median) difference between desired and existing housing equity, again by housing equity and income and for movers and for stayers. This table indicates the housing choices that families would make were there no moving transaction

Table 1.3   Mean (and Median) of Preferred Minus Actual Housing Equity, by Move Status and by Housing Equity and Income Quartiles

	Income Housing Equity				
	Low	2d	3d	4th	Total
All:					
Low	243	50	285	−1,924	−86
	(−29)	(−89)	(0)	(−1,008)	(−64)
2d	866	814	191	−225	468
	(50)	(275)	(427)	(−511)	(30)
3d	1,133	897	1,323	649	1,009
	(71)	(205)	(275)	(269)	(185)
4th	2,497	1,923	2,438	3,940	3,007
	(674)	(552)	(819)	(915)	(721)
Total	827	835	1,165	1,569	1,010
	(24)	(199)	(221)	(151)	(106)
Movers:					
Low	2,054	3,406	718	−2,815	1,210
	(1,048)	(269)	(−2,567)	(−2,912)	(357)
2d	2,812	2,647	2,655	−833	1,775
	(906)	(364)	(−524)	(−3,840)	(37)
3d	4,834	2,586	2,976	−1,566	2,127
	(2,041)	(794)	(1,754)	(−1,487)	(810)
4th	7,625	5,328	4,310	9,337	7,326
	(2,627)	(4,868)	(1,194)	(4,405)	(3,109)
Total	4,044	3,321	2,877	2,822	3,258
	(1,324)	(704)	(930)	(−795)	(854)
Stayers:					
Low	176	−114	264	−1,860	−147
	(−39)	(−94)	(2)	(−939)	(−67)
2d	743	731	46	−175	388
	(26)	(275)	(−126)	(−439)	(30)
3d	843	817	1,238	803	943
	(50)	(183)	(230)	(338)	(176)
4th	1,897	1,762	2,343	3,590	2,736
	(450)	(479)	(801)	(770)	(619)
Total	633	718	1,076	1,481	975
	(5)	(176)	(207)	(185)	(89)

costs and if all families chose housing equity to optimize the allocation of wealth between housing and other assets. The average difference is $1,010, and the median difference is $106. Families with low income and high housing wealth would like to reduce housing equity, but those with high income and low housing equity would like to allocate more wealth to housing.

The predicted mean increase for movers is $3,258; the median is $854. Like the predictions for all households together, those for movers show some reallocations that increase housing equity and others that reduce it. On average, the increases outweigh the reductions. The results in the second panel of the table are very similar in pattern to the findings reported in Venti and Wise (1989), although the magnitudes are smaller here.[12] The mean predicted change in the housing equity of stayers, were they to move, is $975, with a median of $89. Comparison of the panels for movers and for stayers shows that the predicted changes within the cells are typically greater for movers than for stayers.

The averages of predicted percentage differences between actual and desired housing equity are shown in table 1.4. Two features of the table stand out. The

Table 1.4   **Mean (and Median) Percentage Difference between Actual and Preferred Housing Equity, by Move Status and by Housing Equity and Income Quartiles**

	Income Housing Equity				
	Low	2d	3d	4th	Total
All:					
Low	3.4	.3	.9	−3.3	1.3
	(−.4)	(−.5)	(.0)	(−1.9)	(−.5)
2d	10.4	4.1	.7	.0	4.2
	(.5)	(1.3)	(−.4)	(−1.0)	(.2)
3d	10.9	4.3	4.1	1.3	4.8
	(.8)	(.9)	(.9)	(.5)	(.8)
4th	24.9	8.8	7.5	7.0	9.4
	(5.9)	(2.5)	(2.6)	(1.5)	(2.2)
Total	9.1	4.0	3.6	2.9	4.9
	(.3)	(.9)	(.7)	(.3)	(.6)
Movers:					
Low	28.2	17.9	2.2	−3.5	14.3
	(18.2)	(1.2)	(−7.2)	(−6.9)	(2.2)
2d	47.2	14.4	8.3	1.1	18.9
	(13.5)	(1.8)	(−1.7)	(−8.7)	(.2)
3d	44.3	12.4	9.1	−.7	16.1
	(17.6)	(3.7)	(5.4)	(−3.6)	(2.8)
4th	71.9	26.9	12.0	18.7	28.2
	(35.5)	(23.0)	(3.8)	(8.0)	(11.1)
Total	46.2	17.0	8.5	7.2	19.7
	(18.8)	(3.4)	(2.8)	(−1.4)	(3.8)
Stayers:					
Low	2.5	−.5	.8	−3.3	.7
	(−.5)	(−.5)	(.0)	(−1.8)	(−.6)
2d	8.1	3.6	.3	−.1	3.3
	(.3)	(1.3)	(−.3)	(−.8)	(.1)
3d	8.3	3.9	3.8	1.5	4.2
	(.5)	(.9)	(.7)	(.6)	(.8)
4th	19.4	8.0	7.3	6.2	8.2
	(4.3)	(2.2)	(2.5)	(1.3)	(2.0)
Total	6.8	3.4	3.4	2.6	4.1
	(.1)	(.9)	(.7)	(.4)	(.5)

desired changes are positive on average and are greater for movers than for stayers. And the desired increases are much greater for families with high income and low housing wealth than for families with low income and high housing equity. This pattern is especially evident among movers. On average, movers with high income and low housing equity would like to increase housing equity by 72 percent; the average mover with low income and high housing equity would like to reduce housing equity by only 3.5 percent. Were there no moving transaction costs, and if all families moved to optimize the allocation of wealth between housing and other assets, housing equity would increase by 4.9 percent on average; the typical family would not change housing equity, as indicated by the median percent change of .6 percent.

1.4   Summary and Conclusions

Mobility among elderly families is very low. Approximately 8 percent of RHS homeowners move during a two-year period. The percentage increases very substantially, to about 15 percent, at the time of precipitating shocks like change in marital status or retirement. Thus, most elderly people are apparently reluctant to move. In our analysis, this is reflected in large transaction costs of moving. The analysis emphasizes the potential gain in utility to be had by moving and the resulting opportunity to reallocate wealth between housing and other assets, under the presumption that many elderly would like to withdraw wealth from housing to finance current consumption of other types. This potential gain is very small, however, for most elderly. Thus, relative to the potential gain from a reallocation of wealth, the transaction costs of moving are large.

Nonetheless, the transaction costs evidently have very little effect on the housing equity of the elderly. The evidence suggests that, although some elderly would make substantial changes in housing equity were they to choose new housing, some would choose to add to housing wealth and others to reduce it. On balance, were all elderly to move and choose optimal levels of housing equity, the amount of housing equity would be increased slightly. Thus, the results reinforce our earlier findings and those of Feinstein and McFadden (1989). Most elderly are not liquidity constrained. And, contrary to standard formulations of the life-cycle hypothesis, the typical elderly family has no desire to reduce housing equity. This is true even among families with low total wealth, for whom housing equity is a large fraction of total wealth. The desired reduction of housing equity is largest among families with low income and high housing wealth. Even in this case, however, the desired reductions are rather small, and these desired reductions are more than offset by the desired increases of other families, especially those with high income and low housing wealth.

The evidence of high moving transaction costs, however, suggests that some families may be prevented by such costs from moving, even though they would like to reduce housing equity. It is for these families that reverse annuity mortgages would apparently be most beneficial. Limited demand, though, may explain the absence of an active market for such financial instruments.

Appendix
Selection of Estimation Sample and Variable Definitions

The estimates are based on data from the RHS. The survey covered families headed by persons between ages 58 and 63 in 1969. The families were interviewed every two years between 1969 and 1979; there were six waves altogether. The initial sample contained slightly over 11,000 families. Over 8,000 families were interviewed in the last survey in 1979.

To obtain the sample for this paper we began with all families who owned homes in 1969. A family was omitted from the sample if the first move was to a rental unit or if data used in the analysis (other than housing wealth) were missing in any year prior to the first move. The remaining sample consisted of 4,106 families. In addition, housing equity was sometimes missing or misreported. In some cases, housing equity was not reported in one or more years; in other cases, it was apparently either incorrectly reported or incorrectly coded in one or more years. This latter problem is clearly evident in the tremendous year-to-year variation in housing equity. In our model, a large error in reported housing equity for a family that does not move in a given interval means that the family must be dropped from the sample. This is because a family, at each point in time, must choose between its current level of housing equity (inherited from the previous period) and the optimal allocation of housing wealth. If housing equity is incorrectly reported to be unusually high in period t, then in some cases housing equity in period t will exceed total wealth in period $t + 1$. Unless nonhousing wealth is negative or housing values dropped sharply between periods t and $t + 1$, such cases reflect error in year-to-year reported housing equity. Instead of deleting all such cases from the sample, the median of housing equity (in 1979 dollars) over all periods prior to a move is used as the measure of housing equity in each period that the family does not move. If a family moves, the median represents the equity of the old unit; the equity of the new unit is the reported amount. The final sample includes 3,423 families.

Initial estimates were obtained using reported housing equity throughout. This meant that a disproportionate number of families with low housing equity and low total wealth were deleted from the sample. In fact, the central conclusions of the paper are not affected by the sample selection procedure, although individual estimates are.

The definitions of most of the variables are straightforward. Housing equity is the market value of the house less mortgage and other debt on the house.

Nonhousing wealth includes real property (less debt), motor vehicles (less debt), savings bonds, corporate stocks and bonds, checking accounts, savings accounts, and the face value of life insurance. Total wealth is the sum of housing and nonhousing wealth. The changes in health, retirement, and family status pertain to the two-year intervals between surveys.

Notes

1. The findings of the predecessor paper were very similar to those of Feinstein and McFadden (1989), which are based on the Panel Survey of Income Dynamics; our findings were based on the Retirement History Survey (RHS). These findings are also consistent with the results reported earlier by Merrill (1984).

2. More "structural" specifications based on the asset value and the consumption value of housing, and on a budget constraint limiting the user cost of housing to current income, were rejected in favor of this simple specification.

3. In this sense, the model is consistent with models explicitly incorporating both consumption and investment demands for housing, as in Henderson and Ioannides (1983, 1987), e.g.

4. In their work, Feinstein and McFadden strongly reject the null hypothesis of no unobserved household effects on mobility decisions.

5. It is clear from eq. (10) that the specification may be interpreted as a disequilibrium model, where $d(Z)$ represents the extent of disequilibrium in the proportion of wealth allocated to housing. An alternative procedure is to predict desired housing wealth directly as a function of age, current income, and total wealth, without incorporating the term H_{t-1}/W_{t-1}. The use of the predetermined ratio is a way to control directly for heterogeneity; otherwise, it would be concentrated to a greater extent in the disturbance term. Because the estimation procedure does not integrate over possible values of desired housing equity, given the right-hand variables in eq. (10), more accurate predictions can be had by using the procedure that is followed here.

6. For more explanation in the context of a different application, see Butler and Moffitt (1982).

7. In principle, both probabilities might involve integration over possible values of $H_{*\tau}$ since not all families have the same preferences and, even if they did, the optimal housing level may not be available at any point in time. Integration would be over the random term v, when V_* is evaluated. This is the procedure followed in Venti and Wise (1984). It is not done here for two reasons. It adds substantial complexity to the likelihood calculations. And the method used to predict desired H_t already incorporates substantial heterogeneity in housing preferences; the remaining residual variance is small.

8. In this specification, unlike the standard probit model, the error variance is in fact estimated by the coefficient on $\Delta \ln V$.

9. These estimated values are sensitive to errors in reported housing equity. If, instead of the median of the several housing values reported by each family in the biannual surveys before a move (see the appendix), the actual recorded values are used, all these estimates are considerably larger.

10. With $\Delta \ln V$ evaluated at its mean and with all the dummy variables assumed to be zero.

11. In fact, divorce or marriage are associated with a much higher probability of moving, about .43 (see Venti and Wise 1989).

12. The earlier results were actual changes in housing equity among movers by housing equity and income quartile, after controlling for age, calendar year, children, and changes in retirement, health, or marital status. A correction was also made for reporting errors. The predictions here may provide more accurate information because the continuous functional form does not allow measurement error—which would be most prevalent among families who enter the upper right and the lower left portions of the table—to exert as large a force on the results as the dummy variable specification used in our earlier paper. It could also be that the specification used here does not fit the data as well as the flexible form used there.

References

Butler, J. S., and R. Moffitt. 1982. A computationally efficient quadrature procedure for the one-factor multinomial probit model. *Econometrica* 50, no. 3 (May).

Feinstein, J., and D. McFadden. 1989. The dynamics of housing demand by the elderly: Wealth, cash flow, and demographic effects. In *The economics of aging*, ed. D. Wise, 55–86. Chicago: University of Chicago Press.

Henderson, J. V., and Y. M. Ioannides. 1983. A model of housing tenure choice. *American Economic Review* 73 (1):98–113.

———. 1987. Owner occupancy: Investment vs. consumption demand. *Journal of Urban Economics* 21 (2):228–41.

Merrill, S. 1984. Home equity and the elderly. In *Retirement and economic behavior*, ed. H. Aaron and G. Burtless. Washington, D.C.: Brookings.

Venti, S. F., and D. A. Wise. 1984. Moving and housing expenditure: Transaction costs and disequilibrium. *Journal of Public Economics* 23 (½):207–43.

———. 1989. Aging, moving, and housing wealth. In *The economics of aging*, ed. D. Wise, 9–48. Chicago: University of Chicago Press.

Comment   Alan J. Auerbach

The main result of this paper is that, when elderly people move, they do not reduce their housing equity, on average. To the authors, this suggests that programs that allow households to reduce housing equity without incurring moving costs have not really caught on because there is little underlying demand for them.

I believe this finding, that people in the sample do not, on average, wish to reduce their housing equity. I am less convinced that this explains the lack of demand for reverse annuity mortgages. Further, I am troubled by certain details of the model specification that, while not necessarily influencing the

Alan J. Auerbach is professor of economics and chair of the Department of Economics at the University of Pennsylvania and a research associate of the National Bureau of Economic Research.

basic result about housing equity demand, do make it difficult to interpret the paper's two-stage model of housing demand and moving costs.

The modeling approach taken here is quite sensible and straightforward. In each period, each household evaluates its optimal level of housing and compares it to the current level. If the economic benefit from moving exceeds the cost of doing so, the household moves. Loosely speaking, we can identify the determinants of housing demand from the sample of people who move and the determinants of moving costs by imputing housing demand to the entire sample and then seeing who moves.

The first problem one encounters with the model is in the definition of housing. There are really three relevant housing variables: the value of housing owned, the value of housing equity net of mortgages, and the value of housing consumed. Imposing the constraint of owner occupation leaves us with two independent measures since ownership must equal consumption. Still, there are determinants of housing demand distinct from housing equity demand that, because of data limitations, must be ignored in the paper, which considers only housing equity as an argument of utility. Given that household preferences are actually affected by both, how are we to interpret the paper's empirical findings? The answer depends on the relation between these two variables.

My intuition is that there could be present in the population a general desire to decrease housing equity that is hidden by a desire not to decrease housing consumption. To make the argument simple, suppose there were no mortgage market at all, so housing equity would have to equal housing consumption. Then a household wishing to reduce housing equity would have to reduce housing consumption by the same amount. Balancing these two factors might lead to a small average decrease in housing demand; yet, if mortgages were now introduced (or made easier to obtain), we might observe significant decreases in home equity. An important question to which I do not know the answer is how freely households in the sample can vary housing equity and housing consumption if they move or if they do not move. The paper's logic suggests that housing equity can be changed only by moving. If it can be changed without moving, then why *should* we expect housing equity to be related to the moving decision?

Let me turn now to the model itself. Using six waves of the Retirement History Survey from 1969 to 1979, Venti and Wise follow each family until it moves or until the sample period ends. That is, moving is treated as an absorbing state. The decision to omit observations on families that have moved during the sample period does formally constitute choice-based sampling and introduces potential bias into the estimation procedure. Given the low probability of moving in any given year, this may not be a serious problem, but I am not sure what the authors gain in terms of simplicity by omitting such observations.

The ability to observe households several times permits the specification of an error structure that includes household-specific moving costs. One might also have imagined a role for time effects as well, to account for macroeconomic factors such as mortgage rates, overall housing demand, etc. The authors assume that households begin each period with an optimal amount of housing but that preferences drift (according to eq. [8]) because of changes in observable and unobservable household attributes. This leads some households to move, if the desired change in housing is sufficiently large to overcome the costs of moving, which also vary by household. Unfortunately, since few households move in any given period, this specification of the typical household's preferences is not time consistent. Even if it does not move to its optimal point in period t, a household is assumed during period $t + 1$ to have done so.

A more appropriate specification would be a disequilibrium model in which, at the beginning of the sample, households are assumed to have some distribution around their optimal housing equity values. Indeed, the notion of disequilibrium is clearly what Venti and Wise have in mind, even though their model is not formally specified that way. The preference drift function $d(x)$ described in (9) is ostensibly a measure of how preferences change over time to induce movements from a previous optimum to a new one. In fact, the function is based on levels rather than changes in such variables as income and wealth. Indeed, what the estimates in table 1.1 tell us is that high income leads people to wish to consume more housing and low wealth leads them to wish to consume less. This is perfectly consistent with the disequilibrium approach and, I think, only with this approach. My sense is that the model could be reworked to be consistent with this approach without the basic story being fundamentally altered. It is likely that the econometrics of my preferred modeling approach would be more complex, however. This is because one would lose the independence of current from past decisions; that is, the probability of a move would relate to past moving decisions, how long ago the family last moved, etc.

My next problem with the model as estimated deals with the difficulty of distinguishing the determinants of housing demand and moving costs. Certain variables, such as health status, are included in the moving cost function and ought to be there. One could argue for including such variables in the housing demand function, too. Other variables, such as change in marital status, seem appropriate primarily as determinants of demand shifts but instead are included only in the moving cost function. How should one interpret the reported result that moving costs are reduced significantly by a change in marital status? My intuition is that people in this situation move more because of a change in desired housing arrangements than because of a decline in moving costs. The exclusion of this and other variables from the demand shift function seems quite likely to have induced biased estimates of the moving cost function. This may have a significant effect on the model's policy implications, as well, since the apparently small average change in desired housing equity indicated by the model could be an artifact of the decision to put all the demographic variables into the moving cost function and to exclude them from the demand shift function.

In summary, I am reasonably convinced by this paper that the elderly do not, on average, wish to reduce their housing equity. This is an important result in itself. Without intending to diminish this positive contribution, I must confess to being less convinced by the paper's explanation of the determinants of moving costs and the demand for housing equity and its attempt at resolving the puzzling lack of demand for reverse annuity mortgages. More work on these questions seems warranted.

2 The Dynamics of Housing Demand by the Elderly: User Cost Effects

Chunrong Ai, Jonathan Feinstein, Daniel McFadden, and Henry Pollakowski

2.1 Introduction

This paper is the second in a series of reports on the economic environment in which the elderly must make housing decisions, on the choices they make, and on the consequences of these choices. This report concentrates on the construction of housing prices and user costs faced by the elderly. Section 2.4 of the paper reports some preliminary results on elderly behavior, based on analysis in progress on the 1984 wave of the Panel Study on Income Dynamics (PSID).

2.1.1 Housing Decisions and User Cost

Moving between dwellings and buying or selling a residence are major choices in the life cycle of a consumer. Because of high transactions costs in housing decisions, these choices become important instruments for management of risk and will be strongly influenced by expectations of future income, costs, and health. A fully articulated model of life-cycle housing choices will treat the consumer's problem as a dynamic stochastic program. The discreteness of housing choices introduces nonlinearities that in general will make current decisions dependent on the complete distribution of future cost components, conditioned on current information. As a result, there will be no

Chunrong Ai is a graduate student at the Massachusetts Institute of Technology. Jonathan Feinstein is assistant professor at the Graduate School of Business, Stanford University. Daniel McFadden is professor of economics at the Massachusetts Institute of Technology and a research associate of the National Bureau of Economic Research. Henry Pollakowski is an associate at the Joint Center for Real Estate, John F. Kennedy School of Government, Harvard University.

This research was supported by a grant from the Institute on Aging of the National Institutes of Health, with additional support from the National Bureau of Economic Research and from the James R. Killian Fund at the Massachusetts Institute of Technology. The authors thank Edward Norton and Doug Steiger for research assistance and Brian Palmer for data on survival curves.

one-dimensional statistics on costs that are sufficient (in the statistical sense) to explain behavior. Nevertheless, it is likely that summary cost measures, obtained by using population probabilities to form expected present values, will capture the principal component of costs and thus be excellent instruments for explaining behavioral response to expected costs.

The approach of this paper is to define and calculate for an elderly population measures of expected user cost that incorporate considerable detail on the cost components facing each household. These user costs should then be good instruments for explaining housing decisions of the elderly. They will, however, be appropriate inputs to a dynamic stochastic programming model of behavior only as leading components of more inclusive vectors of information.

This study employs the 1984 wave of the PSID. This panel was started in 1968 with approximately five thousand households and has since interviewed these and split-off households annually. The original sample contained one subsample that was a clustered random sample of U.S. households and a second subsample that oversampled the poor and minorities. Aside from this oversampling, the panel appears to remain representative of U.S. households. This paper provides expected user costs by year, as well as ex post realized user costs, for each elderly household in the PSID, from 1975 through 1984. Because of data limitations, we are unable to extend the series back before 1975. Some of the components entering user cost could be obtained, within the scope of this project, only at a state or non-SMSA census region level of geographic detail. To provide a broad base for some of the cost calculations, we have included in the analysis all households with a family member over age 35 in 1968.[1] The analysis in this paper is based on 2,089 households, of which 960 had a member of age above 50, and 193 above 65, in 1968.

2.1.2 Ingredients of User Cost Calculation

The first component in a calculation of the expected present value of user cost of housing is a stream of out-of-pocket costs that will be incurred as long as the current dwelling is occupied. For renters, this is simply rent plus utilities. In a few states, there is some state income tax offset for rental expenses. For homeowners, the out-of-pocket costs include mortgage payments, real estate taxes, utilities, maintenance, and insurance. The deducibility of homeowner interest and real estate tax expenses in federal income taxes and some state income taxes is an important offsetting factor in calculating out-of-pocket expenses.

The second major element in user cost is the transaction cost associated with moves, purchases, or sales. A house purchase involves loan fees, title insurance, and other closing costs. A sale involves real estate broker's fees. Moving between dwellings involves direct moving expenses, less easily measured time and money costs in setting up the household, and psychic costs of disruption.

A third component in user cost for owners is capital gains on the housing asset. An increase in the present value of net equity resulting from sale of a home at a future date, rather than immediately, is an additional component that offsets the cost of ownership. Calculation of capital gains is complicated by their tax treatment, particularly the one-time exemption for elderly households that was in effect during the period of this study. A second complication arises in the treatment of homes sold as part of the household's estate after the death of the household. In our analysis, we take a "Ricardian equivalence" view that bequests, including home equity, have utility to the household, and are determined jointly with lifetime consumption. With further simplifications, this leads us to treat capital gains from sale of a house symmetrically whether the household is living or not. Alternatively, the household may treat bequests as the unintended residual of a "self-insured annuity" that contributes little to utility. This would increase the perceived cost of options in which the household owns its home until death, at least to the extent that increases in home equity are not offset dollar for dollar by decreases in liquid assets. A test that capital gains are weighed differently by the household than other housing cost components, for this or other reasons, can be tested empirically.

In calculating the present value of expected user cost of housing, important factors will be the discount rate that the consumer uses, the length of time the household stays in the current dwelling, and the likely transitions after the household leaves the current dwelling. First, the Fisherian consumer in an imperfect capital market will use a discount rate that depends endogenously on lending or borrowing status, credit limits, and instruments available in each period. The length of time the household stays in the dwelling will be influenced by largely exogenous factors such as death of one or more household members, job changes or retirements, and changes in health status (i.e., ability to live unaided in a dwelling with specific characteristics). It will also be influenced by endogenous response to factors such as realized cost of current dwelling and alternatives and life-cycle issues involving current income, portfolio of assets (including equity in owner-occupied housing), and bequest motives.

The approach taken in this paper is to calculate an annualized expected present value of user cost taking all the factors outlined above into account, in a fashion that mimics the calculations of a representative household. However, the endogenous interactions between life-cycle income and consumption patterns that enter the discount rate, and the endogenous decisions on length of stay that would enter the actual calculation of a consumer that solves a life-cycle dynamic stochastic program, are replaced by exogenous rates and probabilities based on statistical averages from a population of similarly situated individuals. The idea is that this "population average" user cost should be a good instrument for the true, endogenous user cost calculated by the life-cycle optimizer. In fact, if consumers are not rational optimizers but

are rather "Bayesian learners" who use the observed experiences of others as
a basis for forming expectations, then user cost instruments of the form
constructed in this paper may come very close to the form in which information
is synthesized in housing decisions.

2.2   Housing Prices and Operating Costs[2]

2.2.1   Quality-adjusted Housing Costs

Careful analysis of housing cost changes requires the use of a hedonic rental
or housing price index to assure that differences in the unit price of housing
are not confused with differences in housing quality. Recent house selling
values are available in selected metropolitan areas, and the American Housing
Survey (AHS) contains both dwelling characteristics and the occupant's reported rent or property value.[3] However, construction of hedonic costs has
in most cases been limited in location or time. Hedonic indices have been
developed for a single market over time (Ferri 1977; Palmquist 1980; Bryan
and Colwell 1982; and Mark and Goldberg 1984). Metropolitan housing
markets have also been segmented into a number of submarkets, and indices
have been created (Schnare and Struyk 1976; and Pollakowski 1982).
Gillingham (1975), who used census data to develop housing price indices for
1970, was the first to develop price indices for multiple markets. The AHS
SMSA files have been used to develop owner-occupied and rental housing
price indices for up to fifty-nine medium- and large-sized metropolitan areas.
Owner-occupied housing price indices for a single year have been constructed
by Follain and Ozanne (1979), Malpezzi, Ozanne, and Thibodeau (1980),
Ozanne and Thibodeau (1983), and Goodman and Kawai (1984). Blackley,
Follain, and Lee (1986) have used the AHS SMSA files to construct indices
for two points in time, 1974–75 and 1977–78, for thirty-four SMSAs.

To provide cost indices for our analysis that cover all locations in the PSID
and all years from 1974 through 1984, we have done a hedonic analysis of rents
and house prices, using the AHS national sample. Details of the analysis are
given below.

2.2.2   Hedonic Rents

The Bureau of Labor Statistics (BLS) prices a standard rental unit for the
larger cities. However, such a measure is not available for the rest of the nation.
We did not find in the literature any reliable rental price index for the 1974–84
period that covered the entire United States at the required level of geographic
detail or any index that reflected price differentials across dwelling size. To
provide the indices needed, we carried out a hedonic analysis using rental data
from the AHS.

The national file of the American (formerly Annual) Housing Survey
consists of a representative panel of about 75,000 dwelling units, of which

approximately 40 percent are rented. The survey was conducted annually for the years 1974–81. Subsequently, it has been conducted every second year. Data were available for the years 1974–81 and 1983, when this study was undertaken. Description of individual dwellings is quite thorough, although lot size and certain "upscale" housing characteristics were not added until 1985. Metropolitan-area location is identified for the largest 126 metropolitan areas. Remaining locations are identified by census region and metropolitan/non-metropolitan status. The rental unit data were aggregated into five large metropolitan areas and eight remaining zones, each containing approximately 2,000 households. This was the minimum sample size judged necessary to obtain reliable coefficient estimates. The aggregation was carried out by first estimating the hedonic equations at a more disaggregated level, testing for common coefficients across geographically contiguous areas, and combining the areas for which the hypothesis of common coefficients is accepted. The final rental analysis regions are shown in table 2.1.

Table 2.1   **State and County Aggregates for Which Rental Indices Are Defined**

Code	Location
1	Connecticut, Maine, Massachusetts, New Hampshire, New Jersey, New York, Pennsylvania, Rhode Island, Vermont, unless classified elsewhere
2	Illinois, Indiana, Iowa, Kansas, Michigan, Minnesota, Missouri, Nebraska, North Dakota, Ohio, South Dakota, Wisconsin, unless classified elsewhere. Also, Henderson in Kentucky; Brooke, Hancock in West Virginia
3	Alabama, Arkansas, Delaware, District of Columbia, Florida, Georgia, Kentucky, Louisiana, Maryland, Mississippi, North Carolina, Oklahoma, South Carolina, Tennessee, Texas, Virginia, West Virginia, unless classified elsewhere. Also, Belmont in Ohio
4	Arizona, California, Colorado, Idaho, Montana, Nevada, New Mexico, Oregon, Utah, Washington, Wyoming, unless classified elsewhere
7	Alameda, Contra Costa, Marin, San Francisco, San Mateo in California
9	Bronx, Kings, New York, Queens, Richmond, Nassau, Rockland, Suffolk, Westchester in New York
10	Los Angeles in California
13	Cook, Du Page, Kane, Lake, McHenry, Will in Illinois
15	Bucks, Chester, Delaware, Montgomery, Philadelphia in Pennsylvania; Burlington, Camden, Cloucester in New Jersey
19	Albany, Rensselaer, Saratoga, Schenectady, Broome, Tioga, Washington, Erie, Niagara, Madison, Onondaga, Oswego, Livingston, Monroe, Orleans, Wayne, Herkimer, Oneida in New York; Lehigh, Northampton, Erie, Cumberland, Dauphin, Perry, Cambria, Somerset, Lancaster, Allegheny, Beaver, Washington, Westmoreland, Berks, Luzerne, Adams, York in Pennsylvania; Warren, Hudson, Essex, Morris, Union, Bergen, Passaic, Mercer, Salem in New Jersey; Essex, Middlesex, Norfolk, Plymouth, Suffolk, Bristol, Hampden, Hampshire, Worcester in Massachusetts; Fairfield, Hartford, Middlesex, Tolland, New Haven in Connecticut; Bristol, Kent, Newport, Providence, Washington in Rhode Island; New Castle in Delaware; Cecil in Maryland

(continued)

Table 2.1 (continued)

Code	Location
20	Portage, Summit, Stark, Clermont, Hamilton, Warren, Cuyahoga, Geauuga, Lake, Medina, Delaware, Franklin, Pickaway, Greene, Miami, Montegomery, Preble, Lorain, Lucas, Wood, Mahoning, Trumbull in Ohio; Calumet, Outagamie, Winnebago in Wisconsin; Mclean, Henry, Rock Island, Peoria, Tazewell, Woodford, Boone, Winnebago, Madison, St. Clair in Illinois; Boone, Campbell, Kenton in Kentucky; Dearborn, Allen, Lake, Porter, Boone, Hamilton, Hancock, Hendricks, Johnson, Marion, Morgan, Shelby, Marshall, St. Joseph in Indiana; Scott, Polk, Pottawattamie in Iowa; Macomb, Oakland, Wayne, Genesee, Lapeer, Kent, Ottawa, Clinton, Eaton, Ingham, Monroe in Michigan; St. Louis, Anoka, Dakota, Hennepin, Ramsey, Washington in Minnesota; Douglas, Dane, Milwaukee, Ozaukee, Washington, Waukesha in Wisconsin; Cass, Clay, Jackson, Platte, St. Louis, Franklin, Jefferson, St. Charles in Missouri; Johnson, Wyandotte, Butler, Sedgwick in Kansas; Douglas, Sarpy in Nebraska
21	Clayton, Cobb, De Kalb, Fulton, Gwinnett, Richmond, Walker in Georgia; Aiken, Berkely, Charleston, Lexington, Richland, Greenville, Pickens, in South Carolina; Travis, Jefferson, Orange, Nueces, San Patricio, Collin, Dallas, Denton, Ellis, Kaufman, Rockwall, El Paso, Johnson, Brazoria, Fort Bend, Harris, Liberty, Montgomery, Bexar, Guadalupe in Texas; Baltimore, Anne Arundel, Carroll, Harford, Howard, Montgomery, Prince, Georges in Maryland; East Baton Rouge, Jefferson, Orleans, St. Bernard, St. Tammany in Louisiana; Jefferson, Shelby, Walker, Baldwin, Mobile in Alabama; Mecklenberg, Union, Forsyth, Guilford, Randolph, Yadkin, Wake in North Carolina; Hamilton, Anderson, Blount, Knox, Shelby, Davidson, Sumner, Wilson in Tennessee; Broward, Duval, Dade, Orange, Seminole, Hillsborough, Pinellas, Palm Beach in Florida; Cabell, Wayne in West Virginia; Boyd, Jefferson in Kentucky; Lawrence in Ohio; Hinds, Rankin in Mississippi; Pulaski, Saline, Crittenden in Arkansas; Clark, Floyd in Indiana; Hampton, Newport News, York, Chesapeake, Norfolk, Portsmouth, Virginia Beach, Richmond, Chesterfield, Hanover, Henrico, Alexandria, Fairfax, Falls Church, Arlington, Fauquier, Loudoun, Prince William in Virginia; Canadian, Cleveland, Oklahoma, Creek, Osage, Tulsa in Oklahoma; Bossier, Caddo in Louisiana; District of Columbia
22	Bernalillo in New Mexico; Orange, Kern, Fresno, Ventura, Placer, Sacramento, Yolo, Monterey, Riverside, San Bernardino, San Diego, Santa Clara, Santa Barbara, San Joaquin in California; Ada in Idaho; El Paso, Adams, Arapahoe, Boulder, Denver, Jefferson in Colorado; Honolulu in Hawaii; Clark in Nevada; Maricopa, Pima in Arizona; Clackamas, Multnomah, Washington in Oregon; Clark, King, Snohomish, Spokane, Pierce in Washington; Davis, Salt Lake in Utah

Note: States listed in codes 1–4 include all areas in those states except those areas referred to by other codes.

In the hedonic analysis, the logarithm of the contract rent of a dwelling unit is regressed on a set of hypothesized determinants representing characteristics of the structure, land, and location. We assume a linear specification in which the coefficients are the implicit prices of the various characteristics. The specification used here is an adaptation of the specification used in earlier work with the metropolitan files of the AHS (see, e.g., Malpezzi, Ozanne, and Thibodeau 1980; and Blackley, Follain, and Lee 1986). Table 2.2 presents the

Table 2.2   **Explanatory Variables Used in the Hedonic Rental Equation**

Variables	Median
Constant	1.000
One and a half baths	.063
Two baths	.075
More than two baths	.011
Number of rooms	4.000
Multifamily	.721
Age of structure	29.8
Age of structure squared	886
Structure built before 1940	.392
Wall or room heater	.168
Room air conditioning	.298
Central air conditioning	.224
Rooms without electric outlets	.421
Poor structural features index	.105
Poor hallway conditions index	.091
Poor condition index	.487
Length of tenure	3.6
Length of tenure squared	12.9
Black household head	.144
Spanish household head	.052
Abandoned or boarded-up housing on street	.091
Heat included in contract rent	.355
Water included in rent	.043
Dummies for 1975–81 and 1983	
Dummies for 1975–81 and 1983 times	
number of rooms	

Note: Median values are the median, across 34 SMSAs, of SMSA means (from Blackley, Follain, and Lee 1986).

explanatory variables used in the hedonic price equation for rental housing units. Dummy variables for each year enter the equation as intercepts and in interaction with number of rooms, permitting construction of cost indices by size class. Some tenant characteristics are included that are expected to be correlated with unobserved quality variations or with duration-of-residence discounts. In general, the signs and magnitudes of estimated coefficients and the overall fit are comparable to results from earlier studies of selected metropolitan areas. The occurrence of unreasonable coefficients is about what one would expect by chance. Note that a hedonic equation such as this is most appropriately viewed as the reduced form of a structural system containing supply-and-demand equations for housing. As such, its estimated parameters should not be viewed as solely representing either supply or demand factors.

Once the hedonic equations were estimated, rental indices were constructed for a representative rental housing bundle (described in table 2.2 and taken from Blackley, Follain, and Lee [1986]). This bundle is described as the median over thirty-four metropolitan areas of the area means of each characteristic. An index of the marginal rent for an additional room is also calculated at the median bundle. The rent for dwellings of different sizes is then approximately the median bundle rent, multiplied by a year-specific marginal cost factor for size. The resulting average and marginal rents (in current year dollars) are given in table 2.3. Figure 2.1 compares our rental price index for mid-size dwellings in Los Angeles with the BLS rental cost index in a standard unit; the two series are normalized to be equal in 1979. The two series are in close agreement prior to 1980, with our index showing much sharper cost increases in 1980 and 1981. Figure 2.2 makes the same comparison for New York and again shows our cost index rising more sharply than the BLS index after 1980. Comparing figures 2.1 and 2.2, one notes striking differences across the two locations both in the decade growth rate and in the timing of surges; this is typical across regions.

2.2.3 Hedonic Housing Prices

We have constructed quality-adjusted prices of owner-occupied dwellings by a hedonic analysis that parallels the analysis of rental housing. We used the

Table 2.3   **Log of Monthly Rent for "Median" Dwelling and Marginal Rent per Additional Room**

Location	1974	1975	1976	1977	1978	1979	1980	1981	1983
Median dwelling:									
1	4.458	4.625	4.736	4.750	4.733	4.893	4.948	4.996	5.217
2	4.548	4.644	4.714	4.784	4.877	4.910	4.982	5.085	5.194
3	4.435	4.524	4.560	4.669	4.710	4.849	4.926	5.055	5.210
4	4.626	4.782	4.828	4.926	5.022	5.063	5.251	5.254	5.369
7	5.158	5.153	5.248	5.294	5.429	5.482	5.540	5.811	5.907
9	5.281	5.380	5.411	5.478	5.577	5.641	5.705	5.849	6.005
10	4.844	4.904	4.997	5.123	5.211	5.303	5.514	5.630	5.705
13	5.021	5.005	5.065	5.050	5.224	5.327	5.373	5.507	5.618
15	4.678	4.695	4.860	4.891	5.020	4.992	5.111	5.227	5.319
19	4.659	4.744	4.774	4.851	4.969	5.025	5.100	5.245	5.383
20	4.742	4.782	4.833	4.922	4.997	5.065	5.187	5.262	5.396
21	4.464	4.514	4.575	4.675	4.740	4.794	4.939	5.017	5.254
22	4.614	4.732	4.795	4.926	4.999	5.150	5.263	5.360	5.541
Additional room:									
1	.07	.05	.07	.03	.11	.05	.05	−.01	.01
2	.07	.08	.05	.06	.07	.05	.11	.04	.11
3	.05	.06	.09	.08	.08	.08	.09	.08	.06
4	.05	.05	.10	.10	.13	.14	.08	.08	.09
7	.10	.09	.07	.15	.07	.09	.08	.07	.11
9	.06	.11	.07	.09	.07	.04	.05	.05	.04
10	.11	.17	.12	.11	.10	.10	.11	.13	.08
13	.08	.07	.09	.03	.06	.08	.04	.07	.08
15	.04	.07	.11	.10	.13	.10	.14	.13	.14
19	.07	.06	.09	.07	.06	.07	.06	.06	.04
20	.08	.10	.09	.10	.07	.05	.07	.09	.09
21	.07	.09	.10	.07	.07	.06	.08	.07	.09
22	.09	.08	.08	.10	.09	.08	.11	.11	.08

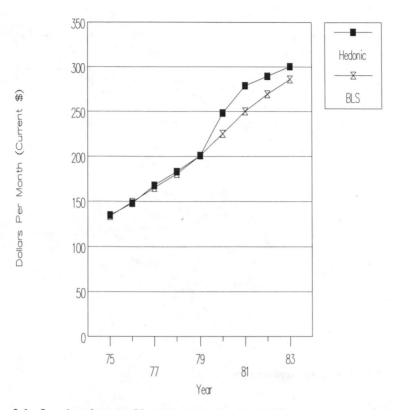

Fig. 2.1 Los Angeles monthly rent

approximately 45,000 owner-occupied dwellings in the national sample of
the AHS. A hedonic regression model linear in housing characteristics, with
the logarithm of owner-reported current dollar house value as the dependent
variable, was estimated. Regressions were done for twelve large metropolitan
areas, along with ten additional zones representing the remainder of the United
States, as shown in table 2.4. Again, the final zones were obtained by first
running the regressions on more disaggregated areas and then combining contiguous areas where the hypothesis of common coefficients could be accepted.

Table 2.5 lists the explanatory variables used in the model. Again, dummy
variables for year are introduced as intercepts and in interaction with number
of rooms to yield a price index sensitive to size. Condominiums are excluded
from the analysis, as are dwellings located on more than ten acres of land.

A median bundle of owner-occupied housing characteristics is defined by
forming area means for each of the twenty-six areas in our final hedonic
analysis and taking the median of these averages.[4] This bundle is described
in table 2.5. The result of this calculation is very close to the median bundle
for owner-occupied dwellings obtained by Blackley, Follain, and Lee
(1986). The average house price and the marginal price per room are then

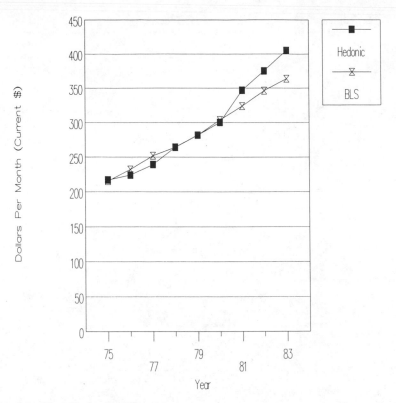

Fig. 2.2 New York monthly rent

Table 2.4   **State and County for Which Price Indices Are Defined**

Code	Location
1	Connecticut, Maine, Massachusetts, New Hampshire, New Jersey, New York, Pennsylvania, Rhode Island, Vermont, unless elsewhere classified
2	Illinois, Indiana, Iowa, Kansas, Michigan, Minnesota, Missouri, Nebraska, North Dakota, Ohio, South Dakota, Wisconsin, unless elsewhere classified. Also, Henderson in Kentucky; Brooke, Hancock in West Virginia
3	Alabama, Arkansas, Delaware, District of Columbia, Florida, Georgia, Kentucky, Louisiana, Maryland, Mississippi, North Carolina, Oklahoma, South Carolina, Tennessee, Texas, Virginia, West Virginia, unless elsewhere classified. Also, Belmont in Ohio
4	Arizona, California, Colorado, Idaho, Montana, Nevada, New Mexico, Oregon, Utah, Washington, Wyoming, unless elsewhere classified
5	Brazoria, Fort Bend, Harris, Liberty, Montgomery in Texas
6	Essex, Middlesex, Norfolk, Plymouth, Suffolk in Massachusetts
7	Alameda, Contra Costa, Marin, San Francisco, San Mateo in California
8	District of Columbia; Montgomery, Prince Georges in Maryland; Alexandria, Fairfax, Falls Church, Arlington, Fauquier, Loudoun, Prince William in Virginia
9	Bronx, Kings, New York, Queens, Richmond, Nassau, Rockland, Suffolk, Westchester in New York
10	Los Angeles in California
11	Baltimore, Anne Arundel, Carroll, Harford, Howard in Maryland

Table 2.4 (continued)

Code	Location
12	Collin, Dallas, Denton, Ellis, Kaufman, Rockwall, El Paso, Johnson in Texas
13	Cook, Du Page, Kane, Lake, McHenry, Will in Illinois
14	Macomb, Oakland, Wayne in Michigan
15	Bucks, Chester, Delaware, Montgomery, Philadelphia in Pennsylvania; Burlington, Camden, Cloucester in New Jersey
16	Anoka, Dakota, Hennepin, Ramsey, Washington in Minnesota
17	Fairfield, Hartford, Middlesex, Tolland, New Haven in Connecticut; Hudson, Essex, Morris, Union, Bergen, Passaic, Mercer in New Jersey
18	Albany, Rensselaer, Saratoga, Schenectady, Broome, Tioga, Washington, Erie, Niagara, Madison, Onondaga, Oswego, Livingston, Monroe, Orleans, Wayne, Herkimer, Oneida in New York; Lehigh, Northampton, Erie, Cumberland, Dauphin, Perry, Cambria, Somerset, Lancaster, Allegheny, Beaver, Washington, Westmoreland, Berks, Luzerne, Adams, York in Pennsylvania; Warren, Salem in New Jersey; Bristol, Hampden, Hampshire, Worcester in Massachusetts; Bristol, Kent, Newport, Providence, Washington in Rhode Island; New Castle in Delaware; Cecil in Maryland
23	Portage, Summit, Stark, Clermont, Hamilton, Warren, Cuyahoga, Geauuga, Lake, Medina, Delaware, Franklin, Pickaway, Greene, Miami, Montegomery, Preble, Lorain, Lucas, Wood, Mahoning, Trumbull in Ohio; Calumet, Outagamie, Winnebago in Wisconsin; Mclean, Henry, Rock Island, Peoria, Tazewell, Woodford, Boone, Winnebago, Madison, St. Clair in Illinois; Boone, Campbell, Kenton in Kentucky; Dearborn, Allen, Lake, Porter, Boone, Hamilton, Hancock, Hendricks, Johnson, Marion, Morgan, Shelby, Marshall, St. Joseph in Indiana; Scott, Polk, Pottawattamie in Iowa; Genesee, Lapeer, Kent, Ottawa, Clinton, Eaton, Ingham, Monroe in Michigan; St. Louis in Minnesota; Douglas, Dane, Milwaukee, Ozaukee, Washington, Waukesha in Wisconsin; Cass, Clay, Jackson, Platte, St. Louis, Franklin, Jefferson, St. Charles in Missouri; Johnson, Wyandotte, Butler, Sedgwick in Kansas; Douglas, Sarpy in Nebraska
25	Clayton, Cobb, De Kalb, Fulton, Gwinnett, Richmond, Walker in Georgia; Aiken, Berkely, Charleston, Lexington, Richland, Greenville, Pickens, in South Carolina; Travis, Jefferson, Orange, Nueces, San Patricio, Bexar, Guadalupe in Texas; East Baton Rouge, Jefferson, Orleans, St. Bernard, St. Tammany in Louisiana; Jefferson, Shelby, Walker, Baldwin, Mobile in Alabama; Mecklenberg, Union, Forsyth, Guilford, Randolph, Yadkin, Wake in North Carolina; Hamilton, Anderson, Blount, Knox, Shelby, Davidson, Sumner, Wilson in Tennessee; Broward, Duval, Dade, Orange, Seminole, Hillsborough, Pinellas, Palm Beach in Florida; Cabell, Wayne in West Virginia; Boyd, Jefferson in Kentucky; Lawrence in Ohio; Hinds, Rankin in Mississippi; Pulaski, Saline, Crittenden in Arkansas; Clark, Floyd in Indiana; Hampton, Newport News, York, Chesapeake, Norfolk, Portsmouth, Virginia Beach, Richmond, Chesterfield, Hanover, Henrico in Virginia; Canadian, Cleveland, Oklahoma, Creek, Osage, Tulsa in Oklahoma; Bossier, Caddo in Louisiana
27	Bernalillo in New Mexico; Kern, Fresno, Placer, Sacramento, Yolo, Riverside, San Bernardino in California; Ada in Idaho; El Paso, Adams, Arapahoe, Boulder, Denver, Jefferson in Colorado; Clark in Nevada; Maricopa, Pima in Arizona; Clackamas, Multnomah, Washington in Oregon; Clark, King, Snohomish, Spokane, Pierce in Washington; Davis, Salt Lake in Utah
28	Orange, Ventura, Monterey, San Diego, Santa Clara, Santa Barbara, San Joaquin in California; Honolulu in Hawaii

Note: States listed in codes 1–4 include all areas in those states except those areas referred to by other codes.

Table 2.5   Explanatory Variables Used in Hedonic Price Equation

Variables	Median
Constant	1
One and a half baths	.174
Two baths	.218
More than two baths	.116
Number of rooms	6.24
Single-family attached	.0147
Garage present	.809
Basement present	.688
Age of structure	28.6
Age of structure squared	818
Age of structure cubed	23,400
Structure built before 1940	.225
Wall or room heater	.0163
Steam or hot water heat	.0386
Electric heat	.0639
Room air conditioning	.325
Central air conditioning	.319
Rooms without electric outlets	.0172
Poor structural features index	.0153
Cook with electricity	.421
Length of tenure	11.6
Length of tenure squared	135
Black household head	.0904
Spanish household head	.015
Abandoned or boarded-up housing on street	.0355
Dummies for 1975–81 and 1983	
Dummies for 1975–81 and 1983 times number of rooms	

Note: Median values are the median, across 34 SMSAs, of SMSA means (from Blackley, Follain, and Lee 1986).

calculated for each location and year. The housing price indices are given in table 2.6. Hedonic housing prices for Los Angeles and New York are shown in figures 2.3 and 2.4. For comparison, the BLS homeowner cost index, available for the years 1975–82, was spliced to a series on sales prices of existing homes (without quality adjustment) from 1982 to 1984. For Los Angeles, the two series are comparable. However, in New York, the hedonic index shows lower increases than the BLS index and sharply lower increases from 1981 to 1983, when the spliced BLS index is not quality adjusted.

2.2.4   Mortgage Rates, Closing Costs, and Selling Expense

Residential real estate markets exhibit substantial transactions costs and capital market restrictions. Closing costs associated with purchases, including mortgage points, title insurance, and legal fees, are typically 1 or 2 percent of

Table 2.6 Log of Price of "Median" Dwelling and Log Marginal Cost of an Additional Room

Location	1974	1975	1976	1977	1978	1979	1980	1981	1983
Median dwelling									
1	3.506	3.510	3.598	3.640	3.796	3.914	3.901	4.073	4.197
2	3.158	3.262	3.364	3.505	3.586	3.741	3.704	3.843	3.860
3	3.150	3.172	3.256	3.425	3.563	3.677	3.784	3.984	4.072
4	3.224	3.320	3.416	3.643	3.888	3.928	3.970	4.334	4.302
5	2.965	3.105	3.213	3.430	3.510	3.595	3.721	3.905	3.979
6	3.614	3.633	3.676	3.778	3.815	3.974	4.038	4.181	4.355
7	3.654	3.703	3.859	4.103	4.290	4.443	4.690	4.806	4.852
8	3.737	3.846	3.905	3.958	4.038	4.184	4.327	4.390	4.397
9	3.727	3.783	3.803	3.829	3.904	3.943	4.040	4.120	4.344
10	3.598	3.660	3.836	4.102	4.334	4.538	4.709	4.790	4.768
11	3.336	3.447	3.518	3.686	3.748	3.884	3.963	4.056	4.088
12	3.001	3.053	3.150	3.275	3.431	3.636	3.737	3.903	4.052
13	3.639	3.721	3.767	3.920	4.079	4.169	4.249	4.208	4.267
14	3.340	3.407	3.433	3.477	3.608	3.779	3.840	3.994	3.958
15	3.489	3.559	3.673	3.737	3.770	3.900	3.983	4.026	4.153
16	3.368	3.455	3.585	3.731	3.903	4.015	4.107	4.199	4.232
17	3.720	3.768	3.845	3.913	4.084	4.189	4.261	4.371	4.516
18	3.298	3.345	3.422	3.560	3.625	3.772	3.832	3.960	4.008
23	3.245	3.340	3.404	3.517	3.671	3.745	3.845	3.960	4.001
25	3.164	3.239	3.290	3.407	3.504	3.612	3.695	3.846	3.944
27	3.204	3.270	3.420	3.595	3.808	3.924	4.078	4.241	4.294
28	3.747	3.892	4.051	4.345	4.451	4.622	4.748	4.979	4.964
Additional room									
1	.05	.08	.06	.09	.11	.09	.12	.08	.02
2	.08	.10	.11	.06	.11	.09	.07	.03	.08
3	.07	.11	.11	.14	.13	.06	.08	.13	.11
4	.06	.06	.03	.04	.02	.02	.03	.08	.05
5	.12	.12	.12	.10	.15	.13	.11	.11	.10
6	.05	.06	.06	.09	.07	.08	.10	.09	.08
7	.13	.09	.09	.13	.09	.08	.08	.09	.11
8	.06	.06	.06	.09	.10	.09	.08	.09	.10
9	.04	.06	.07	.08	.06	.07	.06	.08	.09
10	.07	.08	.11	.14	.15	.14	.11	.12	.03
11	.09	.08	.09	.03	.06	.04	.07	.07	.06
12	.10	.12	.13	.10	.12	.09	.09	.11	.11
13	.05	.07	.07	.08	.09	.12	.09	.08	.09
14	.03	.05	.05	.10	.08	.09	.09	.11	.11
15	.08	.09	.08	.06	.05	.06	.08	.10	.09
16	.07	.07	.05	.07	.06	.05	.06	.04	.06
17	.04	.06	.06	.08	.05	.05	.11	.12	.09
18	.06	.08	.05	.04	.07	.06	.05	.03	.05
23	.08	.08	.08	.07	.07	.07	.07	.06	.07
25	.08	.10	.10	.11	.10	.09	.10	.10	.10
27	.08	.08	.06	.07	.10	.06	.08	.07	.07
28	.03	.06	.08	.06	.10	.14	.08	.10	.10

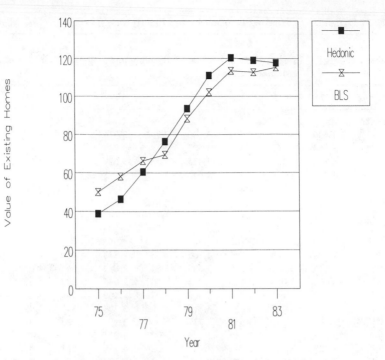

Fig. 2.3   Los Angeles housing prices (current dollars, in thousands)

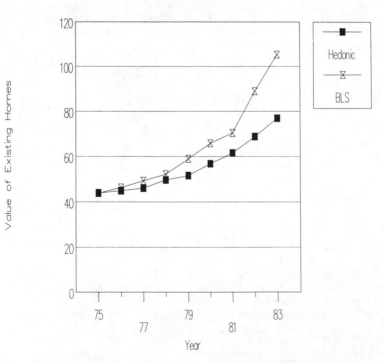

Fig. 2.4   New York housing prices (current dollars, in thousands)

price. Selling expenses, including real estate broker fees, are typically 5–7 percent of price. Mortgages in the period 1974–84 were predominantly issued at fixed interest rates. Prior to deregulation of financial markets, mortgage rates were somewhat more favorable than other interest rates, reflecting restrictions on interest paid on savings deposits, restrictions on lending by savings and loan associations, and federal insurance programs for mortgages. Buyers typically face an earnings test to qualify for a mortgage, and the amount of a mortgage is limited to a fraction of the property value.

For the period 1954–84, we have collected state average data on FHA insured, conventional new-home, and conventional existing-home mortgage interest rates on residential property. These rates are highly correlated, and a sales-weighted rate is close to the conventional existing-home rate. We use the conventional existing-home rate. Where calculations require interest rates after 1984, we assume that the ratio of state to national rates is constant from 1984 on, use data on observed national average mortgage rates from 1984 through 1988 (from the *Federal Reserve Bulletin*), and assume that the real national mortgage rate is constant from 1988 on. Table 2.7 gives the data on mortgage rates through the period of the panel.

For the period 1954–84, the U.S. Federal Home Loan Bank Board *Savings and Home Financing Source Book* gives national average data on initial fees,[5] term to maturity, and loan-to-price ratio. These data are summarized in table 2.8.[6]

Regional data on title insurance and transfer fees for purchasers, or broker fees for sellers, have not been found for the period 1974–84. Consequently, we assume that closing costs other than initial fees (transfer fees, title insurance, and attorney's fees) are 1 percent of purchase price and that real estate brokerage fees paid by sellers are 6 percent of selling price.

2.2.5 Maintenance and Insurance

Dwelling maintenance required to keep quality of a structure constant is typically 1–2 percent of value. Data from the *Construction Reports* published by the U.S. Bureau of the Census give national expenditures on maintenance and repair. Table 2.9 expresses these data as percentages of the value of the residential owner-occupied housing stock. We have not found a source that permits geographic disaggregation of these ratios.

Homeowner insurance rates are typically .2–.5 percent of value. We have not found data on homeowner insurance rates by year and state. Consequently, we have omitted this cost component from the homeowner calculation, leaving its effect to be captured by ownership dummies.

2.2.6 Real Estate Taxes

Property taxes are a significant component of homeowner cost that vary substantially across localities. In some locations, there have also been substantial variations over time. We have collected data from 1974–84 on

Table 2.7 Mortgage Interest Rate (%), by State

State	Code	1968	1969	1970	1971	1972	1973	1974	1975	1976	1977	1978	1979	1980	1981	1982	1983	1984
AL	1	6.9	7.7	8.2	7.5	7.4	7.9	8.8	9.0	8.9	8.8	9.4	10.6	12.5	14.5	14.8	12.3	12.0
AZ	2	6.9	7.7	8.2	7.5	7.4	7.9	8.8	9.0	8.9	8.9	9.4	10.7	12.0	14.2	15.0	12.0	12.1
AR	3	6.9	7.7	8.2	7.5	7.4	7.9	8.8	9.0	8.9	8.8	9.4	10.6	12.5	14.5	14.8	12.3	12.0
CA	4	6.9	7.7	8.2	7.5	7.4	5.4	6.3	6.2	6.1	9.1	9.7	10.9	12.8	14.7	14.6	11.9	11.7
CO	5	6.9	7.7	8.2	7.5	7.4	8.3	9.2	9.1	9.0	9.0	9.7	10.8	11.7	13.1	14.1	12.3	12.0
CT	6	6.9	7.7	8.2	7.5	7.4	7.5	8.5	8.7	8.6	8.5	8.7	9.9	12.2	15.1	15.5	12.4	12.0
DE	7	6.9	7.7	8.2	7.5	7.4	7.7	8.9	9.2	9.1	8.8	9.1	10.2	12.2	14.5	15.0	12.6	12.6
DC	8	6.9	7.7	8.2	7.5	7.4	7.9	8.8	9.1	9.0	8.9	9.5	10.7	12.5	14.1	14.5	12.3	11.7
FL	9	6.9	7.7	8.2	7.5	7.4	3.9	4.5	4.4	4.3	8.5	9.0	10.6	12.9	14.8	15.1	12.2	11.7
GA	10	6.9	7.7	8.2	7.5	7.4	8.0	8.7	8.7	8.7	8.7	9.3	10.4	12.4	14.0	14.5	12.4	11.8
ID	11	6.9	7.7	8.2	7.5	7.4	7.9	8.8	9.0	8.9	8.8	9.4	10.6	12.5	14.5	14.8	12.3	12.0
IL	12	6.9	7.7	8.2	7.5	7.4	7.5	8.2	8.9	8.9	8.7	9.3	10.2	12.3	14.2	14.3	12.3	11.9
IN	13	6.9	7.7	8.2	7.5	7.4	2.5	2.8	3.0	2.9	8.7	9.3	10.4	12.2	13.9	14.2	12.3	11.8
IA	14	6.9	7.7	8.2	7.5	7.4	7.9	8.8	9.0	8.9	8.8	9.4	10.6	12.5	14.5	14.8	12.3	12.0
KS	15	6.9	7.7	8.2	7.5	7.4	7.9	8.8	9.0	8.9	8.8	9.5	10.3	11.9	13.2	13.4	12.0	11.8
KY	16	6.9	7.7	8.2	7.5	7.4	7.9	8.8	9.0	8.9	8.8	9.2	10.2	11.6	14.1	14.4	12.5	11.8
LA	17	6.9	7.7	8.2	7.5	7.4	7.9	8.8	9.0	8.9	8.8	9.4	10.6	12.5	14.5	14.8	12.3	12.0
ME	18	6.9	7.7	8.2	7.5	7.4	7.9	8.8	9.0	8.9	8.8	9.4	10.6	12.5	14.5	14.8	12.3	12.0
MD	19	6.9	7.7	8.2	7.5	7.4	7.8	8.8	9.2	9.0	8.8	9.3	10.5	12.3	14.2	14.7	12.4	12.1
MA	20	6.9	7.7	8.2	7.5	7.4	7.7	8.9	9.1	8.8	8.5	8.9	10.8	13.0	15.8	15.8	12.8	12.8
MI	21	6.9	7.7	8.2	7.5	7.4	7.9	9.1	9.0	9.0	8.8	9.4	10.9	12.7	14.3	14.1	11.7	11.6
MN	22	6.9	7.7	8.2	7.5	7.4	7.8	8.1	8.1	8.5	8.8	9.4	10.3	11.9	13.5	13.7	11.8	11.4
MS	23	6.9	7.7	8.2	7.5	7.4	3.8	4.0	4.5	4.5	8.8	9.4	10.3	12.2	13.9	14.0	12.2	11.9
MO	24	6.9	7.7	8.2	7.5	7.4	7.9	8.8	9.0	8.9	8.8	9.4	10.6	12.5	14.5	14.8	12.3	12.0

MT	25	6.9	7.7	8.2	7.5	7.4	7.9	8.8	9.0	8.9	8.8	9.4	10.6	12.5	14.5	14.8	12.3	12.0
NE	26	6.9	7.7	8.2	7.5	7.4	7.9	8.8	9.0	8.9	8.8	9.4	10.6	12.5	14.5	14.8	12.3	12.0
NV	27	6.9	7.7	8.2	7.5	7.4	7.9	8.8	9.0	8.9	8.8	9.4	10.6	12.5	14.5	14.8	12.3	12.0
NH	28	6.9	7.7	8.2	7.5	7.4	7.7	8.9	9.1	8.8	8.5	8.9	10.8	13.0	15.8	15.8	12.8	12.8
NJ	29	6.9	7.7	8.2	7.5	7.4	7.6	8.7	8.9	8.9	8.6	8.9	10.0	12.2	14.8	15.2	12.5	12.3
NM	30	6.9	7.7	8.2	7.5	7.4	7.9	8.8	9.0	8.9	8.8	9.4	10.6	12.5	14.5	14.8	12.3	12.0
NY	31	6.9	7.7	8.2	7.5	7.4	3.8	4.2	4.3	4.3	8.5	8.6	9.8	12.2	14.9	15.3	12.0	11.3
NC	32	6.9	7.7	8.2	7.5	7.4	7.9	8.8	9.0	8.9	8.8	9.4	10.8	12.3	14.6	14.9	12.4	12.3
ND	33	6.9	7.7	8.2	7.5	7.4	7.9	8.8	9.0	8.9	8.8	9.4	10.6	12.5	14.5	14.8	12.3	12.0
OH	34	6.9	7.7	8.2	7.5	7.4	3.8	4.3	4.5	4.4	8.7	9.4	10.7	12.6	14.1	14.3	12.2	12.2
OK	35	6.9	7.7	8.2	7.5	7.4	7.9	8.8	9.0	8.9	8.8	9.4	10.6	12.5	14.5	14.8	12.3	12.0
OR	36	6.9	7.7	8.2	7.5	7.4	7.9	8.8	9.0	8.9	9.0	9.6	10.6	12.1	13.7	14.5	12.2	11.9
PA	37	6.9	7.7	8.2	7.5	7.4	3.8	4.5	4.6	4.6	8.6	9.1	10.3	12.3	14.5	15.1	12.3	12.1
RI	38	6.9	7.7	8.2	7.5	7.4	7.9	8.8	9.0	8.9	8.8	9.4	10.6	12.5	14.5	14.8	12.3	12.0
SC	39	6.9	7.7	8.2	7.5	7.4	7.9	8.8	9.0	8.9	8.8	9.4	10.6	12.5	14.5	14.8	12.3	12.0
SD	40	6.9	7.7	8.2	7.5	7.4	7.9	8.8	9.0	8.9	8.8	9.4	10.6	12.5	14.5	14.8	12.3	12.0
TN	41	6.9	7.7	8.2	7.5	7.4	7.9	8.8	9.0	8.9	8.8	9.4	10.6	12.5	14.5	14.8	12.3	12.0
TX	42	6.9	7.7	8.2	7.5	7.4	8.1	8.9	8.9	9.0	8.9	9.5	10.0	11.8	13.3	14.1	12.3	11.9
UT	43	6.9	7.7	8.2	7.5	7.4	7.9	8.8	9.0	8.9	9.1	9.7	10.8	11.7	13.3	13.3	12.5	11.8
VT	44	6.9	7.7	8.2	7.5	7.4	7.9	8.8	9.0	8.9	8.8	9.4	10.6	12.5	14.5	14.8	12.3	12.0
VA	45	6.9	7.7	8.2	7.5	7.4	7.9	8.8	9.1	9.0	8.9	9.5	10.7	12.5	14.1	14.5	12.3	11.7
WA	46	6.9	7.7	8.2	7.5	7.4	3.9	4.5	4.7	4.6	9.0	9.6	10.6	12.2	13.9	14.7	12.3	11.8
WV	47	6.9	7.7	8.2	7.5	7.4	7.9	8.8	9.0	8.9	8.8	9.4	10.6	12.5	14.5	14.8	12.3	12.0
WI	48	6.9	7.7	8.2	7.5	7.4	3.9	4.0	4.0	4.2	8.7	9.4	10.5	12.1	14.2	13.9	11.8	11.7
WY	49	6.9	7.7	8.2	7.5	7.4	7.9	8.8	9.0	8.9	8.8	9.4	10.6	12.5	14.5	14.8	12.3	12.0

Source: Federal Home Loan Bulletin, 1968–86, interpolated in missing years and averaged over reported locations in the state. For states without reported locations, the national average is used. Prior to 1973, state data were unavailable.

Table 2.8   **Interest Rate, Fees, Term to Maturity, and Loan/Price Ratio Average over Years 1965–86**

State	Code	Interest (%)	Fees (%)	Term to Maturity	Loan/Price (%)
AL	1	9.40	1.40	25	73.67
AZ	2	9.36	1.61	26	75.10
AR	3	9.40	1.40	25	73.67
CA	4	8.92	1.24	25	70.70
CO	5	9.33	1.38	27	76.13
CT	6	9.32	1.26	25	67.94
DE	7	9.44	1.41	24	71.69
DC	8	9.33	1.32	27	75.44
FL	9	8.56	1.79	24	67.98
GA	10	9.27	2.00	26	76.53
ID	11	9.40	1.40	25	73.67
IL	12	9.27	1.56	24	72.54
IN	13	8.24	1.46	22	64.23
IA	14	9.40	1.40	25	73.67
KS	15	9.19	1.41	26	75.42
KY	16	9.31	1.35	25	73.90
LA	17	9.40	1.40	25	73.67
ME	18	9.40	1.40	25	73.67
MD	19	9.38	1.25	25	73.76
MA	20	9.59	1.06	25	71.25
MI	21	9.38	1.24	26	73.89
MN	22	9.07	1.34	26	73.49
MS	23	8.46	1.30	22	68.03
MO	24	9.40	1.40	25	73.67
MT	25	9.40	1.40	25	73.67
NE	26	9.40	1.40	25	73.67
NV	27	9.40	1.40	25	73.67
NH	28	9.59	1.06	25	71.25
NJ	29	9.38	1.33	25	69.82
NM	30	9.40	1.40	25	73.67
NY	31	8.44	1.20	23	63.75
NC	32	9.43	1.16	25	74.50
ND	33	9.40	1.40	25	73.67
OH	34	8.59	1.57	23	66.81
OK	35	9.40	1.40	25	73.67
OR	36	9.30	1.44	26	75.51
PA	37	8.60	1.36	22	65.86
RI	38	9.40	1.40	25	73.67
SC	39	9.40	1.40	25	73.67
SD	40	9.40	1.40	25	73.67
TN	41	9.40	1.40	25	73.67
TX	42	9.26	1.93	27	78.89
UT	43	9.26	1.50	26	75.35
VT	44	9.40	1.40	25	73.67
VA	45	9.33	1.32	27	75.44
WA	46	8.57	1.49	24	69.30
WV	47	9.40	1.40	25	73.67
WI	48	8.42	1.29	23	66.22
WY	49	9.40	1.40	25	73.67

Source: Conventional first mortgage contract interest rate and terms, Federal Home Loan Bank Board, *Savings and Loan Financing Source Book,* 1967–87.

Table 2.9   **Maintenance as a Proportion of House Value, by Region**

Region	1970	1975	1976	1977	1978	1979	1980	1981	1982	1983	1984
Northeast	.006	.006	.006	.006	.006	.006	.005	.005	.006	.006	.009
North central	.007	.007	.007	.006	.006	.006	.006	.006	.008	.007	.012
South	.008	.008	.008	.007	.007	.007	.006	.005	.005	.006	.008
West	.010	.009	.008	.007	.006	.006	.005	.005	.004	.004	.006

Source: For maintenance, U.S. Bureau of the Census, *Construction Reports,* ser. C-50, various years. For house value, U.S. Bureau of the Census, 1980 Census of Housing, vol. 1. For owner-reported value, adjusted to various years using the median sales price of new one-family homes, U.S. Bureau of the Census, *Construction Reports,* ser. C-25.

average residential property tax rates, by state. There is substantial intrastate variation in property tax rates, but collecting property tax rates and assessment rates by locality was beyond the scope of the project. Statistics on property tax rates are given in table 2.10.

2.2.7 Income Tax Deductions and Treatment of Capital Gains

We adopt the general approach of Hendershott and Slemrod (1983) for the calculation of income tax offsets to mortgage interest and property taxes and the calculation of capital gains taxes. For a given stream of future tenure states and projected income, we calculate the federal and state tax liability of the household in each year, with and without itemization of deductions. We have developed a tax program that determines the federal and state income taxes for a household with specified income, exemptions, mortgage interest, property taxes, and other potential deductible expenses. Inputs to this program are federal and state tax schedules, exemption allowances, and rules for itemizing deductions, by year. Potential deductible expenses other than mortgage interest and property taxes are estimated as a function of income from a sample of individual tax returns in 1982. Let N^* denote nonhomeowner potential deductible expenses, H denote mortgage interest and property taxes for a homeowner, S denote the standard deduction, and Y denote taxable income. Then, the filer itemizes deductions if $N^* + H > S$, in which case $N = N^*$ is observed. Assume N^* given Y is normally distributed in the population with mean $\alpha + \beta Y$ and variance σ^2. Then the probability of itemizing is

$$(1) \qquad P = \Phi[(\alpha + \beta Y + H - S)/\sigma],$$

the density of N given itemization is

$$(2) \qquad \sigma^{-1}\phi[(N - \alpha - \beta Y)/\sigma]/\Phi[(\alpha + \beta Y + H - S)/\sigma],$$

and the expectation of N given itemization is

$$(3) \quad \alpha + \beta Y + \sigma\phi[(\alpha + \beta Y + H - S)/\sigma]/\Phi[(\alpha + \beta Y + H - S)/\sigma].$$

Table 2.10   **Property Tax Rate (percentage of market value) 1974–84, by State**

State	Code	74	75	76	77	78	79	80	81	82	83	84
AL	1	.75	.75	.74	.74	.73	.70	.56	.38	.41	.42	.41
AZ	2	1.54	1.54	1.63	1.72	1.69	1.37	1.16	.74	.56	.71	.71
AR	3	1.41	1.41	1.45	1.49	1.48	1.54	1.53	1.42	1.42	1.29	1.35
CA	4	2.08	2.08	2.14	2.21	2.26	.94	.98	1.04	1.03	1.05	1.02
CO	5	1.99	1.99	1.90	1.80	1.74	1.22	1.05	1.01	1.01	.95	.98
CT	6	1.94	1.94	2.05	2.17	1.94	1.64	1.55	1.53	1.56	1.60	1.68
DE	7	.92	.92	.90	.88	.89	.89	.85	.79	.75	.76	.71
DC	8	1.78	1.78	1.77	1.77	1.76	1.60	1.30	1.22	1.15	1.17	1.14
FL	9	1.18	1.18	1.16	1.13	1.14	1.11	1.02	.92	1.03	.92	.79
GA	10	1.33	1.33	1.30	1.27	1.28	1.23	1.24	1.21	1.21	1.16	1.08
ID	11	1.86	1.86	1.66	1.46	1.57	1.29	.96	.94	1.04	1.02	1.01
IL	12	2.21	2.21	2.06	1.90	1.81	1.48	1.50	1.47	1.59	1.72	1.63
IN	13	1.64	1.64	1.65	1.66	1.61	1.14	1.19	1.13	1.19	1.23	1.22
IA	14	2.20	2.20	2.08	1.76	1.59	1.39	1.48	1.75	1.64	1.67	1.63
KS	15	1.55	1.55	1.46	1.37	1.28	.98	.94	.93	.97	1.00	1.11
KY	16	1.23	1.23	1.24	1.25	1.26	1.26	1.19	1.14	1.11	1.02	.95
LA	17	.64	.64	.62	.61	.47	.29	.26	.28	.15	.14	.16
ME	18	1.86	1.86	1.76	1.65	1.58	1.58	1.25	1.42	1.52	1.52	1.31
MD	19	2.01	2.01	1.85	1.69	1.72	1.53	1.61	1.25	1.37	1.38	1.26
MA	20	3.26	3.26	3.38	3.50	3.64	3.28	2.51	2.43	2.14	1.85	1.57
MI	21	2.38	2.38	2.50	2.63	2.63	2.45	2.54	2.74	2.68	2.68	2.78
MN	22	1.58	1.58	1.49	1.39	1.33	1.04	.93	.79	.77	.85	.99
MS	23	1.12	1.12	1.11	1.10	1.12	.94	.93	.86	.76	.82	.77
MO	24	1.85	1.85	1.72	1.59	1.45	1.03	1.00	.95	1.17	1.09	1.02
MT	25	1.60	1.60	1.45	1.31	1.23	1.05	1.11	1.08	1.14	1.17	1.14
NE	26	2.50	2.50	2.49	2.48	2.43	2.28	2.37	2.31	2.23	2.12	2.11
NV	27	1.53	1.53	1.62	1.71	1.72	1.53	1.22	1.13	.77	.68	.63
NH	28	2.38	2.38	2.24	2.10	1.96	1.82	1.73	2.06	2.39	2.23	2.02
NJ	29	3.15	3.15	3.23	3.31	3.30	2.82	2.60	2.53	2.55	2.54	2.62
NM	30	1.56	1.56	1.60	1.65	1.47	1.30	1.12	1.14	.93	.90	.76
NY	31	2.56	2.56	2.72	2.89	3.02	2.76	2.75	2.75	2.57	2.66	2.80
NC	32	1.51	1.51	1.43	1.35	1.35	1.15	.95	1.07	.97	.96	1.01
ND	33	1.53	1.53	1.40	1.26	1.18	1.01	1.00	1.01	1.10	1.26	1.25
OH	34	1.29	1.29	1.28	1.26	1.20	1.09	1.08	1.07	1.15	1.15	1.03
OK	35	1.27	1.27	1.11	.95	.95	.95	.91	.82	.74	.89	.95
OR	36	2.18	2.18	2.21	2.25	2.18	1.86	1.72	1.56	2.06	2.27	2.22
PA	37	1.71	1.71	1.78	1.85	1.91	1.67	1.57	1.50	1.63	1.71	1.53
RI	38	2.27	2.27	2.12	1.97	1.82	1.67	1.93	1.90	1.88	2.01	2.01
SC	39	1.07	1.07	.95	.82	.80	.83	.81	.84	.92	.85	.81
SD	40	2.14	2.14	1.97	1.79	1.69	1.63	1.70	1.69	1.77	1.75	1.63
TN	41	1.31	1.31	1.35	1.40	1.40	1.27	1.27	1.42	1.24	1.17	.97
TX	42	2.06	2.06	1.95	1.84	1.66	1.60	1.57	1.68	1.40	1.36	1.32
UT	43	1.20	1.20	1.11	1.03	.99	1.05	1.02	1.03	.92	.97	.87
VT	44	2.21	2.21	2.04	1.87	1.70	1.54	1.60	1.60	1.60	1.60	1.60
VA	45	1.32	1.32	1.27	1.21	1.20	1.23	1.26	1.39	1.44	1.28	1.00
WA	46	1.86	1.86	1.81	1.75	1.78	1.50	1.06	.95	1.01	1.03	1.01
WV	47	.78	.78	.71	.64	.56	.49	.43	.37	.52	.68	.68
WI	48	2.63	2.63	2.43	2.22	2.12	1.66	1.67	1.75	2.01	1.90	2.00
WY	49	1.12	1.12	1.01	.87	.76	.58	.50	.47	.48	.45	.45

Source: Property tax rates for selected metropolitan areas, Advisory Committee on Intergovernmental Relations, *Government Fiscal Federalism, 1974–1985.* Missing values are interpolated. State rates average reported areas or the national average for states without covered metropolitan areas.

We estimate this model by maximum likelihood Tobit; the results are given in table 2.11. This model is used to predict nonhomeowner itemized deductions. The household is assigned the lesser of the calculated tax with predicted itemized deductions, including predicted mortgage interest and property tax for owner alternatives, and with the standard deduction.

The mortgage interest deduction for owner housing will depend on the mortgage/price ratio, the interest rate, and the length and age of the mortgage. We assume that new house purchasers always take the maximum mortgage available. We assume that current owners who buy a new dwelling first roll over those capital gains from their previous dwelling that are not exempted from capital gains taxation and then take a mortgage for the remainder of the new dwelling, up to the maximum available. We use the data from table 2.9 for mortgage length and mortgage/price ratio.[7] We use the standard amortization formula

$$(4) \qquad R_t = rM_0(1 - e^{-r(L-t)})/(1 - e^{-rL}),$$

where R_t is interest payment, t is mortgage age, L is mortgage length, M_0 is initial mortgage amount, and r is interest rate, to calculate deductible mortgage interest.

The tax laws in the period 1974–84 gave special treatment to long-term capital gains. Table 2.12 details the year-by-year tax treatment of capital gains from the sale of residential real estate.

We repeat all tax calculations assuming that capital gains in an owned dwelling are realized and taxed immediately and that thereafter the household has no deductible mortgage interest or property taxes. The *difference* of the tax

Table 2.11   **A Tobit Model for Nonhomeowner Income Tax Deductions**

	Status		
	Single	Head	Married Joint and Widows
Standard deduction ($)	2,300	2,300	3,400
Number in sample (total 2,267)	598	82	1.564
Number of itemizers (total 1,305)	202	44	1,049
Estimated coefficients (SE):			
Constant	−658	1295	−1534
	(3,370)	(81,500)	(105)
Taxable income	.195	.125	.150
	(.038)	(.910)	(.0003)
Standard error of regression	3,835	1,574	2,437
	(1,600)	(158)	(5.9)
Weighted sum of squared residuals	1,906	3,820	20,280

Source: Internal Revenue Service, Taxpayer Compliance Measurement Program 1982 database. Four representative geographic districts comprising 2,267 observations (out of approximately 52,000) were selected.

**Table 2.12   Tax on Capital Gains from Resale of Residential Real Estate,
                      By Year**

Tax:
  1974–80   .5 · (capital gain) should be included in taxable income
  1981–84   .4 · (capital gain) should be included in taxable income
Deduction:
  1974–76   Person aged 65 or older can deduct any gains if adjusted selling price is not
                more than 20,000. Otherwise, he or she can deduct (20,000/selling
                price) · capital gain
  1977–78   Person aged 65 or older can deduct any gains if adjusted selling price is not
                more than 35,000. Otherwise, he or she can deduct (35,000/selling
                price) · capital gain
  1979–81   Person aged 55 or older can exclude $100,000 from capital gain
  1982–84   Person aged 55 or older can exclude $125,000 from capital gain

Source: Standard Federal Tax Reports: United States Master Tax Guide, 1974–1985.

streams in these two cases is entered as a component in the out-of-pocket cost stream that appears in the user cost calculation. For renters, this difference is zero; for owners, it is the *incremental* offset, relative to renting, resulting from the tax treatment of ownership.

The statement of tax rates in nominal terms, and the taxation of nominal capital gains, introduces inflationary effects into the calculation of ownership costs. As a consequence, expectations about both future real housing prices and the rate of inflation will enter user cost calculations. We assume that households have perfect foresight on both nominal housing prices and the rate of inflation. To implement this for years after 1984, we assume actual inflation rates through 1988 and inflation at the 1988 rate thereafter. Real housing prices in a region are assumed to grow at rates that are linearly interpolated between a zero annual rate in 1989 and their observed annual rate in 1982–84. After 1989, real housing prices are assumed constant.

2.3   Dynamic Optimization and User Cost

2.3.1   A Definition of User Cost in Life-Cycle Housing Decisions

In this section, we describe a stylized household life-cycle model formulated as a dynamic stochastic program, in which the only discrete decision is tenure and in which the household faces perfect capital markets, except for the fixed costs of real estate transactions. We begin by abstracting from the complexities of tax offsets, letting these be defined implicitly as part of the net out-of-pocket costs of housing. A *life-cycle housing strategy* is defined to be a plan that specifies the current period tenure decision and a probability distribution of future decisions, conditioned on current information. This strategy will take into account contingent responses to future news. The *user cost* of a life-cycle housing strategy will be defined as a nonstochastic life annuity that, if paid by the household in lieu of the actual distribution of current and future out-of-pocket housing costs, would yield the same expected utility. We set out some rather stringent assumptions under which user cost given by this definition can be calculated as a present value, independently of the parameters of the utility function of the household. Our interpretation of this result is that it defines a "point of expansion" of Bellman's equation for the stochastic program in which only the one-dimensional calculated user cost enters the leading term. We believe that this provides a justification for calculated user cost as a good instrument in reduced-form models of housing choices. We have not, however, established that there is a useful solution algorithm for the dynamic stochastic program based on this "expansion"; this question is beyond the scope of this paper.

Suppose discrete time, divided into periods of one year. In period t, the household's consumption policy is described by an indicator for tenure, $d_t = 1$ for a homeowner and $d_t = 0$ for a renter; an "inclusive" out-of-pocket cost for housing, C_t, which depends on current and past tenure and incorporates realized net capital gains from purchase or sale of housing; and a real consumption expenditure level, G_t. The household has an atemporal partial indirect utility function $\psi(G_t - C_t, d_t)$, given consumption expenditures net of housing and tenure. Commodity prices other than housing are assumed constant in real terms and are suppressed as an argument of ψ. Household deaths are assumed to occur at the end of a year, after a full year's consumption, with the liquidation of the household's estate yielding bequests at the time of death. The household has an atemporal utility $\psi^b(B_T)$ for bequests B_T made on death of the household at the end of period T. Let y_t denote income in period t and r_t the one-period real interest rate for liquid assets held from year $t - 1$ to year t. Let δ denote the household's personal discount factor, reflecting impatience. The liquid (nonhousing) assets of the household satisfy the equation of motion

(5) $$A_t = (1 + r_t)A_{t-1} + y_t - G_t .$$

The bequest of a household that dies at the end of year t is the sum of liquid assets and home equity,

(6) $$B_t = A_t + 1(d_t > 0)E_t ;$$

in this formula, $1(Q)$ is an indicator that is one when the event Q is true and zero otherwise, and E_t is end-of-year equity. Equations (5) and (6) imply

(7) $$A_t = A_0 \prod_{\tau=1}^{t} (1 + r_\tau) + \sum_{s=1}^{t} (y_s - G_s) \prod_{\tau=s+1}^{t} (1 + r_\tau).$$

Combining these formulae, the partially indirect utility of a household with a given housing plan (d_t) and expenditure stream (G_t) and with death in period T is

$$(8) \quad U_T = \sum_{t=1}^{T} \delta^{t-1}\psi(G_t - C_t, d_t) + \delta^{T-1}\psi^B[A_T + 1(d_T > 0)E_T].$$

At $t = 1$, the household does not know its date of death or the sequence d_τ for $\tau > 1$. It may also be uncertain about some variables in the economic environment, such as future income, interest rates, and net housing costs. Let λ_t denote the probability of household death in year t, given survival up until t, and let $\kappa_t = (1 - \lambda_1) \cdot \ldots \cdot (1 - \lambda_{t-1})$ denote the probability of survival until t. Then the household seeks to maximize expected utility

$$(9) \qquad \mathcal{U} = E_1 \sum_{t=1}^{\infty} \kappa_t \lambda_t U_t$$

$$\equiv E_1[\sum_{t=1}^{\infty} \kappa_t \delta^{t-1}\psi(G_t - C_t, d_t) + \sum_{t=1}^{\infty} \kappa_t \lambda_t \delta^{t-1}\psi^B(B_t)],$$

where E_1 denotes expectation of future variables and events, conditioned on information available in period 1.

From (7) and (6), a first-order condition for optimization is

$$(10) \qquad 0 = \partial\mathcal{U}/\partial G_n \equiv E_1[\kappa_n \delta^{n-1}\psi_1(G_n - C_n, d_n)$$

$$- \sum_{t=n}^{\infty} \kappa_t \lambda_t \delta^{t-1}\psi_1^B(B_t) \prod_{\tau=n+1}^{t} (1 + r_\tau)].$$

An arbitrage argument gives a useful alternative form for this condition. Suppose that the household survives until t and considers shifting one unit of expenditure to the following year. The marginal utility of the unit of expenditure this year is $\psi_1(G_t - C_t, d_t)$. This foregone unit yields $1 + r_{t+1}$ units in the following year. If the household survives, this has marginal utility with present value $\delta\psi_1(G_{t+1} - C_{t+1}, d_{t+1}) (1 + r_{t+1})$. If the household does not survive, the bequest B_{t+1} rises by the amount $1 + r_{t+1}$, yielding marginal utility with present value $\delta\psi_1^B(B_{t+1}) (1 + r_{t+1})$. Then, arbitrage implies

$$(11) \quad \psi_1(G_t - C_t, d_t) = (1 - \lambda_t)\delta(1 + r_{t+1})\psi_1(G_{t+1} - C_{t+1}, d_{t+1})$$

$$+ \lambda_t\delta(1 + r_{t+1})\psi_1^B(B_{t+1}).$$

Now, suppose that, instead of facing the actual stream of housing costs, the household faces a hypothetical alternative with the same tenure pattern but with equity converted to liquid assets and with a real life annuity implicit rental, or *user cost*, R. In this alternative, the household will adjust life-cycle expenditures to maximize

(12) $$\tilde{\mathcal{U}} = E_1\left[\sum_{t=1}^{\infty} \kappa_t \delta^{t-1}\psi(\tilde{G}_t - R, d_t) + \sum_{t=1}^{\infty} \kappa_t \lambda_t \delta^{t-1}\psi^B(\tilde{B}_t)\right]$$

subject to

(13) $$\tilde{B}_t = (A_0 + E_0)\prod_{\tau=1}^{t}(1 + r_\tau) + \sum_{s=1}^{t}(y_s - \tilde{G}_s)\prod_{\tau=s+1}^{t}(1 + r_\tau).$$

Now, equate the optimized values of $\tilde{\mathcal{U}}$ from (12) and $\mathcal{U}$ from (9). Make a first-order Taylor's expansion of (12), evaluated at its optimal path, around the optimal path for (9), and let ξ denote the remainder:

(14) $$\xi = E_1\left[\sum_{t=1}^{\infty} \kappa_t \delta^{t-1}\psi_1(G_t - C_t, d_t)\left\{\tilde{G}_t - G_t - R + C_t\right\}\right.$$

$$+ \sum_{t=1}^{\infty} \kappa_t \lambda_t \delta^{t-1}\psi_1^B(B_t)\left\{\sum_{s=1}^{t}(G_s - \tilde{G}_s)\prod_{\tau=s+1}^{t}(1 + r_\tau)\right.$$

$$\left.\left. + E_0 \prod_{\tau=1}^{t}(1 + r_\tau) - E_t 1(d_t > 0)\right\}\right].$$

Using (10), this equation yields a solution for R,

(15) $$R = \left\{E_1 \sum_{t=1}^{\infty} \kappa_t \delta^{t-1}\psi_1(G_t - C_t, d_t)\right\}^{-1}$$

$$\left\{E_1\left[\sum_{t=1}^{\infty} \kappa_t \delta^{t-1}\psi_1(G_t - C_t, d_t)C_t + \sum_{t=1}^{\infty} \kappa_t \lambda_t \delta^{t-1}\psi_1^B(B_t)\right.\right.$$

$$\left.\left.\left\{E_0 \prod_{\tau=1}^{t}(1 + r_\tau) - E_t 1(d_t > 0)\right\}\right] - \xi\right\}.$$

Write the marginal utility of bequests in the event of nonsurvival as the marginal utility of expenditure in the event of survival plus a remainder,

(16) $$\psi_1^B(B_t) = \psi_1(G_t - C_t, d_t) + \zeta_t.$$

If the remainder is small, then the household views the marginal utility of an additional unit of bequest in the event of nonsurvival as nearly equal to the marginal utility of an additional unit of expenditure in the event of survival. Combining (16) and (11),

(17) $\psi_1 (G_t - C_t, d_t) = \delta(1 + r_{t+1})\psi_1(G_{t+1} - C_{t+1}, d_{t+1}) + \lambda_t\delta\zeta_t$,

implying

(18) $\psi_1(G_t - C_t, d_t) = \psi_1(G_1 - C_1, d_1)/\delta^{t-1}\prod_{\tau=2}^{t} (1 + r_\tau) + \chi_t$,

with χ_t again denoting a remainder. Substituting in (15) and dropping the remainder, this yields

(19) $$R = \left\{E_1 \sum_{t=1}^{\infty}\kappa_t/\prod_{\tau=1}^{t} (1 + r_\tau)\right\}^{-1}\left\{E_1\left[\sum_{t=1}^{\infty} \kappa_tC_t/\prod_{\tau=1}^{t} (1 + r_\tau)\right.\right.$$

$$\left.\left. + \sum_{t=1}^{\infty} \kappa_t\lambda_t\left\{E_0 - E_t1(d_t> 0)/\prod_{\tau=1}^{t} (1 + r_\tau)\right\}\right]\right\} .$$

Then (19) is simply the value of a life annuity that has the same expected present value as the actual stream of housing costs, including capital gains and losses on transactions during the household's lifetime and including capital gains and losses from liquidation of the housing component of bequests on the death of the household. In this formula, future costs are discounted at a rate reflecting the market interest rate and the household's survival probability. For the critical assumption of a small remainder, the household's marginal utility of expenditure must be relatively insensitive to consumption level; hence, the household must be nearly risk neutral, and the "Ricardian equivalence" property must hold that a unit consumed by descendants in period t has the same marginal utility for the nonsurviving household as own consumption of this unit by the surviving household. If the marginal utility of expenditure is constant and the "Ricardian equivalence" is exact, then (19) is exact.

Our calculated user costs correspond to (19), with some modifications. First, we consider discrete choice among three dwelling sizes, as well as tenure, so that in each year the household has the alternative of not moving or of moving to one of the six possible size/tenure combinations. Second, we incorporate a relatively complete model of the offsets resulting from federal and state treatment of property taxes, mortgage interest, and capital gains. Third, we incorporate concrete models of expectations about future incomes, price levels, interest rates, and mobility. These models assume that households are Bayesian "imitators" who use the experiences of similarly situated house-holds in the past to forecast the distribution of their own responses in the future. We note that these are not necessarily "rational expectations" and that in the implementation they are not based solely on information available prior to the decision year.

2.3.2 Discounting, Mobility, and Survival

The user cost formula (19) assumes discounting at market rates of interest common to all households in a region. In fact, households face a variety of interest rates and credit constraints, with the mortgage rate somewhat above the lending rate on savings and substantially below the borrowing rate on unsecured loans. In our user cost calculations, we use the regional mortgage rate for discounting, independently of the tenure status of the individual household. This will be accurate for most mature or elderly households of at least modest means, who are typically homeowners or who have sufficient liquid assets so a rate near the mortgage rate characterizes their intertemporal trade-off. However, our calculations will understate the effective interest rate to households that are in poverty or who face credit constraints, and thus understate the user cost to these households of alternatives with "front loaded" cost streams.

Consider household expectations on the future path of housing states, conditioned on current information. Mobility among elderly households is relatively low and most commonly has one of the following patterns:

(a) Initial owners either stay until death, move to a rental unit and then stay until death, or move to a new owned unit, followed possibly by a move to a rental unit.

(b) Initial renters either stay until death, move to a new rental unit and then stay until death, or move to an owned unit, followed possibly by a move to a rental unit.

We assume that these are the *only* paths considered in the formation of expectations. By doing so, we are ignoring a small percentage of households that have high mobility rates and may anticipate this mobility in forming their expectations. Table 2.13 gives the frequency of patterns observed over the seventeen years of the PSID panel and provides some empirical justification for limiting paths to patterns a and b.[8] Our motivation for adopting this restriction is first that it drastically limits the branches of future paths the household is assumed to consider when forming expectations, making it practical to calculate expected futures without backward recursion. One could make a "bounded rationality" argument that individuals do prune decision trees before forming expectations about the future, although we cannot claim that the particular pruning we use has behavioral support. Second, the high empirical frequency of patterns a and b reflects unobserved "mover-stayer" heterogeneity in the population, in the presence of which an independent trials Bernoulli hazard model, even with duration dependence, will underestimate survival probabilities in the tail. The restriction to patterns a and b partially compensates for this bias.

We estimate simple discrete-time Bernoulli multiple hazard models for stays or moves to six possible tenure/size states, where tenure is own or rent and size

Table 2.13   Mobility Patterns

Pattern	Number	Percentage
Owner	777	38.0
Owner > renter	36	1.8
Owner > owner	220	10.8
Owner > owner > renter	4	0.2
Renter	292	14.3
Renter > renter	89	4.4
Renter > owner	96	4.7
Renter > owner > renter	6	.3
Subtotal, common patterns	1,520	74.3
Owner > owner > owner	62	3.0
Owner > renter > owner	23	1.1
Owner > renter > renter	25	1.2
Renter > owner > owner	42	1.9
Renter > renter > owner	2	.1
Renter > renter > renter	56	2.7
Owner, 3 moves	51	2.5
Renter, 3 moves	84	4.1
Owner, 4 moves	30	1.5
Renter, 4 moves	51	2.5
Owner, 5+ moves	34	1.7
Renter 5+ moves	65	3.2
Subtotal, complex patterns	525	25.7
Total	2,045	

is small, medium, or large. Define a rental unit of three rooms or fewer as *small* and one of five rooms or more as *large*. Define an owner-occupied house of four rooms or fewer as *small* and one of six rooms or more as *large*. The models are fitted as seven-alternative multinomial logits. The models are specified as functions of age of head and duration of the spell in the current dwelling and are assumed to be stationary with respect to calendar time. They are estimated using data on transitions in the PSID sample. We do not exclude multiple moves in the estimation data set. Thus the probability of moving yielded by this model is elevated slightly owing to the presence of frequent movers, relative to the mobility that would be observed if all households followed patterns *a* or *b*. Table 2.14 summarizes the period-to-period transitions in the sample. Table 2.15 gives multinomial logit transition probabilities for each of the six originating tenure/size states.

The expectation in the user cost formula (19), elaborated to include dwelling size, is approximated using the possible paths *a* and *b* described above. The probability distribution of duration in each state in a path is obtained using the multiple hazard models in table 2.15, conditioned on the destinations available from the state as specified by the possible paths. For example, a current owner in a small dwelling, when evaluating the alternative of staying for at least one more period, will have a probability distribution of moving in future years to

Table 2.14   Transition Frequencies Between Housing State, All Households, 1968–83

	Previous State						
Current State	Rent Small	Rent Medium	Rent Large	Own Small	Own Medium	Own Large	Row Total
Rent small	260	103	91	33	33	63	583
	(10.3)	(4.1)	(2.1)	(.97)	(.6)	(.5)	(1.8)
Rent medium	99	131	117	18	22	41	428
	(3.9)	(5.2)	(2.6)	(.5)	(.4)	(.3)	(1.3)
Rent large	71	144	382	10	19	89	655
	(2.8)	(5.7)	(8.7)	(.3)	(.3)	(.7)	(2.1)
Own small	30	22	34	63	27	54	230
	(1.2)	(.9)	(.8)	(1.86)	(.5)	(.4)	(.7)
Own medium	11	31	62	36	75	75	290
	(.4)	(1.2)	(1.4)	(1.06)	(1.4)	(.6)	(.9)
Own large	26	41	138	34	81	288	608
	(1.0)	(1.6)	(3.2)	(1.0)	(1.46)	(2.1)	(1.9)
Stay	2,033	2,035	3,554	3,192	5,307	13,007	29,128
	(80.4)	(81.2)	(81.2)	(94.27)	(95.4)	(95.5)	(91.1)
Column total	2,530	2,507	4,378	3,386	5,564	13,617	31,982
	(7.9)	(7.8)	(13.7)	(10.6)	(17.4)	(42.6)	

Note: Numbers in parentheses are column percentages.

any of the six tenure/size combinations. Using the patterns in a, if a transition to a rental unit is made, then the household expects to remain there until death. If a transition to another owned unit is made, then, according to a, the household considers further the possibility of a second move to a rental unit but excludes the possibility of a move to a third unit or further moves from a rental unit. The multiple hazard model is again applied to give a distribution of durations in the second owned unit; the *conditional* transition probability from ownership to a rental/size combination, given that the destination is a rental, is used for this calculation.

We define household death for a couple to be the death of the last survivor. Using U.S. mortality tables and demographic projections of future mortality patterns, we calculate survival probabilities $\kappa_S(t; A)$ for males $(S = 0)$ and females $(S = 1)$ starting from period $t = 0$, with starting age A. We use fifth-degree polynomials for interpolation of the mortality tables. The survival probability for a couple is calculated from the survival probabilities of the individuals using

$$(20) \qquad \kappa_H(t; A_0, A_1) = \kappa_0(t, A_0) + \kappa_1(t; A_1) \\ - \kappa_0(t; A_0) \cdot \kappa_1(t; A_1),$$

where κ_H denotes the household survival probability. The survival probabilities κ_0, κ_1, and κ_H enter the discount factor in the user cost formula (19) and

Table 2.15   **Multinomial Logit Transition Probabilities, Variables, and Spline Functions Used in Model**

Variable:
Choice   Choice variable—0, rent small; 1, rent medium; 2, rent large; 3, own small; 4, own medium; 5, own large; 6, stay
dur   Duration since last move

	Spline Functions of Age		
	Center	Left Limit	Right Limit
Variable:			
d1	35	35	45
d2	45	35	55
d3	55	45	65
d4	65	55	75
d5	75	65	85
d6	85	75	98
d7	98	85	98
d51	75	65	98
d61	98	75	98
d42	65	55	98
d52	98	65	98
d23	45	35	98
d33	98	45	98

	Alternative-Specific Variables: Value by Alternative						
	0	1	2	3	4	5	6
Variable:							
q1	0	1	2	0	0	0	0
q2	0	0	0	1	1	1	0
q3	0	0	0	1	2	3	0
q4	0	0	0	0	0	0	1

	Model					
	Rent Small		Rent Medium		Rent Large	
	Coeff.	SE	Coeff.	SE	Coeff.	SE
Variable:						
q1 · d1	−.053	.441	.139	.396	1.161	.327
q1 · d2	−.168	.180	.448	.159	1.128	.149
q1 · d3	−.478	.137	−.092	.147	.799	.142
q1 · d4	−.961	.179	−.216	.218	.325	.211
q1 · d51	−1.065	.290	.300	.322	1.275	.431
q1 · d61	−3.823	1.924	−1.501	1.253	.678	2.221
q2 · d1	2.048	1.978	.303	1.613	−.112	.974
q2 · d2	−1.472	1.032	−.128	.781	.958	.429
q2 · d3	−2.925	1.289	−1.823	.716	−.066	.448
q2 · d4			.943	.924	.699	.616
q2 · d42	−.077	1.293				

Table 2.15 (continued)

	Model					
	Rent Small		Rent Medium		Rent Large	
Variable:	Coeff.	SE	Coeff.	SE	Coeff.	SE
q2 · d51			−.496	1.809	−.758	1.450
q2 · d52	−20.830	12.359				
q2 · d61			.643	11.694	8.441	5.165
q3 · d1	−2.119	1.394	−.705	.874	.521	.337
q3 · d2	−.307	.549	−.730	.418	−.022	.157
q3 · d3	−.646	.753	.061	.341	.157	.173
q3 · d4			−1.520	.592	−.377	.259
q3 · d42	−2.073	.952				
q3 · d51			−.750	1.121	.610	.547
q3 · d52	5.802	4.730				
q3 · d61			−3.980	9.639	−3.956	2.783
q4 · d1	1.822	.591	2.633	584	3.764	.578
q4 · d2	2.049	.226	2.648	.241	4.294	.260
q4 · d3	1.989	.150	2.763	.195	3.900	.238
q4 · d4	2.114	.158	3.423	.270	3.934	.327
q4 · d5	2.196	.226				
q4 · d6	2.144	.409				
q4 · d7	3.958	1.978				
q4 · d51			3.546	.441	5.037	.746
q4 · d61			.735	1.274	3.599	3.806
Sample N	2,451		2,411		4,255	
Log lik.	−1,726.5		−1,676.5		−3,397.1	

	Model					
	Own Small		Own Medium		Own Large	
Variable:	Coeff.	SE	Coeff.	SE	Coeff.	SE
q1 · d1	1.026	.817	.615	1.416	2.716	1.483
q1 · d2	1.335	.328	3.526	1.233		
q1 · d3	1.335	.314	1.374	.511		
q1 · d4	.973	.345				
q1 · d42			.292	.562		
q1 · d51	1.994	0.495				
q1 · d52			4.769	3.930		
q1 · d61	−1.052	1.161				
q1 · d23					1.246	.433
q1 · d33					8.432	5.263
q2 · d1	−2.261	3.120	.461	2.921	.829	3.228
q2 · d2	1.767	.872	6.103	2.484		
q2 · d3	2.154	.751	1.412	1.089		
q2 · d4	1.222	.831				
q2 · d42			1.709	1.021		
q2 · d51	2.244	1.205				

(*continued*)

Table 2.15 (continued)

	Model					
	Own Small		Own Medium		Own Large	
Variable:	Coeff.	SE	Coeff.	SE	Coeff.	SE
q2 · d52			10.607	7.793		
q2 · d61	.131	3.224				
q2 · d23					.918	.879
q2 · d33					17.383	10.495
q3 · d1	.895	1.177	.432	.525	1.841	.560
q3 · d2	− .346	.323	.469	.248	1.008	.136
q3 · d3	− .208	.245	.480	.235	1.066	.107
q3 · d4	.047	.267			1.052	.147
q3 · d42			.355	.202		
q3 · d51	.122	.367			1.207	.239
q3 · d52			− 1.354	1.013		
q3 · d61	− 1.660	1.446			1.218	.662
q4 · d1	.099	1.707	− 2.428	2.743	5.289	2.859
q4 · d2	1.029	.669	7.371	2.422		
q4 · d3	2.069	.607	2.652	.956		
q4 · d4	1.396	.654				
q4 · d42			2.445	.932		
q4 · d51	2.877	.983				
q4 · d52			8.910	7.567		
q4 · d61	− 4.220	2.603				
q4 · d23					2.842	.836
q4 · d33					19.937	10.456
q4 · dur	2.772	.176	2.623	.166	2.680	.123
Sample N	3,489		5,462		12,783	
Log lik.	− 799.62		− 650.64		− 1,041.5	

are also applied to calculate the probability of nonsurvival in a period *before* the multiple hazard model for mobility is applied. Figure 2.5 shows the survival probabilities for a husband-wife household and for a single woman household, conditioned on the individuals being alive at age 60 in 1974.

2.3.3   Assets and Income Expectations

Expectations of future income not only enter household expected wealth, which directly influences life-cycle planning, but also determine expected income tax offsets to housing costs. We model income expectations as a function of current income, wealth, and demographic characteristics. We assume that there is no information available to the household that is unavailable to the econometrician, that there were no macro shocks through the period of the PSID panel that make the life-cycle income patterns observed therein unrepresentative, and that income expectations are stationary once trends are accounted for. Then the ex post distribution of incomes in a future

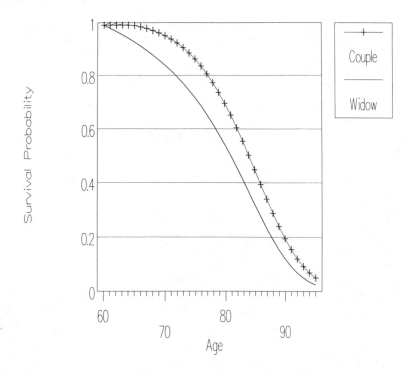

Fig. 2.5   Survival probabilities (households aged 60 in 1974)

period, for the subpopulation with the same history as the household in question, coincides with the ex ante expectation of this household. We can then estimate the ex post distribution and use it in the user cost calculation. However, these assumptions may not be a good approximation of reality. We note that assuming the absence of macro shocks is unpalatable here, as there is certainly correlation of the housing markets seen by geographically proximate households, and ex post house price data from areas such as the Los Angeles SMSA will certainly embody the realizations of market-wide shocks not perfectly anticipated by consumers.

The *taxable* income profiles starting from year t with a head of age A_t are assumed to have the form

$$(21) \qquad y_{t+s} = y_t \exp\left(\sum_{j \in J} \theta_j [d_j(A_{t+s}) - d_j(A_t)] \right),$$

where $s = 1, 2, \ldots$ denotes future years, the θ_j are coefficients, and the d_j are linear spline functions of age,

$$(22) \qquad d(a) = \begin{cases} 1 - c_1(c_0 - a) \text{ if } c_1 (c_0 - a) < 1 \text{ and } a \leq c_0 , \\ 1 - c_2(a - c_0) \text{ if } c_2 (a - c_0) < 1 \text{ and } a > c_0 , \\ 0 \text{ otherwise,} \end{cases}$$

with c_0, c_1, and c_2 specified nonnegative constants. In order to estimate this model using the eleven-year window from 1974 through 1984 in which the PSID has comparable income data, we make the crude approximation that households treat their demographic state as time invariant. For example, a household consisting of a couple with head aged 60 is postulated to assume that changes in its income profile between ages 80 and 90 will resemble the changes over a decade of *couples* that start with head aged 80. In fact, there is a substantial probability that this head will die before age 80 and the household's income profile in this future decade will more closely resemble that of widows that start at age 80. This is not very satisfactory, and a better solution would be to turn to data on full life cycles in which future income profiles could be constructed conditioned on demographic status at comparable ages.

The form of the income profile could have been elaborated to account for additional effects, some of which may be important. A term allowing a chronological trend in real income levels or a function of actual variations in aggregate real income per household in the historical period (replaced in income projections by long-run macroeconomic forecasts) could be added. Base income y_t could be replaced by an exponential distributed lag on current and past income levels; this might more closely approximate the ''nontransitory income'' that the household uses as a base for income forecasts. We have not made these extensions.

The system above is log linear in parameters and is estimated using PSID total household money income data that are available from 1975 through 1984. (Only labor income data are available back to 1968.) These data are stacked by household and by year within household. Then the profile is estimated in log form using all available pairs of years t and $t + s$, conditioned on all income variables appearing in the regression being positive. The cases of zero income almost all correspond to nonsurvival, and for these the regression conditioning corresponds to the conditional forecast needed. The few cases where surviving households have zero labor and pension income are adapted to the functional form by assigning a minimum income of one dollar.

The formulation above of the life-cycle income profile and estimation method differs from the more common autoregressive forecasting model in that we use a direct s-period ahead forecast rather than an s-step ahead iterative forecast. The reason we do this is that we anticipate the existence of persistent individual effects, which can be approximated in an autoregressive model only with a lengthy lag. The trade-off is that we have rather tightly parameterized the tail of the life-cycle income profile. A second variation on conventional analysis is that we combine labor and pension income and do not condition on retirement. Thus, our model gives unconditional income profiles that incorporate sample information on retirement patterns and their interdependence on earnings and pension profiles. This approach circumvents the necessity of specifying a correct structural model of the retirement process and is robust to the nature of this structure. One drawback is that we will not be able to do policy analysis of housing behavior response to structural changes in retirement programs or forecast housing demand in a future where structural changes in retirement programs have occurred. Since our analysis is conditioned only on household survival, not on individual members, it incorporates the expected effect on income of nonsurvival of head or spouse. This avoids structural modeling of, say, income conditioned on the event of future widowhood.

Table 2.16 gives the coefficients of the fitted taxable income forecasting models for twenty demographic categories. Figure 2.6 gives the income profile

Table 2.16   **Explanatory Variables Used in the Income Projection Model**

Spline Function of Age	Center	Left Limit	Right Limit
L40	25	None	40
L45	30	None	45
L50	35	None	50
L55	40	None	55
L60	45	None	60
R60	75	60	None
R65	80	65	None
R70	85	70	None
R75	90	75	None
R80	95	80	None

Classification of Households and Income Forecasting Models

Black Female Head		Nonblack Female Head			Nonblack
					Unmarried
Graduate	Other	Graduate Nonworking	Working	Other	Male Head
2	1	4	5	3	20

Black Male Head

Married		Unmarried		
Working	Nonworking	Nongraduate Nonworking	Graduate *or* Working	Other
7	6	9	10	8

Nonblack Married Nonworking Male Head

Graduate		Nongraduate			
Wife Working	Other	Wife Graduate Working	Wife Nongraduate Nonworking	Wife Nongraduate Working	Other
12	11	13	14	15	11

Table 2.16 (continued)

	Nonblack Married Working Male Head					
	Both Graduate		One Graduate		Neither Graduate	
	Wife Nonworking	Other	Wife Working Graduate *or* Nongraduate	Other	Wife Nonworking	Wife Working
	16	11	17	11	18	19

	Estimated Models						
	1	2	3	4	5	6	7
Constant	.073	.003	.057	.010	.047	−.023	−.078
	(.032)	(.026)	(.020)	(.032)	(.029)	(.019)	(.047)
L40	−2.421	−2.472	−4.540	−1.753	−10.245	3.368	2.665
	(1.516)	(.674)	(1.445)	(2.033)	(3.968)	(.926)	(2.168)
L45	.248	1.712	−1.484	−1.001	−1.781	.130	−1.886
	(.723)	(.406)	(.538)	(.713)	(1.229)	(.327)	(1.170)
L50	.928	−.616	−.115	−.263	.679	.200	−1.437
	(.304)	(.209)	(.278)	(.316)	(.642)	(.163)	(.651)
L55	−1.486	−.366	−.936	−.724	−1.126	−.612	.678
	(.265)	(.225)	(.234)	(.282)	(.500)	(.157)	(.465)
L60	1.072	.312	.741	.494	.045	1.036	−.057
	(.198)	(.178)	(.155)	(.207)	(.309)	(.114)	(.289)
R60	−2.391	.587	−2.403	−2.803	−.306	−3.167	−.306
	(.229)	(.233)	(.133)	(.216)	(.241)	(.140)	(.418)
R65	.917	.096	.910	.049	.403	−.220	−.309
	(.460)	(.595)	(.181)	(.335)	(.308)	(.284)	(.552)
R70	−.854	−.050	.259	−1.160	−.630	−.652	−.446
	(.700)	(.886)	(.208)	(.507)	(.258)	(.730)	(.632)
R75	.784	−20.506	−.904	2.201	.285		−.717
	(1.195)	(6.667)	(.193)	(1.349)	(.350)		(.948)
R80	−5.151			−7.809	−.406		
	(3.901)			(6.531)	(.357)		
Sample N	3,199	2,141	11,523	3,796	5,929	7,632	1,571
R^2	.072	.024	.059	.166	.010	.136	.026

	8	9	10	11	12	13	14
Constant	.076	.003	.140	−.019	−.066	−.044	−.025
	(.046)	(.052)	(.085)	(.009)	(.017)	(.036)	(.032)
L40	−3.633		−.632	1.913	−.724		
	(5.602)		(7.731)	(.615)	(1.277)		
L45	−.922	−1.316	−.548	1.006	1.192	−1.197	3.125
	(.899)	(.954)	(1.963)	(.205)	(.314)	(.765)	(.793)
L50	.444	.654	−.314	−.523	−.884	−.626	.572
	(.498)	(.518)	(1.161)	(.087)	(.141)	(.316)	(.296)

Table 2.16 (continued)

	Estimated Models						
	8	9	10	11	12	13	14
L55	−.607	−.373	−.786	−.120	−.183	1.374	−.056
	(.404)	(.411)	(1.025)	(.081)	(.140)	(.282)	(.258)
L60	.870	.384	1.500	.534	.502	−.666	.164
	(.285)	(.302)	(.666)	(.059)	(.103)	(.206)	(.190)
R60	−3.625	−4.530	−2.967	−2.482	−3.594	−2.934	−1.300
	(.319)	(.386)	(.549)	(.066)	(.124)	(.259)	(.233)
R65	.400	1.491	2.297	.220	−.551	−1.567	−1.188
	(.684)	(.935)	(1.153)	(.103)	(.234)	(.488)	(.466)
R70	2.787	−5.788	.614	2.126	3.467	4.310	−2.309
	(.917)	(2.317)	(1.261)	(.129)	(.355)	(1.100)	(2.022)
R75	−2.234		−2.586	−2.219	−4.780	−4.765	−8.610
	(1.444)		(1.646)	(.134)	(.589)	(99.999)	(2.486)
R80	−9.166		−6.976			−8.000	
	(2.363)		(2.676)			(99.999)	
Sample N	1,304	869	435	37,020	9,555	1,920	2,135
R^2	.169	.256	.136	.075	.196	.171	.095
	15	16	17	18	19	20	
Constant	−.058	−.048	.010	−.024	−.051	.030	
	(.030)	(.046)	(.047)	(.078)	(.052)	(.036)	
L40	4.093						
	(1.000)						
L45	.639	3.071	−1.119			−.388	
	(.557)	(1.439)	(1.626)			(.872)	
L50	−.455	−.882	−.723	−1.777	−3.181	−1.177	
	(.262)	(.735)	(.742)	(1.468)	(2.393)	(.384)	
L55	.439	−1.557	.067	−1.972	7.313	.378	
	(.250)	(.542)	(.659)	(.751)	(1.307)	(.389)	
L60	.164	1.585	−.013	2.074	−3.756	.410	
	(.184)	(.341)	(.512)	(.541)	(.500)	(.282)	
R60	−3.624	−2.817	−1.467	−.601	.399	−1.418	
	(.218)	(.361)	(.490)	(.802)	(.486)	(.289)	
R65	.761	3.519	.259	−6.070	−1.008	−1.248	
	(.382)	(.467)	(.581)	(.957)	(.617)	(.377)	
R70	1.324	−1.026	1.046	4.616	.217	2.363	
	(.714)	(.518)	(.404)	(1.038)	(.445)	(.429)	
R75	−5.077	−6.157	−1.746	−1.993	.192	−1.932	
	(1.576)	(1.478)	(.721)	(1.672)	(.668)	(.371)	
R80	−.507		−3.179	−.950	−.501		
	(3.209)		(2.876)	(1.602)	(.743)		
Sample N	3,417	932	1,566	758	1,871	2,617	
R^2	.155	.109	.031	.218	.047	.049	

Note: Standard errors are in parentheses.
[a]Workng means employed in the last four years. Graduate means graduated from high school.

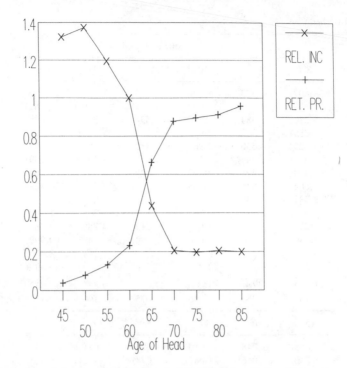

Fig. 2.6   Couple's expected income (relative income and retirement probability)

produced by the model, along with retirement probability for the head obtained from a logistic regression on the same spline functions of age, for a married household (model 11). There is a sharp drop in *taxable income* between 60 and 70 years of age. Figure 2.7 gives a comparable profile for a working widow (model 5).

2.4   The Elderly in the Panel Study of Income Dynamics

2.4.1   Some Features of the Sample

Table 2.17 gives some of the characteristics of the analysis sample and, for comparison, some population statistics on the elderly. The PSID has a slightly higher proportion of nonwhites and is slightly weighted to the older elderly but otherwise appears to resemble the general population of persons aged 65 and over. The PSID shows mean net worths in 1984 for the 65–74 age group that are lower than those found in the Federal Reserve Survey of Consumer Finances for 1983; however, the PSID net worths for the 75 and over group are higher. The latter comparison is surprising in view of the original PSID oversampling of poverty households. Table 2.18 shows the distribution of income by source.

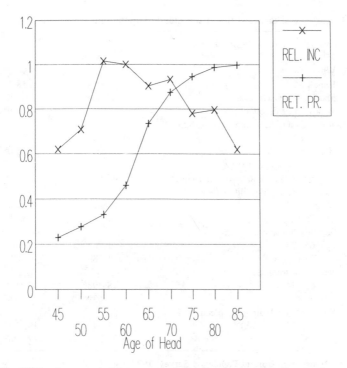

Fig. 2.7   Widow's expected income (relative income and retirement probability)

The PSID shows substantially more social security income and less asset income than the Current Population Reports, due in part to the weighting to older households. Table 2.19 gives net worth and the distribution of assets. For the PSID, these are calculated for the part of the sample (84.2 percent) that has positive assets. Table 2.20 relates 1984 asset income reported in the PSID to reported asset holdings; the coefficients can be interpreted as the gross rates of returns on these assets, not accounting for unrealized net capital gains or reinvestment. In this year, the real rate of return at the prime rate was 6.3 percent. Thus, the PSID households are either underreporting asset income, overreporting assets, reinvesting a substantial portion of asset earnings, or achieving returns well below the market.

2.4.2   User Costs

The method of calculating user costs described in section 2.3 is carried out for each household in our PSID sample, in each year from 1975 through 1984, except for years with missing data. Table 2.21 gives the average user cost of housing by age group for the sample population and for owners and renters separately. There are several factors that are expected to introduce a linkage between age and user cost. First, older households have less time to amortize

Table 2.17   Characteristics of the Elderly Population, Age 65 and Over

Individuals age 65+ (PSID N = 1,054):		
75+ (%)	36.7[f]	38.2[a]
White (%)	81.3[f]	90.2[a]
Female (%)	59.8[f]	58.7[a]
Married, spouse present (%)	59.9[f]	53.5[a]
Widowed or divorced (%)	38.1[f]	39.6[a]
Households age 65+ (PSID N = 823):		
75+ (%)	47.0[f]	41.1[b]
Homeowners (%)	65.9[f]	75.0[c]
Owners mortgage free (%)	80.4[f]	83.0[c]
Median house value, owners, 1983 ($)	48,600[f]	48,800[b]
Income on shelter/utilities (%):		
65–74	. . .	36.6[d]
75+	. . .	35.5[d]
Monthly household income ($):		
65–74	1,362[f]	1,164[e]
75+	1,189[f]	828[e]
Net worth total ($):		
65–74	78,598[f]	63,597[e]
75+	81,639[f]	55,178[e]
Net worth excluding home equity ($):		
65–74	47,546[f]	19,979[b]
75+	28,374[f]	17,025[b]

[a]1986 proportions, from Current Population Survey, 1987.

[b]1983 means, from "Financial Characteristics of the Housing Inventory," Current Housing Reports Series H-150-83, 1983.

[c]1983 means, from Current Population Reports Series P-60, no. 152, 1986.

[d]1984 means, from "Consumer Expenditure Survey: Interview Survey, 1984," Bulletin no. 2267, 1986.

[e]1984 medians, from "Household Wealth and Asset Ownership, 1984," Current Population Reports, P-70, no. 7, 1986. A median family income of $1,518 per month for household age 65 and over, excluding unattached individuals, is reported for 1984 in Current Population Reports, Series P-60. The Survey of Consumer Finances, Federal Reserve, reports for 1983 the following net worths:

Age	Mean	Median
65–74	125,184	50,181
75+	72,985	35,939

[f]PSID 1984 sample tabulation.

the initial costs of purchasing a dwelling so that the relative cost of owning to renting should rise with age, as should the relative cost of moving versus staying. Second, older households have lower taxable income and hence benefit less from income tax offsets to ownership. Third, the present expected value of capital gains from owned housing was large in the period 1975–84, providing an offset to user costs that we assume is attenuated over the remaining life of younger households.[9] Fourth, variations in the geographic distribution of households by age, with the elderly concentrating in lower-cost housing areas, could confound sample age differences in user costs. The panel for all households in table 2.21 shows that user costs do not rise uniformly with age but instead fall for the old. This pattern is repeated when households are classified separately by owners and renters.

In the PSID sample, the relative cost of owning to renting rises until age 65 and after that is nearly constant, as figure 2.8 shows. This graph was obtained by regressing the user cost ratio for four-room dwellings on age, using a quadratic spline. Examination of the survival probabilities shows that, at any age up to 80, expected remaining life is sufficiently long that the effect of

Table 2.18   **Sources of Income, Households Age 65 and Over in 1984**

Social security	60.7[a]	31.6[b]
Asset income	15.2	23.7
Pensions	12.6	15.3
Earnings	8.2	28.6
Other	2.6	.8

[a]N = 806 households with complete data.
[b]U.S. Census, Current Population Reports, Series P-60, 1984.

Table 2.19   **Assets of Household Age 65 and Over in 1984**

Net Worth:		
Percent Distribution (%):		
Home equity	50.3[a]	38.6[b]
Other real estate	7.4	11.2
Cash	33.2	30.3
Stocks	4.1	8.6
Business	3.1	4.5
Other	1.9	6.8
Debt as a % of net worth	1.9	. . .

[a]N = 693 with complete data.
[b]1984 data, ''Household Wealth and Asset Ownership,'' Current Population Reports, Series P-70, U.S. Bureau of the Census.

Table 2.20   **Asset Income Regressed on Asset Holdings, 1984**

Independent Variable	Estimate	Standard Error
Cash	.0504	.0029
Bonds	.0257	.0005
Business nonlabor income	.0259	.0037
Real property	.0251	.0021
Stocks	.0458	.0025
Observations (N)	823	
R^2	.840	

Table 2.21   **Average Annualized User Costs (thousands of 1982$)**

	Rent			Own			
Age	Small	Medium	Large	Small	Medium	Large	Stay
All households:							
35–49	3.733	3.839	4.033	4.780	5.400	6.301	4.111
50–64	3.569	3.703	3.955	5.252	5.926	6.975	4.244
65–79	2.684	2.849	3.100	4.329	5.438	6.392	3.054
80+	2.350	2.524	2.839	4.158	5.213	6.091	2.416
Current owners:							
35–49	5.614	5.746	5.999	6.792	7.672	8.969	6.551
50–64	4.862	5.015	5.309	6.318	7.131	8.452	6.387
65–79	3.475	3.650	3.930	4.778	5.819	6.924	4.765
80+	2.292	2.438	2.709	3.195	3.938	4.626	2.585
Current renters:							
35–49	3.041	3.138	3.309	4.039	4.564	5.320	3.213
50–64	2.803	2.926	3.152	4.620	5.212	6.100	2.974
65–79	2.491	2.653	2.910	4.219	5.345	6.262	2.637
80+	2.356	2.533	2.852	4.254	5.340	6.236	2.399

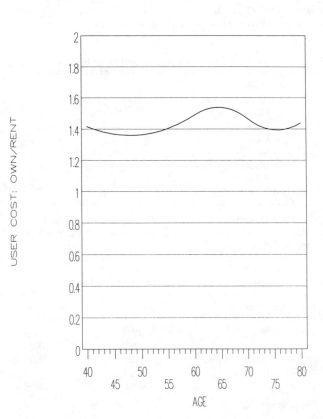

Fig. 2.8   Relative user cost

nonsurvival on present value calculations is small. This may explain the failure of the relative cost to show a strong trend with age.

The relation between user cost of housing and total household income (earned and transfer) is shown in figure 2.9. For comparison, housing cost (including shelter cost and expenditures for fuel, utilities, and public services) from the 1984 Consumer Expenditure Survey (CES) is included. Income drops sharply with age past 60. (This is a cross-sectional comparison, so age differences also contain cohort effects.) The housing cost share from the CES is nearly constant until age 65 and then rises steadily with age. The PSID housing cost share in income, using our construction of annualized user cost, is generally higher than the CES measure, rises more quickly in the 55–65 age range, and is relatively constant past age 70. The PSID share is calculated using the annualized user cost for the alternative of staying in the current dwelling and hence reflects the actual mix of owners and renters in the population. A quadratic spline is used to estimate share as a function of age.

2.4.3   Housing Behavior

The behavioral response of households to housing market conditions should reflect the dual role of owner-occupied housing as a source of shelter services and as an investment in the household's portfolio. Expectations of future price increases will be viewed by the household as increasing out-of-pocket costs but

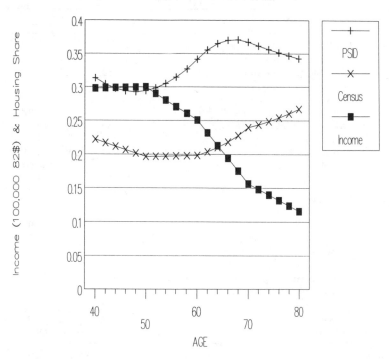

Fig. 2.9   Pretax income and shelter share

as also as increasing the return on the asset via capital gains. Once the expected investment returns are netted out, via the user cost calculations, there should be a relatively unambivalent behavioral response: lower mobility when the user costs associated with moving are relatively high and shifts toward renting when the user costs associated with owning are relatively high.[10]

While it is highly plausible that user costs will influence housing choice behavior at the margin, it is also clear that the circumstances in which prices have an opportunity to operate in housing decisions are limited. Mobility is low, empirically, and in many cases is dictated by noneconomic circumstances. Table 2.22 lists the frequencies with which the PSID sample lists various reasons for moving. Of actual movers, 74 percent give a primary purpose other than a change in dwelling size, which is the most likely to be influenced by costs. While price should be a factor in moves made for other primary reasons, such as involuntary moves (e.g., moves because of demolition of building, condominium conversion, or employment transfers), it may not be strongly correlated with the occurrence of these moves. For these reasons, one might not find statistically significant user cost effects in a relatively small sample. Tables 2.23–2.25 gives seven-alternative multinomial choice models, with the alternatives "stay" or move to one of the six tenure/size combinations (own/rent and small/medium/large), for current previous owners and for

Table 2.22   PSID Sample Reasons for Moving, 1975–84

	N	%
Why the household will or might move:		
Move due to job	207	6.17
Relocate nearer to work	68	2.03
Move to larger dwelling	504	15.02
Move to smaller dwelling	586	17.47
Move from rent to own	400	11.92
Move to better neighborhood	352	10.49
Forced to move involuntarily	493	14.69
Mixed reason	745	22.21
Subtotal	3,355	100.00
No move planned	17,471	83.89[a]
Why the household did move:		
Move due to job	96	5.37
Relocate nearer to work	34	1.90
Move to larger dwelling	278	15.56
Move to smaller dwelling	188	10.52
Move from rent to own	235	13.15
Move to better neighborhood	129	7.22
Forced to move involuntarily	508	28.43
Mixed reason	319	17.85
Subtotal	1,787	100.00
No move planned	19,011	89.14[a]

[a]Percentage of total.

Table 2.23 Multinomial Logit Models of Mobility and Tenure/Size Choice

		Alternative						
Variables	Mnemonic	Rent Small	Rent Medium	Rent Large	Own Small	Own Medium	Own Large	Stay
User cost	ucost	X	X	X	X	X	X	X
Stay dummy	dstay	0	0	0	0	0	0	1
Owner dummy	down	0	0	0	1	1	1	0
Small size dummy	dsmall	1	0	0	1	0	0	0
Large size dummy	dlarge	0	0	1	0	0	1	0
Stay dummy · income	ystay	0	0	0	0	0	0	Y
Owner dummy · income	yown	0	0	0	Y	Y	Y	0
Small size dummy · income	ysmall	Y	0	0	Y	0	0	0
Large size dummy · income	ylarge	0	0	Y	0	0	Y	0

Table 2.24 Choice Model for Previous Owner

A.

Value	Label	Count	%
0	Rent small	14	.61
1	Rent medium	11	.48
2	Rent large	18	.79
3	Own small	9	.39
4	Own medium	12	.52
5	Own large	38	1.66
6	Stay	2,190	95.55

B.

Independent Variable	Estimated Coefficient	Standard Error	Estimated Coefficient	Standard Error
ucost	1.69576e-05	2.82166e-06		
ln(ucost)			1.17957	.27408
dstay	4.93273	.32904	4.87769	.33209
down	−.55890	.31431	−.59912	.32216
dsmall	.56310	.42271	.57259	.42171
dlarge	.68214	.26913	.74638	.26266
ystay	1.06427e-05	9.56519e-06	1.34464e-05	9.75145e-06
yown	1.41865e-05	9.50871e-06	1.72864e-05	9.72394e-06
ysmall	−1.93585e-05	1.42695e-05	−1.98148e-05	1.42886e-05
ylarge	−8.54206e-07	2.55076e-06	−8.68247e-08	2.16556e-06
Sample *N*	2,292		2,292	
Log lik.	−565.47		−575.14	

Table 2.25   Choice Model for Previous Renter

A.

Value	Label	Count	%
0	Rent small	282	5.45
1	Rent medium	177	3.42
2	Rent large	327	6.31
3	Own small	36	.70
4	Own medium	50	.97
5	Own large	74	1.43
6	Stay	4,233	81.73

B.

Independent Variable	Estimated Coefficient	Standard Error	Estimated Coefficient	Standard Error
ucost	1.90477e-06	1.68221e-06		
ln(ucost)			− .44357	.23104
dstay	2.97519	9.42026e-02	2.97544	9.41622e-02
down	− 2.49811	.13480	− 2.22623	.16958
dsmall	.49256	.11626	.46266	.11692
dlarge	.44611	.10615	.48836	.10781
ystay	1.30355e-05	5.94221e-06	1.36404e-05	5.94588e-06
yown	5.98801e-05	5.87533e-06	5.81235e-05	5.94104e-06
ysmall	− 1.41928e-05	7.26346e-06	− 1.43114e-05	7.24157e-06
ylarge	8.88810e-06	5.28270e-06	9.30676e-06	5.26707e-06
Sample N	5,179		5,179	
Log lik.	− 3,824.1		− 3,822.8	

previous renters. In the model for owners, the effect of user cost is positive, suggesting that investment incentives may outweigh consumer substitution effects in "hot" markets. In the model for renters, we find a weak price elasticity of the expected sign and responsiveness to income in choice of dwelling size.

2.5 Conclusions

The primary conclusion of this paper is that carefully constructed user costs for housing, which adjust for income tax offsets and capital gains, show *declining* annualized costs past age 60. While the income of the elderly declines even more rapidly so that the housing share of consumption expenditures rises with age for the elderly, the increase is not sharp, and the housing share appears to level off for the very elderly.

We find that user costs increase sharply with dwelling size. This reflects in part sharp differences in our hedonic price indices for dwellings of different sizes, which may be due in part to quality differences that are correlated with size and that are not captured by the measured features of dwellings. It also reflects the effects of the multiple hazard models (table 2.15) for tenure/size transitions: occupants of large owner-occupied dwellings are more likely to stay in the current dwelling, at high out-of-pocket costs, and are more likely to move to a large dwelling if they move than are occupants of small rental dwellings. We find that the annualized user cost of owner housing generally exceeds that of renting for middle-aged and elderly households. The persistence of ownership in the face of this differential suggests the presence of substantial quality differences in owned and rental housing.

We find little evidence in the relatively small PSID data set that, at the margin, households are modifying choices to avoid relatively high-priced housing. This may be the result of analyzing a relatively small group of movers, many of whom had stated primary motives for moving that were noneconomic. A second possibility is that "supply side" investment incentive effects, with housing prices acting as a proxy for expected capital gains, overwhelm "demand side" consumer response. A third possibility is that the subjective evaluation of the economic costs of choices by households may fail to match the relatively complex model we have used of formation of expectations. On the one hand, the household is likely to have access to more information on its prospective income than is available to us and may have more information on local housing markets. On the other, the household may fail to weigh consistently the contribution of tax offsets and capital gains to user costs or to weigh bequests of real property as we have done in deriving our user cost formula. The analysis of wealth effects on housing choices of the elderly by Feinstein and McFadden (1989) and a macroeconomic paper on housing price expectations and bequest motives by Mankiw and Weil (1988) suggest that households may in fact be more myopic than our user calculations assume.

Notes

1. In the PSID, individuals are identified as *sample* members if they were present in a household at the start of the panel in 1968 or are descendants of sample members. Otherwise, they are *nonsample*. Only sample members are followed through household composition changes. For example, if a sample member marries at a later date, the spouse is not a sample member and is not followed if the sample member dies or they are separated. In this study, we define a PSID household by the following steps. First, we define a *provisional* household for *each* sample member. Then we merge every pair of provisional households such that, when the two sample individuals are both alive, they do not live apart, except temporarily. (A separation for school, institutionalization, or military service or a marital separation that ends in reconciliation is defined to be temporary.) Thus, two sample members that divorce are counted as two households and treated as separate observations, even though part of their history is common. Similarly, a child who leaves home and establishes a separate residence is counted as a different

household than the parent, even if in old age the parent moves in with the child. Nonsample spouses of nonsurviving sample members are treated as a continuation of the household, with missing data. Judgment is used to resolve complex cases; usually, such cases are excluded from the analysis. We include in our analysis sample households where head and spouse are both under 35 in 1968 but where there is another household member over 35. However, the housing choices and user costs we consider are in general not the appropriate ones for a nonhead nonspouse. We exclude from the analysis sample households that attrit before 1984 for reasons *other* than death; approximately three hundred households fall in this category, most of whom attrit within the first few years of the panel.

2. Chunrong Ai and Henry Pollakowski are responsible for the results in secs. 2.2.1–2.2.3 below. The price index construction was supported in part by the Office of Policy Development and Research, U.S. Department of Housing and Urban Development (see Pollakowski 1987; and Pollakowski and Börsch-Supan 1988). We thank Paul Burke, Axel Börsch-Supan, and Thomas Thibodeau for helpful suggestions.

3. For a description of the AHS, see Hadden, Joseph, and Leger (1984).

4. Use of these median values of attributes should be interpreted as follows: for owner-occupied housing, the median dwelling has one and a half baths with a probability of .174, two baths with a probability of .218, more than two baths with a probability of .116, and less than one and a half baths (the base case) with a probability of .508.

5. These are loan origination fees and mortgage points and do not include title insurance, mortgage insurance, and transfer fees.

6. We also investigated the possibility of using data from the PSID to construct regional estimates of mortgage term and the ratio of initial mortgage to purchase price. For the PSID subsample of home purchasers in a year who take mortgages, we use the responses on market value of home, mortgage outstanding, and mortgage payments to construct the needed variables. From the standard amortization formula, mortgage length L satisfies

$$L = -r^{-1}\log(1 - rP_0/m),$$

where P_0 is the initial mortgage outstanding, m is the annual mortgage payment, and r is the state average mortgage rate. (In principle, one could use data on mortgage outstanding in successive years for nonmovers to calculate the interest rate on the individual mortgage. However, the PSID responses are not reliable enough to do this accurately.) In 1973–75 and 1982, the required data were not collected by the PSID. For these years, for 1968 and earlier, and for 1985 and later, L and the ratio of P_0 to house price were calculated by interpolation and extrapolation. In general, the results of this analysis were similar on average to the national statistics and sufficiently noisy so that regional differences could not be distinguished. Therefore, we used the national averages.

7. The mortgage/price ratio distribution is in fact bimodal, with some fraction of households taking no mortgage and the remainder fairly heavily concentrated in the range .6–.9. We have used the average of this distribution, excluding households with zero mortgages, as an approximation to the maximum mortgage available. We have *not* adjusted this statistic for its likely downward bias.

8. For most households, the patterns are right censored before death. Thus, table 2.13 understates to some degree the frequency of multiple moves. Also, only changes in tenure and/or size are counted as "moves."

9. We assume that regional housing prices grow in real terms at a rate that declines linearly from the actual 1984 rate to zero in 1994.

10. Since detailed housing commodities, such as "small rental units," may be inferior goods, classical consumer theory leaves some ambiguity about the sign of response to price.

References

Blackley, D. M., J. R. Follain, and H. Lee. 1986. An evaluation of hedonic price indexes for 34 large SMSA's. *American Real Estate and Urban Economics Association Journal* 14 (Summer):179–205.

Börsch-Supan, A., L. Kotlikoff, and J. Morris. 1988. The dynamics of living arrangements of the elderly. NBER working paper. Cambridge, Mass.: National Bureau of Economic Research.

Bryan, T. B., and P. F. Colwell. 1982. Housing price indexes. In *Research in real estate*, vol. 2, ed. C. F. Sirmans. New York: JAI.

Feinstein, J., and D. McFadden. 1989. The dynamics of housing demand by the elderly: Wealth, cash flow, and demographic effects. In *The economics of aging*, ed. David Wise. Chicago: University of Chicago Press.

Ferri, M. G. 1977. An application of hedonic indexing methods to monthly changes in housing prices: 1965–1975. *American Real Estate and Urban Economics Association Journal* 5 (Winter):455–62.

Follain, J., and J. Ozanne, with V. Alburger. 1979. Place to place indexes of the price of housing. *Urban Institute Paper on Housing*. Washington, D.C.: Urban Institute, December.

Gillingham, R. 1975. Place-to-place rent comparisons. *Annals of Economic and Social Measurement* 4:153–74.

Goodman, A. C. 1978. Hedonic prices, price indices and housing markets. *Journal of Urban Economics* 5 (October):471–84.

Goodman, A. C., and M. Kawai. 1984. Replicative evidence on rental and owner demand for housing. *Southern Economic Journal* 50 (April):1036–57.

Hadden, L., C. Joseph, and M. Leger. 1984. *Codebook for the annual housing survey data base*. Cambridge, Mass.: Abt Associates (prepared under contract H5529 with the U.S. Department of Housing and Urban Development).

Hendershott, Patric, and Joel Slemrod. 1983. Taxes and the user cost of capital for owner-occupied housing. *AREUEA Journal* 10(4):375–93.

Malpezzi, S. L., L. Ozanne, and T. Thibodeau. 1980. Characteristic prices of housing and fifty-nine metropolitan areas. Contract report 1367-1. Washington, D.C.: Urban Institute.

Mankiw G., and R. Weil. 1988. The baby boom, the baby bust, and the housing market. NBER Working Paper no. 2794. Cambridge, Mass.: National Bureau of Economic Research.

Mark, H., and M. A. Goldberg. 1984. Alternative housing price indices: An evaluation. *American Real Estate and Urban Economics Association Journal* 12 (Spring):30–49.

Ozanne, L., and T. Thibodeau. 1983. Explaining metropolitan housing price differences. *Journal of Urban Economics* 13 (January):51–66.

Palmer, B. 1987. Moving and the elderly: Using a stochastic, yet finite planning horizon. Working paper. Cambridge: Massachusetts Institute of Technology.

Palmquist, R. 1980. Alternative techniques for developing real estate price indexes. *Review of Economics and Statistics* 62 (August):442–48.

Pollakowski, H. O. 1982. *Urban housing markets and residential location.* Lexington, Mass.: Lexington.
Pollakowski, H. 1987. Owner-occupied housing price change in the U.S., 1974–1983: A disaggregated approach. Working paper. Cambridge, Mass.: Joint Center for Housing Studies of the Massachusetts Institute of Technology and Harvard University.
Pollakowski, H. O., and A. Börsch-Supan. 1988. Hedonic price indexes for the United States, 1974 to 1983. Working paper. Cambridge, Mass.: Joint Center for Housing Studies of the Massachusetts Institute of Technology and Harvard University.
Schnare, A., and R. Struyk. 1976. Segmentation and urban housing markets. *Journal of Urban Economics* 3 (April):146–66.
Struyk, R. 1977. The housing expense burden of households headed by the elderly. *Gerontologist* 17.
Venti, S., and D. Wise. 1984. Moving and housing expenditure: Transactions costs and disequilibrium. *Journal of Public Economics* 23:207–43.
————. 1989. Aging, moving, and housing wealth. In *The economics of aging,* ed. David Wise. Chicago: University of Chicago Press.
Weisbrod, G., J. Berkovec, J. Ginn, S. Lerman, H. Pollakowski, and P. Reid. 1982. Residential mobility and housing choices of older Americans. Final report. Cambridge, Mass.: Cambridge Systematics.

Comment   Michael D. Hurd

On average, housing equity is the most important component of the bequeathable wealth of the elderly: about 50 percent in the 1984 Panel Study of Income Dynamics, about 57 percent among families in the twentieth to eightieth wealth percentile in the 1984 Survey of Income and Program Participation, and 44 percent in the 1979 Retirement History Survey. Yet our knowledge of the determinants of housing choice is rather limited. For example, we do not know the role of housing choice in life-cycle consumption. Do the elderly desire to decumulate housing wealth as they age, or do they tend to hold housing for purposes of a bequest? Do large transaction costs (both financial and psychic) prevent the elderly from moving? If they do, programs to facilitate downsizing should produce gains, both at the individual level and at the aggregate level, as the existing housing stock is used more efficiently. How large would the gains be? What should be the structure of reverse annuity mortgage programs, and how much benefit could be expected from them? These examples are just a few of many that show the importance of understanding the determinants of housing choice.

The study of housing choice is difficult, however, for at least two different kinds of reasons. The first is that making the best choice is a difficult problem for an individual; housing is lumpy, and its consumption cannot be adjusted smoothly; housing quality varies greatly, and it is not always apparent. A house

Michael D. Hurd is professor of economics at the State University of New York at Stony Brook, and a research associate of the National Bureau of Economic Research.

has both a consumption and an investment component, which means that the decision must consider future economic conditions. Housing decisions must be made in the face of considerable uncertainty about the course of inflation rates, income, health, mortality, rates of return, and income tax rates. For example, if there are fixed costs associated with moving, the decision of a couple to move today will be influenced by the probability that one spouse will die, leaving the other with too much housing. The greater the fixed costs of reversing the move following the death of a spouse, the more the couple will tend not to move. If future inflation destroys the value of nonhousing assets, the couple would want eventually to convert equity to consumption, but anticipated capital gains will be an important factor in the timing of the conversion. A homeowner who moves will probably incur psychic costs associated with neighborhood, climate, family, and the particular house, and he or she probably will find it difficult to factor the psychic costs in with the monetary costs.

The second reason that housing choice is difficult to study is that the researcher has much less information than the individual who makes the choice. Typically, researchers have no information on expectations or tastes or on the full range of choices that were considered but rejected. They may observe with error variables such as health status and the quality of housing. Although they may have quite good information on some financial variables such as Social Security income and bequeathable wealth, other financial variables such as quality-corrected housing prices, neighborhood characteristics, and tax status are bound to be observed with error.

A complete understanding of the determinants of housing choice would involve the solution of the individual's stochastic dynamic program with appropriate adjustments for the difference between what the individual takes to be known and what the researcher takes to be known. Because there are many kinds of uncertainty and several discrete choices over many time periods, this is an exceptionally difficult problem to solve empirically. The nonconvexities require the evaluation of the utility associated with all possible future housing choices (renting and owning housing of various sizes and qualities) in every future time period for all possible outcomes of future uncertainties. The solution would determine the choice of housing today, and it would balance the utility from occupying the housing over the next time period with the requirement that the individual be well positioned to take advantage of new information that is revealed during the time period. Were such a solution obtained, it could be used to answer questions such as how the probability of downsizing today depends on mortality rates and how the choice of renting versus owning depends on uncertainty about income. However, such a complete solution is probably beyond reach as it makes unrealistic demands on modeling, computation, and data.

A different approach, which is taken here by Ai, Feinstein, McFadden, and Pollakowski, is to find the costs associated with choosing various types of housing and to see if the costs are an important determinant of the actual choices made. The costs are, of course, the user costs of the paper, but they are much broader than what we would usually think of as costs.

User cost is found from four components: the cost of occupying a particular housing unit, the cost of changing housing, the probability of occupying a housing unit, and the probability of changing housing. To take a simple example, suppose a couple contemplates moving from a small house to a large house. They will pay costs associated with the transition and out-of-pocket costs while occupying the new house (which may be offset by capital gains and tax advantages). Following the move, however, one of the spouses may die, causing the survivor to move back to a small house, and the transition costs will have been lost. The couple should take this possibility into account when considering the first move.

A way for them to do this is to associate with the first move the discounted probability-weighted cost of the second move. In this example, the calculation of the user cost of the first move is relatively simple because it depends on the out-of-pocket costs of occupying the house, which can be estimated in a straightforward if cumbersome way from outside information; transition costs, which can also be estimated from outside information; and the probability of the second move, which depends on mortality tables. In application, however, the calculation of user cost is much more complicated because not all survivors will choose to move back to a small house: for example, well-to-do widow(er)s may decide to remain in the large house, or some survivors will remain simply because they prefer large houses. The actual probabilities of future transitions will depend on tastes, income, expectations, health, and so forth. To predict what the probabilities are, in order to calculate the user cost, requires the full-scale solution of the stochastic dynamic utility maximizing problem discussed above. If the estimation of user cost were to be implemented in this way, it would offer no simplification over stochastic dynamic programming.

The simplification comes from estimating the transition probabilities of a particular household from the observed transitions of similar households rather than from the solution to the utility maximizing problem. To see why this might be reasonable, consider a population in steady state in which everyone reaching, say, age 65 is identical. As people age and stochastic events unfold, they will make housing choices. By observing the states (housing types) occupied by older people and the transitions they make, a 65-year-old can estimate the probabilities that he will reach each of the states and make each of the transitions. He can then use the estimated probabilities to calculate the user cost associated with a choice to be made at age 65. In panel data, a researcher can duplicate this calculation to arrive at a similar estimate of the probabilities and of user cost.

The calculation does, however, require a number of assumptions. First, if the economic environment is changing, the distribution of older people across housing types will not be a good guide to the future of a 65-year-old because the probabilities of the various paths leading to those states will be different for her than they were for the older people. Second, if people are not identical, the researcher must know how to classify them in the same way the individual classifies herself. For example, suppose an individual knows that she will have high income, and suppose further that high-income people move more often than low-income people. If the researcher has no information on income expectations, user cost cannot vary from individual to individual as income varies, yet the high-income individual will calculate a high user cost (because of the high frequency of moves) and choose housing accordingly. Thus, the data will show no variation in estimated user cost yet variation in housing choice, implying incorrectly that user cost has no effect on choice. Third, this method, in common with many others, relies heavily on constructed variables rather than on actual variables. In complicated models like housing choice, we do not know what effects this will have, so to use this method we must assume that they are small.

These assumptions, and others I have not mentioned, are unlikely to be met strictly in practice. I should emphasize, however, that I think that the user-cost method is a good way to reduce an unmanageable problem to a manageable one. The examples are meant to provide a note of caution.

Most of the results in the paper are the calculations of various parts of the user cost. This is superb work: the attention to detail, the inclusiveness of the components, and the explanation of the methods deserve high praise. These results should prove useful to others in many applications. A good example is the hedonic housing price index for twenty-two locations over nine years, which is an important variable in many kinds of empirical studies.

An important finding is that user cost as a fraction of income peaks at about age 67 and then declines (fig. 2.9), whereas the share of income devoted to housing (from the census) continues to increase with age. The difference comes from the tax and mobility adjustments. The importance of the finding is that most people believe that the elderly devote an increasingly large amount to housing as they age, and people interpret this as evidence against life-cycle behavior. The user cost results show that this view may not be correct. I believe, however, that any interpretation in support of life-cycle behavior should be only tentative because the variation of user cost with age is a cross-sectional result, which can be quite different from a panel result. Furthermore, the decline with age is partly due to the Ricardian equivalence assumption: according to that assumption, except for transaction costs, the value of a house as a bequest is fully as great as its value to the elderly person in consumption. The opposite kind of assumption is that a bequest had no value to the elderly person. Then user cost would tend to rise with age (and increasing mortality rates) because each time period the probability would increase that the house would become worthless. In view of the fact that there is practically no evidence for Ricardian equivalence, the calculation under the alternative assumption (no value from a bequest) should also be made. An extension would be to calculate user cost under Ricardian equivalence for those elderly with children and under the alternative for those elderly without children. Such a variable may provide greater explanatory power in the housing choice equation.

User costs depend heavily on the treatment of capital gains. In view of the fact that housing prices rose rapidly during the sample period, the assumption of perfect foresight in housing prices probably has an important effect on user cost. As a description ex post of what the cost of holding housing was, this is not objectionable, but, as a variable to be used ex ante to explain housing decisions, I believe that the assumption is not justified. A valuable addition to the paper would be to detail the difference that the expectations assumption makes, especially in the housing choice estimation.

Table 2.21 shows that user cost varies with housing size; this is to be expected because the price of a house (or the rent) is imputed from the hedonic equation, which shows increasing price with size. The exhibit also shows substantial variation with age, indicating a good deal of variation by personal characteristics. I believe it would be helpful to detail the source of variation at the individual level: how much is due to taxes, how much to expected transitions, and how much to mortality rates and other factors.

The second kind of result is the effect of user cost on housing choice. Preliminary findings are reported in the final two tables of the paper; more detailed results will be the subject of a future paper. Because they are tentative, my comments on them will be suggestions, not criticisms: as I mentioned above, the method is an interesting and useful alternative to the solution of the stochastic dynamic problem.

The variation in user cost of the different types of housing has two sources. First, the hedonic equations assign a price to each kind of housing that is common to all individuals. Because the housing choice equations (tables 2.23–2.25) have dummy variables for housing types (stay, own, large, and small), the variation in user cost that comes from the hedonic equations will be approximately picked up by the dummy variables in the housing choice equations. Second, each individual has an individual-specific adjustment to the price of each kind of housing that comes from his particular tax and mobility characteristics. That is, a particular house will cost different individuals different amounts to occupy. I imagine that this variation is the main determinant of the estimated effect of user cost. A simple example will show how this could lead to a positive association between housing choice and high user cost.

Suppose there are two types of people, low user cost (20 percent of the population) and high user cost (80 percent of the population), and that their costs and housing choices are given in table 2C.1. Thus, the low-cost types all choose their lowest-cost type of housing, which is type A; the high-cost types also choose their lowest-cost type of housing, which is type B. On average, 20 percent of the population chose housing with an average cost of $90, and 80 percent of the population chose housing with an average cost of

Table 2C.1   **Housing Type**

Person Type	A		B	
	User Cost ($)	% Choosing	User Cost ($)	% Choosing
1 (20 percent)	90	100	100	0
2 (80 percent)	150	0	110	100
Average	90	20	100	80

$100. Estimation that uses the costs of the housing actually chosen will find a positive relation between user cost and choice, whereas estimation that also uses the costs of the housing not chosen will find the true negative relation.

The results in tables 2.23–2.25 do show a positive relation between user cost and choice, which is not what would be expected. The estimation uses only information on the choice taken; in some cases, as the example above shows, this could lead to such a result. I believe that a better specification would describe the costs of all the choices available to the individual, whether taken or not.

I also imagine that "need" should be taken into account. User cost is not a price; it is an estimated fully inclusive expenditure, and people with greater needs will spend more. This could have an effect because both need and user cost are systematically related to age. Similar reasoning suggests that income should have an interaction with income.

Notwithstanding my reservations about the preliminary results, I believe that the approach shows considerable promise, and I look forward to the next paper in the series.

3 A Dynamic Analysis of Household Dissolution and Living Arrangement Transitions by Elderly Americans

Axel H. Börsch-Supan

The dissolution of an elderly person's independent household—either to live in another household or to become institutionalized—is an incisive life event that has many implications for the well-being of the elderly person. Most elderly hold most or all of their wealth in housing (Merrill 1984). In most cases, the dissolution of an elderly person's independent household implies the sale of the house and therefore a substantial change in the elderly's wealth position. In case of institutionalization, some of this wealth may be used to pay for front-loaded fees; in the case of moving to own children, the wealth may be transferred to the next generation by transferring headship of the family home.

The choice of living arrangements by the elderly is also an important aspect of the economics of aging at large because of the side effects in the provision of care and the physical environment that this choice implies. Sharing accommodations, in particular with adult children, will provide not only housing for the elderly but also some degree of medical care and social support. If the elderly perceive sharing accommodations as an inferior housing alternative and remain living independently as long as their physical and economic means allow, this social support and a larger amount of medical care have to be picked up by society at large rather than by the family or close friends. Moving to adult children is also an important substitute for institutionalization. As the private and social costs of institutionalization are skyrocketing, the family may have to become yet again a resort for the elderly.

Axel H. Börsch-Supan is assistant professor of public policy at the John F. Kennedy School of Government, Harvard University; C3-Professor of Economics, Universität Mannheim (West Germany); and faculty research fellow of the National Bureau of Economic Research.

The author is indebted to Peter Schmidt, who provided valuable research assistance, and to Reinhard Kox, who ably managed the file handling. Financial support was received from the National Institutes of Health, National Institute on Aging, grant 1-P01-AG05842.

This is not only a question of distribution—whether the family or society at large pays an otherwise equal bill. One may also argue that independently living elderly are more isolated and incur higher costs for medical care and social support, for example, because of the psychosomatic effects of isolation or a lower interest in preventive care by elderly living alone.

Household dissolution decisions also have important consequences for the intergenerational distribution of housing. In particular in times of tight housing market conditions with very high housing prices for newly developed units, the elderly's willingness to move out of the family home is an important parameter in the supply of more affordable existing homes. If elderly households stay in their family homes well into their 80s, the next generation will have little chance to move into the family homes while their children (the third generation) are being raised and demand for space is largest. If houses of younger families with children are relatively more spacious than those of the elderly, the elderly may be perceived as being "overhoused"—implying a sense of intergenerational inequity.

Household dissolution may change eligibility for certain government programs (Schwartz, Danziger, and Smolensky 1984). Eligibility and transfer level for the food stamp and supplemental social security programs is determined by the income of the household, not by the income of the elderly. Elderly who received supplemental security income may lose this income once they move to children with own income. This may induce elderly to stay living as an independent household longer than they may want to in the absence of these transfer programs.

Finally, Schwartz, Danziger and Smolensky (1984) point out a perverse effect in measured income inequality: if the proportion of independently living elderly increases, then, ceteris paribus, income inequality will rise because there are more small households with low income than if they had lived in a joint household with a combined larger income. The income distribution effect is perverse when it was a slight increase in the elderly's income that produced the increased proportion of elderly living independently. Of course, the effect is purely statistical and vanishes when income inequality is measured, not on the level of households, but on a lower level, for example, on the level of family nuclei (Börsch-Supan 1989).

This paper studies the demographic and economic determinants of the elderly's decision to stay living independently or to dissolve the independent household in order to choose some kind of shared accommodations or to move in an institution such as a nursing home or a home for the aged. The main questions being asked are as follows.

- What are typical sequences of living arrangements in old age? How often do elderly move between their home, their children, and an institution?
- Which events precipitate changes in living arrangements? What are typical living arrangement sequences after retirement, after death of a spouse, after onset of a disability, and in the years preceding death?

- Are there cohort or calendar-time effects in the preferences for certain living arrangements that can be distinguished from pure age effects? Are the elderly becoming more isolated in the last years?
- How many elderly remain living independently until they die? Who are the elderly living independently? Are they younger, are they wealthier, are they isolated?
- Are economic conditions (income, housing prices) important determinants for the choice among living independently, sharing accommodations, and living in an institution? Or is the decision to give up an independent household simply determined by age and health?

This paper is one of a triad of papers on household dissolution and choice of living arrangements of elderly Americans in this volume. It poses some of the same questions (and arrives at very similar answers) as the paper by Ellwood and Kane, using the same data but a very different methodology. The coincidence of all major results yields some confidence in the robustness of my results, in spite of many data problems. Whereas this and Ellwood and Kane's paper concentrate on the demand for dependent and independent living arrangements, the triad's third paper, by Kotlikoff and Morris, is more interested in the supply side and closes a model of living arrangement choices by providing a structural model of dependent living arrangements.

Economic incentives for household formation and, by implication, household dissolution have been extensively studied for the general population in the seventies. A survey of this literature can be found in Börsch-Supan (1985). With a focus on the elderly, this research has been picked up recently by two papers that employ different data sets in order to study determinants of living arrangements for the aged. Schwartz, Danziger and Smolensky (1984) employ the Retirement History Survey (RHS) to estimate a binary choice model between living independently and dependently—that is, in another household, most commonly that of their children. In spite of the size of this data set, their empirical results were mixed, and neither health nor income effects could convincingly be proven, mostly owing to their econometric methodology and the poor health measures available in the RHS. Börsch-Supan (1989) estimated a multinomial logit model of living arrangements on data from the Annual Housing Survey (AHS) that distinguishes several dependent living arrangements rather than just one category. Both papers share two important shortcomings: their data sets prohibited an analysis that takes institutionalization into account, and neither paper performed a dynamic analysis. This paper attempts to overcome these two shortcomings.

The probability of institutionalization per se is the focus of many studies that are reviewed by Garber and MaCurdy's paper in this volume. In contrast to these papers, this paper concentrates on permanent institutionalization as opposed to the more frequent short-term stays in nursing homes. Garber and MaCurdy provide some link between short- and long-term institutionalization by endogenizing duration of stay.

The paper is organized as follows. Since answers to the first three groups of questions enumerated above require panel data, and since answers to all questions demand data with a lot of detail about elderly persons and their living arrangements, I will first describe the data, their novelty, and their problems and present the construction of the essential variables. Section 3.2 provides estimates of transition probabilities for all elderly in my sample. Sections 3.3–3.6 are then devoted to three subsamples, each relating to a particular life event. I first analyze transitions in response to the death of a spouse, then investigate transitions after the onset of a disability in section 3.4, and finally focus on the last five years of life of those elderly who decease during the sample period. Sections 3.2–3.6 are organized as variations on a theme and have a common pattern. First, I will categorize observed sequences of living arrangements and describe their frequencies. Second, multinomial logit models are employed in order to estimate the weights of potential causes for these sequences or choices of living arrangements. The final section summarizes the results and critically discusses the paper's assumptions and data sources.

3.1   Data and Variable Definitions

An empirical investigation of living arrangement transitions faces many technical problems. First, the detection of transitions and an analysis of living arrangement sequences require a longitudinal data set that covers a long time span. There are, however, very few long panels in the United States, the longest being the Panel Study of Income Dynamics (PSID). Second, elderly are particularly prone to become "nonresponses" in a survey for systematic reasons: although their geographic mobility is low, which alleviates the problem of locating elderly respondents, they may become institutionalized or die. In most surveys, these persons are then lost in the sample. Third, a study of living arrangements needs information not only about the immediate household but also about the family of the elderly person, which may provide alternative living arrangements. Similarly, for such a study one needs to know a combination of economic, demographic, and health variables that is unusual for most general purpose surveys. Finally, the very old may have difficulties in answering questions precisely, particularly about their health status, and the interviewer therefore has to phrase questions more carefully and double-check answers. Currently, there is no data set fulfilling all these requirements.

My analysis is based on the new complete family-individual based file of the PSID, 1968–84. This file includes all persons who have ever been interviewed as a member of a PSID family. In contrast to earlier PSID releases, it also includes people who are classified as nonrespondents in the last available interview year (1984), for example, persons who have died in the course of the panel study. The data therefore provide a new opportunity to look at the economic and housing conditions of the very old, particularly those who have died, and the transitions preceding death.

The main advantage of the PSID is its long time horizon of up to seventeen years. This enables us to create event histories, to detect typical sequences of living arrangements, and to estimate transition probabilities that depend on age as well as on calendar time. Another important advantage of the PSID for the study of living arrangement decisions is the collection of at least some data at the individual level (rather than the household level) in the so-called family-individual file and the careful recording of household composition as it relates to the head of household. This makes it possible to detect elderly living as subfamilies or as "secondary individuals" in households headed by their children or other persons. Finally, the nonresponse file keeps records for persons even when they become institutionalized. This is in contrast to all major cross-sectional data sources that comprise either the institutionalized or the noninstitutionalized population and also in contrast to most longitudinal data sources that have only one nonresponse category and do not distinguish between institutionalization, death, and other reasons for nonresponse.[1]

In addition to its extreme unwieldiness,[2] the PSID also has several severe shortcomings that limit the kind of analysis that would be appropriate for the study of the elderly's living arrangements. Most important, the PSID does not contain a systematic record of the functional health status of the elderly. I will depend on age and an indicator for disability status as variables proxying health. The PSID does not record structural housing characteristics that could allow for a precise definition of housing prices corrected for quality differences. Unit housing prices must be assigned from external sources such as the AHS. Also problematic are the many changes and inconsistencies in data collection procedures and variable definitions during the seventeen years in which the PSID has been conducted. Unfortunately, this also includes the classification of persons as institutionalized and the procedures to trace such persons. The creation of an internally consistent file requires a substantial amount of data processing, and it was not always possible to create an unambiguous and consistent variable definition for all included time periods. Finally, though some information (e.g., age, sex, and income) is recorded by individual household member, other information about individuals is either subsumed in a household total or available only for head and spouse. For example, race, number of own children and siblings, and retirement data are recorded only for heads of households and their spouses. Hence, these variables can be assigned to individual sample members only if they have been head or spouse at least once during the sample period. This excludes some kinds of analyses and creates a selectivity bias in other analyses.

As a first step preceding the analysis, the PSID family-individual file was therefore converted into a rectangular file of elderly individuals.[3] Variable definitions common for all waves were employed, and time-invariant data that were collected only for heads and spouses were assigned to these individuals in periods in which they were neither head nor spouse. The "elderly" were defined as individuals who were aged 60 and above in 1968. This includes 1,134 observations. Of those, 956 are in year 1968 in the sample and represent a random sample of the population aged 60 and above.[4] An additional 178 elderly are picked up after 1968, typically, when they join a family from the original PSID sampling frame. This part of the sample is nonrandom as its inclusion in the sample depends on the choice of living arrangement and will be employed only when conditioning on the origin of transition removes this choice bias.

On the basis of the household information collected in the PSID, the main dependent variable in this study—the type of living arrangement—can be classified according to four categories:

- *Independent living arrangements.* The elderly's household does not contain any other adult person beside the elderly individual and his or her spouse, if any (living arrangement *type 1*).[5]
- *Shared living arrangements.* The elderly's household contains at least one other adult person beside the elderly individual and his or her spouse. Two cases can be distinguished. (*a*) The elderly is head of household or spouse of head of household (living arrangement *type 2*). In this case, the relationship between the elderly and all other household members is well documented. (*b*) The elderly is neither head of household nor spouse of head of household (living arrangement *type 3*). In this case, the relationship between the elderly and the other household members cannot be unambiguously determined. Most important, the data do not provide a distinction between an elderly person living in the household of his or her son-in-law and an elderly person living in the household of an unrelated person.[6]
- *Institutional living arrangements.* This category includes elderly who are living on a permanent basis in a health-care-related facility (living arrangement *type 4*). Examples are living in a home for the aged or in a nursing home but not temporary hospital or nursing home stays.[7]

This categorization deserves some comments. First, it would have been desirable to distinguish between adult children/elderly parent households and households in which elderly share accommodations with other related or unrelated persons. This is impossible because of the head-centered recording of family relationships. Most but not all shared accommodations represent adult children/elderly parent households. Based on the national file of the 1983 AHS, 62.1 percent of all composite households including an elderly person were children/elderly parent(s) households (including in-laws). In 27.2 percent of these households, the elderly person shared accommodations with a related individual other than a child (mostly siblings); in the remaining 10.7 percent, at least one unrelated person lived in the composite household (excluding in-laws) (see Börsch-Supan 1989).

Second, it would have been desirable to distinguish between parents who live together with their adult children because the children have not yet left the household (this is a clear possibility for the younger aged who raised children late in their lives) and parents who have been "taken in" by their children but are legal owner of the family home and therefore head of household. This is impossible without a complete life history of all household members. On the other hand, I make a point of distinguishing headship from being a secondary individual in a composite household.

Third, the concentration on permanent nursing home stays as a measure of institutionalization does not correspond to many published numbers that also include temporary nursing home stays. Most nursing home stays are quite brief (e.g., for convalescence) and do not imply that the household was dissolved (e.g., by selling the house or moving out of an apartment). These temporary nursing home stays are treated like hospital stays, and the person's living arrangement is the living arrangement before and presumably after the hospital stay. It is important to keep this in mind when interpreting the relatively small percentages of institutionalized persons in this paper.[8]

3.2   A Markov Model of Living Arrangement Transitions

First, I estimate transition probabilities for the entire random sample of elderly individuals. In addition to establishing some general tendencies, these transition probabilities will serve as a yardstick when we study transition probabilities in special situations such as the years preceding death, the years after death of a spouse, or the years after onset of a disability.

Table 3.1 provides a survey of what happens in the sample: it presents the frequencies of living arrangement sequences among the 956 elderly whose life history can be traced from 1968 on. Of these elderly, 602 died during the sample period, and 354 survived until 1984. The frequencies are reported once for the entire sample and once for the subsample of surviving elderly.

The first result is the stability of living arrangements in spite of the long sample period and the large proportion of elderly who die during this time span. More than two-thirds of the elderly in both samples do not change their living arrangements at all. Most of the elderly live independently through the entire sample period or until their deaths. Of all elderly, 14.4 percent at least once shared a household not being head or spouse of head, and 3.1 percent have been in an institution for at least one entire year during the sample period. Apart from a higher proportion of multiple changes, there is astoundingly little difference between the two subgroups in the sample, the surviving elderly and those who died before 1984.

This large proportion of stayers creates a problem in the specification of transition probabilities. First, with only relatively few transitions, the statistical base for the estimation of parametric transition probabilities is very small. I choose not to employ relatively sophisticated hazard models based on continuous time since they are more likely to generate imprecise results than simple Markovian models. The paper by Ellwood and Kane included in this volume provides an analysis of living arrangements parallel to this one using the same data but duration models based on an exponential hazard. It is

Table 3.1   **Frequencies of Living Arrangement Sequences, 1968–84**
                       (absolute and relative frequencies)

Sequence Type	All Elderly[a]		Surviving Elderly[b]	
	N	*%*	*N*	*%*
No change during sample period	691	72.3	239	67.5
1. Independent	526	55.0	198	55.9
2. With others, as head or spouse	70	7.3	25	7.1
3. With others, as secondary individual	95	9.9	16	4.5
One change during sample period	140	14.6	48	13.5
1 to 2	34	3.6	15	4.2
1 to 3	4	.4	0	.0
1 to 4	6	.6	0	.0
2 to 1	71	7.4	29	8.2
2 to 3	2	.2	1	.3
2 to 4	5	.5	0	.0
3 to 2	11	1.2	2	.6
3 to 4	8	.8	1	.3
More than one change during sample period	125	13.1	67	18.9
Between 1 and 2 only	95	9.9	60	16.9
All others	30	3.1	7	2.0
Total	956	100.0	354	100.0

Source: PSID, 1968–84, including nonrespondents.
[a]All elderly aged 60 and above in 1968.
[b]Elderly aged 60 and above in 1968 who survived at least until 1984.

interesting to note that all important qualitative conclusions from these two papers coincide in spite of the different methodologies.

Second, the large proportion of stayers suggests that a model of simple Markov transitions will not describe the data well. This is so because, even if one-period transitions are estimated correctly, a standard first-order Markov model will predict too many transitions within two or more periods (cf. Amemiya 1985). This effect may be attributed to either unobserved population heterogeneity (certain types of individuals self-select into certain categories of living arrangements) or duration dependence (the likelihood of leaving a living arrangement category decreases with the duration in this category). Because of the few transitions observed in table 3.1, we will not be able to distinguish statistically between these two possibilities. As was mentioned in the preceding section, the data lack some obviously important information (such as detailed health status). Therefore, the heterogeneity model appears most appropriate in this situation.

One solution to the heterogeneity problem that is well suited to this application is the so-called mover-stayer model developed by Goodman (1961) and exposed in Amemiya (1985), which accounts for population heterogeneity by dividing the sample into stayers that never change their living arrangement and movers that may or may not change their living arrangement in any given period. Transition probabilities $P_{ij}(t)$ from living arrangement category I to j for a given individual, not identified as either a mover or a stayer, are then given by

$$P_{ij}(t) = d_{ij}S_i + (1 - S_i)M_{ij}(t),$$

where S_i denotes the proportion of stayers in category i, $M_{ij}(t)$ the transition probability of movers from category i to j, and $d_{ij} = 1$ if $i = j$ and 0 otherwise. I identify stayers as those elderly who do not change their living arrangement in the seventeen years between 1968 and 1984 or between 1968 and their deaths. Note that, unlike in other applications of the mover-stayer model, the long time horizon and the fact that death excludes further changes provide for a reliable estimate of the stayer probabilities (e.g., McCall 1971). I then estimate the matrix of mover transition probabilities M_{ij} by the sample frequencies of observed transitions by movers, the maximum likelihood estimate. Table 3.2 presents the transition probabilities M_{ij} for movers and the resulting unconditional transition probabilities P_{ij} according to the mover-stayer heterogeneity assumption in the above equation.[9]

The unconditional transition probabilities P_{ij} will serve as baseline estimates with which transition probabilities in special situations will be compared. Note that the matrix of two period transitions has a larger diagonal than the square of the transition matrices[10]—it is this feature of the mover-stayer model that helps describe the stability of the elderly's living arrangements.

In order to characterize the stayer population, table 3.3 reports multinomial logit estimates that relate the three stayer probabilities, S_i, 1, . . . , 3, relative to the probability of being a mover to a set of demographic and economic variables. There are no elderly who stay in an institution throughout the entire sample period ($S_4 = 0$). Two sets of estimations are provided: one for the

Table 3.2   Transition Probabilities

	Type of Living Arrangement at Destination:			
Type of Living Arrangement at Origin	1	2	3	4
Transition probabilities for movers, M_{ij}:				
1. Independent	.8987	.0913	.0032	.0069
2. With others, as head/spouse	.1996	.7919	.0019	.0066
3. With others, as secondary individual	.0761	.0711	.7970	.0558
4. Institution	.0345	.0000	.1034	.8621
Unconditional transition probabilities, P_{ij}:				
1. Independent	.9544	.0411	.0014	.0031
2. With others, as head/spouse	.1850	.8071	.0018	.0061
3. With others, as secondary individual	.0685	.0640	.8172	.0503
4. Institution	.0345	.0000	.1034	.8621

Source: PSID, 1968–84, elderly aged 60 and more in 1968, including nonrespondents.

Table 3.3 **A Logit Model of Stayer Probabilities (parameter estimates, *t*-statistics in parentheses)**

		Log Odds of Staying in . . . Rather than Changing					
		(1) Independent		(2) With Others, as Head/Spouse		(3) With Others, as Secondary Individual	
Variable	Sample Mean	All[a]	Surv.[b]	All	Surv.	All	Surv.
CONST	1.0	−.778	1.386	−2.000	−16.687	−8.135	−81.048
		(−.8)	(.7)	(−1.1)	(.0)	(−2.8)	(−.2)
AGE68	68.4	.011	−.020	−.030	−.002	−.031	.069
		(.8)	(−.6)	(−1.3)	(.0)	(−1.1)	(.6)
KIDS	2.7	−.012	.111	.054	.088	.097	.096
		(−.3)	(1.7)	(1.2)	(1.2)	(1.0)	(.8)
NOKIDS	.18	.585	.840	−.300	.010	.960	−10.450
		(2.4)	(2.1)	(−.6)	(.0)	(.8)	(.0)
MDKIDS	.14	−.448	.020	−.100	−12.024	5.149	3.764
		(−1.1)	(.0)	(−.2)	(.0)	(6.2)	(2.1)
SIBS	4.6	.029	−.045	.067	.009	.612	9.380
		(.7)	(−.8)	(1.0)	(.1)	(1.9)	(.2)
NOSIBS	.04	−.162	−.011	−.435	−13.255	−1.652	62.374
		(−.4)	(.0)	(−.4)	(.0)	(.0)	(.1)
MDSIBS	.25	−.510	.036	−.348	−12.018	6.600	75.719
		(−1.5)	(.1)	(−.5)	(.0)	(2.8)	(.2)
NONWHITE	.16	−1.498	−2.380	.735	1.520	−.944	−1.220
		(−6.0)	(−4.8)	(2.3)	(2.8)	(−2.0)	(−1.1)
FEMALE	.54	.349	.467	.512	12.773	.353	.012
		(1.7)	(1.3)	(1.2)	(.0)	(.7)	(.0)
YPERM	2.84	−.026	.008	−.053	.006	.049	−.131
		(−1.5)	(.3)	(−1.1)	(.1)	(.6)	(−.5)
SINGLE	.30	.378	−.404	2.147	2.267	1.375	.415
		(1.8)	(−1.2)	(3.8)	(2.1)	(2.4)	(.4)
MARRIED	.43	1.617	.557	2.928	14.692	.579	−12.486
		(7.3)	(1.4)	(4.8)	(.0)	(1.1)	(.0)

	All	Surv.
Likelihood at convergence, $L(\beta)$	−735.66	−261.06
$Rho^2 = 1 - L(\beta)/L(0)$	.444	.468
Percentage correctly predicted	67.26	64.69
Number of observations	956	354

Source: PSID, 1968–84, elderly aged 60 and more in 1968 who never changed their living arrangement, including nonrespondents.

[a]All elderly aged 60 and above in 1968.

[b]Elderly aged 60 and above in 1968 who survived at least until 1984.

entire sample, combining stayers who died during the sample period and stayers who survived at least until 1984; and one set of estimations for the surviving elderly only.

Most variables employed in table 3.3 are self-explanatory. AGE68 is age in year 1968. SINGLE (MARRIED) is a dummy variable denoting that the elderly was single (married) during the entire sample period. YPERM is the average income during the sample period. NONWHITE includes black, Hispanic, Asian, Pacific, and Native American elderly. KIDS (SIBS) denotes the number of own children (siblings) if reported; NOKIDS (NOSIBS) is a dummy variable denoting that the elderly has no children (siblings). Finally, the dummy variables MDKIDS and MDSIBS indicate missing data on number of children (siblings). The variables KIDS and SIBS are reported only in years when the elderly person was head of household or spouse.[11] Thus data on own children and siblings is unavailable whenever an elderly person was never head of household or spouse during the entire sample period. This lack of precise data about potential family support in this case is a major drawback of the data. The dummy variables MDKIDS and MDSIBS that indicate these cases eliminate any bias in the KIDS and NOKIDS variables (SIBS and NOSIBS, respectively) for those elderly for whom this information is available.

The positive coefficients of the SINGLE (MARRIED) variable indicate that the probability of being "mover" increases by experiencing a marital status change, which in almost all cases represents death of a spouse. This is of course not surprising, and I will analyze the living arrangement adjustments after the death of a spouse in the following section. Male elderly are much more likely to be movers than female elderly. Note that this effect is measured holding marital status constant. As we will see, this effect will become even more pronounced when we study the cases in which a spouse deceased. Race has a very strong effect on the stayer probabilities. Being nonwhite decreases the probability of staying independent or as secondary individual but increases the probability of heading a composite household. There are no measurable income effects, nor does the elderly's age in year 1968 affect the mover-stayer probabilities.[12]

Although the measurement of the "supply-side" variables for shared living arrangements—the number of own children and siblings—is marred by the above-mentioned incomplete information on these two variables, we can ascertain that the probability of being a stayer in the category "Independent Living Arrangements" increases with being childless, just as the presence of children and siblings increases the probability of being a stayer in the two shared accommodation categories. These latter two effects are, however, very small. I conclude that most shared living arrangements are of a transitory nature. The probability of staying as a secondary individual is most strongly affected by the MDKIDS and MDSIBS indicator variables. This is not surprising because by construction these variables work essentially as choice-specific constants for the choice of living arrangement type 3.

There is little significant difference between the two subgroups in my sample. Owing to the smaller sample size, the results for the surviving elderly are less precise. This is particularly true for the third column (staying with others as secondary individual).

We now turn to the transition probabilities of those elderly who changed their living arrangement at least once during the sample period. As is obvious from table 3.2, some of these transition probabilities are very low, and it is therefore impossible separately to relate all sixteen transition probabilities in a meaningful way to the above set of relevant demographic and economic variables. Table 3.4 provides some results for the transitions between living arrangement types 1 and 2 and, most interestingly for our topic household dissolution, the transitions into types 3 (living with others as secondary individual, in most cases being "taken in" by adult children) and 4 (institutionalization). The upper panel describes the binary choice between staying in either a type 1 or a type 2 living arrangement and a transition to type 2 or 1, respectively, conditional on having been identified as a mover at least at some point in time, not necessarily this time. Possible transitions to the other two categories 3 and 4 are ignored, making use of the logit functional form and the independence of irrelevant alternatives. The lower panel pools all origins in order to gain degrees of freedom in estimating the transition probabilities into the latter two living arrangement types.

Most of the variables have already been introduced in table 3.2. In addition, I now measure some demographic and economic changes that occurred concurrently with the transition. DINCOME denotes the magnitude of a real income change; DMARR denotes a change in marital status ($1 =$ becoming married; $0 =$ no change; $-1 =$ loss of a spouse, divorce, or separation); and DLIM indicates a change in limitation status ($1 =$ health status worse than previous year, $0 =$ no change, $-1 =$ health status better than previous year).

I first comment on the left part of the upper panel in table 3.4, which reflects the choice between a transition from living independently to sharing a household as head or spouse of head and staying independent. The loss of a spouse (DMARR),[13] a change in the severity of a disability (DLIM), and a loss in income (DINCOME) are the most important determinants that precipitate this transition. All other things equal, elderly women tend to stay independent, whereas elderly men tend to share accommodations. These results correspond to the same effects in the stayer population. Not being married in the first place strongly increases the likelihood of a transition, as does the presence of children and of siblings (though statistically not significant) and being nonwhite. Neither age nor calendar time significantly alters the transition probabilities between living arrangement types 1 and 2, nor does the level of income.

Not surprisingly, the reverse transition—breaking up a composite household to become independent (right part of upper panel in table 3.4)—is essentially characterized by the opposite mechanisms. Some of these transitions appear

Table 3.4   **Logit Models of Mover Transition Probabilities (parameter estimates, t-statistics in parentheses)**

Variable	Log Odds of Moving . . . Rather than Staying			
	From (1) Independent to (2) Shared as Head		From (2) Shared as Head to (1) Independent	
CONST	−2.614	(−1.67)	.889	(.58)
KIDS	.061	(1.70)	.005	(.16)
SIBS	.030	(.96)	−.041	(−1.45)
NONWHITE	.348	(1.63)	.348	(1.79)
AGE68	.015	(.96)	−.006	(−.39)
FEMALE	−.354	(−1.83)	−.165	(−.90)
INCOME	−.021	(−.65)	.011	(.43)
DINCOME	−.001	(−5.83)	.045	(1.16)
MARR	−.739	(−3.50)	.295	(1.52)
DMARR	−1.529	(−4.34)	1.319	(3.23)
DLIM	.280	(1.62)	−.249	(−1.35)
YEAR	−.013	(−.55)	−.006	(−.25)
$L(\beta)$	−544.6846		−501.9912	
Rho^2	.5780		.2969	
% correct	90.92		79.71	
NOBS	1,862		1,030	

Variable	Log Odds of Moving to . . . Rather Than Staying or Moving Elsewhere			
	To (3) Sharing as Secondary Individual		To (4) Institutionalized	
CONST	15.324	(4.6)	−17.501	(−3.3)
KIDS	.187	(3.1)	−.245	(−1.3)
NOKIDS	1.943	(3.8)	−.875	(−.9)
MDKIDS	3.444	(4.9)	−1.542	(−1.2)
SIBS	.057	(.6)	−.131	(−.8)
NOSIBS	2.232	(2.8)	.017	(.0)
MDSIBS	1.610	(2.3)	3.750	(3.2)
NONWHITE	.824	(2.3)	−.223	(−.3)
AGE68	.045	(1.7)	.175	(3.7)
FEMALE	−.931	(−2.5)	−2.225	(−3.1)
INCOME	−.030	(−.4)	−1.595	(−4.2)
DINCOME	.022	(.3)	−1.688	(−4.5)
MARR	−2.033	(−5.1)	−2.324	(−3.0)
DMARR	−1.606	(−2.6)	−5.800	(−5.6)
DLIM	.103	(.2)	−.103	(−.1)
ORIGIN1	−3.430	(−6.3)	−1.691	(−2.7)
YEAR	−.265	(−5.2)	.072	(1.5)
$L(\beta)$	−132.1030		−55.3071	
Rho^2	.6029		.7832	
% correct	89.38		96.20	
NOBS	480		368	

Source: PSID, 1968–84, elderly aged 60 and more in 1968 who at least once changed their living arrangement, including nonrespondents.

to be statistical artifacts, such as marriage with a person who was already living in the household as an unrelated secondary individual. This may be indicated by the strong coefficient of DMARR. Note that nonwhite as well as male elderly are more likely to change living arrangements, as was the case in the reverse transition.

The lower panel indicates the probabilities of being taken in by others and becoming institutionalized. As is evident, both probabilities increase with age, in particular, the risk of institutionalization. Being or becoming single and being male also increase these probabilities. The presence of children or siblings decreases the risk of institutionalization and increases the likelihood of being taken in, as is expected. Again, the measurement of this "family support–supply effect" suffers from the large number of observations for which a precise number of children or siblings cannot be ascertained (as indicated by the variables MDKIDS and MDSIBS). Most transitions into institutionalization or subfamily status are from living arrangement types 2–4, as indicated by the strong negative coefficient on the variable ORIGIN1 that denotes transitions from living independently, once again reflecting the stability particularly of the independent living arrangement category. Finally, and this is worth emphasizing, we observe a strong negative income effect on the likelihood of entering an institution. Institutions are clearly viewed as inferior living arrangements.

As opposed to the probabilities in the upper panel, the transition probabilities into institutions and being taken in are nonstationary. This is indicated by the effect on the variable YEAR, which measures calendar time. The probability of institutionalization, controlling for all other factors included in the lower panel, exhibits an increasing trend, although measured imprecisely. The likelihood of being taken in, however, decreases between 1968 and 1984, with a large and statistically highly significant coefficient. This result has a strong and important implication: there appears to be a decreasing inclination of the family or friends to take care of "their" elderly and an increasing reliance on institutions such as nursing homes with their related private and social costs. The parameter estimate of the risk of institutionalization is not measured statistically precisely because it is based on relatively few transitions. If one takes this estimate as best available guess anyway, then it translates to a yearly increase of about 7 percent, that is, a doubling of the risk of institutionalization within ten years.[14]

3.3 Living Arrangement Changes after Death of a Spouse

The analysis in the preceding section suggested that death of a spouse is the most important life event precipitating a change in living arrangements. The logit regressions in table 3.4 related living arrangement adjustments to a concurrent change in marital status. This section will take a closer look at the dynamics of what happens after the death of a spouse by studying changes not only in the concurrent year but also in consecutive years.

In my sample, 317 elderly experienced the death of their spouses and survived at least one further year. Table 3.5 presents the frequencies with which living arrangement transitions occur in the year of the spouses' death and in the following years.

Clearly, the transition probabilities in the year of the spouse's death (panel B) are quite different from what they are in the general population (panel A, from table 3.2). Starting from living independently, the transition probability of joining another household as head of household becomes twice as large. The transition probabilities to subfamily status and into an institution increase even more than tenfold (first row in panel B). If the elderly couple headed a composite household, the death of the spouse also resulted in a much elevated likelihood that this common household is broken up, leaving the surviving

Table 3.5   **Transition Probabilities after Death of a Spouse**

	Type of Living Arrangement at Destination			
Type of Living Arrangement at Origin	1	2	3	4
A. Unconditional transition probabilities (from table 3.2):				
1. Independent	.9544	.0411	.0014	.0031
2. With others, as head/spouse	.1850	.8071	.0018	.0061
3. With others, as secondary individual	.0685	.0640	.8172	.0503
4. Institution	.0345	.0000	.1034	.8621
B. Year concurrent with death of spouse (317 observations):				
1. Independent	.8565	.0826	.0217	.0390
2. With others, as head/spouse	.3556	.6000	.0000	.0444
3. With others, as secondary individual	.0244	.1220	.8049	.0488
4. Institution	.0000	.0000	.0000	1.000
χ^2 statistic B − A: 1,005.6				
C. One year later (301 observations):				
1. Independent	.9362	.0638	.0000	.0000
2. With others, as head/spouse	.2041	.7959	.0000	.0000
3. With others, as secondary individual	.0000	.0000	.9670	.0330
4. Institution	.0000	.0000	.3333	.6667
χ^2 statistic C − A: 47.8				
D. Two years later (267 observations):				
1. Independent	.9656	.0287	.0000	.0057
2. With others, as head/spouse	.1429	.8771	.0000	.0000
3. With others, as secondary individual	.0000	.0000	1.000	.0000
4. Institution	.0000	.0000	.0000	1.000
χ^2 statistic D − A: 57.1				
E. Three years later (239 observations):				
1. Independent	.9542	.0458	.0000	.0000
2. With others, as head/spouse	.1860	.8140	.0000	.0000
3. With others, as secondary individual	.0000	.0000	1.000	.0000
4. Institution	.0000	.0000	.0000	1.000
χ^2 statistic E − A: 40.6				

Source: PSID, 1968–84, 317 elderly aged 60 and more in 1968 who lost their spouse, including nonrespondents.

spouse either alone in the family home or as a new independent household (second row in panel B). Note that the probability of becoming institutionalized is very high in the year in which the spouse deceases. In a formal test, the equality of panels A and B is strongly rejected.[15]

A comparison of the panels in table 3.5 clearly shows that most living arrangement adjustments in response to death of a spouse have taken place already in the concurrent year. Though panels C–E are still statistically different from panel A, the size of the chi-squared test statistic is much lower as compared to the test between panels A and B. One year after the spouse's death, the probabilities of a transition between shared and independent living are still elevated, but this is reversed in the second year.

Table 3.6 presents some logit estimation results for the first year transitions. They confirm the general tendencies detected in table 3.4 for all movers also for this special case of transitions most likely precipitated by the death of a spouse. Unfortunately, the small sample size prevents a more detailed analysis, for instance, a stratification by living arrangement prior to death of spouse.

The presence of children or siblings increases the probability of being taken in after the spouse's death. Old age, low income to begin with, or an income loss increase the likelihood of a transition into an institution. Female elderly are more likely to stay living in the family home than widowers. If a health limitation develops concurrently with the death of a spouse, the surviving elderly is most likely taken in by the family or by friends rather than being institutionalized. Nonwhite elderly are less likely to stay independently than white elderly.

Living arrangement prior to the spouse's death is accounted for by the variable ORIGIN1 (if independent) and, though indirectly, by the missing data indicators. Note that, because MDKIDS and MDSIBS essentially serve as indicator variables for categories 2 and 3, introduction of variables such as ORIGIN2 and ORIGIN3 would result in almost perfect collinearity with MDKIDS and MDSIBS. The negative sign of ORIGIN1 (the reference case) and the positive signs of the statistically significant missing data variables indicate the smaller likelihood of a change as compared to staying in living arrangements 1, 2, and 3.

Stationarity of these transition probabilities is clearly rejected: the results confirm the existence and the direction of the time trends already discovered in table 3.4. All other determinants being equal, institutionalization is becoming more likely and being taken in by family or friends less likely as time proceeds from 1968 to 1984.

3.4 Living Arrangement Changes after Onset of a Disability

The logit estimates for all elderly movers in table 3.4 also confirmed the commonsense notion that disability status is an important factor determining an elderly's living arrangement. This section makes an attempt to identify

Table 3.6   **Logit Transition Probabilities: After Death of Spouse (parameter estimates, *t*-statistics in parentheses)**

| | Log Odds of Transition to . . . Rather Than to (1) Independent | | |
Variable	(2) With Others, as Head/Spouse	(3) With Others, as Secondary Individual	(4) Institution
CONST	14.555	−3.676	−23.051
	(3.1)	(−.4)	(−2.2)
AGE68	−.022	.029	.123
	(−.7)	(.6)	(2.4)
KIDS	.085	.248	.121
	(1.1)	(1.5)	(.7)
NOKIDS	−.369	1.387	.630
	(−.5)	(1.0)	(.6)
MDKIDS	.653	5.650	−.466
	(.5)	(3.1)	(−.3)
SIBS	−.079	.191	−.130
	(−.8)	(.8)	(−.5)
NOSIBS	−.165	−5.485	1.643
	(−.2)	(−.1)	(.9)
MDSIBS	−.951	3.374	4.670
	(−.8)	(1.7)	(2.8)
NONWHITE	1.283	.510	1.620
	(2.7)	(.6)	(1.8)
FEMALE	−.560	−2.533	−2.344
	(−1.2)	(−2.7)	(−2.3)
INCOME	−.156	−.748	−.841
	(−1.1)	(−1.5)	(−2.1)
DINCOME	.016	.343	−.935
	(.1)	(1.1)	(−2.2)
DLIM	.630	2.333	−.585
	(1.1)	(2.4)	(−.6)
ORIGIN1	−2.856	−2.237	−.581
	(−6.3)	(−2.0)	(−.6)
YEAR	−.165	−.021	.171
	(−3.1)	(−.2)	(1.6)

Likelihood at convergence, $L(\beta)$	−140.0808
$\mathrm{Rho}^2 = 1 - L(\beta)/L(0)$	.6812
Percentage correctly predicted	85.80
Number of observations	317

Source: PSID, 1968–84, 317 elderly aged 60 and more in 1968 who lost their spouse, including nonrespondents.

cases in which a disability occurs suddenly in order to investigate the time pattern of living arrangement adjustments precipitated by this event.

In fact, changes in disability status are quite hard to measure, in general and particularly in the PSID. The question in the survey (''Are you limited by a health condition?'') provides four answers (''A lot,'' ''Somewhat,'' ''A little,'' and ''No'') that depend on the subjective self-rating of the elderly person. Prior to 1976, only two categories were provided (''Yes'' and ''No'').[16] Not too surprisingly, limitation histories are characterized by a lot of ups and downs that may reflect partly actual subjective feelings and partly arbitrariness in the choice of categories. In addition, many elderly experience a gradual decline in health status with no clear onset of a disability that could be classified as ''one event.''

I define the onset of a disability quite conservatively as a permanent change in disability status: in order to qualify, disability status must be ''No'' for at least five years, then ''Yes,'' ''Somewhat,'' or ''A lot'' for at least another five years. With this definition, I count 237 elderly in the sample who experience a well-defined and sudden change in health status. Table 3.7 presents the actual number of transitions that occur in the year of the health change and in the three years thereafter. Elderly persons who are in a nursing home are excluded in this sample because their limitation status is not recorded.

Unfortunately, the main conclusion to be drawn from these transitions is that the number of actual changes is too small from which to draw reliable conclusions. A formal test of whether the corresponding conditional transition probabilities are equal to those predicted in the lower panel of table 3.2 is significant in the period concurrent with the disability change, barely significant one year later, and insignificant two and three years later.[17] If a reliable

Table 3.7   **Transitions after Onset of a Disability**

Type of Living Arrangement at Origin	Type of Living Arrangement at Destination		
	1	2	3
A. Year concurrent with onset of disability:			
1. Independent	147	9	3
2. With others, as head/spouse	3	41	2
3. With others, as secondary individual	0	0	31
B. One year later:			
1. Independent	135	4	0
2. With others, as head/spouse	5	41	1
3. With others, as secondary individual	0	0	22
C. Two years later:			
1. Independent	109	5	0
2. With others, as head/spouse	5	37	0
3. With others, as secondary individual	0	0	19
D. Three years later:			
1. Independent	84	6	0
2. With others, as head/spouse	4	28	0
3. With others, as secondary individual	0	0	17

Source: PSID, 1968–84, 237 elderly aged 60 and more in 1968 who experienced a well-defined onset of a disability, including nonrespondents.

result can be extracted from table 3.7, then it is a larger probability to stay in living arrangements type 2 and 3 (i.e., living together with children, other relatives, or unrelated persons) in response to a sudden health change to the worse. Unfortunately, the lack of disability data for institutionalized persons made it impossible to detect transitions into nursing homes after the death of a spouse.

It should be noted that these weak results are only apparently in contrast to the strong significance of the variable DLIM (change in the severity of limitation relative to the previous period) in the previous logit analyses. This section limits itself to the obviously rare cases of sudden well-defined unidirectional health changes, whereas the variable DLIM picks up many small changes. In fact, the idea of a sudden onset of a disability rather than a gradual change that eventually necessitates living arrangement adjustments may be inappropriate, or, if such a thing as a sudden onset exists, the measurement of it by a subjective self-rating rather than a functional index of ability may be misleading. Some evidence for the latter explanation can be found in Börsch-Supan, Kotlikoff, and Morris (1988). They show that, among the health variables available in their data set, functional ability is the one that best explains living arrangement changes, rather than subjective health indexes or indicators of actual medical conditions.

3.5 Living Arrangement Changes in the Years Preceding Death

This last section investigates where the elderly spend the last five years of their lives. I count time backward (measuring something like "negative age") and construct a panel that starts with the year of each elderly's death for those 602 elderly for whom date of death is observed. Of those, 448 elderly have at least five years of complete data. Table 3.8 presents the cross-sectional distribution of living arrangement types by year before death, and table 3.9 displays the frequency of all living arrangement sequences observed in this sample.

The main message from these two tables is, once again, the stability of living arrangements—even in the years immediately preceding death. Almost four out of five elderly (79.7 percent) do not change their living arrangements during this time. Note that this fraction is even larger than in the elderly population as a whole. Though one might expect a decreasing mobility with very old age in general,[18] there is also an increase in the necessity to adjust living arrangements in this segment of life, for instance, induced by an increasing frailty in the years preceding death. Obviously, at least in this PSID sample, the first mechanism is stronger than the second.

More than half (55.4 percent) the elderly have been living independently until their deaths. Every fifth of all elderly (20.1 percent) has been taken in by his or her children, relatives, or friends at least once through the last five years before death, most of them (15.2 percent) at least for these five years. Finally,

Table 3.8   **Living Arrangements by Year before Death (percentages)**

Year	(1) Independent	(2) With Others, as Head/Spouse	(3) With Others, as Secondary Individual	(4) Institutionalized
5	64.1	16.7	18.5	.07
4	64.7	15.8	18.3	1.1
3	65.2	15.8	17.6	1.3
2	64.7	15.8	17.6	1.8
1	62.5	16.1	16.3	5.1

Note: Year 1 represents year of death.

Table 3.9   **Living Arrangement Sequences: Last Five Years before Death (absolute frequencies)**

Sequence	Frequency	Sequence	Frequency
11111	248	22111	6
11112	11	22114	2
11113	1	22211	4
11114	5	22214	1
11121	1	22221	7
11122	5	22222	39
11144	2	22224	3
11211	2	24333	1
11221	1	24444	1
11222	3	32222	2
12111	1	33211	1
12122	2	33222	1
12211	1	33331	1
12221	1	33332	2
12222	2	33333	68
14111	1	33334	4
21111	5	33344	1
21112	1	33433	1
21122	1	33444	2
21222	3	43333	1

Source: PSID, 1968–84, elderly aged 60 and more in 1968 who died before 1984.
Note: Sequence 11112 denotes the choice of living arrangement type 2 in the year of death and of type 1 in the preceding four years. The four living arrangement types are denoted as follows: 1 = independent; 2 = with others, as head/spouse; 3 = with others, as secondary individual; 4 = institutionalized.

about 6 percent of the elderly became institutionalized during this time period, almost all of whom stay so until their deaths.

The few changes observed in the sample would put any dynamic analysis on a very weak footing. Hence, I recur to cross-sectional analysis in this section. Table 3.10 provides a cross-sectional analysis of where the elderly choose to live within their last five years of life. The sample consists of all observations with complete data.[19]

Table 3.10   **Cross-sectional Choice Probabilities: Five Years before Death (logit parameter estimates, *t*-statistics in parentheses)**

	Log Odds of Living in . . . Rather Than in (1) Independent		
Variable	(2) With Others, as Head/Spouse	(3) With Others, as Secondary Individual	(4) Institution
CONST	6.640	12.038	−26.803
	(4.0)	(2.4)	(−4.1)
AGE68	−.018	−.043	.030
	(−1.5)	(−1.2)	(.7)
KIDS	.139	.211	−.076
	(5.5)	(4.3)	(−.5)
NOKIDS	−2.447	−1.777	−2.305
	(−6.7)	(−1.4)	(−1.7)
AGEKID	−.047	−.042	−.029
	(−6.2)	(−1.6)	(−1.1)
SIBS	−.085	−.134	−.543
	(−2.5)	(−1.3)	(−2.7)
NOSIBS	.298	1.468	1.641
	(1.1)	(2.0)	(2.0)
NONWHITE	1.359	1.832	.358
	(7.8)	(4.4)	(.5)
FEMALE	−.471	−1.676	−1.873
	(−2.5)	(−3.7)	(−3.3)
INCOME	−.018	−.024	−.757
	(−1.2)	(−.5)	(−4.1)
MARRIED	−1.029	−4.493	−3.523
	(−5.8)	(−6.6)	(−6.0)
LIMITED	−.014	−.497	−.704
	(−.2)	(−2.3)	(−2.3)
HBURDEN	.012	−.061	.023
	(2.5)	(−.9)	(1.7)
YEAR	−.057	−.120	.352
	(−2.4)	(−1.7)	(4.0)
Likelihood at convergence, $L(\beta)$		−911.1028	
$Rho^2 = 1 - L(\beta)/L(0)$		.6326	
Percentage correctly predicted		80.60	
Number of observations		1789	

Source: PSID, 1968−84, elderly aged 60 and more in 1968 who died before 1984.

The analysis in table 3.10 confirms what we have learned so far and shows that some of these effects are particularly pronounced for the very old and most vulnerable elderly. Female elderly are more likely to live independently than male elderly. Black or Hispanic elderly have a higher likelihood of living in shared accommodations, as do elderly with many children. Being married has the expected strong positive effect on living independently. Finally, the variable YEAR that indicates calendar time (not time before death) once again displays the trend toward institutionalization and away from composite households. Note that in this sample of the very old the magnitude of this trend is particularly pronounced. This is a disturbing finding as it appears to indicate a trend toward isolation of those who are particularly vulnerable.

A new variable included is denoted by AGEKID and measures the age of the oldest child. The strong negative coefficient of this variable in the left-most column that characterizes composite households headed by the elderly person appears to indicate the presence of adult children who have never left home. As was mentioned already in section 3.1, it would have been desirable to separate these cases from other shared living arrangements. However, the lack of complete life histories of all household members makes this impossible.

Two economic variables are included. The elderly person's income has a measurable effect only on the probability to become institutionalized; the negative sign shows the inferiority of this alternative—a familiar result by now. The newly introduced variable HBURDEN is the proportion of income that the household must spend on housing; actual gross housing costs (either rent or user costs of homeownership plus utilities) are divided by household income. For institutionalized persons, it measures the last housing burden before institutionalization. For elderly heads, a large burden is a small but significant incentive to share housing. A large housing burden appears also to be a factor that increases the likelihood of entering an institution.

3.6   Summary and Conclusions

I employed the newly available nonresponse file of the PSID to study the living arrangements of elderly Americans. In spite of being a general purpose study that contains some eleven hundred elderly aged 60 and above, this file is on first sight particularly suited to studying the elderly's living arrangements since it includes long histories of living arrangements and their demographic and economic determinants and since it keeps the elderly in the sample when they decease during the sample period or, most important, become institutionalized. No other representative data set combines such a long time horizon as the PSID with a complete recording of nonresponses owing to death or institutionalization. On the other hand, problems with the data—being only partly individual oriented with an incomplete recording of family relationships once secondary individuals are living in a composite household, inconsistencies in the treatment of institutionalization, and a sample size too small for the few observed transitions—substantially inhibited the possible kinds of longitudinal analyses. A longitudinal study specifically for the elderly is still highly desirable for dynamic analyses of the elderly's living arrangement transitions.

The main result of the paper is the stability of living arrangements. Even after incisive life events such as death of a spouse or onset of a disability, and even within the last five years before death, often associated with a quick deterioration of health, only very few elderly adjust their living arrangement, say, in order to move into the household of their children or to live in an institution.

This stability, however, puts the analyst in an awkward position as the resulting small absolute number of changers in the PSID creates a problem for the dynamic analysis. It is my opinion that there are just too few people to support a rich dynamic analysis. A good example for this point is the analysis in the preceding chapter. A well-suited statistical model would have been a fixed effects model that accounts for time-invariant but unobserved differences ("heterogeneity") among the elderly, such as frailty.[20] However, the conditioning on fixed effects necessary for consistent parameter estimation also removes all other time-invariant determinants because these are collinear with the fixed effects. To put it simply, only time variation identifies the dynamics of a dynamic model. Little time variation in the remaining variables and few transitions observed in the sample render the resulting fixed effects model completely unsatisfactory.[21]

I therefore employed very simple models, hoping that simplicity would ensure robustness. Baseline transition probabilities were estimated using a mover-stayer model that accounts in the most simple way for unobserved heterogeneity, and the transition probabilities in the three special cases investigated were parametrized as parsimoniously as possible. I think that this strategy is more appropriate than employing continuous-time hazard models. On the one hand, the data appear to be too weak to allow for proper identification of heterogeneity and state dependence, which could provide the rich dynamics that hazard models are able to generate. Ignoring state dependence and unobserved heterogeneity, however, may render hazard models inappropriate when important variables such as health are unobserved.

In spite of all these problems, I arrived at quite a few results that appear to be robust and are important for the assessment of where the elderly chose to live and what implications this choice has for their well-being. These results are robust as they can be drawn not only from the different models in this paper but also from Ellwood and Kane's analysis (ch. 4, in this volume), which is based on a simple exponential hazard model. They are important as they indicate where, if at all, public policy could improve the well-being of the elderly: there appear to be only a few intervention points—most important, death of a spouse—when active decisions about living arrangements are being made:

- Loss of a spouse is the most important event that precipitates living arrangement transitions. Almost all these transitions take place in the same year as the spouse's death.
- Living in an institution is clearly an inferior living arrangement in terms of income, even in the years immediately preceding death, when medical attention is most valued.
- Male elderly are more likely to live with others or to become institutionalized than female elderly, who most likely stay living independently until their

deaths. This is holding all other determinants, particularly marital status, constant.

* There is a pronounced difference in the choice of living arrangements between white and nonwhite elderly. Nonwhite elderly are much more likely to live with others in a composite household.
* In spite of the perceived inferiority of institutions, the risk of institutionalization has risen substantially from 1968 to 1984, while the likelihood of being "taken in" by relatives or friends has fallen dramatically.

This disturbing tendency toward isolation of the elderly—particularly pronounced among the very old, who are also the most vulnerable—is the most important message of this paper. As pointed out in the introductory section, this growing isolation of the elderly has downstream consequences in terms of medical expenses and social support that are rather costly for society at large and that have to be borne by a decreasing proportion of younger people—not to mention the psychological and physical problems for the elderly themselves caused by growing isolation.

Notes

1. For example, the Longitudinal Retirement History Survey (LRHS), the Survey of Income and Program Participation (SIPP), and the AHS for the noninstitutionalized population and the National Nursing Home Survey (NNHS) and the Survey of Institutionalized Persons (SIP) for the institutionalized population. One exception is the longitudinal study by the Hebrew Rehabilitation Center for the Aged; for an analysis, cf. Börsch-Supan, Kotlikoff, and Morris (1988).
2. The complete family-individual file has almost six-hundred megabytes. To make matters worse, owing to moving in and out, panel members sharing the same household are scattered throughout the file.
3. The data-processing programs are available on request for a fee covering duplication and handling charges.
4. Excluded is a small percentage of elderly individuals whose living arrangement history could not be ascertained because of interview refusal or failure to locate them.
5. There are a few cases where an elderly household had children under 18. These are included in this category.
6. With the exception of the years 1982–84.
7. I perceive entering an institution as an active choice that possibly depends on demographic and economic characteristics as well as health. This does not necessarily imply, however, that the elderly person has to make the choice alone.
8. For an analysis of lengths of nursing home stays, see Garber and MaCurdy (ch. 6, in this volume).
9. Unconditional in the sense that they describe the transition probability of an individual not identified as either a mover or a stayer.
10. For a proof, cf. Amemiya (1985, p. 419).
11. In addition, KIDS is not reported at all in 1968.

12. From a retrospective point of view when date of death is known, remaining years to death ("negative age") may be a more interesting variable than AGE68. If this were so, there should be a significant difference between the coefficients in the two subgroups, which is not the case.

13. This is a loose spoken characterization. Almost all cases of DMARR $= -1$ are deaths of spouses, but there are also a few divorces in old age.

14. The parameter estimate of the risk of being taken in implies a yearly decrease of over 26 percent at sample average. This percentage change—this is a relative change, not a change in absolute percentage points—is too large to be meaningfully extrapolated for ten years because in the highly nonlinear logit model the effect of a change depends on the magnitudes of the choice probabilities.

15. The test is constructed as a joint test of the sixteen conditional transition probabilities. Because only the rows, not the columns, in each table are adding up, the chi-squared statistics have twelve degrees of freedom. At 99 percent confidence, the critical value is 26.22.

16. To make matters worse, in some years, limitation status was asked only for head and spouse, resulting in missing data for those elderly who changed disability status while not being head or spouse of household.

17. At 99 percent confidence.

18. The results in tables 3.3 and 3.4 neither prove nor reject this hypothesis. Feinstein and McFadden (1989) report increasing mobility rates for elderly aged 75 and above on the basis of PSID data, but they do not investigate the very old. Venti and Wise (1989) cannot find systematic age differences in the narrow age distribution of the RHS.

19. There are two econometric problems with these estimates: selectivity bias and panel bias. Both appear innocent in this case. The way in which data on children and siblings is imputed implies that elderly who live as secondary individuals in a composite household and institutionalized elderly have a larger than proportional share of missing data. However, the resulting sample selectivity is innocent owing to inclusion of constants and the logit functional form (McFadden 1978). The pooling of cross sections in this nonlinear model may also result in biased coefficients. The bias appears to be of no quantitative importance in this case as coefficients estimated from single cross sections are of similar magnitude and equal signs.

20. For the development of this model, cf. Chamberlain (1980). For some applications, see Börsch-Supan (1987).

21. See also the difficulties experienced by Schwartz, Danziger, and Smolensky (1984) and the large standard errors in Ellwood and Kane (ch. 4, in this volume).

References

Amemiya, T. 1985. *Advanced econometrics*. Cambridge, Mass.: Harvard University Press.

Börsch-Supan, A. 1985. Household formation, housing prices, and public policy impacts. *Journal of Public Economics*, vol. 25.

———. 1987. *Economic analysis of discrete choice*. Berlin, Heidelberg, and New York: Springer.

———. 1989. Household dissolution and the choice of alternative living arrangements among elderly americans. In *The economics of aging*, ed. David Wise. Chicago: University of Chicago Press.

Börsch-Supan, A., L. Kotlikoff, and J. Morris. 1988. The dynamics of living arrangements of the elderly. NBER Working Paper no. 2787. Cambridge, Mass.: National Bureau of Economic Research.

Chamberlain, G. 1980. Analysis of covariance with qualitative data. *Review of Economic Studies* 47:225–38.

Feinstein, J., and D. McFadden. 1989. The dynamics of housing demand by the elderly: Wealth, cash flow, and demographic effects. In *The economics of aging,* ed. David Wise. Chicago: University of Chicago Press.

Goodman, L. A. 1961. Statistical methods for the "mover-stayer" model. *Journal of the American Statistical Association* 56:841–68.

McCall, J. J. 1971. A Markovian model of income dynamics. *Journal of the American Statistical Association* 66:439–47.

McFadden, D. 1978. Modelling the choice of residential location. In *Spatial interaction theory and planning models,* ed. A. Karlquist. Amsterdam: North Holland.

Merrill, S. R. 1984. Home equity and the elderly. In *Retirement and economic behavior,* ed. H. J. Aaron and G. Burtless. Washington, D.C.: Brookings.

Schwartz, S., S. Danziger, and E. Smolensky. 1984. The choice of living arrangements by the elderly. In *Retirement and economic behavior,* ed. H. J. Aaron and G. Burtless, 229–54. Washington, D.C.: Brookings.

Venti, S. F., and D. A. Wise. 1989. Aging, moving, and housing wealth. In *The economics of aging,* ed. David Wise. Chicago: University of Chicago Press.

Comment   Herman B. Leonard

Those who think they know that elderly Americans want to (and, for the most part, do) live by themselves, accepting a move to live with their children only reluctantly and a move to an institution only in desperation, owe Axel Börsch-Supan a great debt. They are right, and they can now proceed to know what they know with greater assurance than they formerly had any right to feel.

Börsch-Supan's paper provides a readable and comprehensive description of what we can learn about transitions among various living arrangements for the elderly from the new nonresponse files of the PSID. The inclusion of (unfortunately incomplete) data about those who did not survive the sample period permits far more detailed examination of the final and crucial transitions in living arrangements by aging families and individuals.

Börsch-Supan is careful not to extract more than is there from his data. In particular, he emphasizes a number of gaps in the data frame that prevent developing large enough sample sizes to permit confident estimation and inference for at least some of the important issues these data permit approaching. For some questions—for example, which elderly families are living with

Herman B. Leonard is the Baker Professor of Public Sector Financial Management at Harvard University's Kennedy School of Government.

children who are still dependent on them, and which are dependent on the children with whom they are living—these data provide only tantalizingly indistinct hints. Throughout the paper, we get glimpses of what we will be able to learn with more complete data and clear indications of how valuable it would be to have data constructed with these important research issues in mind.

Nonetheless, to dwell on the gaps in these data is to emphasize entirely the wrong feature of this paper. As interested researchers, we perhaps always tend to have our attention drawn to the paper that might have been, to the data that might yet be. But if we indulge that instinct here we will miss what is most important about this paper: that these data are better than those we have previously had, that they allow us to get at questions of profound consequence with regard to public policies about aging, that the results developed from or pointed to by these data are almost certain to be confirmed by any subsequent analysis from whatever better data we may eventually be able to get, and—most important—that we do not have the luxury of waiting because these questions are of deep moment now. What better data will show is what Börsch-Supan is able at least to sketch here. Given the importance of his findings, they deserve to have their implications explored now as guides to the actions we will surely be taking in the meantime, while better data are sought.

The Backdrop: Society's Preferences

Börsch-Supan is able to show us enough to tell a very important story. To understand its importance and implications, it has to be viewed against the backdrop of what society and the elderly want for the last years of life. To be sure, these tastes are value laden and culture bound. It may seem odd to think about what society's preferences about individuals' preferences might be—as a profession, economists usually take individual preferences as given and inquire about how well alternative decisions or social decision mechanisms serve them. But, if given a choice about what people's preferences might be, society as a whole would surely prefer that individuals aspire to forms of consumption that are relatively low in resource intensity and would surely like to avoid having individuals prefer heavily resource-intensive forms of consumption that produce a relatively low quality of life. Hence, society might well have a strong preference for individuals to prefer avoiding institutionalization in the last years of life. If most individuals strongly prefer either independent living or living in the company of others—and, importantly, if those with whom they may live also prefer shared arrangements—then it is both widely believed and plausible that a reasonable quality of life for the elderly or the disabled can be provided at considerably lower real cost than if, by contrast, all or some of the relevant parties strongly prefer institutionalization (either for themselves or for those who might otherwise live with them).

It seems reasonable to suppose that society has a strong preference for independent and shared living arrangements instead of institutionalization. Institutions are not merely expensive; they are also almost inherently capable of providing only a relatively low quality of life, almost irrespective of their cost. To minimize the social cost of such inefficient arrangements, society might then actively seek to support a social culture of independence and shared living.

Results

Against the backdrop of that conception of social interest, what news does Börsch-Supan provide? The good news is that the news is generally good. The bad news is that it is deteriorating.

First, Börsch-Supan finds high levels of independent living. It appears that people very strongly seek to avoid institutionalization, and this suggests that they may be responsive to programs that seek to provide options through which they can remain independent.

Second, Börsch-Supan finds that the rates of independent living and of shared living have been falling, and the risk of institutionalization rising, over the last twenty years. This is no great surprise to those who have looked at the increase in the institutionalized population, but it is particularly strikingly laid out in Börsch-Supan's careful analysis. Holding other factors constant, the hazard of institutionalization has markedly increased. This implies that the rapid growth of the institutionalized population is due not merely to the rapid growth in the population of very old people but also to a conditional growth in the fraction of those institutionalized, holding fixed age and other factors. We should be very interested, as a society, in finding ways to check this increase. The size of the at-risk population will continue to rise rapidly; if the rate at which that group enters institutions also continues to grow, the prospects both for the elderly and for society are quite unattractive.

Börsch-Supan also develops the very important result that living patterns are very stable. The mixed movers/stayers model reveals that a large component of the relevant population has substantial inertia. This is an extremely important (though not terribly surprising) result because it suggests that if we help people toward preferred outcomes—independent living or shared living in composite households—the results may be durable.

It would be very valuable from a policy perspective to have additional evidence on this point. What Börsch-Supan observes is that, under current incentives, there is substantial inertia in changing patterns of living. This is hopeful, but it does not immediately indicate that social interventions to influence the choice of living pattern will have long-term effects. If the choice is induced (e.g., by suasion or by a financial incentive), it may fit less well, wear less comfortably, and persist for a shorter time. Since this is an issue of substantial consequence for policy-making regarding the elderly and disabled, it provides a fertile area for additional research.

Börsch-Supan also finds, again not surprisingly, that a major risk point of transition is the death of a spouse. This is well known; Börsch-Supan's results simply demonstrate how disruptive this transition is. Again, this is an important result from a policy perspective. Through Börsch-Supan's lens, we come to see living patterns as stable and durable over long periods but punctuated by relatively short periods of tumultuous transition. The effects of the transition triggers damp out relatively rapidly across time—for example, those who continue to live independently for two years past the death of a spouse begin to have transition probabilities that resemble those who have had no transition in marital status. Having survived a period of high hazard for living pattern change (triggered by death of the spouse), the survivor emerges into a possibly long and stable period of independent life. In Börsch-Supan's data, traumas either have effects on living patterns that are relatively immediate or have none at all.

This suggests that a policy of active social intervention targeted at high-risk points might be effective and valuable. If the newly widowed can be helped in forming a new independent household, they may be able to maintain their independent status indefinitely. If, by contrast, their transition in marital status induces a change in living arrangement, that effect is likely to be largely irreversible. Once again, we cannot tell from Börsch-Supan's results whether a programmatic intervention targeted at such high-risk points would be effective—but they do suggest that, if we could find an effective short-term intervention, it might repay dividends over a long period.

Finally, Börsch-Supan demonstrates that cultural and social factors seem to be important in determining the rates at which people choose particular living arrangements. Race and sex have strong effects on the propensity to choose particular arrangements and to make transitions among them. While this is not surprising and is well known, we do not have a clear idea of what the underlying cause is. Are we seeing people's expectations about themselves reflected in their choices? Are social or cultural factors central determinants? Are demographic forces dominant (e.g., healthy unmarried men are substantially outnumbered by women among the elderly and so may have more opportunities to develop shared living arrangements)?

While we do not know the causes, the fact that the rates differ across population subgroups suggests that different influences are operating—and, thus, perhaps that these influences could be changed. Our society has done relatively little to shape people's expectations about how they should live in their later years or to shape their preferences. It has done even less to shape the sense of obligation felt by children, siblings, or others who might be able to provide either support of continued independent living or a shared living arrangement. It is not clear that any effective intervention on these dimensions could be crafted—but, if society cares enough about influencing the pattern of living arrangements among the elderly and disabled, the fact that the outcomes differ across population subgroups gives us a place to start in assessing what seems to influence people's preferences and senses of obligation.

Conclusion

Institutionalization holds very unattractive prospects for the elderly and for society. It threatens to consume a high fraction of the life savings of those at risk and of their offspring and to provide them with a low quality of life in spite of its high cost. If it becomes common—if many of us find that our friend's parents are living in institutions—it may erode whatever sense of obligation or preference it is that currently leads many to provide a shared living arrangement for older or disabled siblings, parents, or friends. Even comparatively, institutionalized living provides, in the view of many, what is on the whole a poor way to die.

Society has limited possibilities for intervening in these outcomes. From a public policy perspective, Börsch-Supan's results raise major questions about what role society can and should take. First, it might choose to try to reduce reliance on institutional living arrangements. If so, it will have to do somewhat more than just say no to institutionalization. It will have to seek to build a culture of self and mutual reliance. If it is successful in doing so and more of the frail and sick remain at home, society will also confront additional ethical challenges. For example, can we adapt to letting people die at home of illnesses or conditions from which they might be saved in a hospital, in order to avoid their being institutionalized thereafter, if they would prefer it?

In addition, Börsch-Supan's work frames important questions about the advisability of programs to support independent and shared living arrangements for those at risk of institutionalization. The judicious use of public support to enhance the possibility of continuing in independent or shared living status might have durable effects and might provide manyfold returns in both private and public savings from institutionalization. But it could also feed what may become an insatiable appetite for expensive assistance for those capable of remaining independent without it. Once such help exists, much of the elderly population may come to see it as an entitlement, even if they are not truly at risk of being unable to function independently without it. Moreover, there is a substantial moral hazard. Many are now capable of living alone only because of support (running errands, helping with cooking, and so on) from their children, siblings, or friends. The provision of these private services is costly to the provider. If the public comes forward to provide or to pay for some of these services, some of these volunteer workers supporting the independent living arrangements of elderly or disabled people may disappear, graciously accepting the public's unintended offer to substitute public help for their current private actions. Such programs are potentially extremely costly and would not necessarily even expand the services available to those in need of them. Their desirability is, then, an open question, and we must await further research on people's reactions to these kinds of programs before we can tell whether society's interests—and the elderly's—would be well served by introducing them.

Questions like these go well beyond the scope of Börsch-Supan's work, but he has taken us a very useful step toward framing the relevant questions more clearly and toward having a more definitive data base for knowing what many thought they already knew. We can now proceed with more confidence about what we know—and, therefore, with less trepidation—into the policy terrain, fraught though it may be with cultural and sociological as well as economic considerations.

4   The American Way of Aging: An Event History Analysis

David T. Ellwood and Thomas J. Kane

Women who reach age 65 can expect to live eighteen more years on average, men fourteen more years. Yet economists have largely ignored that part of the life cycle after age 65. By 65, most American men and women have retired, but changes linked to marital status, health, economic support, living arrangements, institutionalization, and death lie ahead. This paper represents an attempt to bring into much sharper focus the timing and incidence of events past age 65.

The ideal data set for studying the event history of aging might carry thirty-five years of longitudinal information on several cohorts of 65-year-olds. Since such data do not exist, we used the seventeen-year Panel Study of Income Dynamics (PSID), piecing together different slices of old age from individuals entering and exiting the survey at different ages. Imposing a general statistical structure, we estimated parameters that allowed us then to simulate thirty-five years of longitudinal data for a cohort of 65-year-olds. By estimating our models and then simulating life events for a sample of 65-year-olds, we have essentially brought together the disparate segments of old age captured within the window of the PSID to draw a smoothed profile of the events of aging.

In order to do the simulations, we estimated models of marriage and widowhood, disability, economic status, shared living arrangements, institutionalization, and death. We then applied the model to generate 8,880 simulated lifetimes, using a representative sample of 444 65-year-olds as the starting point.

David T. Ellwood is professor of public policy at the Kennedy School of Government and a research associate of the National Bureau of Economic Research. Thomas J. Kane is Ph.D. candidate in public policy at the Kennedy School of Government.

With our simulations, we are able both to compare the futures of people with various characteristics at age 65 and to explore what people in particular end states looked like in previous years. For instance, we were able to ask how the aging process differs for those who are white and black, rich and poor, healthy and disabled at age 65. We also analyzed the histories of poor elderly widows and asked what had led them there. Were poor elderly widows formerly middle-class married women or poor married women, or were they already widowed and poor at age 65? Who enters nursing homes? Are they people who are reasonably well to do when they turned 65 who become widowed and whose health failed? Or are they persons who have mostly been poor and sickly for an extended period?

In the paper, we will describe the models we estimated and explore their power and plausibility. We believe that with refinement one may well be able to use models such as this one for a much more detailed understanding of the later years of the life cycle.

4.1   The Data

Trying to estimate the effects of aging with cross-sectional data confuses cohort effects. Particularly with regard to economic status, such effects are likely to be large. For example, in our data, persons turning 65 in the early 1970s had considerably higher poverty rates than those turning 65 in the 1980s. Thus, some of the apparent rise in poverty observed in cross-sectional data among older age groups may reflect the fact that earlier cohorts earned less during their working lives than later ones.

To trace the event histories of those in their old age, we needed a panel data set following a nationally representative sample over an extended period. The PSID is an on-going survey begun in 1968 following an original sample of 5,000 families with annual interviews. We used the seventeen-year sample, following people up through 1984. Our sample consisted of all those who were over 65 for at least three years during the survey (since some of our models use two-year lags). Ultimately, we had a sample of 1,671 persons, 745 men and 926 women.

Until recently, the PSID suffered a major flaw, rendering it inappropriate for use in studying longitudinal patterns of aging. When persons left the sample because of institutionalization, death, or any other reason, their records—including all previous years' information—were dropped from the sample. Thus, the only elderly left on the PSID were the survivors, presenting a potentially serious sample selection problem. Recently, however, a nonresponse sample has been released that includes all people ever surveyed. Most important for our purposes, the nonresponse sample contains information on reason for nonresponse, such as death or institutionalization. Still, we were forced to do a considerable amount of recoding to identify the institutionalized and those who were dependents sharing the household of others. (For a description of our recoding of PSID data, see the appendix.)

4.2 Methodology

Our methodology consisted of three steps. First, we modeled income dynamics and the odds of several discrete events (widowhood and remarriage, disability and return to good health, death, institutionalization and dependent household sharing) separately for men and women. Except when modeling income, where we used a simple OLS estimator, we used hazard models allowing for time-varying covariates. In each case, realizations of other past and contemporaneous events (such as marital status or health) were included as independent variables.

Next, we applied the models to sequentially simulate the paths of aging for a representative sample of 65-year-olds. Each year, we used the models to predict a new set of outcomes for the following year. The simulated results for one year were then used to predict outcomes for the next year and so on for thirty-five years. Because we used a random sample of people and their reported characteristics on turning 65 as the seeds for the simulations, our simulated life expectancies and institutionalization rates should match the actual aggregates for the cohort reaching age 65 during the period 1980–84.

As a final step, we tabulated the simulated data set to study alternative paths of aging. We could compare the lives of those who were disabled and healthy, widowed and married, rich and poor at 65. Taking persons at age 65, we could ask how many were widowed, disabled, poor, dead, or institutionalized by ages 80, 85, 90, and so on. Similarly, we could look at where people ended up and ask what had led them there. Thus, we could ask whether poor elderly widows were formerly middle-class wives. And we could ask whether those entering institutions had been rich or poor, married or unmarried, disabled or healthy, living independently or as a dependent in earlier years.

In effect, our models pull together the experiences of succeeding cohorts within the PSID, capturing the cross-event, intertemporal relations found in the data. We are able to pool the experiences of various cohorts by putting restrictions on the form of the cohort effect. The simulations then reproduce those relations, summarizing the lessons learned in a more intelligible way than might be gotten from piles of cross-tabulations from the original data. In effect, we have projected a thirty-five-year event history for people just turning 65, reflecting the relations gleaned from the original data.

There are important limitations, however. Since the relations observed in current data are assumed to hold into the future, unmodeled trends will lead our projections astray. On the other hand, any projection suffers from these flaws. Our method, at least, allows us to exploit the full longitudinal and cross-sectional information available from the PSID.

4.3   General Modeling Strategy

We used two different types of models in this paper: hazard models for discrete events such as death and institutionalization and a separate model for income dynamics. We discuss the hazard models first.

4.3.1   Hazard Models

In order to predict discrete events such as death and widowhood, we estimated single and multiple-risk hazard models using fixed and time-varying covariates.[1] The odds of death, institutionalization, and dependent household sharing were estimated within a multiple-risk framework. Chances of moving into and out of marriage and into and out of good health were each modeled individually as single risks.

Only a small fraction of the sample was exactly age 65 at the start of the survey. Some turned 65 late in the survey and thus were followed for only a few years; others turned 65 long before the survey began, providing a glimpse of the later years of the aging process but carrying no information on the earlier years. In limiting ourselves to any one cohort, we might have observed at most seventeen years of the aging process, ignoring either the earlier or the later years of the aging process.

We sought a way to learn from all the scattered segments of old age observed within the PSID. In defining aged "spells" and their distributions, we imposed a general statistical structure on the problem, which allowed us to pool the experiences of the succeeding cohorts to come up with a portrait of the dynamics of aging. We define a spell as the number of years we observed a person in a particular state starting at age 65 or the first year he or she was observed in the state (if he or she was 65 at the beginning of the survey). Each period, the probability of an event was a function of $Z(t)$, a vector of time-varying covariates (such as age, marital status, and health status), and X, a vector of fixed characteristics (race and education). Note that t is the number of years in which we saw them in a particular state, not the number of years they have lived past 65.

We assume t to have an exponential baseline hazard. In effect, the baseline hazard was assumed to be constant, exhibiting no duration dependence. But, by including age dummies among the time-varying covariates, we allow for a very general form of age-varying failure rates. Our single-risk hazard function takes the simple form below, with an exponential baseline hazard, fixed characteristics X, time-varying covariates $Z(t)$, and no unobserved heterogeneity:

$$h[t; X, Z(t)] = \phi \cdot \exp[X\beta_1 + Z(t)\beta_2].$$

Because age is a time-varying covariate, the hazard is allowed to shift up or down with changes in age. Thinking in terms of a spell of old age, this amounts to a nonparametric form of duration dependence. Changes in other variables such as health or marital status will shift the hazard as well.

In most of our models, there was only a binary choice, but, as will be discussed below, we jointly estimate the odds of death, institutionalization, and sharing models. For simplicity, we assume that each alternative—death, institutionalization, and sharing—is independent of the other alternatives in that period.

4.4 Models and Results

Before discussing the simulation results, we will briefly highlight the models and estimated parameters. The coefficient estimates and asymptotic standard errors are given in the appendix tables. Table 4.1 shows the specification of each one of our models.

4.4.1 Disability Models

We modeled movements into and out of disability as a function of income, age, marital status, and race.[2] By including a dummy for disability status last period, we allowed for the possibility that the newly disabled or the newly healthy might be more likely to change states again, either because of some short-term event or because of some measurement error.

An 80-year-old healthy man who reported being disabled one year earlier had a much higher likelihood of becoming disabled again right away (37 percent) than men in their second or later year of good health (12 percent).

Table 4.1   **Model Specification**

	Hazard Models: (at time t)			
Variables:	Into and Out of Disability	Into and Out of Marriage	Into Death, Institutional- ization, and Dependent Sharing	From Sharing to Death, Institutional- ization
Disability$_{t-1}$		X	X	
Disability$_{t-2}$	X	X	X	
Income/needs$_{t-1}$	X	X	X	
Age Group$_{t-1}$	X	X	X	X
Marital status$_{t-1}$	X		X	
Newly married$_{t-1}$	X		X	
Newly unmarried$_{t-1}$	X		X	
Year of survey$_t$	X	X	X	
Years of school completed	X	X	X	
Race	X	X	X	X
Sex[a]				X

[a]All models except those from sharing into institutionalization and death are estimated separately for men and women.

(For the probabilities of becoming disabled, other characteristics held at their means for those who were not disabled at age 80, see table 4.2.) Disabled men aged 80 who only recently entered disability status had a 40 percent chance of becoming healthy again right away and had a 13 percent chance thereafter. (Estimated probabilities for movements out of disability are not shown since they are largely symmetric to those in table 4.2.)

Persons of both sexes who were more educated or richer were less likely to become disabled. White women were less likely to become disabled and more likely to become healthy again once disabled.

4.4.2   Marriage Models

We modeled movements both into and out of marriage as well. By far, the most common reason for becoming unmarried was widowhood, but the rare cases of divorce were treated in the same model. Our models are based on only the characteristics of the individual. In more complex models, one might

Table 4.2   **Predicted One-Year Probabilities of Moving into Disability from Good Health For 80-Year-Old Men and Women Living Independently**

Characteristic	Men	Women
Grand mean	.1597	.2187
Previous disability status:		
Disabled one year ago	.3672	.4699
Not disabled two years	.1233	.1944
Marital status:		
Married	.1682	.2343
Unmarried	.1570	.2136
Newly unmarried	.0521	.1893
Income:		
At poverty level	.2266	.2752
2 times poverty	.1974	.2269
3 times poverty	.1819	.2021
4 times poverty	.1716	.1859
5 times poverty	.1640	.1742
Age:		
65–69	.1143	.1877
70–74	.1220	.2037
75–79	.1419	.2245
80–84	.1597	.2187
85–89	.2340	.3076
90+	.0898	.4076
Race:		
White	.1585	.2151
Nonwhite	.1813	.2974

Note: When varying each characteristic, other characteristics are held at sample means.

include spousal characteristics such as age or disability in modeling widow-hood, but that would greatly complicate the simulations.

In modeling movements out of marriage, we included disability this year and last, age, race, and income. Table 4.3 reports the probability of becoming unmarried, varying one characteristic at a time, holding all else at the mean for those who were married at age 80. Not surprisingly, the most important predictor of widowhood was age. Holding other characteristics at their means for married men at age 80, the annual chances of becoming unmarried for men increased from 1.2 percent at age 65 to 3.8 percent at age 90. For two reasons—because they have longer life expectancies and because they are typically younger than their mates—women are much more likely to be widowed. Again holding other characteristics at their mean for women age 80, women's annual chances of widowhood increased from 3.2 percent to 14 percent between ages 65 and 90.

Income was an important predictor of a woman's chances of becoming widowed. An 80-year-old married woman who was poor had a 17 percent annual chance of widowhood; an otherwise similar woman with income five times the poverty level had only a 11 percent chance.

4.4.3   Death, Institutionalization, and Dependent Sharing

We modeled the transition from independent living to death, institutional-ization, and dependent sharing separately for men and women. As shown in

Table 4.3   **One-Year Probabilities of Becoming Unmarried for Currently Married 80-Year-Old Men and Women Living Independently**

Characteristic	Men	Women
Grand Mean	.0383	.1337
Income:		
At poverty level	.0463	.1668
2 times poverty	.0425	.1413
3 times poverty	.0404	.1281
4 times poverty	.0390	.1195
5 times poverty	.0379	.1131
Age:		
65–69	.0117	.0323
70–74	.0220	.0431
75–79	.0212	.0759
80–84	.0383	.1337
85–89	.0306	.0593
90+	.0377	.1397
Race:		
White	.0387	.1330
Nonwhite	.0346	.1598

Note: When varying each characteristic, other characteristics are held at sample means.

table 4.1, the variables used to predict were health status in the past two periods, income, marital status, and recent changes in marital status, age, and race. For those who became dependent sharers, we also had to model transitions into death and institutionalization.[3]

Death

Marital status, age, and especially disability were the most important predictors of death rates for men and women. The average 80-year-old man who was disabled in both of the past two years had a 13 percent chance of dying in the next year as compared to 4 percent for those who were healthy (see table 4.4).

Marriage had opposite implications for men and women. Marriage helped men's and hurt women's chances of survival. This may reflect the traditional

Table 4.4   **Probability of Death, Institutionalization, or Dependent Sharing for 80-Year-Old Men and Women Currently Living Independently**

Characteristic	Men			Women		
	Death	Institution	Share	Death	Institution	Share
Grand Mean	.0819	.0036	.0067	.0314	.0124	.0044
Disability:						
Disabled at least 2 years	.1265	.0041	.0120	.0941	.0519	.0069
Healthy at least 2 years	.0418	.0028	.0030	.0236	.0085	.0038
Newly disabled	.0823	.0069	.0020	.0538	.0355	.0071
Marital status:						
Married	.0751	.0029	.0041	.0380	.0121	.0019
Unmarried	.1010	.0053	.0202	.0292	.0125	.0057
Newly unmarried	.0927	.0158	.0448	.0311	.0163	.0212
Newly married	.0675	.0029	.0041	.1546	.0121	.0019
Income:						
At poverty level	.0952	.0206	.0058	.0346	.0164	.0061
2 times poverty	.0883	.0085	.0062	.0310	.0121	.0042
3 times poverty	.0844	.0051	.0065	.0291	.0101	.0034
4 times poverty	.0818	.0035	.0067	.0278	.0089	.0029
5 times poverty	.0799	.0026	.0068	.0268	.0080	.0026
Age:						
65–69	.0395	.0005	.0022	.0187	.0025	.0034
70–74	.0429	.0008	.0019	.0232	.0038	.0028
75–79	.0561	.0017	.0040	.0246	.0048	.0047
80–84	.0819	.0036	.0067	.0314	.0124	.0044
85–89	.0928	.0042	.0100	.0481	.0117	.0076
90+	.1605	.0122	.0107	.1486	.0543	.0076
Race						
White	.0831	.0035	.0064	.0323	.0138	.0042
Nonwhite	.0733	.0041	.0095	.0242	.0051	.0061

Note: When varying each characteristic, all other characteristics are held at the means for 80-year-old men or women.

roles of husband and wife. Married men live longer because they are cared for by their wives. In the process, wives' health may be endangered lifting and helping a disabled husband.

As expected, death rates for both men and women rose with age.

Institutionalization

As described in the appendix, we coded someone as institutionalized in several ways. Our data may understate the extent of institutionalization for several reasons. First, nursing home stays that are expected by family members to be short will not be reported. Second, those who enter nursing homes and die in the interval between annual interviews will be counted as nonresponse due to death, so the spell of nursing home residence will be missed. Third, those from single person households entering nursing homes after living alone are likely to be undercounted. PSID interviewers often pursued a single-person household into an institution and provided no direct indicator where they were (until 1984, when an institutionalization indicator was added). We worked with PSID staff to develop a recoding scheme to capture this third group, as described in the appendix. Still, we are uncertain whether we have fully resolved the problem.

While exits from nursing homes would be observed in some cases, most could not have been traced, given PSID procedures. As a result, we treated institutionalization as an absorbing state.

Age, disability, income, and marital status were the best predictors of nursing home entry for men and women. Ninety-year-olds were twenty times more likely to enter nursing homes than 65-year-olds. Disability also had a moderate effect.

Wealthier men and women were less likely to enter nursing homes. For instance, a woman with the mean characteristics of an 80-year-old but with income at the poverty level was twice as likely as a woman with income five times the poverty level to enter an institution within a year (1.6 vs. .8 percent).

With a spouse to care for them, married men were less likely to enter institutions; recently widowed men were more likely. We found similar results for women, but with large standard errors.

Dependent Sharing

Adult children often return to their parents' home temporarily. To maintain the distinction between those who were dependents and those who were merely sharing their home, we adopted the label "dependent sharing." To be a "dependent sharer," one not only lived with others but depended on others who owned or rented the house and accounted for more than half the income.

Marital status, income, and age were the most important predictors of dependent sharing. For both men and women, being married sharply reduced the chances of becoming a dependent sharer. Newly widowed women were especially likely to move in with their children.

There is a broad literature relating the increase in independent living among the elderly to higher incomes (see, e.g., Schwartz, Danziger, and Smolensky 1984; Michael, Fuchs, and Scott 1980; and Pampel 1983). Our models provide consistent results that those with higher incomes were less likely to become dependent sharers.

Unlike death and institutionalization, dependent sharing was not assumed to be absorbing. We estimated separate models of the movement from dependent sharing to death and to institutionalization. (Virtually no one returned to independent living.) Because of small sample sizes, we pooled observations of males' and females' dependent sharing and modeled transitions into death and institutionalization as a function of age and race alone. We also included a sex dummy. Holding constant race and age, female dependent sharers were less likely to die and to enter nursing homes in a given year than men.

4.4.4   Income Dynamics

The major factor affecting the standard of living of the elderly is changed marital status. Since spousal benefits for Social Security are considerably lower than those of the primary beneficiary, one would expect a large fall in income for women if their husband dies. Pensions usually offer even less protection to widows. For men, we would also expect a fall in income since the spouse's benefits are lost, but not nearly as great a fall as for women.

In all our models, we use income relative to the poverty line as a simple indicator of economic well-being. Since the poverty line differs by family size, dividing income by the poverty need standard adjusts for family size. Alternatively, one could have modeled income separately and then divided by family size. We have estimated the models both ways, and the results are similar. In the end, we used income/needs ratios because the coefficients are more readily interpretable.

We modeled the log of income relative to needs as a function of past disability, current marital status, recent and past changes in marital status, race, education, age, and survey year (to account for cohort differences). We also included three years of lagged income/needs (in logs), restricting their coefficients to sum to one so that the model would not create regression to the mean due to measurement error.[4]

The poverty line in 1985 was $5,156 for a one-person household and $6,503 for a two-person home. Since the poverty line for a one-person home is 79 percent of that for a two-person one, income relative to the poverty/needs ratio would fall when a person became widowed only if income fell by more than 21 percent.

New widowers and new widows face very different changes in economic status on the death of a spouse. When a man loses his wife, his standard of living (income relative to needs) is estimated to fall by 10 percent initially (implying that total income fell by roughly 30 percent). It remains 10 percent lower in succeeding years.

In sharp contrast, widows experience a 56 percent drop in standard of living initially (created by a 77 percent drop in income!). But more than half the loss is recovered in the next year, presumably as survivors' benefits of various sorts are paid. Ultimately, we estimated that women experience a 20 percent drop in their standard of living on the death of their husband (caused by a 41 percent decline in their income). It is clear that the current system of income support leaves women at far greater risk than men.

4.5   Simulation Results

We used the parameter estimates to simulate the events of old age for a representative sample of 65-year-olds. Starting with the 444 PSID sample members who turned 65 between 1980 and 1984, we used each individual as the seed for twenty different simulated life histories. In doing the simulation, we estimated the probability of each event in the subsequent year. Drawing from a uniform (0,1) distribution, we modeled the occurrence of each event. We also estimated expected income/needs ratios for those at age 66 using the income model. Taking a draw from a normal distribution with mean zero and variance equal to the estimated variance of the disturbance term in the income equation, we reproduced the observed distribution of incomes. Proceeding sequentially, we used simulated characteristics at age 66 to predict characteristics at age 67 and so on. Generating twenty equiprobable lifetimes for each of the 444 sample members, we eventually had 8,880 simulated spells of old age to study.

In table 4.5, we compare our simulated life expectancies with those reported by the U.S. National Center for Health Statistics (NCHS).[5] This is a rough measure of the external validity of our predictions. With the exception of nonwhite females, our predictions were close for all groups. For instance, for white females, our simulations show a life expectancy at age 65 of 18.5 years as compared to the NCHS estimate of 18.7 years. For white men and for nonwhite men, our estimates were also very close for those aged 65: 14.9 simulated versus 14.5 in the life tables for white men; our simulations of life expectancies for nonwhite men at age 65 were equal to that in the life tables, 13.4 years. Nonwhite females, though, had a simulated life expectancy of 19.4, though the life table estimate was only 17.3.

In many respects, the close correspondence between our simulated and the actual life expectancies is remarkable. Each year, for each individual, life events are being simulated within ten different models. Realizations in one year for each event help predict changes in all other events in future years. Poor predictions in one model would distort the entire simulation since each simulated event would be used to predict other events in later years. That such a large-scale serially dependent model would correspond with life-table estimates is reassuring.

Table 4.5   Comparison of Simulated Life Expectancies with Life-Table
                     Estimates

	Life Expectancy at Age:				
	65	70	75	80	85
White females:					
Life table	18.7	15.1	11.8	8.8	6.5
Simulated	18.5	15.7	12.6	9.8	6.9
Nonwhite females:					
Life table	17.3	14.1	11.5	9.0	7.4
Simulated	19.4	16.1	12.5	9.7	7.1
White males:					
Life table	14.5	11.5	9.0	6.9	5.2
Simulated	14.9	12.6	9.9	8.3	6.0
Nonwhite males:					
Life table	13.4	10.9	9.0	7.1	6.0
Simulated	13.4	11.3	8.7	7.1	5.8

Note: Life-table estimates drawn from U.S. Bureau of the Census, Statistical Abstract of the
United States, 1987 (Washington, D.C.: U.S. Government Printing Office, 1986), table 108.
Life-table estimates are for blacks, simulations for nonwhites.

4.5.1   Looking Forward from Age 65

The extent of institutionalization is much higher than might be expected on
an initial inspection of those who were in institutions at a point in time. For
instance, according to the 1980 census, only 4 percent of the population 75–79
and 12 percent of the population 80 and over were in institutions (drawn from
Bureau of the Census 1984). But the size of the stock of elderly and institutions
leaves a false impression that only a few of the elderly ever enter. In the
simulations, 12 percent of men and 38 percent of women aged 65 were
eventually institutionalized. These estimates are in fact quite consistent with
alternative estimates of 25–50 percent for both sexes combined (see, e.g.,
Vicente, Wiley, and Carrington 1979; and McConnell 1984).

We wanted to compare the prospects of those who were rich and poor,
disabled and healthy, married and unmarried, white and nonwhite at age 65.
In tables 4.6 and 4.7, we report the status at age 80 for those with selected
characteristics at age 65.

With the simulated data, we were able to pose a number of questions not
answerable with cross sections. Reassuringly, the answers were for the most
part as expected. For example, men and women who were disabled at age 65
were much more likely to be dead or in nursing homes by age 80 than those
who were healthy. Further, men and women who were married at age 65 lived
two years longer than men and women who were unmarried. (Although
marriage lowers women's chances of survival after controlling for income,
married women tended to have higher standards of living.) White men were
less likely to be institutionalized by age 80 than nonwhite men, white women

Table 4.6   Simulated Status at Age 80 for Those with Selected Characteristics at Age 65 (Men)

Characteristic at Age 65	Of Persons Alive at 65			Of Persons Alive at 80, % Sharing	Of Persons Alive and Independent at 80		
	Life Expectancy at Age 65	% Dead by Age 80	% Institutional by Age 80		% Unmarried	% Disabled	% Below 2 Times Poverty
All Persons	14.7	53	4	20	15	43	28
White	14.9	52	4	18	15	41	26
Nonwhite	13.4	55	7	34	17	72	35
Disabled	12.7	59	6	16	17	54	35
Not Disabled	16.0	48	3	16	15	39	23
Married	14.9	52	4	16	14	43	28
Unmarried	12.9	60	6	21	44	61	30
Income < 2 times poverty	12.4	58	10	49	18	76	61
Income 2–5 times poverty	14.3	54	4	17	19	48	36
Income 5+ times poverty	16.8	46	2	12	11	30	10

more likely. White men and women were much less likely to be dependent sharers by age 80 than nonwhites.

The differences in the prospects for those who were low and high income at age 65 were most dramatic. (Low income is defined as having income less than two times the poverty level, high income as having income greater than five times the poverty level.) Those who were low income at age 65 lived four fewer years on average, were much more likely to be in a nursing home or dependent sharers by age 80, and were much more likely to be disabled.

4.5.2.   Looking Backward

We were also interested in tracing back the life histories of those in particular end states. Two were of particular policy interest: institutionalization and poor widowhood. For instance, were those who ended up in institutions identifiable at age 65? Were they rich or poor, healthy or disabled, married or unmarried? What changes in disability status, marital status, and income did they see in the few years preceding their institutionalization? How many of those who were poor widows at age 80 were middle-class wives at age 65?

We have already noted that, in our simulations, 12 percent of men and 38 percent of women alive at age 65 eventually entered institutions. Table 4.8 compares the characteristics of the ever institutionalized with the average characteristics at age 65. Men who were eventually institutionalized were

Table 4.7   Simulated Status at Age 80 for Those with Selected Characteristics
at Age 65 (Women)

Characteristic at Age 65	Of Persons Alive at 65			Of Persons Alive at 80, % Sharing	Of Persons Alive and Independent at 80		
	Life Expectancy at Age 65	% Dead by Age 80	% Institutional by Age 80		% Unmarried	% Disabled	% Below 2 Times Poverty
All Persons	18.6	26	12	16	69	42	34
White	18.5	26	13	13	68	40	31
Nonwhite	19.4	26	8	38	80	64	57
Disabled	17.2	28	15	14	70	42	41
Not Disabled	19.8	22	11	9	68	42	29
Married	19.3	25	10	11	55	41	28
Unmarried	17.9	24	18	10	97	44	43
Income < 2 times poverty	16.3	32	15	34	84	52	70
Income 2–5 times poverty	19.6	22	12	9	69	43	28
Income 5+ times poverty	20.8	22	7	6	56	33	9

Table 4.8   Comparison of Characteristics of Persons Who Eventually Become
Institutionalized with the Characteristics of All Persons at Age 65
by Sex

Characteristics at Age 65	Men		Women	
	All	Ever Institutionalized	All	Ever Institutionalized
Unmarried	5	7	37	41
Disabled	38	41	38	38
< 2 times poverty	17	29	33	37
2–5 times poverty	49	50	43	40
5+ times poverty	34	21	24	22

disproportionately low income. However, their disability status was very
similar to that of persons who did not enter institutions. We suspect that this
results from the fact that disabled men die more quickly, often not living long
enough to be institutionalized.

The results for women are even more interesting. By the criteria shown in
the table, women who eventually became institutionalized are virtually
indistinguishable from those who do not. Once again, the result almost

certainly reflects differential mortality. Low-income women are more likely to be institutionalized if they get very old, but they are less likely to reach very old age. Those who eventually enter institutions thus appear to be a real cross section of American women at age 65.

In table 4.9, we report the characteristics of the institutionalized in the few years immediately preceding their institutionalization. Over one-third (38 percent) of men who were institutionalized were dependent sharers the year before entering institutions. For men who enter the nursing home from living independently, there is a sudden jump in widowhood and disability in the last year before institutionalization. Still, 68 percent of men who were institutionalized were married only the year before.

Women who enter nursing homes were more likely to have been living independently and more likely to have been widows for a while. Theirs seems to be a gradual deterioration, not a sudden change. Only 18 percent of women were sharing the year before institutionalization. Among eventually institutionalized women who were living independently, 72 percent were widows as many as five years before institutionalization, and two-thirds (66 percent) were widows nine years before.

We also looked at the past history of poor, unmarried women at age 80. In our simulations, these women were often relatively disadvantaged even at age 65. About 60 percent had been below the poverty line fifteen years before. Only 3 percent had had incomes five times the poverty level. Even more interestingly, over half the poor unmarried women at age 80 were not married at age 65. In our results, few middle-class wives became poor elderly widows.

Table 4.9   **Simulated Characteristics of Persons in Various Years Prior to the First Year of Institutionalization (persons who were simulated to enter institutions only)**

	Years before Institutionalization				
	1	2	3	4	9
Percentage of all men dependent sharing	38	34	31	27	22
Of all men who were not dependent sharing:					
Percent unmarried	32	22	21	21	19
Percent disabled	66	45	51	47	45
Percent < 2 times poverty	71	66	62	54	46
Percent 2–5 times poverty	23	28	29	37	37
Percent 5 + times poverty	5	6	8	9	16
Percentage of all women dependent sharing	18	16	15	13	11
Of all women who were not dependent sharing:					
Percent unmarried	81	78	77	72	66
Percent disabled	80	64	53	43	38
Percent < 2 times poverty	47	45	46	44	40
Percent 2–5 times poverty	32	44	33	35	40
Percent 5 + times poverty	21	21	21	21	21

4.6 Conclusion

Even in this initial effort, we have noted some intriguing results. For example, rich and poor at age 65 face very different experiences in old age, higher-income persons living more than four years longer on average. Second, widowhood created a 20 percent drop in the standard of living of women as compared to a 10 percent drop for men. Third, women who ultimately enter institutions have very similar incomes, rates of disability, and rates of marriage at age 65 to women who do not enter nursing homes. Finally, poor widows were likely to have been widowed or low income already at age 65.

We see this paper as a pioneering effort to use recursive simulation models to explore the events of aging. It remains experimental. Nonetheless, we were surprised at the close correspondence between our results and external estimates. We outline a methodology for piecing together the disparate slices of old age captured within a panel survey covering a number of cohorts. Rather than wait twenty more years for a long-term panel of a single cohort to trace the events of aging, the methodology described allows one to develop a smoothed profile of the aging process by pooling the experiences of a number of cohorts.

Appendix
Data Recoding on the PSID

We describe here our recoding scheme in more detail.

Nonresponse

A sample member of the PSID can become a nonrespondent for a number of reasons: death, institutionalization, refusal, disability, inability to locate, etc. We treated nonrespondents for reasons other than death and institutionalization as right-censored observations.

Women's Health Status

In six out of seventeen years, disability status data on wives, but not female heads, was missing. Since we would have had disability status for female heads but not for wives, measured disability would have been capturing marital status differences. As a result, we treated disability status as missing for all women in those years.

Institutionalization

There are four different ways to identify the institutionalized on the PSID. First, someone is coded as institutionalized if remaining sample members of a household report the absence of a household member perceived to have left the household for a long-term stay in a nursing home. Those who are temporarily out of the household at the time of the interview—for instance, on a short-term hospital stay—will not be coded as "institutionalized." Second, if a single person household enters a nursing home and there are no remaining sample family members outside, the PSID interviewers will still attempt to obtain an interview. If they fail, the household should be coded as nonresponse due to institutionalization. Third, if the PSID staff succeeded in obtaining an interview in the nursing home, there is an indicator of institutionalization in 1984. We reverse coded anyone who was coded as institutionalized in 1984 as institutionalized until his or her previous move.

Before 1984, however, there are no direct indicators of institutionalization for single person households who were interviewed in nursing homes. We worked with PSID staff in developing a method for identifying such households. If a single person moves into a housing type "other" (as opposed to an apartment, house, condominium, or trailer) for involuntary reasons (such as health), if there are two rooms or less, and if the household size never grows past one before the person moves, than we coded that person as "institutionalized."

Because we checked each recode by hand, we are confident that we have not overcounted institutionalization. However, we are uncertain about the degree of undercounting. We are particularly likely to miss short-term stays. Those who are in what are perceived to be short-term stays will not be reported as institutionalized when reported absent by household members. In addition, those who enter nursing homes and die between interviews will be reported as dead, the spell of nursing home use missed. For all the above reasons, our estimates of ever institutionalization should be treated as lower bounds.

Dependent Sharing

We sought to distinguish between living arrangements where adult children move back in with their parents and cases where elderly parents move in with others, becoming economically dependent on them. Having noted the frequency of adult childrens' return to their parents' home, we wanted to avoid treating both dependent sharers and household heads similarly.

At the start of the survey, who was designated as head did reflect the degree of economic independence. For instance, the head was often the person who owned the home. As a result, at the start of the survey, the elderly who were designated as nonheads were dependent sharers. However, if a person started the survey as a family head, it was rare that they would ever become a nonhead, even if they became dependent. The key to understanding coding procedures is to note that the PSID is a family-centered survey that carries a host of questions specifically for family heads. In trying to maintain a consistent series of data for each head, PSID interviewers rarely changed the household status of those who ever were designated heads, except for reasons of marriage.

We identified three different groups of dependent sharers. The first group was those who were explicitly categorized as parents of the head or other relatives of the heads. Most of these started the survey in that status.

The second group was made up of family heads that moved in with other sample members. When a sample household moves in with another sample household, there is often no direct indicator that the other family is present. For instance, if an elderly parent moves in with an adult child who had been part of the original sample family in 1968 and both parent and child had been followed over the years, the PSID often did not recombine the two households' records if they moved back in with each other. Indeed, there was often no direct indicator that the other family was present. We worked with the PSID staff to develop a method for detecting such shared living arrangements. If the family composition was described as "other" (rather than as a primary family with relatives or nonrelatives included within the family unit), if the person neither owned nor rented his or her housing, and if the reason he or she neither owned nor rented was not that housing was some form of compensation or gift, then we considered that person a dependent sharer.

Third, we tried to identify sample heads moving in with nonsample families. In such cases, the PSID usually carries no indicator that the other family is present. Even if someone in the nonsample household owns or rents the home, the sample head is listed as an owner or renter. Eventually (often in the second year of coresidence), the PSID will indicate the nonsample members as "moving in" with the sample person's household, even if sample member had moved in with them. The sample head would have remained listed as head. Again, we worked with the PSID staff to develop a way of identifying such living situations. We coded people as dependent sharers if all the following conditions are met: they are unmarried; they move; a child or grandchild is shown to move in with them; family size never returns to one before their next move; and the head's income is less than half the family's income over the period of coresidence.

One other problem arose. Little information is reported on nonheads. As a result, we had limited information on disability, marital status, and even income on sharing dependents if they were not heads. Thus, we did not model these characteristics for sharers.

Table 4A.1   **Hazard Models for Movements into Disability**

Variable	Men, Healthy → Disabled		Women, Healthy → Disabled	
	Coefficient	Standard Error	Coefficient	Standard Error
White	−.147	.125	−.377	.160
Education	−.021	.012	−.034	.016
Disabled ($t − 2$)	1.255	.093	1.077	.132
log inc/need ($t − 1$)	−.224	.075	−.323	.093
Married ($t − 1$)	.026	.133	.101	.118
Newly unmarr ($t − 1$)	−1.210	.781	−.141	.410
Year of survey	.040	.011	.007	.012
Newly married ($t − 1$)	.538	.452	−.161	1.429
Health missing ($t − 2$)			.348	.127
Age 70–74	.070	.111	.091	.131
Age 75–79	.232	.136	.201	.154
Age 80–84	.360	.173	.171	.203
Age 85–89	.787	.238	.570	.255
Age 90+	−.254	.645	.924	.369
Phi	.305	.017	.308	.018
Observations	832		1,227	

Note: All standard errors are asymptotic.

Table 4A.2   **Hazard Models for Movements Out of Disability**

Variable	Men, Disabled → Healthy		Women, Disabled → Healthy	
	Coefficient	Standard Error	Coefficient	Standard Error
White	.016	.144	.291	.166
Education	−.001	.014	.019	.018
Disabled ($t − 2$)	−1.320	.098	−.939	.143
log inc/need ($t − 1$)	.320	.086	.121	.106
Married ($t − 1$)	−.065	.140	.301	.135
Newly unmarr ($t − 1$)	.535	.302	.104	.342
Year of survey	.010	.011	−.024	.014
Newly married ($t − 1$)	−.136	1.010		
Health missing ($t − 2$)			−.490	.149
Age 70–74	−.005	.125	−.040	.146
Age 75–79	−.301	.151	−.293	.180
Age 80–84	−.105	.177	.304	.187
Age 85–89	−.502	.301	−.014	.301
Age 90+	−.307	.518	−.390	.607
Phi	.295	.017	.274	.017
Observations	932		1,243	

Note: All standard errors are asymptotic.

Table 4A.3   Hazard Models for Becoming Unmarried

Variable	Men, Married → Unmarried		Women, Married → Unmarried	
	Coefficient	Standard Error	Coefficient	Standard Error
White	.113	.341	−.199	.314
Disability $(t - 1)$	−.239	.317	−.294	.246
Disability $(t - 2)$	.314	.283	−.311	.283
log inc/need $(t - 1)$	−.127	.203	−.260	.154
Year of survey	.031	.030	.020	.021
Health missing $(t - 1)$			−.048	.193
Health missing $(t - 2)$			.053	.195
Age 70–74	.639	.325	.295	.222
Age 75–79	.601	.357	.877	.234
Age 80–84	1.200	.372	1.475	.296
Age 85–89	.975	.600	.621	.773
Age 90+	1.186	1.029	1.523	3.262
Phi	.014	.003	.038	.005
Observations	712		541	

Note: All standard errors are asymptotic.

Table 4A.4   Hazard Models for Becoming Married from Unmarried

Variable	Men, Unmarried → Married		Women, Unmarried → Married	
	Coefficient	Standard Error	Coefficient	Standard Error
White	.037	.565	.343	.974
Education	.055	.058		
Disabled $(t - 1)$	−.160	.620	−.831	1.775
Disabled $(t - 2)$	.320	.622	1.494	1.392
log inc/need $(t - 1)$	.302	.363	−.082	1.028
Year of survey	.032	.054	−.047	.109
Health missing $(t - 1)$			−.667	1.481
Health missing $(t - 2)$			.779	1.117
Age 70–74	−.453	.561	−.328	.976
Age 75–79	−.409	.558	−1.647	1.518
Age 80+	−1.738	.804	−1.687	1.751
Phi	.024	.007	.003	.002
Observations	216		687	

Note: All standard errors are asymptotic.

Table 4A.5   **Hazard Models of Elderly Living Arrangements**

	Transition to Death			
	Men		Women	
Variable	Coefficient	Standard Error	Coefficient	Standard Error
White	.131	.184	.295	.235
Education	.007	.019	.003	.026
Disability $(t - 1)$	.700	.180	.839	.217
Disability $(t - 2)$	.454	.177	.580	.211
log inc/need $(t - 1)$	−.114	.108	−.161	.144
Married $(t - 1)$	−.312	.151	.265	.175
Newly unmarr $(t - 1)$	−.093	.428	.067	.525
Newly married $(t - 1)$	−.112	1.023	1.470	.734
Year of survey	.005	.015	−.057	.018
Health missing $(t - 1)$			.710	.223
Health missing $(t - 2)$			.202	.212
Age 70–74	.085	.180	.218	.204
Age 75–79	.359	.183	.278	.225
Age 80–84	.752	.196	.525	.264
Age 85–89	.882	.259	.962	.304
Age 90+	1.468	.364	2.144	.407
Phi	.037	.004	.022	.003
Observations	745		926	

Note: All standard errors are asymptotic.

Table 4A.6   **Hazard Models of Elderly Living Arrangements**

	Transition to Institutionalization			
	Men		Women	
Variable	Coefficient	Standard Error	Coefficient	Standard Error
White	−.160	.472	.998	.495
Disability $(t - 1)$	.920	.738	1.439	.521
Disability $(t - 2)$	−.525	.489	.388	.366
Log inc/need $(t - 1)$	−1.280	.373	−.448	.184
Married $(t - 1)$	−.562	.450	−.028	.313
Newly unmarr $(t - 1)$	1.129	.703	.276	.800
Year of survey	.050	.048	.052	.335
Health missing $(t - 1)$			1.398	.508
Health missing $(t - 2)$			−.246	.401
Age 70–74	.369	.870	.406	.420
Age 75–79	1.149	.733	.652	.476
Age 80–84	1.883	.695	1.605	.435
Age 85–89	2.047	.897	1.541	.508
Age 90+	3.116	.910	3.101	.471
Phi	.0012	.0007	.0029	.0010
Observations	738		921	

Note: All standard errors are asymptotic.

Table 4A.7   **Hazard Models of Elderly Living Arrangements**

	Transition to Dependent Sharing			
	Men		Women	
Variable	Coefficient	Standard Error	Coefficient	Standard Error
White	− .401	.896	− .373	.606
Disability (t − 1)	− .423	.612	.621	.630
Disability (t − 2)	1.820	1.004	− .033	.748
log inc/need (t − 1)	.105	.494	− .536	.446
Married (t − 1)	− 1.585	.657	− 1.053	.574
Newly unmarr (t − 1)	.834	1.113	1.376	.639
Year of survey	− .033	.098	− .041	.068
Health missing (t − 1)			1.440	.593
Health missing (t − 2)			.611	.642
Age 70–74	− .112	.915	− .178	.530
Age 75–79	.621	.857	.335	.545
Age 80–84	1.130	.879	.256	.561
Age 85–89	1.540	1.154	.818	.791
Age 90 +	1.605	1.273	.818	.791
Phi	.0014	.0007	.0028	.0011
Observations	737		917	

Note: All standard errors are asymptotic.

Table 4A.8   **Hazard Models of Elderly Living Arrangements**

	Men and Women, Dependent Sharing → Death		Men and Women, Dependent Sharing → Institut.	
Variable	Coefficient	Standard Error	Coefficient	Standard Error
White	− .459	.242	− .270	.469
Male	.492	.233	.844	.385
Year of survey	.003	.027		
Age 70–74	.330	.354		
Age 75–79	1.002	.324		
Age 80–84	1.344	.335	3.211	.976
Age 85 +	2.301	.318	3.780	.961
Phi	.0329	.0048	.0029	.0019
Observations	194		194	

Note: All standard errors are asymptotic.

Table 4A.9   Ordinary Least Squares Estimates of Determinants of Log of Income/Needs Ratio

	Men		Women	
Variable	Coefficient	Standard Error	Coefficient	Standard Error
Intercept	−.0375	.0275	.0580	.0269
Disab $(t - 1)$	−.0059	.0143	.0016	.0166
Disab $(t - 2)$	.0103	.0144	.0007	.0166
Unmar (t)	.0022	.0162	.0129	.0100
New unm (t)	−.0991	.0447	−.5621	.0307
New unm $(t - 1)$	−.0493	.0460	.0600	.0321
New unm $(t - 2)$	−.0134	.0460	.0761	.0313
New unm $(t - 3)$	.0263	.0450	.0997	.0320
New mar (t)	.1799	.0820	.4118	.1118
New mar $(t - 1)$	.0453	.0750	.3668	.0915
New mar $(t - 2)$	−.0391	.0780	.1287	.0889
New mar $(t - 3)$	−.0799	.0750	−.0569	.0773
Health missing	.0250	.0799	−.0375	.0119
Education	−.0018	.0014	−.0021	.0014
Log inc/need $(t - 1)^a$	.5707	.0160	.5392	.0138
Log inc/need $(t - 2)^a$	.2432	.0180	.2464	.0151
Log inc/need $(t - 3)^a$	.1860	.0160	.2143	.0135
White	−.0118	.0158	−.0021	.0135
Age 70–74	.0281	.0130	−.0001	.0109
Age 75–79	.0193	.0150	.0114	.0133
Age 80–84	.0160	.0200	.0038	.0170
Age 85–89	.0698	.0320	.0376	.0260
Age 90+	.0131	.0720	−.0003	.0546
Year of survey	.0018	.0016	−.0033	.0014
Observations	3,538		4,886	
R^2	.8063		.8114	
MSE	.1004		.0979	

[a]The coefficients on lagged income were constrained to sum to one.

Notes

1. We gratefully acknowledge the help of Bruce Meyer of Northwestern University, who provided us with the software for estimating the hazard models and offered much helpful advice.

2. People were categorized as disabled if they reported some limitation on the type or amount of work they could do.

3. We did not model movements from dependent sharing back to independent living as they were quite rare in our data.

4. We also estimated the model without these constraints, with little effect on the results.

5. Our simulated "life expectancy" is the expected number of years before death or institutionalization in the simulations. To the extent that people live a while longer once

entering institutions, we should understate life expectancies for those who are institutionalized. This should be less of a problem for men, who are much less likely to become institutionalized.

References

Bureau of the Census. 1984. 1980 Census of the population, Subject reports, *Persons in institutions and other group quarters,* PC80-2-4D.
McConnell, C. E. 1984. A note on the lifetime risk of nursing home residency. *Gerontologist* 24:193–98.
Michael, Robert T., Victor Fuchs, and Sharon Scott. 1980. Changes in the propensity to live alone: 1950–76. *Demography* 17:39–56.
Pampel, Fred C. 1983. Changes in the propensity to live alone: Evidence from consecutive cross-section surveys, 1960–76. *Demography* 20:433–47.
Schwartz, Saul, Sheldon Danziger, and Eugene Smolensky. 1984. The choice of living arrangements by the elderly. In *Retirement and economic behavior,* ed. Henry Aaron and Gary Burtless. Washington, D.C.: Brookings.
Vicente, L., J. Wiley, and R. A. Carrington. 1979. The risk of institutionalization before death. *Gerontologist* 19:361–67.

Comment   James H. Schulz

Ellwood and Kane state two primary objectives at the beginning of their paper. First, they seek to move beyond the limitations of cross-sectional data by utilizing seventeen years (1968–84) of longitudinal survey data to study certain life events for various cohorts of persons over age 64. Second, they develop a simulation modeling process in order to "compare the futures of people" as they move from being young old to old old and also to look backward to help explain where elderly people started with regard to the life events that actually occurred later in life. This is certainly an ambitious pair of tasks.

The increasing use of longitudinal data sets by researchers to investigate various questions is certainly a welcomed development. And the use of various simulation techniques to generate longitudinal data streams and to explore variable interactions is, in my opinion, one of the most important methodological developments in recent years—especially with regard to policy research. In the absence of longitudinal data, researchers have had to make major inferences about the behavior of individuals and institutions based on

James H. Schulz is professor of economics and Kirstein Professor of Aging Policy, Brandeis University.

cross-sectional information. This has certainly been true with regard to research concerning the biological and social processes of aging.

In their now classic inventory of gerontological research findings, Riley and Foner (1968) emphasized and warned us of the dangers. Their conclusions are still relevant today: "[Aging research using cross-sectional information has promoted] a tragic stereotype of the older person as destitute, ill, facing irreparable losses, no longer integrated into society, and no longer subject to society's controls and sanctions. Old age appears as the nadir: the end of a long decline that follows peaks that occur at the early life stages in intelligence, capacity for work, income, sexual capability, and so on" (7). Riley and Foner discuss the early research and the incorrect conclusions that were drawn from various cross-sectional data: "Fallacies such as these pose a particular problem for social scientists because they produce distortions in substantive and theoretical understanding of the aging process" (9).

Certainly, much of the improvement recently documented in the living situation of the elderly is a result of explicit changes that have occurred in pension, health, and service delivery programs. But part of the change in our image of the aged is a result of our ability to get closer to the realities of aging through better research methods. Ellwood and Kane's paper is an attempt to bring both improved data and innovative research methods to bear on a set of familiar research questions. What are good predictors of death, disability, institutionalization, and financial dependency in old age? What is the effect of a spouse's death on a survivor's well-being? To what extent does economic status change as people age?

It was the pioneering efforts of Guy Orcutt (Orcutt et al. 1961) that encouraged the use of micro-simulation techniques in the social sciences. Ellwood and Kane's efforts join a now long history of simulation models developed by economists—for example, the Brookings Institution tax model, the Urban Institute TRIM and DYNASIM models, and the pension models by James Schulz, ICF Inc., the Social Security Administration, and the Brookings Institution. Ellwood and Kane have learned what others before them have learned; development of these models is difficult, time consuming, and expensive.

Unlike the efforts referred to above, Ellwood and Kane have tried to economize in their efforts by using only one data set, one basic estimating technique (hazard models),[1] a truncated simulation cohort of people ages 65 and over, and a very small number of variables in the model. This approach severely limits what they can do and the quality of their results.[2] For example, they find that the major factor affecting the standard of living of the elderly is changed marital status but reach that result after ignoring the effect of employment on income because labor force participation is not modeled.

Almost all the findings from their simulations will be very familiar to researchers in the field of gerontology. Nonwhites tend to die sooner, are more likely to be disabled, and are less likely to live independently as they grow very old. The incidence of disability rises with age, and the disabled are more likely to die at an earlier age. Unmarried older males are a clearly disadvantaged group, both economically and health-wise. And the poorer elderly are more vulnerable than those with more income. It is useful to have this confirmation, based on the PSID longitudinal data, of prior research in these important areas.

Ellwood and Kane give a lot of attention to the issue of poverty among women. Their simulation indicates that the death of a spouse in the retirement years results in a sharp drop in income and, furthermore, that the drop is significantly greater for surviving women than for widowers. They also find that unmarried older women are often relatively disadvantaged even at age 65—with 60 percent of this group already in poverty. Again, however, this finding will not be surprising to gerontologists since such findings have been reported repeatedly over the years (see, e.g., Sass 1979).

To explain the deterioration of economic status among widows, the authors correctly draw attention to the decline in public and private pension income that results when a spouse dies. However, they incorrectly attribute the effect on Social Security benefits to low spouse benefits[3] rather than to the modest levels of ''worker benefits'' that put many older couples *close to* the poverty level—creating a situation of extreme vulnerability if the survivor does not have access to a private pension supplement. As the life insurance industry can verify, another part of the problem has been a difficulty over the years in getting people to adequately insure themselves to supplement pension survivor benefits.

With regard to private pension supplementation, Burkhauser, Holden, and Feaster (1988) have recently shown that there are dramatic differences in the economic status of older widows eligible only for Social Security and those eligible also for an employer-sponsored benefit. However, a major problem is the low coverage in the past (and still today) of women under such private pension plans. Moreover, the Tax Reform Act of 1986 probably makes the situation worse—given the pension coverage disincentives unintentionally built into it. While the 1986 act's new minimum coverage rules will expand coverage under some plans, many pension experts think that other provisions of the act discourage plan creation and liberalization of coverage provisions.

We cannot expect to see most women covered by good private pension plans in the near future, if ever (in the absence of government compulsion). To get the supplemental income necessary to stay out of poverty in retirement, women would do well to marry a covered male, be sure to stay married, and then opt for survivor's protection. But that is easier said than done. Many men are still not covered in private employment; rates of divorce (currently at historically high levels) show no sign of abating; and families often gamble on foregoing survivor protection in order to get higher pension benefits at retirement.

But having pointed out the coverage, divorce, and survivor protection issues, many people forget to point out another equally important matter. Even if all women were covered by private plans, it is highly unlikely that many would earn the benefits they need to ensure an adequate income in retirement—given their employment histories. The Social Security Administration released in 1986 longitudinal information on the work histories of recent beneficiaries that graphically illustrates the problem (Snyder 1986). Looking at women receiving their first Social Security benefit between June 1980 and May 1981, 43 percent were covered by an employer-sponsored pension plan on their *longest* job. Of those women with coverage, more than half (52 percent) had less than twenty years' service on that job. This means that, to get an adequate retirement income in their own right, many women have to piece together pensions from more than one plan. But employer-sponsored pensions in the United States (both public and private) are not indexed when vested. The result is that vested pensions accumulated early in the work career are typically worth little at retirement. Thus, the problem of inadequate income for widows is extremely complicated.

To help us understand and deal with complex issues like the high rates of poverty among older women, Ellwood and Kane would have to expand their modeling effort significantly. Short of that, however, their approach provides a way of checking the accuracy of many prevailing views on the elderly that are based on cross-sectional analysis.

Notes

1. There is one exception, where they use ordinary least squares techniques.
2. They are encouraged by how well their estimates track actual data for life expectancies. But, as other simulation modeling efforts have shown, this is one of the easiest variables to simulate accurately over short periods of time. Other variables, such as the occurrence of disability, are notorious for the difficulty arising in tracking actual disability experience among subgroups of the population.
3. When a primary earner husband dies, the surviving wife gets 100 percent of his benefit (not her former, and lower, spouse benefit).

References

Burkhauser, Richard V., K. C. Holden, and D. Feaster. 1988. Incidence, timing, and events associated with poverty: A dynamic view of poverty in retirement. *Journal of Gerontology: Social Sciences* 43 (March): S46–S52.
Orcutt, Guy, M. Greenberger, J. Korbel, and A. Rivlin. 1961. *Microanalysis of socioeconomic systems: A simulation study.* New York: Harper and Row.
Riley, Matilda White, and Anne Foner, eds. 1968. *Aging and society.* Vol. 1, *An inventory of research findings.* New York: Russell Sage.
Sass, Tim. 1979. Demographic and economic characteristics of nonbeneficiary widows: An overview. *Social Security Bulletin* 42 (November):3–14.
Snyder, Donald C. 1986. Pension status of recently retired workers on their longest job: Findings from the new beneficiary survey. *Social Security Bulletin* 49 (August): 5–21.

5   Why Don't the Elderly Live with Their Children? A New Look

Laurence J. Kotlikoff and John N. Morris

Perhaps no single statistic raises more concern about postwar changes in the U.S. family than the proportion of the elderly living alone. Since 1940, the proportion of unmarried noninstitutionalized elderly living alone has risen from less than 25 percent to over 60 percent. For the old old, those over 85, the proportion has increased from 13 percent to 57 percent (Sandefur and Tuma 1987). The proportion of the old old living in institutions has also increased dramatically; in 1940, only 7 percent of those over 85 lived in institutions; today's figure is almost 25 percent. Part of the reason the current elderly are much less likely to live with children is simply that they had relatively few children and that they have outlived some or all of their children. In 1940, for each person age 80 and over there were four people age 60–65. In 1985, for each person age 80 and over there were fewer than two people age 60–65. When the baby boomers are in their 80s, there will be only one person age 60–65 for each baby boomer (Current Population Reports 1984).

   While demographics appear to explain much of the change in the living arrangements of the elderly, the rising income of the elderly is viewed by many as the chief or at least a chief reason why the elderly live alone. This argument has been made by Beresford and Rivlin (1966), Carliner (1975), Chevan and Korson (1972), Kobrin (1976a, 1976b), Soldo and Lauriat (1976), Michael, Fuchs, and Scott (1980), Tissure and McCoy (1981), and Wolf (1984). One difficulty in interpreting these studies is that they fail to control for charac-

Laurence J. Kotlikoff is professor of economics and chairman of the Department of Economics at Boston University and a research associate of the National Bureau of Economic Research. John N. Morris is the associate director of the Department of Social Gerontological Research at the Hebrew Rehabilitation Center for the Aged.

   This study was conducted as part of the National Bureau of Economic Research's Project on Aging, which is funded by the National Institute of Aging, grant 1P01AG05842-01. The authors thank Jinyong Cai, Jagadeesh Gokhale, and Dan Nash for excellent research assistance.

teristics of children. Since incomes of parents and children are correlated, the measured effects of parents' income on living arrangements may be capturing, at least in part, the influence of children's incomes. In contrast to the standard view, it may be that increases in children's incomes have lowered the likelihood of shared living. The fact that more than half the aged living with their children are themselves the homeowners (Schorr 1980) suggests that many adult children live with their elderly parents for financial reasons.

This study uses new data on the characteristics of the elderly and their children to study the effects of children's and parents' income as well as other characteristics on the shared living decision. The new data are the 1986 HRCA Elderly Survey and the 1986 HRC-NBER Child Survey. The 1986 HRCA Elderly Survey is part of an ongoing panel survey of the elderly in Massachusetts that is being conducted by the Hebrew Rehabilitation Center for the Aged (HRCA). The 1986 HRC-NBER Child Survey is an interview of the children of those elderly who participated in the 1986 HRCA Elderly Survey.

The research reported here considers 297 cases of elderly parents who have a single living child. Our first approach to studying the living arrangements of these 297 parent-child observations is to estimate reduced-form logit and probit models. Estimates of these models indicate that child characteristics such as income and marital status are as important as parent characteristics in explaining living arrangements. The probit and logit results point to the principal determinants of shared living, but understanding the precise role of income and other variables in this decision requires a structural model. Our second approach is thus to develop and estimate a structural model of shared living. The model trades off the economies to scale in shared living against the (potential) disutility of parents and children from living together. Analysis of the model indicates that, regardless of the precise form of preferences, the decision concerning shared living is economically separate from the decision concerning how much housing the parent and child should purchase and how much the parent and child should each consume; that is, living arrangements can be studied without simultaneously specifying the precise nature of parent-child bargaining. The model also clarifies how the parent's and child's income jointly affect the shared living decision. In contrast to the logit or probit specifications, in the structural model the effects of increases in income of either the parent or the child depend on the parent's and child's preferences regarding living together. By introducing error terms in the model, these preferences can be estimated. The error terms in the model are specified quite naturally as unobserved (to the econometrician) taste parameters concerning shared living.

The paper proceeds in sections 5.1 and 5.2 with a presentation of the structural model and an analysis of how changes in parent and child incomes affect the decision to live together. Section 5.3 demonstrates how the model can be empirically estimated. Sections 5.4–5.7 describe the HRCA and

HRC-NBER surveys, summarize some general findings from the two new surveys, and present cross-tabulations from our sample of 297 parents and their single children. Section 5.8 presents probit and logit models of the choice of the elderly to live with children, to live in an institution, or to live alone. Section 5.9 reports and interprets maximum likelihood estimates of the structural model. Finally, section 5.10 summarizes and concludes the paper.

5.1   A Model of Family Living Arrangements

Consider a single surviving parent who has only one child. Let U_p and U_c stand, respectively, for parent and child preferences over goods, housing services, and living arrangements. If the parent and child live alone, the parent maximizes U_p, and the child maximizes U_c. When they choose to live together, they are assumed to maximize U_F (given in [1]), which is a weighted average of their preferences, where the weight θ that is chosen by the parent and child reflects the outcome of parent-child bargaining:

(1) $$U_F = \theta U_p + (1 - \theta)U_c .$$

This is a general expression for family preferences in the case of shared living since θ can take any value between zero and unity. Formulating the problem in this manner only restricts the solution to be efficient; that is, the maximization of U_F subject to the collective family (parent and child) budget produces a Pareto-efficient solution, and all Pareto-efficient solutions to the shared living choice problem can be represented as the maximand of U_F for a particular choice of the utility weight θ.

Consider the following Cobb-Douglas characterization of U_p and U_c:

(2) $$U_p = A \log(C_p H_p),$$

$$U_c = B \log(C_c H_c).$$

In (2), C_p and C_c are the respective levels of consumption of the parent and child, while H_p and H_c are the respective housing services enjoyed by the parent and child. The coefficients A and B describe the parent's and child's preferences for shared living. If the parent and child live apart, A and B both equal unity; if they live together, A or B can be greater than, equal to, or less than unity, depending on whether the parent and child enjoy living together, are indifferent to shared housing, or prefer living apart. We are particularly interested in cases in which $A > 1$ and $B < 1$, or vice versa; that is, when one family member prefers living together and the other prefers living apart.

We first consider the maximization of (1) for given values of θ and then examine the choice of θ as well as the conditions under which the parent and child choose to live together. When the parent and child live together, their combined budget is

$$(3) \qquad C_p + C_c + qH = Y_p + Y_c \, .$$

In (3), q stands for the relative price of housing services, and Y_p and Y_c are the incomes of the parent and child, respectively. H stands for the quantity of housing services jointly consumed by the parent and child; that is, equation (3) incorporates the assumption that housing services are a public good that can be simultaneously consumed by both the parent and the child without congestion. While one could assume some marginal congestion from shared housing, which could be modeled as a higher effective price of H, as long as the effective price of H is less than $2q$ there is an economic incentive for shared housing. In this study, we assume zero marginal congestion.

The economic gain from shared housing, which is modeled here as a lower effective price of housing, is compared with the disutility from shared housing (in which case A and/or B will be less than unity) in determining whether the parent and child will live together. More precisely, the parent and child each compare their utility when they live together with their utility if they live alone. The necessary condition for shared living is that both the parent and the child be at least as well off living together as they would be if they lived apart.

Figure 5.1 illustrates the parent-child utility possibility frontier from shared living. The point Q lies outside the frontier. If the utilities of the parent and child from living apart are given by point Q, the two will choose to live apart. If, on the other hand, separate living produced utility levels indicated by point R, the parent and child can do better by living together. The assumption that when they live together the child and parent choose efficient and mutually advantageous levels of housing and consumption means that the utility

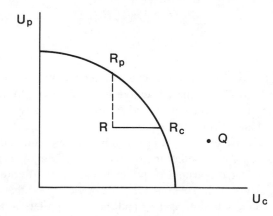

Fig. 5.1   The parent-child utility possibility frontier

outcome lies on the frontier between and including points R_p and R_c. At one extreme, point R_p, the parent receives all the gains from shared housing, while at the other extreme, R_c, all gains go to the child, and the parent is no better off than if he or she lived alone. Points on the frontier between R_p and R_c involve both the parent and the child sharing the gains from living together. The choice of the weight θ used in maximizing (1) subject to (3) determines the point chosen on the utility possibility frontier.

While the exact point chosen on the frontier requires an explicit specification of the child-parent bargaining process, the decision to live together can be examined without any reference to the specific bargaining solution. Given the assumption that efficient bargaining occurs, one can decide whether the parent and child live together simply by determining whether their utility position if they live apart lies inside or outside the utility possibility frontier available if they live together. This is a general proposition that holds regardless of the precise form of preferences. In terms of equations (1) and (3), one need show only that there is a range of values of θ that, when used in (1), imply a Pareto improvement over living apart. Knowledge of the particular value of θ actually chosen is not required. The fact that one can study living arrangements independently from studying nonaltruistic parent-child decision making (bargaining) is a great advantage since estimating this process would place greater demands on the data.

A simple procedure for determining whether the utility position from living apart lies inside or outside the frontier involves calculating two critical values of θ, θ_p and θ_c. θ_p is the value of θ that if used in maximizing (1) subject to (3) leaves the parent with the same utility from shared living as he or she receives from living alone; θ_c is defined symmetrically for the child. If $\theta_p = \theta_c$, the utility position from living apart lies on the utility frontier available if they live together. If $\theta_c > \theta_p$, then the utility position from living apart lies inside the frontier. If $\theta_p > \theta_c$, the utility position from living apart lies outside the frontier. To see this, note that, if $\theta_p > \theta_c$, the choice of $\theta \geqslant \theta_p$ produces a lower level of utility for the child than he or she enjoys from living alone, while choosing $\theta < \theta_p$ produces a lower level of utility for the parent than is available from living alone.

The conditions under which $\theta_p = \theta_c$ are of interest because they indicate the circumstances in which the parent and child would be just indifferent between living together and living apart. As demonstrated below, given Y_p, Y_c, and q, the condition $\theta_c = \theta_p$ (the utility position from living apart is on the frontier) occurs for combinations of the utility parameters A and B defined by a function $G(A, B) = 0$. Hence, the conditions under which the parent and child choose to live together can be expressed in terms of critical values of thepreferences (A and B) of the parent and child regarding shared living. While the preference parameters A and B are not observed, their determinants can be estimated.

Maximization of (1) subject to (3) yields the following demand relations when the parent and child live together:

$$(4) \qquad H = \frac{Y}{2q}, \quad C_p = \frac{\theta A Y}{[\theta A + (1 - \theta)B]2},$$

$$C_c = (1 - \theta) \frac{BY}{[\theta A + (1 - \theta)B]2},$$

where $Y = Y_p + Y_c$. Note that the demand for housing services, in this formulation, is independent of the bargaining solution, θ. Larger values of θ, the weight applied to the parent's preferences, means more parent consumption (larger C_p) and less consumption by the child (smaller C_c). Without loss of generality, we measure H in units such that $q = 1/4$.

The indirect utility functions of the parent, V_p, and child, V_c, from shared living are given by

$$(5) \qquad V_p = \log\left\{\frac{\theta A Y^2}{[\theta A + (1 - \theta)B]}\right\}^A,$$

$$V_c = \log\left\{\frac{(1 - \theta)BY^2}{[\theta A + (1 - \theta)B]}\right\}^B.$$

The indirect utilities of the parent and child from living alone, V_p and V_c, respectively, are

$$(6) \qquad V_p' = \log Y_p^2$$

$$V_c' = \log Y_c^2$$

The critical values of θ, θ_p, such that $V_p = V_p'$, and θ_c, such that $V_c = V_c'$, are given by

$$(7) \qquad \theta_p = \frac{BY_p^{2/A}}{AY^2 + (B - A)Y_p^{2/A}},$$

$$\theta_c = \frac{BY^2 - BY_c^{2/B}}{(A - B)Y_c^{2/B} + BY^2}.$$

From (7), one can show that $\delta\theta_p/\delta A < 0$ and $\delta(1 - \theta)/\delta B < 0$; the smaller the parent's disutility from shared living, the smaller is the critical weight θ_p that leaves the parent indifferent between living apart and living together. The critical child weight, $1 - \theta_c$, is correspondingly negatively related to the child's utility from shared living.

Equating θ_p and θ_c provides the relation $G(A, B) = 0$ given in (8). Values of A and B satisfying $G(A, B) = 0$ leave the parent and the child indifferent between living together and living apart. If $G(A, B) > 0$, the parent and child choose to live together. They choose to live apart if $G(A, B) < 0$. Note that the asymptotes of the $G(\;\;)$ function occur at $\bar{A} = 2 \log Y_p / \log (Y^2 - 1)$ and $\bar{B} = 2 \log Y_c / \log(Y^2 - 1)$. When Y_p becomes very large relative to Y_c, $\bar{A}$ approaches one, and $\bar{B}$ approaches one when Y_c becomes very large relative to Y_p.

$$(8) \qquad\qquad G(A, B) = Y^2 - Y_c^{2/B} - Y_p^{2/A} = 0.$$

Along the locus defined by $G(A, B) = 0$, we have

$$(9) \qquad\qquad \frac{\delta A}{\delta B} = \frac{-Y_c^{2/B} A^2 \log Y_c^2}{Y_p^{2/A} B^2 \log Y_p^2} < 0.$$

Figure 5.2 graphs the values of A and B satisfying (8). The point D defined by $A = 1$, $B = 1$, lies above the $G(A, B) = 0$ locus and involves shared living. To see this, one need only observe from (7) that, when $A = 1$ and $B = 1$, $\theta_p / \theta_c = Y_p^2 / (Y_p^2 + 2Y_pY_c) < 1$, which is the condition for shared living. Combinations of A and B lying northeast of the $G(A, B) = 0$ locus satisfy $G(A, B) > 0$ and entail shared living, while combinations lying southwest of the locus satisfy $G(A, B) < 0$ and entail separate living. Consider points in which the parent prefers to live together $(A > 1)$ and the child prefers to live alone $(B < 1)$. As Y_p rises relative to Y_c, the $G(A, B)$ curve approaches a vertical line at $A = 1$ leaving all such points in the area for which $G(A, B) > 0$. Hence, when parents prefer living together, but their children do

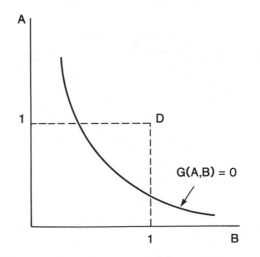

Fig. 5.2   The living together–living apart indifference curve

not, they are able eventually to bribe their children if their incomes are sufficiently high relative to their children. The opposite situation in which the child's preferences always dominate arises when Y_c is very very large relative to Y_c.

5.2   Income Effects and Living Arrangements

The $G(A, B)$ function can be used to analyze the effect of increases in the parent's or child's income on the decision to live together. The technique is to consider how income changes shift the $G(A, B) = 0$ locus. The $G^*(A, B) = 0$ and $G^{**}(A, B) = 0$ loci in figure 5.3 are examples of such shifts. Given a distribution of family pairs of A and B in the population, the $G^*(\ )$ locus clearly involves less shared living than the $G(\ )$ locus since all A, B pairs lying between the two curves now involve living apart.

The $G^{**}(A, B) = 0$ locus, on the other hand, involves less living together among families in which both the child and the parent dislike shared living $(A < 1)$ but possibly more shared living in cases in which either the parent or the child prefers living together $(A > 1$ or $B > 1)$.

To examine shifts in the $G(A, B)$ locus, we consider the implicit function $A = F(B, Y_p, Y_c)$ defined by $G(A, B) = 0$ and determine how this function changes with changes in Y_p and Y_c, holding B constant. For example, if changes in the function $F(\ )$ arising from a particular income change are positive at each level of B, the $G(A, B)$ curve shifts outward. We first consider the effect of a uniform proportional increase in Y_p and Y_c. Let λ represent a positive factor multiplying Y_p and Y_c. Equation (10) presents the derivative $\delta A/\delta \lambda = \delta F(B, \lambda Y_p, \lambda Y_c)/\delta \lambda$ evaluated at $\lambda = 1$ and values of A and B satisfying $G(A, B) = 0$.

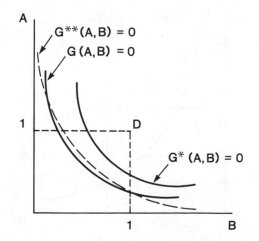

Fig. 5.3   Shifts in the living together–living apart indifference curve

(10)
$$\frac{\partial A}{\partial \lambda} = \frac{\dfrac{(1-B)}{B}Y_c^{2/B}}{\dfrac{1}{2A^2}Y_p^{2/A}\log Y_p^2} + \frac{(1-A)}{A}Y_p^{2/A}.$$

This derivative is clearly positive for $A < 1$ and $B < 1$. Hence, equal proportional increases in Y_p and Y_c reduce shared living among families in which both the parent and the child dislike living together ($A < 1$ and $B < 1$). On the other hand, among families where there is disagreement about shared living ($A > 1$ and $B < 1$ or $B > 1$ and $A < 1$), such income increases may or may not increase shared living.

We next consider how redistribution from the child to the parent shifts the $G(A, B) = 0$ locus. This derivative, which holds Y constant and raises Y_p by the same amount, ϕ, that Y_c is lowered is given by

(11)
$$\frac{\partial A}{\partial \phi} = \frac{2[Y_p^{(2/A)-1} - Y_c^{(2/B)-1}]}{\dfrac{1}{A^2}Y_p^{2/A}\log Y_p^2}$$

This derivative is negative if $A > B$ and $Y_p < Y_c$. Hence, among families in which the parent is relatively poor and has a relative preference for living with the child, redistribution from the child to the parent increases the extent of shared living. In terms of figure 5.2, such redistribution leads to a counter-clockwise rotation of the $G(A, B) = 0$ locus.

Finally, we consider changes in the $G(A, B) = 0$ locus arising from changes in the income of one family member, holding constant the income of the other member. Equation (12) examines the effect of raising Y_p:

(12)
$$\frac{dA}{dY_p} = \frac{-2Y + \dfrac{2}{A}Y_p^{(2/A)-1}}{\dfrac{1}{A^2}Y_p^{2/A}\log Y_p^2}$$

This derivative is negative for values of $A \geq 1$ and is positive for sufficiently small values of A. Hence, a rise in the income of the parent produces a counterclockwise rotation in the $G(A, B) = 0$ locus, thereby raising the frequency of shared living among families whose parents prefer living with their children ($A > 1$) and reducing the frequency of shared living among families whose parents prefer to live apart ($A < 1$). Increases in the child's income, holding the parent's income constant, produce a clockwise rotation in the $G(A, B) = 0$ curve, giving more weight to the child's preferences in determining living arrangements.

To summarize, in the structural model the effects of income changes on living arrangements depend in a nonlinear manner on the relative incomes of parents and children and on both their preferences. This feature differs greatly from the implicit assumption in logit and probit specifications that the effects of income changes are the same sign regardless of the particular parent-child observation in question.

5.3 Empirical Specification

Preferences toward living arrangements are likely to differ greatly across as well as within families. Hence, it seems reasonable to model the preference parameters A and B as depending partly on observable characteristics and partly on unobservable (at least to the econometrician) components. Specifically, we assume that A and B can be represented as

(13) $$A = \alpha_p X_p + \mu_p ,$$

$$B = \alpha_c X_c + \mu_c .$$

In (13), X_p and X_c are vectors of characteristics determining the parent's and child's preferences, respectively.

The terms μ_p and μ_c in (13) are random errors, which, to simplify the exposition, are assumed here to be independent standard normal deviates. Referring to figure 5.2, the likelihood that a parent and child live apart corresponds to the probability that $G(A, B)$ is negative, which is given by

(14) $$P[G(A, B) < 0] = \int_{-\infty}^{\infty} P(A = A^*)P[G(A^*, B) < 0]dA^*.$$

From figure 5.2, for values of A below the horizontal asymptote $\bar{A}$, G (A, B) is negative. Hence, we can write (14) as

(15) $$P[G(A, B) < 0] = F(\bar{A} - \alpha_p X_p)$$

$$+ \int_{\bar{A} - \alpha_p X_p}^{\infty} f(\mu_p) F\left\{ \frac{2 \log Y_c}{\log[Y^2 - Y_p^{2/(\alpha_p X_p + \mu_p)}]} - \alpha_c X_c \right\} d\mu_p .$$

In (15), $F(\ )$ stands for the standard normal distribution function, and $f(\ )$ stands for the standard normal density function. The probability of living together is simply $1 - P[G(A, B) \leq 0]$. These expressions can be used to form the likelihood of observing a sample of parents some of whom live with their children and some of whom do not. Hence, the parameter vectors α_p and α_c can be estimated by maximum likelihood. Note that this probability statement is quite different from the standard reduced-form logit specification that one might posit. For example, parent's income enters in a complex, nonlinear fashion in the probability statement, and its influence on the probability of shared living interacts with the level of the child's income and the parent's and child's preferences for shared living.

5.4   The Data

As mentioned, this paper uses data from the 1986 HRCA Elderly Survey and the 1986 HRC-NBER Child Survey. The former survey was conducted by the Hebrew Rehabilitation Center for the Aged (HRCA), while the latter was conducted by the authors and HRCA. The 1986 HRCA Elderly Survey is part of an ongoing panel survey of Massachusetts elderly that began in 1982. In addition to the 1982 and 1986 surveys, the elderly sample was reinterviewed in 1984, 1985, and 1987. The 1986 HRC-NBER Child Survey is a survey of the children of those elderly interviewed in the 1986 HRCA Elderly Survey. One child of each elderly respondent was interviewed and asked a set of questions concerning his (her) household, his (her) parents, and his (her) siblings.

The original 1982 stratified sample of 3,856 elderly individuals was drawn from two populations. The first population (the community sample), accounting for 2,674 of the elderly in the total sample, was drawn from communities in Massachusetts. The second population (the health care sample), which accounts for the remaining 1,182 elderly in the 1982 survey, was drawn from elderly participants of all twenty-seven Massachusetts home health care corporations. Both samples were stratified to produce an overrepresentation of the older old. The sample's selection is described in more detail in Kotlikoff and Morris (1989) and Morris et al. (1987). The 1982 sample of the elderly included only the noninstitutionalized elderly, but each subsequent survey has followed the initial sample as they changed residences, including moving into and out from nursing homes.

Each of the HRCA Elderly Surveys includes detailed questions about living arrangements and health status. The 1986 reinterview of the elderly also contains a series of questions of the elderly about their children. These questions include the names, sexes, and locations of all children, frequency and type of contact with children, the extent of financial aid given to and received from children, and the amount of assistance given by children to their elderly parents in performing activities of daily living. In addition, the 1986 survey contains a set of questions about the elderly respondent's income and wealth.

At the close of the HRCA Elderly Survey, we asked elderly respondents in the community sample for permission to contact one of their children to conduct our Child Survey. While we would have preferred to randomly select the child to be interviewed, we felt that we would receive more cooperation if we allowed the parent to make the selection. Like the HRCA Elderly Surveys, the HRC-NBER Child Survey is a telephone interview. The Child Survey is roughly forty-five minutes in length. Interviews with the child's spouse were conducted if the child was unavailable. The questions in the Child Survey concerning the respondent's characteristics include age, geographic location, marital status, number of young children, work and health status, occupation, industry, education, grades in high school, income, and wealth. These questions are also asked of the respondent about his or her siblings. In addition, the child was asked to indicate (1) the frequency of contact between each sibling and each sibling's spouse and the HRCA elderly respondent parent, (2) the amount of financial assistance each sibling and his spouse give to or receive from the HRCA elderly respondent parent, and (3) the amount of time each sibling and his spouse spends helping the HRCA elderly respondent. The child was also asked about his parents' health status as well as his parents' income and net wealth.

The sample size of the initial 1982 Elderly Survey is 3,856. In contrast, the 1986 completed sample size of elderly was 2,889, with most of the attrition since 1982 due to deaths. In the 1986 data, over 90 percent of the elderly are above age 70, over 40 percent are the old old (above age 85), and over two-thirds are females. The size of the HRC-NBER Child Survey is 850. Of these 850 children, 341 have no living siblings. In this study, we consider these 341 children with no siblings and their elderly parents who were also interviewed in 1986. Of the 341 single child/parent observations, 297 have complete data. The remaining 45 observations are missing data, typically on the income of either the child, the elderly parent(s), or both.

5.5   Some Initial Findings from the 1986 HRCA Elderly Survey and the HRC-NBER Child Survey

Since the 297 observations examined here represent only a portion of the data, it may be useful to summarize some of the initial findings reported in Kotlikoff and Morris (1989) based on the entire 1986 Elderly and Child Surveys. These data paint a bimodal picture of contact and assistance of the elderly by their children, with a majority of elderly receiving significant attention and care and a significant minority receiving little or no attention or care. Clearly, the realities of demographics limit the potential support that children can provide parents. Over one-fifth of the HRCA elderly in 1986 had no children, and another fifth have only one child. Elderly couples are more likely to have children than the single elderly; over a quarter of the single elderly have no children. Daughters are often viewed as more important providers of care to the elderly than sons. But, in total, 40.5 percent of the elderly have either no daughters or just one daughter, and over half the elderly either have no daughters or have no daughters who live within an hour.

Only 13.1 percent of all elderly and only 15.4 percent of vulnerable elderly live with their children. Of those elderly with children, fewer than one-fifth live with their children. Indeed, over half of single elderly males and females and over 40 percent of single elderly males and females who were deemed vulnerable based on an ADL ability score live completely alone. The fraction of respondents in institutions in 1986 is 11.8 percent for the entire sample and over 25 percent for the vulnerable elderly. Taken together these figures suggest only modest support of the elderly by children in the form of shared living quarters.

The geographic location of parents obviously limits their access to their children. Over one-third of the elderly either have no children or have no children who live within an hour. Despite their health problems, the vulnerable elderly are only slightly more likely to live with or near their children. Of those elderly who have children but are not living with them, only 44.6 percent have more than one child within an hour. In a typical month, over a quarter of children of the elderly do not physically spend time with their children; in contrast, almost a quarter of children, including those living with the HRCA elderly, spent over thirty hours in the previous month in physical contact.

While physical contact may, in some instances, be limited, most elderly with children have some form of contact, be it telephone contact or visits, during the week. Of the elderly with children, 84 percent either live with their children or have daily or weekly contact with one or more children. The institutionalized, the group with perhaps the greatest need for child contact, sometimes receive the least attention. Almost one-third of the institutionalized elderly either have no children or have very little contact with their children over the course of a year. For the noninstitutionalized, the corresponding fraction is less than one-quarter.

Although many of the elderly in the HRCA sample are quite poor, direct financial support of elderly parents by children is rare. Only 3 percent of the HRCA elderly report receiving regular monthly financial help from their children. Of the elderly that are very poor (annual incomes below $5,000), the corresponding percentage is only 4 percent. These figures seem surprising, and what is even more surprising is that there are few transfers to the poor elderly even in cases where there are a large number of middle- and upper-income children.

5.6   Characteristics of the Selected Sample—the Elderly

There are 297 elderly respondents in the 1986 HRCA Elderly Survey corresponding to the 297 children. Ten percent of these respondents live in nursing homes, 20 percent live with their children, and the rest, 70 percent, live alone, which in this context means either completely alone, with their spouse, or with other individuals who are not their children. The 297 elderly respondents are typically quite old; over half, 150, are age 85 and over. For those age 85 and older, the proportion living in nursing homes is 16 percent, the proportion living with children is 23 percent, and the proportion living alone is 61 percent. Two-thirds of the elderly are females; interestingly, only one of the thirty institutionalized elderly is a male. The elderly sample is disproportionately white (94 percent) and single (72 percent).

We have created five dummy variables to characterize the elderly respondents' health status. These are Independent (H1), Minor Functional Problems (H2), Requires Assistance with Independent Activities of Daily Living (H3), Requires Some Assistance with Activities of Daily Living (H4), and Requires Substantial Assistance with Activities of Daily Living (H5). Each of the elderly was allocated to one of these categories on the basis of responses to over thirty questions on functional ability, ability to perform independent activities of daily living, and objective information about ongoing diseases and infirmities. We also considered several other health variables, including dummies for neurological problems, inability to move from a chair without assistance, and Alzheimer's disease. These variables did not add significantly to the prediction of living arrangements given the dummies H1–H5. Of the thirty institutionalized elderly, twenty-eight have positive H4 or H5 health indicators. Of the fifty-eight elderly living with their children, twelve (21 percent) have positive H4 or H5 indicators. Of the 209 elderly living alone, twenty-one (10 percent) have positive H4 or H5 indicators.

The incomes of the elderly are typically fairly low. Slightly over half the elderly reported income below $7,500. Another 39 percent reported incomes between $7,500 and $20,000. Only twenty-three of the elderly, 8 percent, report incomes over $20,000. It is interesting to note that none of these twenty-three higher-income elderly live in nursing homes and that only two of the twenty-three live with their children.

5.7   Characteristics of the Selected Sample—the Children

The ages of the 297 children of the elderly range from twenty-seven to seventy-nine. A surprisingly high number, 185, of the 297 children in the sample (all of whom were referred by the HRCA elderly respondent) are female. Slightly over half are younger than 55; over two-thirds are between ages 45 and 65. Children living with their parents tend to be somewhat older; 19 percent of children living with parents are age 65 or older, compared to 8 percent for children whose parents live alone. Most of the children, 76 percent, are married; but, among children living with their parents, the proportion married is only 45 percent. Over half the children went to college, and only thirty of the 297 children failed to complete high school. There is no clear correlation in the raw data between child's education and the living arrangements of the parents.

In contrast to the parents, whose median income is approximately $7,000, the median income of children is approximately $30,000. A total of sixty-one children reported incomes above $50,000, and twenty-one reported incomes below $10,000. Of the sixty-one elderly whose children have incomes above $50,000, fifty-three, 87 percent, live alone. This figure contrasts with the 70 percent figure for the overall sample. Most of the children, 85 percent, report their health to be good, 14 percent report their health to be fair, and only 1 percent report their health to be poor.

5.8   Logit and Probit Estimates

Table 5.1 reports results for a logit model specifying the probability of living alone, living in an institution, and living with children. The independent variables are the age of the parent, Age; the sex of the parent, Male = 1 for

Table 5.1   **Estimates from the Logit Model**

	Coefficients for the Probability of Living in an Institution		
	Variable	Coefficient	t-Statistic
	Constant	1.468	.290
	Marry	NA	NA
	Income	.093	.915
	Age	− .037	− .545
	Male	− .911	− .723
	H1	NA	NA
	H2	NA	NA
	H3	− 3.175	− 3.129
	H4	− .626	− .736
	KMarry	1.590	2.067
	KIncome	.631E-2	.363
	KAge	.664E-2	.142
	KMale	1.054	1.564
	KHealth	.594	.693
	KEd	.531	.774

	Coefficients for the Probability of Living Alone		
		Coefficient	t-Statistic
	Constant	− .167	− .060
	Marry	.916	1.686
	Income	.456E-1	1.135
	Age	− .184E-1	− .500
	Male	.102	.233
	H1	.651	.910
	H2	1.158	1.460
	H3	.796	1.029
	H4	.568	.654
	KMarry	1.608	4.047
	KIncome	.211E-1	1.825
	KAge	− .483	− .173
	KMale	.806	2.039
	KHealth	− .226	− .441
	KEduc	.273	.722

a male, 0 otherwise; the marital status of the parent, Marry = 1 for married, 0 otherwise; the income of the parent, Income; four health dummies for the parent, H1, H2, H3, and H4; the age of the child, KAge; the marital status of the child, Kmarry = 1 married, 0 otherwise; the sex of the child, Kmale = 1 for a male, 0 otherwise; the income of the child, KIncome; the years of education of the child, KEduc; and the self-reported health status of the child, KHealth = 1 if the child reported excellent or good health, 0 otherwise.

Surprisingly few of the parent coefficients from the logit model are significant, but the signs of the coefficients of parent variables generally accord with previous findings. In particular, higher levels of parent's income increase the probability of living alone, as does being married and being male. Compared to those elderly with severe health problems (those in the fifth health category), other elderly are more likely to live alone and are less likely to live in a nursing home.

The new child variables in the logit indicate that those elderly whose children have higher incomes, are married, or are male are more likely to live alone or live in an institution. Both KMarry variables are significant, as is the KMale coefficient in determining the probability of living alone. The KIncome variable in the probability of living alone is almost significant.

The probit model presented in table 5.2 considers the subsample of 267 elderly who are not in nursing homes. As in the logit results, table 5.2 indicates that the probability of living with children rather than living alone decreases with the parent's and child's income. This probability is smaller if the child

Table 5.2   **Estimates from the Probit Model**

	Coefficients for the Probability of Living with Children versus Living Alone	
Variable	Coefficient	t-Statistic
Constant	.084	.052
Marry	−.574	−1.899
Income	−.218E-1	−1.176
Age	.956E-2	.446
Male	−.653E-1	−.260
H1	−.390	−.934
H2	−.661	−1.465
H3	−.503	−1.127
H4	−.313	−.600
KMarry	−.989	−4.231
KIncome	−.115E-1	−1.800
KAge	.460E-2	.289
KHealth	.128	.431
KEduc	−.178	−.808
KMale	−.450	−2.028

is male or if the child or parent are married. Surprisingly, the parent health variables are not significant, although they have the expected sign. The child health coefficient is also insignificant; according to the table, parents whose children are in excellent or good health are more likely to live with their children. While the age neither of the parent nor the child is significant, older parents are more likely to live with their children, as are parents with older children. Finally, parents with more educated children are less likely to live with their children, although this coefficient is also insignificant. In sum, the logit and probit coefficients, although often insignificant, generally accord with our priors and suggest that child characteristics are important codeterminants of the living arrangements of the elderly.

5.9   Results from Estimating the Structural Model

The estimated coefficients from the structural model based on the 267 observations of children and their noninstitutionalized parents are presented in table 5.3. A likelihood ratio test indicates that, as a group, the coefficients are highly significant. The variable Health is a dummy that takes on the value one if the parent's health indicator is H4 or H5 and zero otherwise. The first five coefficients in the table multiplied by their respective variables correspond to the term $\alpha_p X_p$ in (13), while the second five coefficients multiplied by their respective variables correspond to the term $\alpha_c X_c$ in (13). Hence, positive coefficients in the table mean that the expected value of either A or B is larger, as is the probability of shared living. According to the table, this probability is smaller for married parents or parents with married children. It is also smaller if the child is male. In contrast, the probability of shared living is larger for male parents, older parents, parents with older children, parents with less well educated children, and parents who fall into the worst two health categories.

The estimated coefficients from the structural model can be used to determine values of $\alpha_p X_p$ and $\alpha_c X_c$ for each observation. The mean values of

Table 5.3   **Estimates from the Structural Model**

Variable	Coefficient	t-Statistic
α_p Constant	-1.911	$-.731$
Marry	$-.673$	-1.424
Age	.353E-1	1.068
Male	.316E-1	.764E-1
Health	.178	.276
α_c Constant	1.356	1.201
KMarry	-1.565	-2.443
Kage	.118E-1	.802
KMale	$-.768$	$-.291$
KEduc	$-.452E-1$	$-.165$

$\alpha_p X_p$ and $\alpha_c X_c$ across all observations are .848 and .482, respectively. Since both these figures are less than unity, both children and parents prefer, on average, to live apart, but children have a stronger preference toward separate living. Not all parents and children have values of $\alpha_p X_p$ and $\alpha_c X_c$ less than unity. Quite the contrary; 129 of the 267 parents (48 percent) and sixty-four children (24 percent) have estimated values of $\alpha_p X_p$ and $\alpha_c X_c$, respectively, in excess of unity. Hence, almost half of parents and almost one-quarter of children appear to prefer shared living. Figure 5.4 presents the distribution of pairs of $\alpha_p X_p$ and $\alpha_c X_c$ for each parent-child pair. Points in the southeast and northwest quadrants indicate parent-child pairs in which there is a conflict with respect to preferences regarding shared living. Points in the northwest quadrant correspond to cases in which parents prefer to live with their children (assuming $\mu_p = 0$) and children prefer to live apart from their parents (assuming $\mu_c = 0$). Points in the southeast quadrant correspond to parents who prefer to live apart from their children but children who prefer to live with their parents. Since 129 of the 267 parents want (assuming $\mu_p = 0$) to live with their children but only fifty-eight do so, it appears that a large number of parents live alone against their will. According to the model, if their incomes were sufficiently high, these parents could persuade their children to live with them.

Another issue that can be explored using the model's estimated coefficients is the effect on the probability of living together of changes in income. In this exercise, reported in table 5.4, we evaluate $\alpha_p X_p$ and $\alpha_c X_c$ at the mean values of X_p and X_c and consider different combinations of Y_p and Y_c. The table

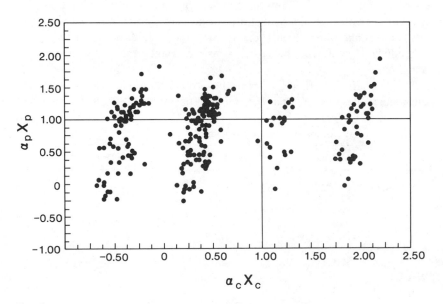

Fig. 5.4   Distribution of $\alpha_p X_p$ and $\alpha_c X_c$

Table 5.4   **Probability of Living with Children for Selected Combinations of Parent and Child Incomes**

Y_p ($)	Y_c ($)	Probability	Y_p ($)	Y_c ($)	Probability
1,000	1,000	.549	1,000	1,000	.549
5,000	1,000	.327	1,000	5,000	.269
10,000	1,000	.311	1,000	10,000	.253
20,000	1,000	.306	1,000	20,000	.247
50,000	1,000	.302	1,000	50,000	.243
1,000	50,000	.244	50,000	1,000	.303
5,000	50,000	.207	50,000	5,000	.237
10,000	50,000	.192	50,000	10,000	.211
20,000	50,000	.181	50,000	20,000	.191
50,000	50,000	.175	50,000	50,000	.175

indicates that, at the mean values of $\alpha_p X_p$ and $\alpha_c X_c$, significant changes in the probability of living together occur only if the child's or parent's income is fairly low. Stated differently, because the mean preferences indicate a mutual dislike for shared living, the income of the parent or the child must be quite low to produce a reasonably large probability of shared living.

A related experiment is to ask how equalizing the incomes of children and parents, while keeping the total constant, affects the probability of living together. To analyze this question, we used the estimated values of $\alpha_p X_p$ and $\alpha_c X_c$ for each parent and child and computed the probability of shared living given current income positions. We then computed the probability based on equalized income. The differences in probabilities for the 267 observations are quite small. For 173 observations, the probabilities changed by less than 1 percentage point. For forty-four observations, the probabilities changed by between 1 and 2 percentage points. For forty-one observations, the probabilities changed by between 2 and 10 percentage points; and for only two observations did the probabilities change by more than 10 percentage points.

Taken together, these two experiments suggest that the intrinsic preferences of the parent and child regarding shared living rather than the relative or absolute incomes of the two are most important in determining the probability of shared living. In terms of figure 5.1, the position of curve $G(A, B)$ is not highly sensitive to even substantial variations of Y_p and Y_c around observed values, and the key determinant of the living arrangement is the location of A and B in the axis. This finding that income effects play a rather minor role in determining living arrangements is supported as well by the probit results. Evaluated at the mean levels of income, which are $36,704 for children and $9,719 for parents, the probability of shared living is .170. If the child's income is reduced from $36,704 to $12,000, the probability of shared living only increases to .230. If the child's income is raised to $65,000, the probability only declines to .088. Holding the child's income at the mean, if the parent's income is increased to $20,000, the probability of living together only declines from .170 to .101; lowering the parent's income to $4,000 raises the probability to only .191.

5.10 Summary and Conclusion

This paper uses new data on the characteristics of children and parents to study their decision to live together. Theoretical analysis of this decision indicates that living arrangements can be studied separately from the question of child-parent bargaining. The analysis also points out that income effects with respect to living arrangements are likely to be family specific; in some families, increases in the incomes of children or parents will lead them to live apart, in others to live together.

Empirical findings from logit and probit models as well as the structural model suggest that characteristics of children are important codeterminants of living arrangements. They also support a view that income differences are not as important as may previously have been thought in explaining living arrangements.

References

Beresford, J. C., and A. M. Rivlin. 1966. Privacy, poverty and old age. *Demography,* 3 (1):247–58.

Carliner, G. 1975. Determinants of household headship. *Journal of Marriage and the Family* 37:28–38.

Chevan, A., and J. H. Korson. 1972. The widowed who live alone: An examination of social and demographic factors. *Social Forces* 51 (September):45–53.

Kobrin, F. E. 1976a. The fall in household size and the rise of the primary individual in the United States. *Demography* 13:127–38.

———. 1976b. The primary individual and the family: Changes in living arrangements in the United States since 1950. *Journal of Marriage and the Family* 8:233–38.

Kotlikoff, L. J., and J. N. Morris. 1989. How much care do the aged receive from their children? A bimodal picture of contact and assistance. In *The economics of aging,* ed. D. A. Wise, 151–75. Chicago: University of Chicago Press.

Michael, R. T., V. R. Fuchs, and S. R. Scott. 1980. Changes in the propensity to live alone, 1950–1976. *Demography* 17:39–56.

Morris, J. M., C. E. Gutkin, C. C. Sherwood, and E. Bernstein. 1987. Interest in long term care insurance. Final Report in connection with HCFA Cooperative Agreement 18-C-98375/1, June.

Sandefur, G. D., and N. B. Tuma. 1987. Social and economic trends among the aged in the United States, 1940–1985. February. Typescript.

Schorr, A. L. 1980. Filial responsibility in the modern American family. Social Security Administration, Division of Program Research.

Soldo, B. J., and P. Lauriat. 1976. Living arrangements among the elderly in the United States: A loglinear approach. *Journal of Comparative Family Studies* 7 (Summer):351–66.

Tissure, T., and J. L. McCoy. 1981. Income and living arrangements among poor aged singles. *Social Security Bulletin* 44:3–13.
Wolf, D. 1984. Kin availability and the living arrangements of older women. *Social Science Research* 13 (1):72–85.

Comment   Axel H. Börsch-Supan

The elderly's choice of living arrangements is the subject of three papers in this volume. My papers and that by Ellwood and Kane follow the traditional approach in much of the housing literature: they are empirical investigations of the elderly's demand for several types of living arrangements, in particular, living with their own adult children as an alternative to living independently, on the one hand, and becoming institutionalized, on the other hand. But there are two sides of the market for housing as well as for living arrangements, in particular, two parties who make an elderly parent-adult child living arrangement possible: the elderly parent on the demand side and the adult child on the supply side. It is the merit of the paper by Larry Kotlikoff and John Morris to make this simultaneous choice explicit.

The two sides have to match, and the likelihood of a match will depend on characteristics of the elderly parent as well as of the adult child. Thus, the least one should do is to relate all these characteristics to observed choices in some kind of reduced form of the complicated matching process. Kotlikoff and Morris are much more ambitious. They model the matching process explicitly and rather boldly by postulating a structural model derived from first economic principles. The model is quite ingenious as it succeeds in separating the preferences of elderly parent and adult children from the mechanics of the bargaining process that makes or breaks the match. This allows Kotlikoff and Morris essentially to ignore how this bargaining process comes about and yields a fairly simple characterization of the probability of living together that fits nicely in random utility theory.

The formalism of the model can be stripped down to five essential ingredients: two parameters that characterize the preference between privacy and joint living, one for the elderly, A, and one for the child, B; the elderly's income, Y_p, and the income of the child, Y_c; and a bargaining weight θ that represents the elderly's say in the joint household's decisions. The main logic of the model is as follows. If there is a bargaining weight θ such that the resulting joint utility dominates the utility of living alone for both elderly and child, they will find out about it one way or another, and we, the econometric

Axel H. Börsch-Supan is assistant professor of Public Policy at the John F. Kennedy School of Government, Harvard University; C3-Professor of Economics Universität Mannheim (West Germany); and faculty research fellow of the National Bureau of Economic Research.

observers, do not have to worry about its magnitude. We just have to check whether there is at least one value of θ such that the above condition holds.

Postulating such a model is one thing; testing it is yet another challenge. The authors are to be applauded for doing both. Most important, one needs a data set of elderly and their living arrangements that includes characteristics describing the elderly person *and* his or her adult children. As such data were not available, Kotlikoff and Morris collected the data themselves, complementing a panel of elderly in Massachusetts that was started in 1981 by Morris with data collected from the children. It is worth noting that this is the first, and it is to be hoped not the last, major data collection effort in the Economics of Aging Project. As the results of this paper show, more data on elderly *and* their children are badly needed.

The data include some 300 elderly parent–adult child pairs of predominantly vulnerable elderly in Massachusetts. The authors include only elderly with one adult child since they decided that they should exact the burden of an additional interview on only one child per elderly, a child chosen by the elderly, not randomly. The restriction on elderly with only one child may well bias the results as elderly with more than one child ever born are more likely to live jointly with one of their children. In short, this is a small, very specific, and possibly self-selected sample. One should keep this in mind when generalizing the results of this paper.

The authors transform their behavioral model in a testable probability equation by postulating that the preference parameters A and B are linear combinations of observable characteristics such as marital status, sex, age and health of parent and child, denoted by the vectors X_p and X_c, plus unobservable normally distributed preference components. Utility maximization subject to the budget constraint at given incomes Y_p and Y_c for all possible values of the bargaining weight θ produces an implicit function in A and B, denoted by $G(A, B)$, that characterizes the locus of indifference between living jointly and living separately. A positive $G(A, B)$ implies living together, a negative $G(A, B)$ implies living alone. Thus, the $G(A, B)$ function acts like a very specific, nonlinear indirect utility function in the familiar random utility model. The maximum likelihood estimation follows directly from this interpretation.

Let me now turn to the empirical results. Unfortunately, after all the effort and the admirable set-up of the structural model, the reader is rather disenchanted detecting only one significant coefficient in the tightly specified structural model. Even if the parameters of the structural model are jointly significant, this is the more frustrating as reduced-form logit and probit models produce considerably better results. The small and specific sample may explain the disappointing results, but it appears to me that these poor results are indicators for other problems as well.

What distinguishes the reduced-form logit and probit models from the structural model? The key is the functional form of the indirect utility difference between living alone and living together. Logit and probit are based on a linear combination of the deterministic components in A and B *and* income plus unobservables:

(i) $u^R(X_p, X_c, Y_p, Y_c) = \alpha_p X_p + \alpha_c X_c + \beta_p Y_p + \beta_c Y_c + \mu_p + \mu_c$,

where ϵ is logistic in the logit model and normal in the probit model. The structural model imposes a much more specific nonlinear functional form:

(ii) $u^S(X_p, X_c, Y_p, Y_c) = (Y_p + Y_c)^2 - Y_p^{2/(\alpha_p X_p + \mu_p)} - Y_c^{2/(\alpha_c X_c + \mu_c)}$

(eq. [8] in the paper). Most notably, in the reduced-form models the effect of income on living arrangement choice is governed by separate parameters β_p and β_c, while in the structural model income does only indirectly enter this choice and is consequently "missing" in table 5.3. (Why the authors also change some of the X_p and X_c in this table remains inconceivable.)

The lack of freedom in the pattern and magnitude of income effects is my main criticism of the structural model and appears to be the most likely cause of the inferior performance relative to the two reduced-form models. The functional form of the income effects result from one assumption: the Cobb-Douglas specification of direct utility (eq. [2]) with a common exponent for housing and other consumption. It restricts the budget share of housing to a constant 50 percent. This is rather unrealistic. First, the share of housing expenditures varies widely among elderly as some live in owned homes that are long paid off and others in rental housing. Moreover, the sheer magnitude of this share is much too large. In a structural model as tightly specified as this one, this misspecification is rather likely to lead to a poor fit and to a bias in the other coefficients.

It is worth noting that the direct utility function can easily be changed to be more general without spoiling the model's simplicity—a utility function separable in housing and consumption but with A and B affecting only housing and not consumption will do the trick. I would also prefer this specification for other reasons—why should the elderly (the child, respectively) enjoy all other consumption just as much more or less as shared housing when living jointly?

A second, more general criticism of the structural model is its built-in pure selfishness. However, asks the moralist, if there is no altruism in parent-child relations, where else should it be in this world? Should it not at least be conceivable that the child has a higher utility from helping a parent who needs it compared to one who does not need it—for example, by taking in a sick or a poor parent? None of the parent's characteristics such as health or income enter the child's utility in this selfish model world.

Since the structural model has no interaction between the two utilities, the model is also unable to test the assumption of pure selfishness. The basic econometric problem is that interaction effects—say, elements of X_p also included in the exponent of Y_c in (ii)—are hard to identify, effectively only by functional form. However, if interaction terms are not identified, we are back at reduced forms such as (i). Hence, another possible explanation of the superior performance of the reduced-form equations is a certain degree of altruism in parent-child relations.

In summary, it appears to me that the structural model imposes too many restrictions that are not reflected in the data. More flexibility in the utility specification would allow for more realistic budget shares and some degree of altruism without going all the way to reduced forms—although the econometric maneuvering room is tight. Notwithstanding this criticism, I admire the model for its simplicity and the bold attempt to cut through the mesh of bargaining and joint utility maximization.

An important and robust result is that childrens' characteristics matter in the elderly's choice of living arrangements. This finding should be a strong incentive to include information on children in new surveys of the elderly such as the authors did for this study.

The structural model produces a very useful categorization of elderly-child pairs into four groups: those who agree in either living together or living separately, and those pairs in which one partner would like sharing but the other refuses to join. The possibility of this categorization is the main attraction of the authors' model, and it is a very relevant one for policy analysis. The paper's main substantive message results from this categorization. It is a sad message about the isolation of the elderly in our society and worth repeating as it confirms a message relayed by the other two studies on living arrangements in this volume: many elderly live alone not because they prefer to live alone but because their children prefer not to live with them.

Issues in the Economics of Aging

Edited by   David A. Wise

The University of Chicago Press

Chicago and London

6 Predicting Nursing Home Utilization among the High-Risk Elderly

Alan M. Garber and Thomas MaCurdy

How likely is nursing home admission for an elderly person? How long does institutionalization last? These questions concern the elderly and their families, private insurers, and government agencies. The dearth of affordable, comprehensive insurance coverage makes long-term care (LTC) the leading cause of catastrophic health costs among the elderly. Private insurance rarely covers the costs of care received in nursing homes, which accounts for about 90 percent of LTC expenditures. Medicare and private insurance pay for only 1.7 percent and 1 percent, respectively, of all U.S. nursing home expenditures (Lazenby, Levit, and Waldo 1986), and Medicaid is available only to those who have become impoverished. The remaining burden falls on the elderly, their friends, and their families, who often provide "informal" care as well as financial assistance. Even unpaid care can have severe financial consequences; taking care of an impaired elderly relative frequently means reducing or abandoning paid employment (Muurinen 1986). Private LTC insurance, government LTC programs, and novel mechanisms for insuring and financing LTC have been proposed to alleviate these problems (Meiners 1983; U.S. Department of Health and Human Services 1986; Blumenthal et al. 1986). Insurers are becoming interested in offering comprehensive LTC insurance, and many of the elderly seem willing to consider the purchase of such plans. Whether the funds for LTC come from insurance payments, direct private

Alan M. Garber is assistant professor in the Department of Medicine at Stanford University School of Medicine, a staff physician at Palo Alto Veterans Administration Medical Center, and a research associate at the National Bureau of Economic Research. Thomas MaCurdy is both a professor in the Department of Economics and a senior fellow of the Hoover Institution at Stanford University as well as a research associate at the National Bureau of Economic Research.

This research was supported by a FIRST Award from the National Institute on Aging (1 R29 AG07651-01), a grant from the Veterans Administration (HSR&D Project IIR no. 86-118G), National Science Foundation Grant SE 85-13455, and grant 12761 from the Robert Wood Johnson Foundation. Bart Hamilton and Holly Prigerson provided valuable research assistance.

savings, or public coffers, financing can improve only if accurate projections of future LTC utilization become available. Inadequate information about expected nursing home utilization of the elderly impedes the development of these alternatives.

Demographic trends heighten the need to develop accurate predictions of nursing home utilization. Between 1980 and 2030, the number of Americans aged 65 and over is projected to increase from 24,927,000 to 55,024,000, as their fraction of the total U.S. population reaches 18.3 percent (Doty, Liu, and Wiener 1985). The number of Americans aged 85 and over—who are apt to be disabled, to live alone, to require frequent hospitalization, and to be found in nursing homes (Rosenwaike 1985)—is expected to quadruple in the same period (Taeuber 1983).

Although many authors have attempted to predict the risk of institutionalization, their estimates are often based on geographically limited populations of the elderly. Their data sources have sometimes been unsatisfactory, and many of these studies have used methods that do not lend themselves to forecasting. We report below the results of a new investigation of predictors of utilization, based on a national longitudinal sample of elderly persons at high risk of entering nursing homes. Our analysis of data from the National Long-Term Care Demonstration (Channeling) addresses the following questions. What is the probability of nursing home admission, and the expected number of annual nursing home days, for an elderly individual living in the community who possesses high-risk health characteristics? What is the distribution of lengths of stay in the nursing home for these individuals? How do these aspects of utilization vary with other personal characteristics?

Our answers to these questions are based on an analysis of data obtained in the early 1980s. These data reflect the current health care environment, which may change dramatically in the coming years. Current policy initiatives suggest that, in the future, nursing homes, home health care, and LTC insurance will be very different than they are today. We do not attempt to model the effects of these changes directly. We do not estimate, for example, the effects of moral hazard or adverse selection on future utilization. We emphasize instead the correlates of current nursing home utilization, an essential first step in any attempt to forecast future demand for LTC.

Our analysis proceeds as follows. First, we describe previous studies of nursing home utilization, identifying some of the issues that they have been unable to address. We then describe the data used for our study of nursing home utilization. The third and fourth sections explain the empirical approach and the estimation procedure, respectively. Since limitations in the data set make standard longitudinal models inappropriate, the methods applied in this study have unusual features. Results of the statistical analysis are described in section 6.5, along with simulations that show distributions of nursing home utilization for various categories of individuals.

6.1   Previous Studies of Nursing Home Utilization

6.1.1   The Likelihood of Nursing Home Admission

While few studies have fully investigated the determinants of nursing home length of stay, several have examined the likelihood of institutionalization (for a review, see Wingard, Jones, and Kaplan 1987). Insofar as they do not examine duration, these studies are of limited value for analyzing nursing home utilization; insurers and others concerned with the financial risks tied to LTC need to be able to distinguish very short nursing home admissions from stays that last for years. From their point of view, the several studies of the lifetime risk of nursing home admission are least useful since they neither predict the risk in specific age intervals nor distinguish short posthospital discharge stays, which Medicare usually reimburses, from prolonged institutionalization.

The studies of lifetime risk of nursing home admission have shown, however, that many of the elderly—25 percent–50 percent—will eventually be admitted to a nursing home (Palmore 1976; Vicente, Wiley, and Carrington 1979; McConnel 1984).

Several studies of the likelihood of admission in fixed intervals assess the effect of age, demographic characteristics, health status, and other variables. Logistic regression has been used to assess the probability of admission to nursing homes from the community (Branch and Jette 1982; Nocks et al. 1986; Cohen, Tell, and Wallack 1986a) and from hospitals (Kane and Matthias 1984) during fixed time intervals. Several other studies have used life-table methods or Markov models to predict the likelihood of nursing home admission (Manton, Woodbury, and Liu 1984; Liu and Manton 1984; Shapiro and Webster 1984; McConnel 1984; Lane et al. 1985; Manheim and Hughes 1986; Cohen, Tell, and Wallack 1986b). Several of these (Cohen, Tell, and Wallack 1986a; Lane et al. 1985; Manheim and Hughes 1986; McConnel 1984) do not control for individual characteristics. Generalizations based on studies that do not control for individual characteristics are particularly speculative; if health status, income, or other population characteristics change over time, the utilization patterns observed in the studies may no longer apply. Furthermore, the first-order Markov assumption is unlikely to be satisfied in a heterogeneous population unless there is an adjustment for determinants of institutionalization.

6.1.2   Duration of Nursing Home Admissions

Much of the previous literature on the duration of nursing home admission is based on demonstration projects. Several demonstrations have tested whether intensive community services could forestall nursing home admission or hasten discharge. Most studies of duration employ case-control methods to assess the effect of the community care interventions on nursing home utilization (e.g., Yordi and Waldman 1985; Branch and Stuart 1984; Hughes, Cordray, and Spiker 1984; Gaumer et al. 1986). For most of these investigations, the determinants of nursing home utilization are of less interest than the effectiveness of the intervention. The results of these studies seldom generalize to other areas since they are based either on single communities or on small areas that may offer community services not available elsewhere. Furthermore, the study populations differ greatly; rates of institutionalization in the control groups of the eight community-based LTC interventions reviewed by Weissert (1985) varied tenfold. Hence, this literature does not provide a basis for predicting either the likelihood or the duration of institutionalization that can be confidently applied elsewhere.

These and other studies of the duration of institutionalization have made it clear that there are at least two distinct groups of nursing home patients: those who are admitted for a short stay, either for convalescence from hospitalization or to die; and those who will become long-term residents of nursing homes because they are severely, chronically disabled but not dying (Keeler, Kane, and Solomon 1981). Liu and Manton (1984) found that 50 percent of a cohort of nursing home admissions were discharged within ninety days of entry, while 14 percent were institutionalized for over three years. Liu and Manton presented results for certain subgroups such as patients with particular diagnoses and disabilities. However, like most other studies of duration, their paper did not report a multivariate analysis that would enable the reader to infer the independent effects of personal characteristics.

6.1.3   Who Is at Risk of Institutionalization?

Despite their varied methods and data sources, published studies show remarkable agreement about the factors that are important determinants of institutionalization. These factors fall into four categories.

Demographic Factors

Virtually every study that controls for age has found that advancing age is associated with a rising risk of institutionalization; the prevalence of institutionalization rises with age, in univariate analyses, and it has a smaller but still significant effect in multivariate analyses. Sex also seems to be an important factor; univariate analyses find that elderly women are more likely than elderly men to enter a nursing home (Greenberg and Ginn 1979; Vicente, Wiley, and Carrington 1979). Since women are far more likely than men to survive their spouse, the effect of living alone may be confounded with the sex effect.

Health and Functional Status

Other studies have found that certain health conditions, such as cancer and dementia, raise the risk of institutionalization. Also important is functional status. Existing measures of functional status have important drawbacks: most have not been validated; they are coarse measures, insensitive to large changes in physical functioning; they are not usually cardinal scales, though they have been used that way (Spitzer 1987; Feinstein, Josephy, and Wells 1986). These flaws should weaken the ability of functional status measures to predict health events. Nevertheless, the most widely used measures are clearly associated with the risk of institutionalization.

Two measures are widely used to assess chronic disability in the elderly. The first of these, "activities of daily living" (ADL), describes the ability to perform basic functions such as dressing, eating, and walking without assistance. Functional status evaluation using this measure dates to the late 1950s (Katz et al. 1963). The second measure is based on limitations in "instrumental activities of daily living" (IADL). The IADLs measure the ability to perform more complex tasks without assistance, such as shopping, handling finances, and cooking. Most nursing home residents suffer from at least one ADL impairment, and nearly all have an IADL impairment. Previous investigations have found that ADL and, to a lesser extent, IADL limitations predict subsequent nursing home admission rates well.

Financial Status

Few studies have examined whether wealth or income affects nursing home utilization. Vicente, Wiley, and Carrington (1979) found that individuals whose family income was "inadequate" were more than twice as likely to be admitted to a nursing home as individuals of "very adequate" means. Greenberg and Ginn (1979) found that the coefficient of a binary variable for poverty was of borderline statistical significance in a multiple logistic regression predicting the probability of nursing home admission. Increased utilization of home health services may explain why wealthier people are less likely to enter institutions.

Living Arrangement, Marital Status, and Informal Supports

Being married is associated with a lower likelihood of nursing home admission (Cohen, Tell, and Wallack 1988), while living alone is associated with an increased risk of institutionalization (Kovar 1988). A spouse often provides substantial aid for a disabled person. The elderly who live alone have fewer disabilities than others of the same age who live with a spouse or other family members (Feller 1983), suggesting that they cannot continue to live independently in the face of severe disability. The National Long-Term Care Survey revealed that the likelihood that a disabled elderly individual who lives alone will be in a nursing home two years later is more than half again as great as for a similarly disabled person living with a spouse (Kovar 1988).

Collectively, these studies show that the elderly are likely to be admitted to a nursing home at some time, though the risk of prolonged institutionalization is distributed unequally. Studies that forecast utilization need to analyze duration as well as the probability of admission. It is important to explore the sources of the heterogeneity in nursing home utilization. We next describe a data set particularly suited for this purpose, the National Long-Term Care Demonstration.

6.2 The Channeling Data

Our analysis of the determinants of nursing home utilization is based on data from a sample of very frail elderly Americans. The data were collected as part of the evaluation of the National Long-Term Care (Channeling) Demonstration. This project, which was organized by the Department of Health and Human Services in 1980, was designed to demonstrate and evaluate the efficacy of "case management" in improving the LTC of the elderly. The advocates of case management hoped that it would control the costs of LTC while providing valuable services to the frail elderly. Channeling incorporated a total of ten study sites throughout the country. Within these sites, patients were randomized to usual care or assigned to a case manager. Case management could take one of two forms. At five sites, the case manager assumed responsibility for evaluating the elderly and planning and obtaining specific services. At five other sites, the case manager was also responsible for LTC expenditures on behalf of the enrollee. Other differences between the two forms that channeling took are detailed in Kemper et al. (1986) and Carcagno et al. (1986).

Like most large studies of community care interventions, Channeling enrolled individuals at high risk for institutionalization. Had the investigators studied a random sample of elderly individuals, either a much longer follow-up or a substantially larger sample would have been required to obtain reliable statistical estimates. Furthermore, as detailed in table 6.1, the criteria for enrollment in the Channeling demonstration were specified clearly. Other demonstration projects enrolled individuals who applied for particular services or who met other criteria of uncertain generalizability. Finally, unlike most other demonstration projects Channeling was performed at geographically diverse sites.

Table 6.1   **Eligibility Criteria for Channeling Demonstration**

Age	65 or over.
Functional disability	Two moderate ADL limitations or three severe IADL limitations or two severe IADL limitations and one severe ADL limitation.
"Unmet needs"	Must need help with at least two categories of service affected by functional disabilities or impairments for six months (such as meals or personal care), or informal supports may no longer be able to provide needed care.
Residence	Must be living in community or, if in nursing home, certified to be likely to be discharged within three months.
Medicare coverage	Must be eligible for Medicare Part A.

Source: Adapted from Kemper et al. (1986, 36).

We did not examine the effect of the Channeling intervention as part of this study. Previous studies have reported that the intervention had negligible effects on nursing home utilization and health outcomes (Kemper 1988). Our interest focuses instead on the utilization of nursing home services by the entire enrolled population. Data in the Channeling study were collected by surveying the participants and family members. These data were augmented by Medicare and Medicaid records, death certificate data, and data from providers. The baseline and followup data included the following:

- *Baseline* (September 1982–July 1983). Information about level of function (ADL and IADL impairments), health status, health service use, availability of informal care, basic demographic information, financial resources, health insurance (sample size 5,626);
- *Six-month follow-up* (September 1982–February 1984). Insurance coverage, health status, housing conditions, expenditures, health service use, community service use, nursing home admissions, income and assets, disability (sample size 4,593);
- *Twelve-month follow-up* (March 1983–July 1984). Same as six-month (sample size 4,752);
- *Eighteen-month follow-up* (September 1983–July 1984). Same as six-month (sample size 2,248).

To be included in this follow-up, a sample member had to be in the cohort of individuals enrolled in the first half of the demonstration and to have completed both the six- and the twelve-month follow-ups.

Summary statistics for the baseline characteristics of the sample, displayed in table 6.2, reveal that the average age of the Channeling participant was 80 years and that nearly 72 percent were female. Both physical and mental disability were common; nearly half the participants had moderate or severe cognitive impairments (dementia), and most had multiple and severe functional limitations. Although 42 percent owned their homes, 55 percent had very low (< $500) monthly incomes, and only 10 percent reported monthly incomes that exceeded $999.

The population included in the Channeling Demonstration was not selected randomly. Their uniqueness is evident in the outcomes during the first year of the study; in that period, 26 percent of the participants died, and about 16 percent entered nursing homes. The results presented below characterize utilization for this high-risk segment of the population. Because this group is so unusual, one should draw only limited conclusions about utilization in the general population from this set of data.

Despite limited generalizability, analysis of the Channeling data can lead to several insights. These insights depend on the application of suitable statistical models to a data set with unusual characteristics. In the next section, we describe a method for obtaining more precise estimates of mortality and of nursing home utilization for various subgroups of the Channeling population.

Table 6.2   **Baseline Characteristics**

Variable	Mean	Standard Deviation	Min	Max
Age	79.5797	7.6981	64.0	103.0
Male	.2850	.4514	.0	1.0
Married	.3186	.4660	.0	1.0
Living alone	.3717	.4833	.0	1.0
Has living children	.6569	.4748	.0	1.0
Education	8.2552	4.0670	.0	18.0
Nonwhite	.2641	.4409	.0	1.0
Severe cognitive impairment	.1532	.3603	.0	1.0
Moderate cognitive impairment	.3193	.4662	.0	1.0
Mild or no cognitive impairment	.4697	.4991	.0	1.0
No ADLs and some IADLs	.1177	.3222	.0	1.0
No severe ADLs	.2083	.4061	.0	1.0
1 severe ADL	.2236	.4167	.0	1.0
2 or more severe ADLs	.5808	.4935	.0	1.0
Weighted number of ADL impairments	5.4801	3.8841	.0	12.0
Weighted number of IADL impairments	5.0815	3.6926	.0	14.0
No assets	.5524	.4973	.0	1.0
Assets $1–$5,000	.2442	.4296	.0	1.0
Assets $5,001–$10,000	.0826	.2754	.0	1.0
Assets > $10,000	.1208	.3259	.0	1.0
Income < $500 per month	.5508	.4975	.0	1.0
Income $500–$999 per month	.3508	.4773	.0	1.0
Income > $999 per month	.0984	.2979	.0	1.0
Own a home	.4206	.4937	.0	1.0
Receive Medicaid	.2277	.4194	.0	1.0
Receive private insurance	.5902	.4918	.0	1.0
In nursing home at baseline	.0407	.1976	.0	1.0
Any nursing home stays six months prior to baseline	.0847	.2784	.0	1.0
Dead at end of six months	.1545	.3614	.0	1.0
Dead at end of twelve months	.2608	.4391	.0	1.0
Dead at end of eighteen months	.3514	.4775	.0	1.0

$N = 5,625$

Note: Number of observations for dead at end of eighteen months = 2,820.

6.3   An Empirical Framework

This section develops a statistical model that enables us to predict nursing home utilization over a wide range of ages. The measure of utilization predicted in this analysis is the number of weeks spent in a nursing home by subgroups of the elderly, classified by demographic and other characteristics. A transition probability model (TPM), of the sort found in the analysis of Markov chains,[1] serves as the statistical foundation for this model. The absence of information on spell lengths significantly complicates estimating a

TPM using the Channeling data (with the public-use files currently available). This data source provides information on the total days an individual resides in nursing homes during each month, and it is possible to infer the number of admissions during this month, but the duration of individual admissions is unknown. Consequently, standard duration models cannot be applied to estimate a TPM with the Channeling data available. The following discussion proposes an alternative estimation procedure that can be implemented using the available information.

6.3.1   Transition Probabilities

A TPM to describe nursing home utilization must specify the probabilities that an elderly man or woman occupies particular "states of the world" and the transition probabilities for moving from one of these states to another. In our formulation, an individual may occupy any one of three states in a given week: if an elderly person resides in a nursing home for any part of a week, we classify him or her as being in state n; we assign this individual to occupancy in state c if he or she lives in the community (i.e., outside a nursing home); finally, we assign persons who have died to state d. Occupancy in state c captures a wide variety of circumstances, including hospitalization.

To characterize the stochastic process governing the transitions between states, let $\delta(t)$ and $y(t)$ denote two discrete random variables that can take the values of either zero or one in each week t. An individual is alive in week t if $y(t) = 1$ and is dead if $y(t) = 0$. Given $y(t) = 1$, an elderly person resides in a nursing home in week t if $\delta(t) = 1$ and lives in the community if $\delta(t) = 0$. Specifying the intertemporal stochastic properties of $\delta(t)$ and $y(t)$ determines the probabilities relevant to our TPM.

To introduce these probabilities, let $Z(t)$ represent the attributes of an individual that are deemed to influence the distributions of $\delta(t)$ and $y(t)$. Define

(1) $P[n \rightarrow c \mid Z(t)] = \text{prob}[\delta(t) = 0 \mid \delta(t-1) = 1, y(t) = 1, Z(t)],$

(2) $P[c \rightarrow n \mid Z(t)] = \text{prob}[\delta(t) = 1 \mid \delta(t-1) = 0, y(t) = 1, Z(t)],$

and

(3) $P[(n, c) \rightarrow d \mid Z(t)] = \text{prob}[y(t) = 0 \mid y(t-1) = 1, Z(t)].$

Expression (1) gives the probability that an elder moves from state n in period $t - 1$ to state c in period t given $Z(t)$ and survival until period t. Expression (2) provides an analogous relation for moving from state c to state n, and (3) shows the probability that an elderly person dies in week t. Because there is no return from state d (i.e., death is an absorbing state),

(4) $\text{prob}\,[y(t) = 1 \mid y(t-1) = 0, Z(t)] = 0,$

which simply indicates that y cannot return to one after it equals zero. Note that the relations given by (1)–(3) are not conventional transition probabilities. Expressions (1) and (2) condition on not being in state d in period t, and (3) provides the joint probability of moving from either state n or state c to state d. One can interpret this formulation as a nested two-state TPM. At the first level, the value of $y(t)$ determines whether state d or states (n, c) obtain. At the second level, $\delta(t)$ allocates individuals who are not in state d between the states n and c.

Our empirical analysis incorporates two categories of variables in $Z(t)$. The time-varying category contains only a single variable representing a person's age in week t, which we denote by $A(t)$ with $A(t) = A$ for all weeks in which an individual is A years old (i.e., a person between 70 and 71 is assigned $A = 70$ until he or she actually turns 71). The second category includes attributes of individuals reflecting their functional status, living arrangements, the presence of certain chronic conditions, and financial status, which are interpreted to be characteristics that do not change over time. Grouping this latter set of variables into the quantity X, we have $Z(t) = [A(t), X] = (A, X)$. The lack of data on spells limits the variables that can be included in $Z(t)$. Because we do not have data on spell lengths, we cannot allow for elaborate forms of duration dependence. Models of these forms of duration dependence require the inclusion of measures of spell durations in $Z(t)$.

This choice of Z effectively introduces three assumptions concerning the stochastic processes generating the discrete variables $\delta(t)$ and $y(t)$. The first is that these processes satisfy a Markov property; the second is that past values of $\delta(t)$ do not influence the value of $y(t)$;[2] and the third is that transition probabilities are constant over the period of time during which an individual is at a given age. With i and j denoting arbitrary states, this last assumption allows us to introduce the shorthand notation

$$(5) \qquad P[i \rightarrow j \mid Z(t)] = P_A(i \rightarrow j \mid X) \equiv P_A(i \rightarrow j)$$

for all t such that $A(t) = A$. This property amounts to assuming that weekly exit rates are stationary over any T-week period (with $T \leq 52$) in which a person's age does not change. While these assumptions imply that the discrete variable $y(t)$ follows a Markov process given a person's age, it does not imply this property in broader context because A is included as one of the characteristics determining probabilities. This admits a form of duration dependence in the distribution generating y that permits the likelihood of death to increase with age.

6.3.2   Predicting Nursing Home Utilization

Knowledge of the transition probabilities provides sufficient information to infer the distribution of the total time spent in nursing homes by a group of elderly persons over any age range and period. Given $P_A(n \rightarrow c)$, $P_A(c \rightarrow n)$,

$P_A[(n, c) \rightarrow d]$, and a set of characteristics X and starting values for δ and y, one can simulate a large number of sample paths for the variables $\delta(t)$ and $y(t)$ over time and, in doing so, can estimate the distributions of quantities that are averages of these variables such as the total weeks spent in nursing homes occurring in an age range.

The simulations for a person with a given set of characteristics proceed as follows. First, calculate the predicted values of the transition probabilities corresponding to the set of characteristics. Second, generate a random variable whose value determines that transition occurs; the probability of generating a random number that will yield a particular transition is equal to the transition probability. For example, if the probability of survival is .90 and only the transition to death is being considered, a uniformly distributed random number between zero and one might be drawn, and a transition to death would occur only if the number exceeded .9. After the simulated individual is assigned to a state for the next period, another random number is drawn to determine the following transition. This process is repeated until the simulated individual dies. At that point, the process begins again with a new person. By repeating this process (the results described here are based on five thousand repetitions), it is possible to generate the distributions of survival and of nursing home utilization.

6.4   An Estimation Procedure

In this section, we describe the procedure for estimating the transition probabilities that are used in the simulation. We first describe an approach for estimating $P_A(n \rightarrow c)$ and $P_A(c \rightarrow n)$ using the type of information provided by the Channeling data. We then describe a procedure for estimating $P_A[(n, c) \rightarrow d]$.

6.4.1   Specifying the Distribution of Accumulative Utilization

Over a fixed period of time (say, six months), the Channeling data offer sufficient information to infer the following three aspects of an individual's nursing home utilization: whether this person begins the period in or out of a nursing home; the total number of weeks of residence in a nursing home; and the total number of admissions. To use this information to estimate the probabilities associated with transitions between the states n and c, we require a formulation for the likelihood function describing these data.

Other measures of utilization can be constructed using the Channeling data. Consider a population of elderly individuals who are at the same age, over a period of observation of T weeks, who possess a common set of characteristics X, and who are alive for the entire period. Let S_n denote the number of distinct nursing home admissions experienced by an individual from this population during the weeks 1 to T; let S_c represent the number of distinct spells not in a nursing home; and let L denote the total number of weeks spent in a nursing home over this period. The variable S_n (or S_c) is incremented by one if a person is in a nursing home (not in a nursing home) in week 1 and each time thereafter that she transits from state c to state n (from n to c). Thus, S_n represents the number of nursing home admissions, and S_c represents the number of noninstitutional spells. The variables S_n and S_c need not be equal because spells may be interrupted either at the start or at the end of the sample period (i.e., there may be either left or right censoring). From the three informational items provided by the Channeling data listed above, one can construct observations for the variables $\delta(1)$ (i.e., whether an individual starts the period in a nursing home or not), L, S_n, and S_c.

To develop the implied specification of the likelihood function associated with these variables, consider the distribution for that segment of the population that resides in a nursing home during week 1, i.e., for which $\delta(1) = 1$. Let $G_A[S_n, S_c, L \mid \delta(1) = 1, T]$ denote the probability that a randomly drawn individual from this subpopulation experiences S_n nursing home spells, S_c spells outside a nursing home, and L total weeks in the nursing home over the period 1 to T conditional on living until period T. Given the statistical model introduced above, the implied specification for this joint probability is

(6)
$$G_A[S_n, S_c, L \mid \delta(1) = 1, T]$$
$$= K_n P_A(n \rightarrow n)^{L-S_n} P_A(n \rightarrow c)^{S_c} P_A(c \rightarrow c)^{T-L-S_c} P_A(c \rightarrow n)^{S_n-1},$$

where the quantity $K_n \equiv K_n(S_n, S_c, L, T)$ represents the number of unique ways in which the variables S_n, S_c, and L can occur in the T-week period. The quantity $P_A(n \rightarrow n) = 1 - P_A(n \rightarrow c)$ in this expression corresponds to the transition probability associated with staying in a nursing home from one week to the next, and, similarly, $P_A(c \rightarrow c) = 1 - P_A(c \rightarrow n)$ represents the probability of remaining in the community state. The probability function (6) determines the fraction of the elderly population who reside in nursing homes in week 1 who will eventually experience S_n and S_c spells and L weeks of occupancy.

Now consider the analogous distribution for the segment of the population that does not reside in a nursing home during week 1. Let $G_A[S_n, S_c, L \mid \delta(1) = 0, T]$ represent the probability of observing S_n, S_c, and L conditional on being in the community in week 1 and living until period T. This probability takes the form

(7)
$$G_A[S_n, S_c, L \mid \delta(1) = 0, T]$$
$$= K_c P_A(n \rightarrow n)^{L-S_n} P_A(n \rightarrow c)^{S_c-1} P_A(c \rightarrow c)^{T-L-S_c} P_A(c \rightarrow n)^{S_n},$$

where $K_c = K_n(S_c, S_n, T - L, T)$. This expression determines the fraction of the elderly who reside in the community in week 1 who will eventually experience S_n and S_c spells and L total weeks of institutionalization during the T-week period.

Combining these probability functions associated with the two segments of the elderly population achieves the goal of formulating a likelihood function that links the three aspects of nursing home utilization provided by the Channeling data. The implied specification is

$$(8) \qquad \mathcal{L}[S_n, S_c, L \mid \delta(1), T, A, X] =$$
$$G_A[S_n, S_c, L \mid \delta(1) = 1, T]^{\delta(1)} G_A[S_n, S_c, L \mid \delta(1) = 0, T]^{1-\delta(1)}.$$

Maximum likelihood estimation using (8) yields estimates of the transition probabilities $P_A(n \to c)$ and $P_A(c \to n)$. One can infer how these probabilities vary as functions of the age variable A and the characteristics X by introducing explicit functional forms for $P_A(n \to c)$ and $P_A(c \to n)$ in this estimation procedure. We use a binary logit functional form for these probabilities.

6.4.2 Specifying the Distribution of the Length of Life

The third transition probability that we need to know determines the time of death. The Channeling study provides information on the week that an elderly person dies if he or she does not survive until the end of the observation period. This information can be used to estimate $P_A[(n, c) \to d]$.

To develop a specification for the likelihood function describing the time of death, consider a population of elders who are at the same age over a period of T^* weeks and who possess a common set of characteristics X. To be included in this population, a person must be alive in week 1, i.e., $y(1) = 1$. The probability that a member of this population survives exactly T weeks for $T < T^*$ is

$$(9) \quad \text{prob}[y(T) = 0, y(T - 1) = 1, \ldots, y(2) = 1 \mid y(1) = 1, A, X]$$
$$= P_A[(n, c) \to (n, c)]^{T-1} P_A[(n, c) \to d],$$

where the quantity $P_A[(n, c) \to (n, c)] = 1 - P_A[(n, c) \to d]$ corresponds to the transition probability associated with remaining alive from one week to the next. The probability that a population member survives that entire $T = T^*$ weeks is

$$(10) \qquad \text{prob}[y(T) = 1, \ldots, y(2) = 1 \mid y(1), A, X]$$
$$= P_A[(n, c) \to (n, c)]^{T-1}.$$

The Channeling study includes information on T, the number of weeks that a sample member survives during an observation period of T^* weeks. According to (9) and (10), the likelihood function describing the distribution of T is given by

$$(11) \qquad \mathcal{L}[T \mid y(1) = 1, A, X]$$
$$= P_A[(n, c) \to (n, c)]^{T-1} P_A[(n, c) \to d]^{1-y(T^*)},$$

where $y(T^*) = 1$ if $T = T^*$ (i.e., if an individual survives the entire period). Applying maximum likelihood, using specification (11) enables one to estimate the transition probability $P_A[(n, c) \to d]$. With an explicit functional form for $P_A[(n, c) \to d]$ substituted into (11), one can further estimate the relation linking this probability to the age variable A and to the characteristics X. For the estimates we report below, we have used logit functions. To derive the predicted length of life, we employed simulation methods as described in the preceding section.

6.5   Empirical Analysis

The construction of the data sets for nursing home transitions and for transitions from living to dead is described in the appendix. The estimation procedure uses the maximum number of observations available for each follow-up period; that is, all individuals with complete information on the six-month follow-up are included, even though many were not included in the eighteen-month follow-up.

6.5.1   Estimating Transition Probabilities

The functional forms assumed for the transition probabilities are the following binary logistic equations:

$$(12) \qquad P_A(n \to c) = 1 / \left[1 + \exp\left\{ -\left(\sum_{i=0}^{5} A^i \beta_{11} + X\gamma_1 \right) \right\} \right],$$

$$(13) \qquad P_A(c \to n) = 1 / \left[1 + \exp\left\{ -\left(\sum_{i=0}^{5} A^i \beta_{12} + X\gamma_2 \right) \right\} \right],$$

$$(14) \qquad P_A[(n, c) \to d] = 1 / \left[1 + \exp\left\{ -\left(\sum_{i=0}^{5} A^i \beta_{13} + X\gamma_3 \right) \right\} \right].$$

The results of the logit estimates appear in tables 6.3–6.5. Variables included are demographic characteristics (i.e., race and sex); health and functional status measures (ADL and IADL impairments, dementia, other measures of cognitive impairment); social supports (marital status, number of living children); Medicaid and supplemental insurance coverage; and measures of financial well-being (variable for income below $500 per month, home ownership) and educational attainment. The specification allows for interactions between the severity and number of ADL impairments.

Table 6.3 presents estimates for the transition from community to nursing home. Notably, the factors that influence nursing home admission are largely distinct from those that are generally expected to influence health. Homeownership markedly diminishes the probability of nursing home entry. Having

Table 6.3   **Parameter Estimates for $P_A(c \to n)$**

Variable	Estimate
Constant	−4,229.9537
	(1,595.5759)
Age/10	2,570.5673
	(985.9692)
Age^2/10^3	−6,219.6365
	(2,426.4012)
Age^3/10^5	7,478.5185
	(2,972.6041)
Age^4/10^7	−4,468.4258
	(1,813.0247)
Age^5/10^9	1,061.3707
	(440.4258)
Education—9–11 years	−.079870
	(.076576)
Education—12 years	−.029645
	(.075007)
Education—over 12 years	−.043779
	(.092108)
Male	.105647
	(.061570)
Married	−.065005
	(.072989)
Living children	−.199735
	(.054644)
Nonwhite	−.887912
	(.073200)
Dementia	.520179
	(.098012)
ADL score	.137180
	(.062315)
Dementia • ADL score	−.014364
	(.014422)
1 severe ADL	.528313
	(.192858)
2 or more severe ADLs	.779851
	(.131734)
ADL • 1 severe ADL	−.218540
	(.087713)
ADL • 2 or more severe ADLs	−.131557
	(.063323)
Income less than $500 per month	.103728
	(.073897)
Own home	−.388055
	(.056903)
Medicaid	.581507
	(.064207)
Private insurance	.106319
	(.062844)

Note: Standard errors in parentheses. Total number of observations = 8,596.

Table 6.4   Parameter Estimates for $P_A(n \to c)$

Variable	Estimate
Constant	3,363.6942
	(1,999.0484)
Age/10	−2,109.0280
	(1,227.8786)
$Age^2/10^3$	5,258.6005
	(3,003.3717)
$Age^3/10^5$	−6,523.2438
	(3,656.8733)
$Age^4/10^7$	4,026.0538
	(2,216.5447)
$Age^5/10^9$	−989.0995
	(535.0832)
Education—9–11 years	.036003
	(.109582)
Education—12 years	.054864
	(.097245)
Education—over 12 years	−.323784
	(.123172)
Male	−.011968
	(.087073)
Married	.316133
	(.096487)
Living children	.185329
	(.077202)
Nonwhite	−.034065
	(.104408)
Dementia	−.484524
	(.130421)
ADL score	−.091484
	(.068393)
Dementia • ADL score	.020004
	(.019351)
1 severe ADL	−.052812
	(.221783)
2 or more severe ADLs	−.098761
	(.180023)
ADL score • 1 severe ADL	.165044
	(.093898)
ADL score • 2 or more severe ADLs	.094215
	(.069748)
Income less than $500/month	−.115566
	(.091941)
Own home	.144524
	(.075214)
Medicaid	.008409
	(.085629)
Private insurance	.175246
	(.081411)

Note: Standard errors in parentheses. Total number of observations = 8,596.

Table 6.5   **Parameter Estimates for $P_A[(n, c) \to d]$**

Variable	Estimate
Constant	249.4911
	(1,586.1160)
Age/10	−184.9339
	(981.1263)
$Age^2/10^3$	524.4331
	(2,416.9041)
$Age^3/10^5$	−730.9426
	(2,963.8794)
$Age^4/10^7$	501.7803
	(1,809.4293)
$Age^5/10^9$	−135.8604
	(439.9563)
Education—9–11 years	.028640
	(.082634)
Education—12 years	.044137
	(.080369)
Education—over 12 years	.036470
	(.089636)
Male	.617575
	(.062476)
Married	−.062005
	(.074941)
Has living children	−.068667
	(.058975)
Nonwhite	−.034362
	(.066414)
Dementia	.050580
	(.114349)
ADL score	−.008919
	(.081203)
Dementia • ADL score	.008523
	(.014900)
1 severe ADL	−.115739
	(.199950)
2 or more severe ADLs	−.184681
	(.152688)
ADL score • 1 severe ADL	.124168
	(.098132)
ADL score • 2 or more severe ADLs	.123985
	(.081870)
Income less than $500 per month	.108454
	(.073513)
Owns home	−.054480
	(.058230)
Medicaid	−.189711
	(.078321)
Private insurance	−.042883
	(.064451)

Note: Standard errors in parentheses. Total number of observations = 10,722.

living children and being nonwhite are associated with decreased risk of nursing home admission. As might be expected, Medicaid participation is associated with a markedly increased likelihood of transition to the nursing home, as are advanced age, functional impairments, and dementia. Income does not appear to have a major independent association with institutionalization.

As table 6.4 shows, the factors that are associated with increased duration of admission are not necessarily the factors that indicate strong risk of admission. Being married and having living children are associated with an increased probability of leaving a nursing home, confirming the important role of social supports, but owning a house is no longer significant, and Medicaid coverage does not seem to matter once an individual is in a nursing home. Even though supplemental insurance does not usually provide significant nursing home coverage, individuals who have such insurance appear to leave nursing homes earlier, although this variable is only marginally significant. Dementia is associated with a diminished probability of discharge.

Table 6.5 presents results for the survival probabilities. Note the diminished roles of socioeconomic factors and social supports. Being male markedly diminishes the likelihood of surviving, while Medicaid coverage is associated with increased survival. Functional limitations do not seem to affect mortality. The age variables are jointly significant.

Several findings emerge from these estimates. First, since the factors that influence survival are so different from the variables associated with nursing home utilization, future changes in nursing home utilization are likely to be highly dependent on the effects of new medical technology. Life-prolonging technology, for example, may have no effect on age-adjusted disability from chronic illness. Dementia does not increase mortality, at least in this population, and dementia is likely to be more common in the future as long as old-age survival continues to improve. Because there are no effective preventive measures or treatments for the most common causes of dementia, life-prolonging health interventions are likely to increase the demand for nursing home care. Similarly, since functional impairment is not closely related to mortality, any increases in its prevalence are sure to lead to more nursing home use.

Numerous studies have documented the association between socioeconomic factors and health status. The most important socioeconomic factors have been education and, to a lesser extent, income, wealth, occupation, and race. The Channeling data are not ideal for measuring the effects of these factors, particularly because the population studied was predominantly low income and had limited education. Nevertheless, our analysis found no evidence that these factors were closely tied to nursing home utilization, with two exceptions. Advanced education was associated with longer stays, and nonwhite race was associated with a lower probability of nursing home admission. The latter finding could reflect poor access to nursing home care for nonwhites, but by many measures utilization of acute health services is higher for nonwhites (some authors argue that increased utilization may not reflect adequate access to health care since low-income, nonwhite, and less educated people may have a much greater need for health care). These findings emerge in an analysis that controls for Medicaid coverage, which is more common among nonwhites.

6.5.2   Predicting Accumulative Utilization

The effects of these variables on measures of utilization are not readily interpreted from the logit parameters. Being male, for example, increases the transition probability to death, and it also raises the likelihood of nursing home admission (although its logit parameter in the community to nursing home transition is not statistically significant at the 5 percent level). Is total nursing home utilization greater for men or women of a given age and set of functional limitations? Questions such as these are best answered by the results of the simulations that generate cumulative utilization figures (accumulative measures) for specific subgroups. These results are reported in tables 6.6–6.9. The simulations are based on the transition probabilities estimated from the logit equations above.

Simulation results for several sets of representative individuals are presented in tables 6.6–6.9. The simulations are performed as described in section 6.3.2. In each simulation, transition probabilities are updated as an individual ages, but other variables (the X's in eq. [12]–[14]) are held at fixed values over time. In these tables, the utilization figures are divided into age categories. Each now gives the distribution of nursing home utilization associated with the indicated age category experienced by an individual who starts in the simulation at age 65. The expected number of weeks in nursing homes at the older ages is very small because the probability of surviving to very old age in this high mortality population is low.

In each table, the first set of simulations is for an individual with Medicaid coverage, and the second is for an otherwise identical person without Medicaid. Findings for individuals who have private health insurance are not presented; private insurance had little effect on predicted nursing home utilization in the simulations, except at advanced ages. Very few individuals are expected to survive that long, so this disparity has little effect on predicted overall utilization.

Table 6.6 simulates the distribution of nursing home use for a very high-risk individual—a severely impaired, unmarried 65-year-old male on Medicaid who does not own his home. The chance that he will enter a nursing before the age of 70, if he is on Medicaid, exceeds 70 percent; if he did not have Medicaid, he would have had a 54 percent chance of entering a nursing home in the same interval. On entering the nursing home, the Medicaid patient is expected to stay longer than his uninsured counterpart; the length of stay for nursing home admissions is forty-six weeks for the men on Medicaid and thirty-three weeks for the uninsured men, between the ages of 65 and 70. In

Table 6.6   **Distribution of Nursing Home Use**

Description of population characteristics:
    Demographic   Male, white, unmarried, living children, high school graduate
    Health status   Cognitively impaired, 2 severe ADL impairments
    Financial attributes Income over $500 per month, does not own home, Medicaid/no
                       Medicaid, no private insurance

Summary Statistics

	Probability of Not Entering a Nursing Home	Fraction Alive at Initial Age	Distribution of Nursing Home Utilization Given at Least One Admission			
			Mean Number of Weeks in Nursing Home	Quartiles for Number of Weeks		
				Q1	Q2	Q3
Medicaid:						
Age 65–70	.271	1	45.65	17	38	66
Age 70–75	.758	.289	50.82	20	42	74
Age 75–80	.940	.075	47.15	15	39	68
Age 80–85	.985	.019	51.45	22	44	76
Age 85–90	.996	.005	42.78	16	46	72
Age 90–95	.999	.001	43.50	7	80	80
Age 65–95	.265	1	61.44	20	47	94
No Medicaid:						
Age 65–70	.456	1	33.24	10	24	47
Age 70–75	.855	.212	36.00	11	27	53
Age 75–80	.976	.041	31.91	11	23	43
Age 80–85	.996	.006	34.43	8	29	38
Age 85–90	.999	.002	39.00	13	42	63
Age 90–95	1	0	. . .	. . .	. . .	. . .
Age 65–95	.443	1	42.99	11	29	62

every age category, both the likelihood and the duration of admission are longer for the Medicaid men.

At the older ages, the probability of nursing home admission is very low. This sample is not only at high risk of institutionalization but also dies at an increased rate. Fewer than 1 percent of the non-Medicaid men at age 65 are expected to live to age 80, so they are not likely to utilize nursing homes at advanced age, unless they are among the very few individuals who survive for more than a decade.

Less-impaired men with better social and economic supports are represented in table 6.7. The 65-year-old men represented here are married, have only one severe ADL impairment, and own their homes. About 58 percent of Medicaid men with these characteristics will enter a nursing home by the age of 70, while their non-Medicaid counterparts have a 38 percent chance of entering a nurs-

Table 6.7   **Distribution of Nursing Home Use**

Description of population characteristics:
  Demographic   Male, white, married, living children, high school graduate
  Health status   Cognitively impaired, 1 severe ADL impairment
  Financial attributes Income over $500 per month, owns home, Medicaid/no Medicaid, no
                      private insurance

			Summary Statistics			
				Distribution of Nursing Home Utilization Given at Least One Admission		
	Probability of Not Entering a Nursing Home	Fraction Alive at Initial Age	Mean Number of Weeks in Nursing Home	Quartiles for Number of Weeks		
				Q1	Q2	Q3
Medicaid:						
Age 65–70	.419	1	21.55	7	16	30
Age 70–75	.747	.397	22.40	8	17	32
Age 75–80	.914	.137	20.14	6	15	28
Age 80–85	.965	.052	22.80	8	18	34
Age 85–90	.988	.018	22.43	10	21	28
Age 90–95	.998	.004	25.42	6	13	20
Age 65–95	.377	1	33.69	10	23	47
No Medicaid:						
Age 65–70	.623	1	16.65	6	12	23
Age 70–75	.848	.329	18.77	6	14	26
Age 75–80	.962	.094	16.81	5	12	24
Age 80–85	.988	.025	18.02	7	15	25
Age 85–90	.996	.007	22.86	3	10	17
Age 90–95	.999	.001	16.67	2	4	44
Age 65–95	.560	1	22.98	7	16	31

ing home. For the men who are admitted to a nursing home, the distribution of length of stay is substantially shorter than for the men in table 6.6; both median and mean durations are roughly half as large.

The logit estimates suggest that women utilize nursing homes more heavily than men, but the size of this effect is not readily apparent. Women have significantly lower mortality rates, but sex seems to have no effect on duration of nursing home admission, independent of the other variables, and surviving men may have a higher risk of entering a nursing home. However, the coefficient of sex falls short of statistical significance at the 5 percent level of the logit regression predicting institutionalization. A comparison of table 6.6 and table 6.8, which gives predicted utilization for a high-risk woman who differs from the man in table 6.6 only in sex, clarifies the effects of sex on utilization in the severely impaired elderly. Medicaid coverage continues to be

Table 6.8   Distribution of Nursing Home Use

Description of population characteristics:
  Demographic   Female, white, unmarried, living children, high school graduate
  Health status   Cognitively impaired, 2 severe ADL impairments
  Financial attributes Income over $500 per month, does not own home, Medicaid/no
                       Medicaid, no private insurance

Summary Statistics

	Probability of Not Entering a Nursing Home	Fraction Alive at Initial Age	Mean Number of Weeks in Nursing Home	Distribution of Nursing Home Utilization Given at Least One Admission		
				Quartiles for Number of Weeks		
				Q1	Q2	Q3
Medicaid:						
Age 65–70	.192	1	50.07	22	42	73
Age 70–75	.562	.498	56.16	25	50	82
Age 75–80	.799	.233	51.72	21	45	76
Age 80–85	.903	.111	56.60	24	50	78
Age 85–90	.953	.052	62.86	26	56	93
Age 90–95	.983	.019	55.78	15	49	93
Age 65–95	.181	1	75.75	29	75	146
No Medicaid:						
Age 65–70	.348	1	36.97	13	29	53
Age 70–75	.677	.432	39.00	14	31	57
Age 75–80	.874	.176	35.65	12	29	49
Age 80–85	.952	.067	43.17	16	36	61
Age 85–90	.978	.027	41.16	12	30	57
Age 90–95	.995	.008	46.54	19	28	74
Age 65–95	.311	1	59.90	20	46	91

associated with increased utilization. At any age, a woman is more likely to enter a nursing home than a comparable man. If she enters a nursing home, she will tend to stay longer than her male counterpart. Of course, elderly women are not comparable to elderly men. They are more likely to be unmarried (because they usually survive their spouses) and to have functional impairments, so their nursing home utilization tends to be even higher, relative to men, than these results suggest.

The "best-risk" case is examined in table 6.9. This is a woman who may have IADL impairments but has no ADL or cognitive impairments. She is married, has children, and owns her home. While her projected mortality greatly exceeds that of the general population, it is less than that of the other categories examined here. Compared to the other simulated cases, she has better chances of staying out of a nursing home and spends less time there if

Table 6.9   **Distribution of Nursing Home Use**

Description of population characteristics:
Demographic   Female, white, married, living children, high school graduate
Health status   No cognitive impairment, no ADL impairments
Financial attributes Income over $500 per month, owns home, Medicaid/no Medicaid, no
                private insurance

Summary Statistics

			Distribution of Nursing Home Utilization Given at Least One Admission			
	Probability of Not Entering a Nursing Home	Fraction Alive at Initial Age	Mean Number of Weeks in Nursing Home	Quartiles for Number of Weeks		
				Q1	Q2	Q3
Medicaid:						
Age 65–70	.618	1	11.93	4	9	16
Age 70–75	.723	.647	12.78	4	9	17
Age 75–80	.834	.402	11.57	4	9	16
Age 80–85	.891	.250	12.52	4	9	17
Age 85–90	.929	.152	12.48	4	10	18
Age 90–95	.962	.086	13.49	4	10	20
Age 65–95	.417	1	21.92	7	16	31
No Medicaid:						
Age 65–70	.770	1	10.68	3	8	15
Age 70–75	.833	.600	10.91	4	8	15
Age 75–80	.904	.347	9.93	3	7	13
Age 80–85	.948	.195	11.45	4	8	16
Age 85–90	.967	.111	10.71	4	8	14
Age 90–95	.985	.050	10.84	4	9	15
Age 65–95	.594	1	15.66	5	11	22

she is admitted. While Medicaid coverage is associated with longer stays, the mean weeks in nursing home conditional on admission are never more than one week longer under Medicaid, over a five-year period, than for the non-Medicaid women. At any age, the probability of admission remains higher for Medicaid women.

These simulations demonstrate that a small number of characteristics distinguish groups of people with very different expected utilization patterns. Medicare partially covers nursing home stays that last one hundred days or less; this exceeds the median number of nursing home days in a five-year period for the "low-risk" women in table 6.9 who are admitted to nursing homes. They would be under the Medicare maximum even if all the days were incurred in a single admission. However, men like the individual in table 6.6 have a 70 percent chance of being admitted to a nursing home between the ages of 65 and 70; if they are admitted, they will spend nearly eleven months, on average, in a nursing home over that five-year period.

Although all the underlying characteristics ("*X* variables") have been held constant in these simulations, it is straightforward to allow the variables to change with time. For example, the utilization figures could be recalculated for a man initially free of functional impairments who faces a 5 percent annual risk of developing a severe ADL limitation.

Only a limited number of patterns of underlying characteristics are represented in these simulations. A much wider variety is possible, of course, but simulation for low-risk individuals is hazardous since the logit estimates were obtained from a sample of elderly people who had very high risks of institutionalization and death.

6.6   Conclusions

The population included in the Channeling Demonstration is not representative of elderly Americans. Because the inclusion criteria were designed to select a population that would use nursing homes heavily, Channeling participants were relatively sickly, disabled, cognitively impaired, and lacking in social and financial supports. Our analysis reveals the hazards of targeting a population this way: although Channeling participants were at high risk of entering a nursing home, they were also very likely to die. During the first twelve months of follow-up, more of them died than entered a nursing home. Furthermore, those who entered institutions often had short admissions.

Is it possible to select a population that is likely to utilize nursing homes more heavily than the Channeling population? We believe that it is possible since the determinants of institutionalization appear to be distinct from the factors associated with earlier death. In the Channeling population, mortality rates varied with age but not with many of the important determinants of nursing home admission, such as functional impairment and social supports. While advancing age is associated with a rising risk of institutionalization in the general population, within this sample age did not have large effects on nursing home utilization when functional status and support measures were taken into account. By emphasizing the factors that are associated with institutionalization but not death, one can define a population that is likely to use nursing homes heavily.

In summary, we find that the most disabled, sickly elderly may not be the heaviest utilizers of nursing homes. Such individuals die early. When they are admitted to nursing homes, death cuts their stays short. Our analysis leads us to speculate that a properly selected population less disabled than the Channeling participants would spend more time in nursing homes as a consequence of their greater life expectancy.

Appendix
The Channeling Data and Its Arrangement

From the original sample of 6,326 individuals, 700 were dropped because they did not complete the baseline interview. One person was dropped because he or she did not provide age data. The remaining individuals formed the research sample. About half (2,820) were followed for eighteen months after the baseline interview, while the rest were followed for twelve months or until death. The overall data set included baseline and six-month follow-up data on 5,625 individuals; twelve-month follow-up on 4,756 individuals (869 individuals died during the six months after the baseline interview); and eighteen-month follow-up on 2,075 individuals (2,820 less the 745 who died during the first twelve months).

To estimate the transition probabilities, we pooled data from each follow-up sample. This gave 12,456 observations of six-month periods. Observations were also deleted if they were missing data on key variables: education (840 dropped); functional limitations (466 dropped); income (287 dropped); home ownership (14 dropped); marital status (16 dropped); race (16 dropped); and Medicaid (95 dropped). The remaining 10,722 observations were used to estimate the transition probabilities to death. Because 2,126 observations lacked data on nursing home use, only 8,596 observations were included in the estimates of transitions between nursing home and community.

The following notes explain how the nursing home variables were constructed.

1. Skilled, intermediate, and other LTC facilities were included in the definition of nursing home stays.

2. Days in the nursing home were rounded to the nearest week.

3. The Channeling data did not report the dates of admission and discharge for each nursing home stay. The following assumptions were made to determine whether an individual was in a nursing home at the beginning of each period. The baseline survey recorded whether the individual was in a nursing home, so the initial status could be determined for the first six months of follow-up. For months 7–12, the individual was considered to be in a nursing home at the beginning of the interval if he or she was in the nursing home at the end of month 6 and was in a nursing home for any part of month 7. For months 13–18, the initial status was considered to be in nursing home if the individual was in a nursing home at the end of month 12 and was in a nursing home during months 13–18.

4. An individual who died during the first twelve months was considered to have died in a nursing home if he or she (*a*) was in a nursing home during the month of death or (*b*) was in a hospital during the month of death and had been in a nursing home the prior month.

5. An individual who died during months 13–18 was considered to have died in a nursing home if he or she (*a*) died in month 13 and was in a nursing

home during month 13 or (*b*) died during months 14–18 and spent more than half the days that he or she was alive during those months in a nursing home.

6. The number of community spells was assumed to equal the number of nursing home stays if the participant was in a nursing home at the beginning of the period but not at the end. If the participant was in a nursing home at both the beginning and the end of the period or died during the period, the number of community spells was assumed to equal the number of nursing home stays minus one. If the person was in the community at the beginning and the end of the period, the number of community spells was the number of nursing home stays plus one.

Notes

1. For further discussion of Markov chain models, see the textbooks by Bartholomew (1982) and Howard (1971).

2. Stated more precisely, $\delta(t)$ does not Granger-cause $y(t)$ so that

$$\text{prob}[y(t)|y(t - 1), \delta(t - 1), A(t), X] = \text{prob}[y(t)|y(t - 1), A(t), X].$$

References

Bartholomew, D. J. 1982. *Stochastic models for social processes.* 3d ed. New York: Wiley.

Blumenthal, D., M. Schlesinger, P. B. Drumheller, and the Harvard Medicare Project. 1986. The future of Medicare. *New England Journal of Medicine* 314:722–28.

Branch, L. G., and A. M. Jette. 1982. A prospective study of long-term care institutionalization among the aged. *American Journal of Public Health* 72:1373–79.

Branch, L. G., and N. E. Stuart. 1984. A five-year history of targeting home care services to prevent institutionalization. *Gerontologist* 24:387–91.

Carcagno, G. J., R. Applebaum, J. Christianson, et al. 1986. *The evaluation of the national long-term care demonstration: The planning and operational experience of the Channeling projects,* vol. 1. Princeton, N.J.: Mathematica Policy Research.

Cohen, M. A., E. J. Tell, and S. S. Wallack. 1986a. Client-related risk factors of nursing home entry among elderly adults. *Journal of Gerontology* 41:785–92.

———. 1986b. The lifetime risks and costs of nursing home use among the elderly. *Medical Care* 24:1161–72.

———. 1988. The risk factors of nursing home entry among residents of six continuing care retirement communities. *Journal of Gerontology* 43:S15–S21.

Doty, P., K. Liu, and J. Wiener. 1985. An overview of long-term care. *Health Care Financing Review* 6:69–78.

Feinstein, A. R., B. R. Josephy, and C. K. Wells. 1986. Scientific and clinical problems in indexes of functional disability. *Annals of Internal Medicine* 105:413–20.

Feller, B. A. 1983. Need for care among the noninstitutionalized elderly. In *Health, United States, 1983*. Department of Health and Human Services Publication no. (PHS) 84-1232. Washington, D.C.: U.S. Government Printing Office.

Gaumer, G. L., H. Birnbaum, F. Pratter, et al. 1986. Impact of the New York long-term home health care program. *Medical Care* 24:641–53.

Greenberg, J. N., and A. Ginn. 1979. A multivariate analysis of the predictors of long-term care placement. *Home Health Care Services Quarterly* 1:75–99.

Howard, R. 1971. *Dynamic probabilistic systems*, vols. 1, 2. New York: Wiley.

Hughes, S. L., D. S. Cordray, and V. A. Spiker. 1984. Evaluation of a long-term home care program. *Medical Care* 22:460–75.

Kane, R., and R. Matthias. 1984. From hospital to nursing home: The long term care connection. *Gerontologist* 24:604–9.

Katz, S. K., A. B. Ford, R. W. Moskowitz, B. A. Jackson, and M. W. Jaffe. 1963. Studies of illness in the aged: The index of ADL: A standardized measure of biological and psychosocial function. *Journal of the American Medical Association* 185:914–19.

Keeler, E., R. Kane, and D. Solomon. 1981. Short- and long-term residents of nursing homes. *Medical Care* 11:363–69.

Kemper, P. 1988. The evaluation of the national long-term care demonstration: 10. Overview of the findings. *Health Services Research* 23:161–74.

Kemper, P., M. Harrigan, R. S. Brown, et al. 1986. *The evaluation of the national long-term care demonstration: Final report*. Princeton, N.J.: Mathematica Policy Research.

Kovar, M. G. 1988. Aging in the eighties, people living alone—two years later. In *Advance Data from Vital and Health Statistics*, no. 149. Department of Health and Human Services Publication no. (PHS) 88-1250. Hyattsville, Md.: Public Health Service.

Lane, D., D. Uyeno, A. Stark, E. Kliewer, and G. Gutman. 1985. Forecasting demand for long-term care services. *Health Services Research* 20:435–60.

Lazenby, H., K. R. Levit, and D. R. Waldo. 1986. *Health Care Financing Notes*. HCFA Publication no. 03232. Washington, D.C.: U.S. Government Printing Office, Office of the Actuary, Health Care Financing Administration.

Liu, K., and K. G. Manton. 1984. The characteristics and utilization pattern of an admission cohort of nursing home patients (II). *Gerontologist* 24:70–76.

Manheim, L. M., and S. L. Hughes. 1986. Use of nursing homes by a high-risk long-term care population. *Health Services Research* 21:161–76.

Manton, K. G., M. A. Woodbury, and K. Liu. 1984. Life table methods for assessing the dynamics of U.S. nursing home utilization: 1976–1977. *Journal of Gerontology* 39:79–87.

McConnel, C. E. 1984. A note on the lifetime risk of nursing home residency. *Gerontologist* 24:193–98.

Meiners, M. R. 1983. The case for long-term care insurance. *Health Affairs* 3:56–78.

Muurinen, J.-M. 1986. The economics of informal care: Labor market effects in the national hospice study. *Medical Care* 24:1007–17.

Nocks, B. C., R. M. Learner, D. Blackman, and T. E. Brown. 1986. The effects of a community-based long term care project on nursing home utilization. *Gerontologist* 26:150–57.

Palmore, E. 1976. Total chance of institutionalization among the aged. *Gerontologist* 16:504–7.

Rosenwaike, I. 1985. A demographic portrait of the oldest old. *Milbank Memorial Fund Quarterly* 63:187–205.

Shapiro, E., and L. M. Webster. 1984. Nursing home utilization patterns for all Manitoba admissions, 1974–1981. *Gerontologist* 24:610–15.

Spitzer, W. O. 1987. State of science, 1986: Quality of life and functional status as target variables for research. *Journal of Chronic Diseases* 40:465–71.

Taeuber, C. M. 1983. America in transition: An aging society. In *Current Population Reports,* ser. P-23, no. 128. Washington, D.C.: Census Bureau.

U.S. Department of Health and Human Services. 1986. *Report to the President: Catastrophic illness expenses.* Washington, D.C.: Department of Health and Human Services.

Vicente, L., J. A. Wiley, and R. A. Carrington. 1979. The risk of institutionalization before death. *Gerontologist* 19:361–67.

Weissert, W. G. 1985. Seven reasons why it is so difficult to make community-based long-term care cost-effective. *Health Services Research* 20:423–33.

Wingard, D. L., D. W. Jones, and R. M. Kaplan. 1987. Institutional care utilization by the elderly: A critical review. *Gerontologist* 27:156–63.

Yordi, C. L., and J. Waldman. 1985. A consolidated model of long-term care: Service utilization and cost impacts. *Gerontologist* 25:389–97.

Comment   Joseph P. Newhouse

This paper is motivated by a desire to improve the ability to predict nursing home utilization among the elderly; its premise is that the primitive methods and results in the literature with respect to this issue have impeded the development of long-term care insurance.

The methodology used in this paper is an improvement over the existing literature in several regards, as pointed out by the authors. Many studies look only at admission and do not study duration. Those that do study duration do not control for detailed patient characteristics. Further, the results in the literature tend to be based on data from single areas, which naturally raises an issue of generalizability.

I wish to focus my comments on two issues: the degree to which these estimates are generalizable and then, even if the estimates are generalizable, whether a lack of such estimates has been a major impediment in developing long-term care insurance.

Suppose for the moment that we accept the argument that estimates of the transition probabilities such as those in this paper are important in developing long-term care insurance. Should we believe the estimates in the paper?

It is clear from the title of the paper, which includes the term "high-risk elderly," that the authors have a nonrepresentative sample of the elderly. The sample was limited to the high-risk elderly, as defined by the criteria in table 6.1, because, as the authors explain, with a random sample of the elderly either

Joseph P. Newhouse is the John D. and Catherine T. MacArthur Professor of Health Policy and Management at Harvard University and director of the Division of Health Policy Research and Education. He is also the founding editor of the *Journal of Health Economics.*

a longer follow-up or a larger sample would have been required to obtain reliable estimates of the effect of channeling, the purpose for which the data were collected. The advantages of this sample for estimating the effect of channeling, however, do not carry over for the authors' purposes.

The channeling sample is not a representative sample from the population that will be insured by long-term care insurance, and apparently these results cannot be reweighted to reflect the population that will be covered. Thus, I consider trying to use these estimates to predict the cost of a universal public long-term care insurance plan, and simply note that I think it would be even more difficult to apply them to a likely private insurance scenario, namely, an employer who provided long-term care insurance as a fringe benefit to employees and to retirees.

The main point is that suitably reweighted estimates are likely to be very different from the estimates here. For example, table 6.9 presents, among other things, the predicted likelihood of death for a cohort of white females who are high school graduates, who are married with living children, and who have an income over $500 per month and own their own home. Based on results for these covariates in table 6.5, which certainly accord with expectations, this subgroup of white females should have a more favorable mortality experience than the average for all white females. In 1980, the annual death rate for all white females 65–74 was .020666 (USDHHS 1985, table 10). Approximating cumulative mortality by treating the death rate as constant within the interval, 81 percent of an average white female cohort alive at age 65 should be alive at age 75. Using the same method to project to age 85 (and the 75–84 annual mortality rate of .054017), 47 percent of that white female cohort would be alive at age 85.

Yet the predicted fraction alive in this sample at age 75 is 37 percent, less than half as large as for an average cohort, and at age 85 is 11 percent, less than a quarter as large as the average. Thus, as the authors say in their conclusion, it seems likely that nursing home experience will be greater among a cohort of women with 47 percent alive at age 85 than among a cohort with 11 percent alive at age 85.[1]

Although the mortality differences between this sample and the general population make the point of unrepresentativeness, it is emphasized by other major differences between the sample and the over-65 population. For example, the percentage white among the elderly over 65 in 1980 exceeded 90 percent (USDOC 1986, 34), but in this sample it is only 74 percent. Only 12 percent of this sample had assets greater than $10,000, but median wealth among the over 75 in 1983 was $36,000 (USDOC 1986, 451). Over half the over 65 have no limitations attributable to health (USDHHS 1985, table 31), but in this sample (according to table 6.1) all the participants were to have a limitation in the activities of daily living (ADL) (though table 6.2 tells us that at least 12 percent in fact had no such limitation; the ''at least'' refers to the fact that 12 percent had no ADLs but some instrumental activities of daily living [IADL]).

Now I would like to turn to the broader issue of long-term care insurance. Suppose that in fact this study had been carried out on a large national probability sample rather than the sample from the Channeling Demonstration. Suppose further that duration data were available. If the methods used here (or rather the improved methods that would exploit the duration data) were applied to such data, how useful would the results be to a potential long-term care insurer? Instead of estimates of use, such an insurer needs estimates of cost, unless the insurance policy is of the form that the insurer pays a fixed number of dollars per day in the nursing home. Bringing cost into the picture, however, both complicates the data collection and means that it is cost rather than duration of stay that should be estimated.

But suppose one had collected cost data so that one could give an estimate in dollars rather than days. Is the lack of a reliable estimate of that sort why we do not observe private long-term care insurance? I doubt it, although I think it is well worth pondering why there is so little private insurance for long-term care. One explanation is misperception on the part of the elderly that Medicare covers long-term care (Task Force on Long Term Health Care Policies 1987). This explanation is hardly satisfying to an economist; among other things, it cannot explain why an insurer has not sought to educate the elderly. (Of course, for any one insurer there is a free-rider problem, but that is the case for advertising in any industry with several firms.) Another possibility is that the availability of Medicaid stifles the private market, but this should apply only to elderly with little wealth to protect from the Medicaid spendown rule. Pauly (1989, 1990) has cited other reasons: the elderly might not wish to transfer income to the sick state or may not want to make it too easy for children to substitute formal care for their own care.

My guess, though it is only a guess, is that the problem lies deeper than a lack of good cost estimates. It is likely that, if one sold individual long-term care insurance among the elderly, there would be a serious adverse selection problem, and there would probably be a moral hazard problem as well.

An alternative to individual insurance among the over 65 is to sell to groups under 65 (e.g., have an employer purchase such insurance as a fringe). But selling insurance to groups under 65 might pose two types of systematic risk that could lead to high loadings. Both risks arise because, unlike traditional group health insurance, the payout is several years downstream from the premium. The first risk concerns the relative price of nursing home services in the future. If the insurance company is to bear the risk of price changes (or, say, 80 percent of them through a coinsurance rate), the risk for the insurance company would be systematic across all policies. An insurer can avoid such risk by limiting payouts to X per day, and, apparently, many policies now on the market in fact do this; that the policies do this suggests to me that this type of risk may be a problem. Of course, such a policy leaves the insured bearing the risk of incorrect estimates of future nursing home prices and may therefore be unattractive as insurance (i.e., there may not be much demand for such policies).

A second type of systematic risk in selling to the under 65 is a change in disease, for example, an increase in the incidence of Alzheimer's disease, or a marked change in mortality. The fragility of predicting is emphasized by the change in mortality rates; between 1980 and 1984 mortality for white males over 65 fell 6.25 percent, but for white females over 65 it fell only 1.7 percent; by contrast, between 1970 and 1980 the percentage reductions for each sex were virtually identical, a little over 16 percent for each (USDHHS 1985, table 10). Changes in mortality risk are a problem in life insurance as well, but payouts in long-term care insurance will be more sensitive to changes in mortality rates among the very old (e.g., over 85) because of the concentration of long-term care use there (see n. 1 above). Mortality rates among the very old are likely to be more variable than mortality rates across all age groups because of the low mortality rates among the under 65.

Another problem with private insurance is uncertainty about a future public program. Because so little is known about what such a program might look like, it would be difficult, one would think, to write a contingent contract.

In sum, good estimates of utilization of long-term care services are necessary for developing long-term care insurance but may not be the key obstacle to private long-term care insurance. This emphatically does not mean that we should not be working on estimates of demand for long-term care. I think we should especially want to know what the insurance elasticity of demand is for purposes of costing possible public programs, if nothing else. Toward that end, what I take away from this effort is that at a minimum we need a sample that is representative of a general population, and it would be even better if there were some exogenous variation in insurance in that sample.

Note

1. This claim relies on the fact that in the general population nursing home use rises sharply with age. The probability in 1977 of an average female's 65–74 being in a home is .016, for a female 75–84 it is .086, and for females 85 and over it is .252 (USDHHS 1985, table 56). Nonetheless, it is possible that utilization in this very sick cohort would be greater, especially if future utilization is discounted.

References

Pauly, Mark V. 1989. Optimal public subsidies of nursing home insurance in the United States. *Geneva Papers in Risk and Insurance* 14 (January):3–10.
———. 1990. The rational nonpurchase of long-term-care insurance. *Journal of Political Economy* 98, no. 1 (February):153–68.

Task Force on Long Term Health Care Policies. 1987. *Report to the Congress and the Secretary.* Washington, D.C.: U.S. Government Printing Office, 21 September.

U.S. Department of Commerce (USDOC). Bureau of the Census. 1986. *Statistical Abstract, 1987.* Washington, D.C.: U.S. Government Printing Office, December.

U.S. Department of Health and Human Service (USDHHS). 1985. *Health, United States, 1985.* Publication no. (PHS) 86-1232. Washington, D.C.: U.S. Government Printing Office.

7   The Pension Inducement to Retire: An Option Value Analysis

James H. Stock and David A. Wise

The labor force participation rates of older workers have declined dramatically in recent years. The data for men show the trend:

	Age			
Year	50–54	55–59	60–64	65+
1971	92.8	88.8	74.1	25.5
1986	88.9	79.0	54.9	17.5

A great deal of analysis has emphasized the role of Social Security provisions in encouraging earlier retirement. Recent examples are Blinder, Gordon and Wise (1980), Burkhauser (1980), Hurd and Boskin (1981), Gustman and Steinmeier (1986), Burtless and Moffitt (1984), Burtless (1986), and Hausman and Wise (1985). Several of these papers direct attention to the large increases in Social Security benefits in the early 1970s. These papers for the most part show only a modest effect of these increases on labor force participation rates; Hurd and Boskin (1981) is an exception.

Largely ignored have been firm pension plans. Firm pension plans were introduced rapidly beginning in the 1950s. Now about 50 percent of employees

David A. Wise is the John F. Stambaugh Professor of Political Economy at the John F. Kennedy School of Government, Harvard University, and a research associate and director of the Economics of Aging Project at the National Bureau of Economic Research. James H. Stock is associate professor of public policy at the John F. Kennedy School of Government, Harvard University, and a faculty research fellow at the National Bureau of Economic Research.

The authors wish to thank Vivian Ho and Robin Lumsdaine for their considerable research assistance. Financial support was provided by the National Institute on Aging, the National Science Foundation, and the Hoover Institution.

are covered by firm plans. The proportion of retiring workers that is covered by a firm pension has risen rapidly. It increased from about 4 to 25 percent between 1950 and 1980 and is still increasing. About 75 percent of covered employees have defined benefit plans. The benefit under such a plan is the promise by the employer to pay the worker a specified amount at retirement. The amount is typically determined by final salary and years of firm employment. Bulow (1981) described pension wealth accrual under these plans, and Lazear (1983) emphasized the potential role of plan provisions in inducing early retirement, as a substitute for mandatory retirement. The very substantial incentive effects of these plans have been emphasized most recently by Kotlikoff and Wise (1985, 1987, 1989), who summarize the incentives of approximately 2,500 plans covered by the Bureau of Labor Statistics Level of Benefits Survey and consider in great detail the effects of the provisions of a large *Fortune* 500 firm. This work demonstrates that the typical firm plan provides a large reward for remaining with the firm until some age, often the early retirement age, and then a substantial inducement to leave the firm, often as early as 55. Almost all plans incorporate a large penalty for working past age 65. The gain in wage earnings from working an additional year is often offset in large part by a loss in the present value of future pension benefits.

There has been very little analysis of the actual effects of these incentives on retirement, however. Exceptions are Burkhauser (1979), Fields and Mitchell (1982), Lazear (1983), Kotlikoff and Wise (1987), and Hogarth (1988). One reason for the limited attention has been the absence of appropriate data. The analysis in this paper is based on the personnel records of a large *Fortune* 500 firm. The firm pension plan was described in detail by Kotlikoff and Wise (1987), who also related the plan provisions to departure rates from the firm.

The goal of this paper is to quantify the effects of pension plan provisions on departure rates from the firm and, in particular, to demonstrate the effect of potential changes in plan provisions. A particularly important component of the analysis is to demonstrate the relative effects of changes in Social Security versus firm pension plan provisions. The analysis is based on the "option value" model developed in Stock and Wise (1988).

The primary conclusions are:

- Firm plans have a much greater effect than Social Security provisions on employee retirement decisions.
- The effect of changes in Social Security provisions that are intended to prolong the labor force participation of the elderly, like the planned increase in the retirement age, may be offset by the response of firms to the change.

We begin in section 7.1 with a description of the incentive effects faced by workers in the firm. The description of the incentive effects is also used to motivate our method of analysis. The option value model and parameter estimates are summarized in section 7.2. Simulations of the effect on departure rates of changes in firm pension plan and in Social Security provisions are discussed in section 7.3. A summary and concluding discussion is provided in the last section.

7.1   The Firm Pension Plan and Retirement Incentives

The analysis in this paper is based on salesmen who are at least 50 years old and have been employed for at least three years.[1] To understand the effect of the pension plan provisions, consider several figures. Figure 7.1 shows the expected future compensation of a person from our sample who is 50 years old and has been employed by the firm for twenty years.[2] It is important to consider total compensation—including wage earnings, the accrual of pension benefits, and the accrual of Social Security benefits. As compensation for working another year, the employee receives salary earnings. He also receives compensation in the form of future pension benefits. The annual compensation in this form is the change in the present value of future pension benefits, due to working an additional year. This accrual is comparable to wage earnings. The accrual of Social Security benefits may also be calculated in a similar manner and is also comparable to wage earnings. Figure 7.1 shows the present value at age 50 of expected future compensation in all three forms. The line labeled earnings represents cumulated earnings, by age of retirement.[3] For example, if the person were to retire at age 62, his cumulated earnings between age 50 and age 62, discounted to age 50 dollars, would be about $300,000. The slope of the earnings line represents annual earnings discounted to age 50

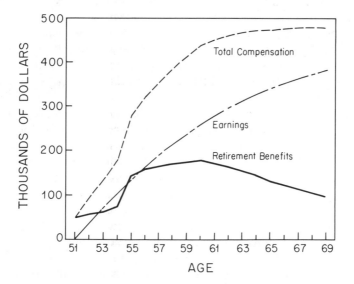

Fig. 7.1   Future compensation of a typical employee

dollars. Earnings decline rather slowly through age 60 and much more rapidly thereafter.

The solid line shows the present value of pension plus Social Security benefits, again discounted to age 50 dollars. The shape of this profile is determined primarily by the pension plan provisions. The most important provisions are described here.[4] An employee could leave the firm at age 53, for example. If he were to do that, and if he were vested in the firm's pension plan—which occurs after ten years of service—he would be entitled to normal retirement pension benefits at age 65, based on his years of service and *current* dollar earnings at age 53. He could start to receive benefits as early as age 55, the pension early retirement age, but the benefit amount would be reduced actuarially. If he started to receive benefits at age 55, they would be only 36 percent of the dollar amount he would receive at age 65. If, however, he were to remain in the firm until the early retirement age, the situation would be quite different. He would be entitled to normal retirement benefits based on his years of service and salary at age 55. But, if he were to start to receive them at age 55, the benefits would be reduced less than actuarially, about 3 percent for each year that retirement precedes age 65, instead of 6 or 7 percent. In addition, the plan has a Social Security offset provision. Pension benefits are offset by a specified amount, depending on the firm estimate of Social Security benefits. But if the person takes early retirement, between 55 and 65, the Social Security offset is not applied to benefits received before age 65. These two provisions create the large discontinuous jump in retirement benefits at age 55; there is an enormous bonus for remaining with the firm until that age. After age 55, however, the person who does not retire forgoes the opportunity of taking pension benefits on very advantageous terms—thus the minimal change in the discounted value of benefits between 55 and 60. If a person has thirty years of service at age 60, he is entitled to full normal retirement benefits. No early retirement reduction is applied to benefits if they are taken then. That is, by continuing to work he will no longer gain from fewer years of early retirement reduction, as he did before age 60. Thus, the kink in the profile and the decline thereafter.

The top line shows total compensation. The large jump at 55 reflects the early retirement provisions of the pension plan. Total compensation declines modestly each year through age 60 and very rapidly thereafter. After age 62 or 63, total compensation is close to zero. Under these circumstances, it would be surprising if this person were to continue to work until age 65.

The graph can also be used to motivate the option value model used in the subsequent analysis. Suppose that the person depicted in figure 7.1 is considering whether to retire now, at age 50. If he does, he will receive utility indirectly from the retirement benefits that he will receive until he dies. (In fact, he will not be able to receive firm pension benefits until age 55, and Social Security benefits cannot be taken until age 62.) If he leaves the firm at age 50, though, he forgoes the option of retiring at some future age. In this case, there will be a large increase in pension benefits at age 55, and thus a jump in total lifetime income, if he postpones retirement until then. Some later age may be even more advantageous. In particular, if he does not retire, he maintains the option of retiring at the future age that for him yields the highest expected utility. The central feature of the option value model is that the person will postpone retirement at age 50 if, based on his expectations at age 50, the best of the future possibilities is better than retiring now. That is, he postpones retirement if the value of the option to retire later exceeds the value of retiring today. At each subsequent age, he will make the same comparison. At some age, future retirement possibilities will look worse than immediate retirement, and he will leave the firm.

It is clear that the early retirement provisions in this firm are likely to have an important effect on retirement decisions. The qualitative effect of changing the early retirement age can be seen by comparing figures 7.1 and 7.2. Figure 7.2 describes the expectations of the same person considered in figure 7.1, except that the firm early retirement age has been shifted from 55 to 60, with all other plan provisions remaining unchanged. It is apparent that the person would under these provisions be much less likely to retire before age 60. Estimates of the effects of such a change are presented below.

To calculate the amounts graphed in figures 7.1 and 7.2, future income is discounted at a 5 percent real interest rate and no distinction is made between individual valuation of wage earnings versus pension benefits. To predict retirement, however, the relevant values are not these but rather the discounted value of future utilities based on the weights that individuals assign to future income streams in determining whether to retire. Such values are estimated in

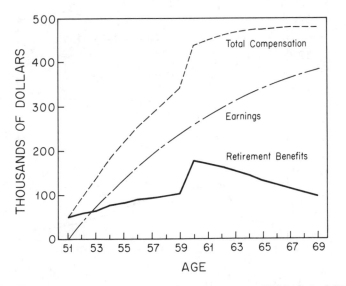

Fig. 7.2   Future compensation with early retirement at 60 instead of 55

the subsequent analysis. As it turns out, the estimated discount rate is much higher than 5 percent, and individuals value a dollar of retirement benefits much more than a dollar of wage earnings; a dollar without work is better than a dollar with work. Based on our parameter estimates, the graph, from the point of view of the individual, would look like figure 7.3 instead of figure 7.1. Based on these valuations of future income streams, the person depicted in figure 7.1 would be much more likely to retire before age 60, say, than is in fact suggested by figure 7.1.

Persons of the same age face very different options depending on years of service and earnings histories. A comparison of figures 7.1 and 7.4 demonstrates this point. The person whose expected future options are shown in figure 7.4 has only three years of service when he is 50 years old. He will not have thirty years of service until he is 77. He will not be vested until he is 57. Compared to the person in figure 7.1, this person would apparently be much less likely to retire before age 65.

Finally, consider a person who is still working at age 58 in 1980. He has eighteen years of service. His expected future options are shown in figure 7.5. Although his wage earnings will decrease only slightly in the next ten years, the present value of retirement benefits will decline almost continuously. The graph suggests that retirement would be likely around 63 or 64. It was clear from a comparison of figures 7.1 and 7.2 that changing the firm early retirement age from 55 to 60 would have a substantial effect on retirement. The potential effect of changes in Social Security provisions can be seen by altering the options faced by the person described in figure 7.5. The current Social Security rules reduce benefits by 5/9 of a percent for each month that benefits

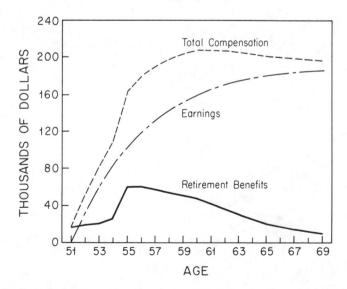

Fig. 7.3   Future compensation based on estimated valuation of future income

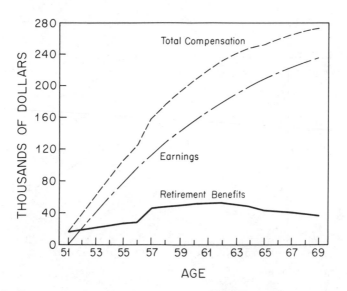

Fig. 7.4   Future compensation for a person with only three years of service at age 50

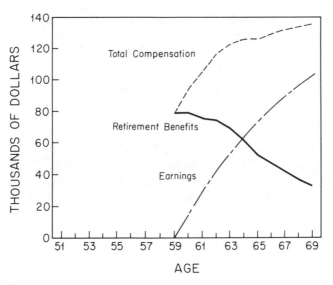

Fig. 7.5   Future compensation from age 58

are taken before age 65. Suppose that the reduction were 1 percent per month instead of 5/9. The effect on the options faced by the figure 7.5 person are shown in figure 7.6. The effect is noticeable, but not extreme. The value of retirement benefits before age 65 has been shifted downward, and thus total income associated with retirement before age 65 has been shifted downward.

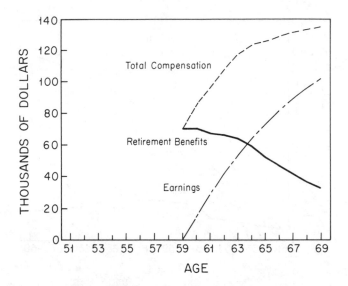

Fig. 7.6 Future compensation from age 58 with the Social Security early retirement reduction at 1 instead of 5/9 percent

The result would apparently be a lower likelihood of retirement between 62 and 65, judging by the change in the graph. Actual estimates of the effect of such a change in Social Security provisions are presented below.

7.2   The Option Value Model and Estimation Results

7.2.1   The Model

The details of the option value model are presented in Stock and Wise (1988). The key elements of the model are summarized here.[5] Assume that the value $V_t(r)$ of working from age t to age $r - 1$ and then retiring can be measured by the indirect utility from future earnings and retirement benefits. It is described by

$$(1) \qquad V_t(r) = \sum_{s=t}^{r-1} \beta^{s-t} U_w(Y_s) + \sum_{s=r}^{S} \beta^{s-t} U_r[B_s(r)].$$

If the person continues to work, his wage earnings in year s are given by Y_s and the indirect utility from these earnings by $U_w(Y_s)$. The weight assigned to future utility, in the determination of the retirement decision, is β. If he retires in year r, he will receive retirement benefits $B_s(r)$ in subsequent years s, which he values according to the function $U_r[B_s(r)]$. As explained above, a person's retirement benefits will depend on his age and years of service at the time of retirement r as well as on his earnings history—thus the notation indicating that

B_s is a function of r. (We adopt the convention that, if s is the first calendar year during which the person has no wage earnings, he is assumed to have retired at the age that he was on 1 January of year s.)

Thus $E_t V_t(r)$ is the expected value at age t from working through age $r - 1$ and retiring at age r, and $E_t V_t(t)$ is the expected value associated with current retirement. Suppose that r^* is the value of r that maximizes $E_t V_t(r)$. The person postpones retirement at age t if $G_t(r^*) > 0$. That is, the decision rule that we assume is: Postpone retirement if

$$(2) \qquad\qquad G_t(r^*) = E_t V_t(r^*) - E_t V_t(t) > 0.$$

If $G_t(r^*) < 0$, the person retires at age t. Thus $G_t(r)$ is the retirement decision function.

Following Stock and Wise (1988), the two indirect utility functions are specified as

$$(3) \qquad\qquad U_w(Y_s) = Y_s^\gamma + \omega_s ,$$

$$U_r(B_s) = [kB_s(r)]^\gamma + \xi_s ,$$

where ω_s and ξ_s are individual-specific random effects. The parameter k is to recognize the possibility that a dollar with leisure—while retired—is better than a dollar that is only had together with work. The random terms reflect a variety of unobserved differences among individuals. The values that individuals attach to wage and pension income may differ. Some persons may enjoy work more than others; some may enjoy retirement more than others. Both may be affected by health status, for example. Retirement decisions are likely to be affected by assets, other than pension wealth, which we do not measure. Such differences will be reflected in different values of ξ. In addition, we consider retirement to be the alternative to continued employment with the firm. For some, especially the younger persons in the sample, the alternative may well be another job. The utility of the alternative to work in such cases will presumably be greater than the utility represented by $U_r(B_s)$ for the typical person. These differences too will be reflected in different values of ξ. (The heteroskedastic error structure that the model implies, as explained below, is well suited to capture the effects of alternatives other than retirement, with the likelihood of such an alternative greatest for younger employees.)

Differences in preferences for work versus retirement, differences in health status, and other individual differences are likely to persist. Thus, these terms are assumed to follow a random walk over time. That is,

$$(4) \qquad\qquad \omega_s = \omega_{s-1} + \epsilon_{\omega s} , \quad E_{s-1}(\epsilon_{\omega s}) = 0,$$

$$\xi_s = \xi_{s-1} + \epsilon_{\xi s} , \quad E_{s-1}(\epsilon_{\xi s}) = 0.$$

We adopt the convention that at time s the individual knows ω_s and ξ_s; his forecasts of future ω and ξ are based on (5). The random walk assumption means, for example, that, if a person's health status worsens between periods t and $t + 1$, his expected health status in period $t + 2$ is not what it was in period t but rather what it was in period $t + 1$.

As shown in Stock and Wise (1988), with the substitution of the specifications (3) and (4), $G_t(r)$ may be decomposed into two terms, one depending on the individual-specific random terms ω_s and ξ_s, the other depending only on forecasts of measured variables. They are given by

$$(5) \qquad g_t(r) = \sum_{s=t}^{r-1} \beta^{s-t} \pi(s|t) E_t(Y_s^\gamma) + \sum_{s=r}^{S} \beta^{s-t} \pi(s|t) \{E_t[kB_s(r)]^\gamma\}$$

$$- \sum_{s=t}^{S} \beta^{s-t} \pi(s|t) \{E_t[kB_s(t)]^\gamma\}$$

and

$$(6) \qquad \phi_t(r) = \left[\sum_{s=t}^{r-1} \beta^{s-t} \pi(s|t)\right](\omega_t - \xi_t) = K_t(r)v_t \ ,$$

where $v_t = (\omega_t - \xi_t)$, $K_t = \sum_{s=t}^{r-1}\beta^{s-t}\pi(s|t)$, and $\pi(s|t)$ denotes the probability that the person will be alive in year s, given that he is alive in year t. The further r is in the future, the larger is $K_t(r)$. That is, the more distant the potential retirement age, the greater the uncertainty about it. This yields a heteroskedastic disturbance term.

In short, $G_t(r)$ may be written simply as

$$(7) \qquad G_t(r) = g_t(r) + K_t(r)v_t \ .$$

The probability of retirement is easily described using this expression. If $r^\dagger$ is the r that yields the maximum value of $g_t(r)/K_t(r)$, the probability of retirement becomes

$$(8) \qquad \Pr[\text{retire in year } t] = \Pr[g_t(r^\dagger)/K_t(r^\dagger) < -v_t].$$

To predict whether a person in the sample in year $t - 1$ retires in year t, equation (8) is all that is needed. Finally, we assume that v_t is normally distributed with variance σ_v^2. The parameters to be estimated are γ, k, r (where $\beta = 1/[1 + r]$), and σ_v.

In fact, we are able to follow persons in the sample for five consecutive years. The analysis in this paper, however, is based only on data for one year. Retirement probabilities for several years may be derived as a simple extension of (8); they are shown in Stock and Wise (1988), together with estimates based on several consecutive years for each person.[6]

7.2.2   Parameter Estimates

Evaluation of $g_t(r)/K_t(r)$ requires estimates of future earnings. Individual forecasts are based on a second-order autoregression that recognizes individual differences in earnings potential and accounts for past evidence of earnings increases. The autoregression was estimated using the individual earnings histories of all salesmen employed at least three years, with earnings converted to 1980 dollars using the Consumer Price Index. The parameters of the forecasting model depend on age, years of service, and an interaction term. The option value model parameter estimates (and standard errors) are[7]

γ	k	β	$\sigma_\nu(\times 10^5)$	$\mathscr{L}$
.632	1.25	.781	.099	-506.86
(.088)	(.28)	(.121)	(.018)	

All the parameters are measured quite precisely, with the possible exception of the weight β. The estimated γ of .632 means that the utility function exhibits modest risk aversion. The estimated value of k means that a dollar without work is worth 1.25 times a dollar gotten by working. In other words, the typical person would be willing to exchange a dollar with work for eighty cents without work. This suggests, loosely interpreted, that retirement benefits that replaced 80 percent of wage earnings would make a person indifferent between work and retirement. In the retirement decision, the estimated weight given to income one year in the future versus now is .781; income five years hence is given about half as much weight as income today. The variance term σ_ν, \$9,900, should be interpreted relative to the present value of future income. Typical values are indicated by the graphs at the beginning of the paper.

In general, the model fits the data well. Actual versus predicted retirement rates are shown in table 7.1 and in figure 7.7. As discussed in Stock and Wise (1988), the simulated average retirement rates by age are typically not significantly different from the sample averages. The only exceptions are at ages 62 and 65. There is apparently a "customary retirement age" effect that is not captured by the model. Unlike other models of retirement, age enters the option value model only indirectly—through the survival probabilities, the earnings forecasts, and the firm pension plan and Social Security rules.

The proportion of those in the firm at age 50 that would remain at age 54, based on actual retirement rates, is .179; the predicted proportion is .190. This suggests that, even though measured variables may often not evaluate correctly the alternative to continued work in the firm for younger employees, the error specification allows enough flexibility that the model predictions are still quite accurate. At older ages, the model predicts quite well the proportion of employees who have left the firm, as shown in figure 7.7.[8]

Table 7.1   Predicted and Actual Retirement Rates by Age for 1980[a]

Age	Number of Observations	Retirement Rates		Cumulative Rates	
		Actual	Predicted	Actual	Predicted
50	108	.037	.057	.037	.057
51	132	.030	.052	.066	.105
52	121	.041	.046	.105	.146
53	107	.047	.031	.147	.173
54	107	.037	.020	.179	.190
55	126	.087	.119	.250	.286
56	129	.116	.129	.337	.378
57	114	.123	.160	.419	.478
58	111	.126	.156	.492	.560
59	118	.153	.194	.570	.645
60	102	.206	.207	.658	.719
61	71	.197	.247	.726	.788
62	70	.471	.339	.855	.860
63	49	.286	.365	.896	.911
64	19	.474	.385	.945	.945
65	12	.583	.286	.977	.961
66	4	.750	.306	.994	.973

[a]The retirement rates were computed for the 1,500 persons used to estimate the model.

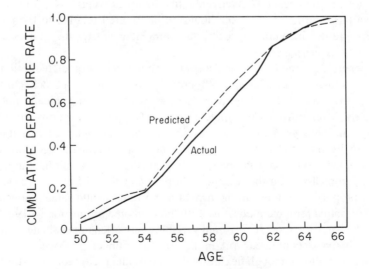

Fig. 7.7   Actual versus predicted cumulative departure rates

7.3   Simulations of the Effects of Changes in Pension and Social Security Provisions

We have used the model to simulate the effect of several potential changes in the firm pension plan and in Social Security provisions. We conclude that potential changes in the firm pension plan have a much greater effect on retirement rates than changes in Social Security rules. Four changes are considered.

7.3.1   Increase the Firm Early Retirement Age from 55 to 60

The effect of increasing the firm's early retirement age from 55 to 60, leaving other provisions as they were, is shown in table 7.2 and is graphed in figure 7.8. Under the current plan, 64.5 percent of those employed at 50 have left by 59. Only 42 percent would have left by age 59 if early retirement had been at 60 instead of 55. Only 13.6 percent of employees leave between 55 and 59 if early retirement is at 60, whereas 45.5 percent leave between these ages under the current system. On the other hand, because the early retirement "bonus" is now farther in the future, more employees leave the firm between 50 and 54. This is the result of the greater weight given to current versus future income. In short, many more workers would be employed between the ages of 57 and 65 if the early retirement age were 60 instead of 55.

Table 7.2   Simulation: Increase the Firm Early Retirement Age from 55 to 60

	Retirement Rates			Cumulative Rates		
Age	Base	Simulation	Difference	Base	Simulation	Difference
50	.057	.065	.008	.057	.065	.008
51	.052	.065	.013	.105	.126	.021
52	.046	.067	.021	.146	.185	.039
53	.031	.062	.031	.173	.235	.062
54	.020	.067	.047	.190	.286	.096
55	.119	.056	−.063	.286	.326	.040
56	.129	.049	−.080	.378	.359	−.019
57	.160	.050	−.110	.478	.391	−.087
58	.156	.035	−.121	.560	.413	−.147
59	.194	.016	−.178	.645	.422	−.223
60	.207	.207	a	.719	.542	−.177
61	.247	.247	a	.788	.655	−.133
62	.339	.339	a	.860	.772	−.088
63	.365	.365	a	.911	.855	−.056
64	.385	.385	a	.945	.911	−.034
65	.286	.286	a	.961	.936	−.025
66	.306	.306	a	.973	.956	−.017

[a]For persons employed at age 60 and older, the simulated alternative is the same as the base case.

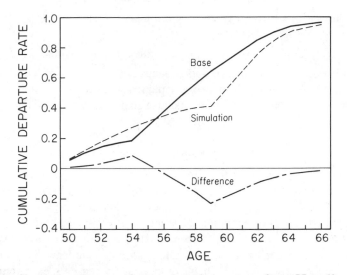

Fig. 7.8   Simulation: increase firm early retirement age from 55 to 60

7.3.2   Increase the Social Security Early Retirement Reduction Factor

The current Social Security rules include a benefit reduction of 5/9 percent per month of retirement before age 65. We consider the effect of increasing the reduction factor to 1 percent per month. The results are shown in table 7.3 and graphically in figure 7.9. It is clear that the effect of this change is small relative to the effect of the change in the firm early retirement age. This is primarily because only a small fraction of firm employees are still working at age 62, only 14 percent in the base case. The retirement rates of those still employed at age 62, however, are considerably lower—about 29 percent— with the higher reduction factor. They are also lower at 63. Still, the net result on the employment of persons covered by the firm's pension plan is negligible.

7.3.3   Increase the Social Security Retirement Ages by One Year

Current plans are to increase the Social Security retirement age from 65 to 67 by 2027. To judge the effect of such a change on workers with pension plans like the one in our firm, we simulate the effect of increasing the normal retirement age from 65 to 66 and the early retirement age from 62 to 63. The results are in table 7.4 and in figure 7.10. Again, the effect on the retirement rates of persons in our firm is small. This is true even though the effect on the annual retirement rates of 62- and 65-year-olds is substantial. The retirement rate of 62-year-olds is reduced from 33.9 to 25.2 percent. The rate at 65 is reduced from 28.6 to 25.1. But only a few workers remain in the firm to be affected by these changes.

Table 7.3   **Simulation: Increase of Social Security Early Retirement Reduction Factor**

Age	Retirement Rates			Cumulative Rates		
	Base	Simulation	Difference	Base	Simulation	Difference
50	.057	.057	.000	.057	.057	.000
51	.052	.052	.000	.105	.106	.001
52	.046	.046	.000	.146	.146	.000
53	.031	.031	.000	.173	.173	.000
54	.020	.020	.000	.190	.190	.000
55	.119	.119	.000	.286	.286	.000
56	.129	.129	.000	.378	.379	.001
57	.160	.160	.000	.478	.478	.000
58	.156	.156	.000	.560	.559	− .001
59	.194	.193	− .001	.645	.645	.000
60	.207	.207	.000	.719	.718	− .001
61	.247	.247	.000	.788	.788	.000
62	.339	.290	− .049	.860	.849	− .011
63	.365	.328	− .037	.911	.899	− .012
64	.385	.371	− .014	.945	.936	− .009
65	.286	.286	.000	.961	.955	− .006
66	.306	.306	.000	.973	.968	− .005

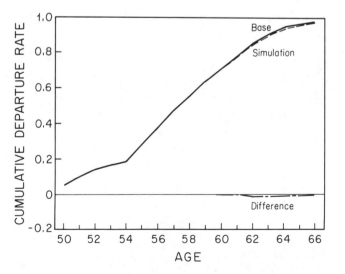

Fig. 7.9   Simulation: increase Social Security early retirement reduction factor

Table 7.4   **Simulation: Increase the Social Security Retirement Age by One Year**

	Retirement Rates			Cumulative Rates		
Age	Base	Simulation	Difference	Base	Simulation	Difference
50	.057	.057	.000	.057	.057	.000
51	.052	.052	.000	.105	.105	.000
52	.046	.045	−.001	.146	.146	.000
53	.031	.031	.000	.173	.172	−.001
54	.020	.020	.000	.190	.189	−.001
55	.119	.119	.000	.286	.285	−.001
56	.129	.129	.000	.378	.378	.000
57	.160	.159	−.001	.478	.477	−.001
58	.156	.155	−.001	.560	.558	−.002
59	.194	.192	−.002	.645	.643	−.002
60	.207	.206	−.001	.719	.716	−.003
61	.247	.246	−.001	.788	.786	−.002
62	.339	.252	−.087	.860	.840	−.020
63	.365	.355	−.010	.911	.897	−.014
64	.385	.369	−.016	.945	.935	−.010
65	.286	.251	−.035	.961	.951	−.010
66	.306	.306	.000	.973	.966	−.007

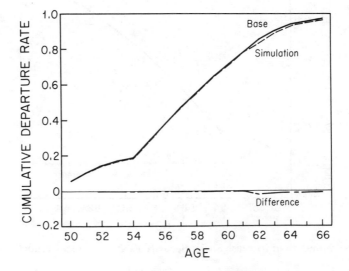

Fig. 7.10   Simulation: increase Social Security retirement ages by one year

7.3.4. Increase Social Security Retirement Ages by One Year and Start the Social Security Offset at 66

If the Social Security retirement age were increased to 66, the firm might be expected to begin the Social Security offset at 66 instead of 65. Thus, we have simulated the effect of increasing the Social Security retirement ages by one year *and* beginning the Social Security offset to the firm pension benefits at 66 instead of 65. The result is reported in table 7.5 and shown graphically in figure 7.11. Increasing the Social Security retirement ages reduced retirement rates by a small amount, as shown in table 7.4. But even these small effects effects would essentially be counteracted if the firm were to respond by delaying the imposition of the Social Security offset. For example, increasing the Social Security retirement ages reduced the retirement rate at age 62 by .087; the reduction is only .049 if the Social Security action is accompanied by the firm response that we have simulated.

7.4 Summary and Concluding Comments

The option value model developed in Stock and Wise (1988) has been used to simulate the effects on retirement of changes in a firm's pension plan and of changes in Social Security rules. Several important conclusions are supported by the analysis.

Table 7.5   **Simulation: Increase Social Security Retirement Ages by One Year *and* Start the Social Security Offset at 66**

	Retirement Rates			Cumulative Rates		
Age	Base	Simulation	Difference	Base	Simulation	Difference
50	.057	.057	.000	.057	.057	.000
51	.052	.052	.000	.105	.105	.000
52	.046	.046	.000	.146	.146	.000
53	.031	.031	.000	.173	.173	.000
54	.020	.020	.000	.190	.189	− .001
55	.119	.120	.001	.286	.287	.001
56	.129	.131	.002	.378	.380	.002
57	.160	.160	.000	.478	.479	.001
58	.156	.155	− .001	.560	.560	.000
59	.194	.192	− .002	.645	.644	− .001
60	.207	.206	− .001	.719	.718	− .001
61	.247	.246	− .001	.788	.787	− .001
62	.339	.290	− .049	.860	.849	− .011
63	.365	.370	.005	.911	.905	− .006
64	.385	.369	− .016	.945	.940	− .005
65	.286	.295	.009	.961	.958	− .003
66	.306	.265	− .041	.973	.969	− .004

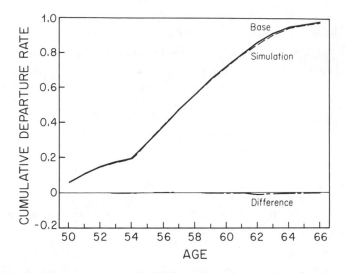

Fig. 7.11   Simulation: increase Social Security retirement ages by one year and start the Social Security offset at 66

- The provisions of the firm's pension plan have a much greater effect than Social Security regulations on the retirement decisions of the firm's employees.
- Increasing the firm's early retirement age from 55 to 60, for example, would reduce by almost 35 percent, from .645 to .422, the fraction of employees that is retired by age 60.
- The effect of changes in Social Security rules, on the other hand, would be small. Raising the Social Security retirement ages by one year, for example, has very little effect on employee retirement rates. The proportion retired by age 62 is reduced by only about 3 percent.
- Changes in Social Security provisions that would otherwise encourage workers to continue working can easily be offset by countervailing changes in the provisions of the firm's pension plan. Firm responses, like delaying the Social Security offset to correspond to a later Social Security retirement age, may simply be a logical revision of current firm plan provisions.

Thus, in considering the effect of changes in Social Security rules, like the retirement age, it is important to understand the implications of private pension plan provisions. In particular, if the effect on retirement decisions of changes in Social Security rules is to be predicted, the potential response of firms to the changes cannot be ignored.

Although the analysis is based on the retirement experience in a single large firm, the firm's pension plan is typical of defined benefit plans. Approximately 75 percent of the employees who are covered by a firm pension have defined benefit plans. Thus, the results suggest that pension plans in general have had a very substantial effect on the labor force participation rates of older workers.

In addition to the simulations, the paper describes the option value model of retirement. Comparisons of actual versus predicted retirement rates demonstrate that the model predicts complicated retirement patterns with considerable precision. That the model fits observed data well increases our confidence in the simulated results.

Notes

1. The criterion that they be employed three years facilitates the forecasting of future wage earnings on an individual basis. We plan in later work to consider other employee groups.

2. For convenience, the graphs assume a 5 percent real discount rate and zero inflation. In the empirical model that is estimated, the discount rate is estimated, and the inflation rate is assumed to be 5 percent.

3. Departure from the firm would be a more accurate description than retirement because for some employees the alternative to continued employment at the firm is likely to be another job rather than retirement.

4. Full details of the plan provisions are presented in Kotlikoff and Wise (1987).

5. Antecedents for the model begin with Lazear and Moore (1988), who argue that the option value of postponing retirement is the appropriate variable to enter in a regression equation explaining retirement. Indeed, it was their work, and analysis of military retirement rates by Phillips and Wise (1987), that motivated us to pursue this approach. Our model is also close in spirit to the much more complicated dynamic programming model of Rust (1989). A dynamic programming model of employment behavior has also been proposed by Berkovec and Stern (1988).

6. The estimates based on several years are very close to those reported here. Implementation using two or more consecutive years is only slightly more complicated than the exposition here, with $v_s = v_{s-1} + \epsilon_s$, ϵ_s i.i.d. $N(0, \sigma_\epsilon^2)$, v_t i.i.d. $N(0, \sigma_v^2)$, where v_t and ϵ_s, $s = t + 1, \ldots, S$ are independent. The covariance between v_τ and $v_{\tau+1}$ is $\text{var}(v_\tau)$, and the variance of v_τ for $\tau \geq t$ is $\sigma_v^2 + (\tau - t)\sigma_\epsilon^2$. (See Stock and Wise 1988.)

7. The estimates were obtained by maximum likelihood, using 1,500 observations. For more detail, see Stock and Wise (1988).

8. Further details on the model fit are presented in Stock and Wise (1988).

References

Berkovec, James, and Steven Stern. 1988. Job exit behavior of older men. (Forthcoming in *Econometrica*.)

Blinder, Alan, Roger Gordon, and Donald Wise. 1980. Reconsidering the work disincentive effects of Social Security. *National Tax Journal* 33 (December):431–42.

Bulow, J. 1981. Early retirement pension benefits. NBER Working Paper no. 654. Cambridge, Mass.: National Bureau of Economic Research.

Burkhauser, Richard V. 1979. The pension acceptance decision of older workers. *Journal of Human Resources* 14 (1):63–75.

_____. 1980. The early acceptance of Social Security: An asset maximization approach. *Industrial and Labor Relations Review* 33:484–92.

Burtless, Gary. 1986. Social Security, unanticipated benefit increases, and the timing of retirement. *Review of Economic Studies* 53 (October):781–805.

Burtless, Gary, and Robert A. Moffitt. 1984. The effects of Social Security on the labor supply of the aged. In *Retirement and economic behavior,* ed. H. Aaron and G. Burtless, 135–74. Washington, D.C.: Brookings.

Fields, Gary S., and Olivia Mitchell. 1982. The effects of pensions and earnings on retirement: A review essay. In *Research in Labor Economics,* vol. 5, ed. R. Ehrenberg, 115–56. Greenwich, Conn.: JAL.

Gustman, Alan, and Thomas Steinmeier. 1986. A structural retirement model. *Econometrica* 54:555–84.

Hausman, Jerry A., and David A. Wise. 1985. Social Security, health status, and retirement. In *Pensions, labor, and individual choice,* ed. D. Wise, 159–90. Chicago: University of Chicago Press.

Hogarth, Jeanne M. 1988. Accepting an early retirement bonus: An empirical study. *Journal of Human Resources* 23 (1):21–33.

Hurd, Michael, and Michael Boskin. 1981. The effect of Social Security on retirement in the early 1970s. *Quarterly Journal of Economics* 46 (November):767–90.

Kotlikoff, Laurence J., and David A. Wise. 1985. Labor compensation and the structure of private pension plans: Evidence for contractual versus spot labor markets. In *Pensions, labor, and individual choice,* ed. D. Wise, 55–87. Chicago: University of Chicago Press.

_____. 1987. The incentive effects of private pension plans. In *Issues in pension economics,* ed. Z. Bodie, J. Shoven, and D. Wise, 283–339. Chicago: University of Chicago Press.

_____. 1989. Employee retirement and a firm's pension plan. In *The economics of aging,* ed. D. Wise. Chicago: University of Chicago Press.

Lazear, Edward P. 1983. Pensions as severance pay. In *Financial aspects of the United States pension system,* ed. Z. Bodie and J. Shoven. Chicago: University of Chicago Press.

Lazear, Edward P., and Robert L. Moore. 1988. Pensions and turnover. In *Pensions in the U.S. economy,* ed. Z. Bodie, J. Shoven, and D. Wise, 163–88. Chicago: University of Chicago Press.

Phillips, Douglas, and David A. Wise. 1987. Military versus civilian pay: A descriptive discussion. In *Public sector payrolls,* ed. D. Wise, 19–46. Chicago: University of Chicago Press.

Rust, John. 1989. A dynamic programming model of retirement behavior. In *The economics of aging,* ed. D. Wise. Chicago: University of Chicago Press.

Stock, James H., and David A. Wise. 1988. Pensions, the option value of work, and retirement. NBER Discussion Paper no. 2686. Cambridge, Mass.: National Bureau of Economic Research. (Forthcoming in *Econometrica.*)

Comment   Edward P. Lazear

This is a very good paper. The model is sound, the estimates are reasonable, and the results are enlightening. Of course, every discussant must find some

Edward P. Lazear is Isidore Brown and Gladys J. Brown Professor of Urban and Labor Economics at the University of Chicago Graduate School of Business and a senior fellow at the Hoover Institution.

things to point out, and I have managed to collect a few; but, before doing that, I would like to start with a more general discussion of the option value approach that is used in this paper to model retirement.

The primary virtue of the option value approach that was introduced in Lazear and Moore (1988) is that it recognizes that turnover at a point in time depends on future considerations as well as current ones. A standard spot market labor supply analysis cannot take into account the effect of work today on future pension accumulation without a great deal of modification. Ignoring these life-cycle considerations leads to grossly inappropriate conclusions. In order to see this, consider an example from the U.S. military. The armed forces have pensions that cliff vest at twenty years of service. Workers who leave the service at any time before twenty years receive nothing, and those who leave at twenty years or after receive a significant pension. This means that the pension value as a function of years of service is as shown in figure 7C.1. (The function drawn in figure 7C.1 assumes for simplicity that soldiers are not permitted to stay beyond twenty years of service.)

Figure 7C.1 implies that pension accruals defined as

$$V(t) \equiv P(t) - P(t - 1)$$

have exactly the same shape as the pension value. That is, accruals are zero until year 20, and then in year 20 the full pension is accrued. Consider the distribution of turnover within the military. It is likely to look something like figure 7C.2.

Suppose that we took the individuals who left the military at some point before the twentieth year of service. Suppose further that we hypothesize that pensions affect turnover in the military because of the extreme cliff-vesting nature of the pension accrual formula. The dependent variable would be turnover rates, whereas the independent variable might be the pension value

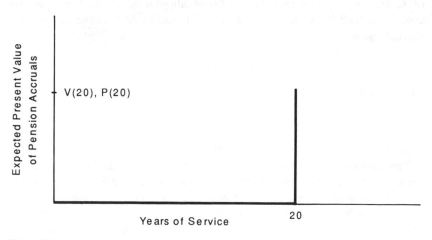

Fig. 7C.1

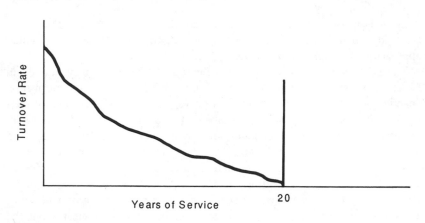

Fig. 7C.2

itself as a function of years of service or the accrual in a particular year as a function of years of service. But for years 0–19, both $P(t)$ and $V(t)$ are zero and do not vary over those nineteen years. The turnover rate, on the other hand, declines for the most part throughout the period. Thus, a regression of turnover rates on either version of an independent variable would not yield the conclusion that pensions affect turnover. Yet merely eyeballing the graphs in figure 7C.1 and figure 7C.2 makes clear that virtually no soldiers leave in the eighteenth and nineteenth years of service because hanging on for another couple of years will result in a very large pension value.

The reason that we are led astray is that the measure of pension accrual is inappropriate. It takes as relevant the change in pension amount associated with a given year of service, without being forward looking. What is being ignored is that serving, say, the eighteenth year gives the soldier the option to retire in the nineteenth year and take the pension associated with nineteen years of service or to go on to serve the twentieth year and to take the pension associated with the twentieth year. Thus, the relevant variable for pension accrual should be

$$V^*(t) \equiv M(t) - [P(t - 1)](1 - r),$$

where r is the discount rate and

$$M(t) \equiv \max\{P(t), M(t + 1)/1 + r\}$$

is defined recursively with $M(20) = P(20)$.

The definition of $V^*(t)$ takes into account that the individual need not accept the pension associated with year t but instead can serve additional years and enjoy the pension associated with longer years of service. In the case of the military, the function $V^*(t)$ is shown in figure 7C.3. A regression of turnover rates against $V^*(t)$ for soldiers who leave at some time between zero and

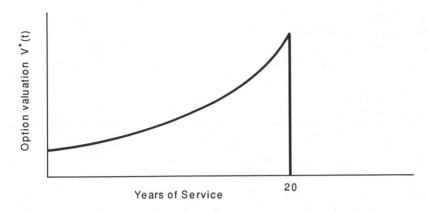

Fig. 7C.3

nineteen years will give an excellent fit because $V*(t)$ takes into account that work in the eighteenth year is valuable by bringing the worker close to work during the twentieth year.

This approach has major advantages over other labor supply models that are designed to deal with retirement. The most common alternative is the work-leisure analysis with a kinked budget constraint. The work-leisure model is fine as far as it goes, but it falls short in a number of dimensions. First, it cannot address the timing of work over the life cycle. At best it tells us that the worker will take, say, twenty years of leisure, total; but it does not speak to the issue of when those years will be taken. Second, it is not easily adapted to changes in the pension formula. Each time there is a small change, the analysis must be completely reworked, and budget constraints must be redrawn. The shape of the $P(t)$ function in no way alters the option value analysis. Of course it will change the values associated with $V*(t)$, but nothing need be done beyond that. Third, it is quite difficult to incorporate uncertainty into the work-leisure approach, and trivial to do so in the option value approach. All that is necessary is that the pension values are weighted by either exogenous or endogenous probabilities of continued work offers in the relevant years. Fourth, the work-leisure approach cannot deal with changes from one job to another. Workers frequently retire in their mid-50s and pick up secondary jobs. Part of those movements may be pension induced, but they are virtually impossible to analyze within the work-leisure context. A change in the alternative use of time must be parameterized as a change in tastes, which is extremely awkward. In the option value approach, one merely compares the value of working here with the alternative use of time, which is a straight-forward calculation.

A second alternative model is myopic life-cycle labor supply. The worker is assumed to choose work and leisure over the life cycle, taking the age/wage relation as exogenous and given. Taken to the extreme, the model would imply that workers should have low participation in the military during years 0–19 and high participation in year 20. Of course that makes no sense since one cannot work the twentieth year without having already worked years 1–19. So a myopic model does not build in the forward-looking aspect of the compensation profile.

A third approach is to solve a dynamic programming problem in stochastic environments. This is most closely related to the option value approach but is computationally much more difficult. It essentially evaluates each potential work-leisure decision and selects the best for each worker over the range of possibilities. The option value approach is merely a simplification of this, recognizing that the relation of one value to another has to bear a particular form and that, once retirement in year T_0 is dominated by retirement in year T_1, it is unnecessary to consider year T_0 again.

Still, there is a significant body of literature where retirement behavior is estimated in a spot labor supply or kinked budget constraint work-leisure model. It is interesting to compare how the Stock-Wise estimates do, relative to some of these others. Unfortunately, Stock and Wise do not do as much comparison as I would like to see done, but they do make a convincing case that their model fits their data extremely well, and it is difficult to imagine that other models would come close to this kind of fit. Some of their claims, however, are a bit too strong. First, the authors claim that their model does well because it beats using only four variables a model that contains seventeen age dummies but ignores future income. Perhaps, but the option value approach is not the only way to take economic variables into account. A better comparison is between the option value approach and the kinked budget constraint model, on the same data, because the kinked budget constraint model also builds in these economic effects. Since the authors emphasize the point that the option value model fits the jumps very well, the kinked budget constraint model (which also fits jumps) is probably the best benchmark.

In the same vein, option values are sensitive to changes in pensions, early retirement values, and vesting provisions, and this of course is the main strength of the option value approach. But the work-leisure kinked budget constraint model is also sensitive to these changes. It would be useful to see which is more volatile and which fits the data the best.

Partial retirement and reentry into the labor market were not handled in a clean way in this paper. Partial retirement can be incorporated into the reservation value, but then income and benefits need to be defined as net of what is available on the other job. This is especially problematic if the other job has a pension or upward-sloping age earnings profile itself. Under these circumstances, the worker might want to retire early enough to start the other job so that vesting can be achieved there.

It was unclear how the authors allowed illness to affect income in the model. The random-walk error structure allows illness to have permanent effects, but some mean reversion process may be more appropriate in the health context.

The most serious empirical disappointment is that the model misses badly on retirement at age 65. This made me wonder whether there was some mandatory retirement constraint either explicit or implicit associated with the pension plan. Also, timing is particularly important here because old workers enjoyed a wealth increase as a result of changes in ADEA legislation that permitted them to work beyond age 65.

While the descriptive statistics that Stock and Wise provide are compelling, perhaps the kappa measure of prediction should be used to get a better feel for how well the model actually does predict retirement ages. Finally, the authors talk about policy changes in Social Security, but they treat the Social Security changes as having no effects on the rest of the compensation profile. However, previous work has taught us that firms and workers will optimize against the Social Security and unemployment compensation system in a way that makes both sides better off. This means that the pension plan and the rest of the compensation profile will switch. For example, if Social Security age of entitlement rises from age 65 to age 67, then it will be optimal to induce most workers to retire at age 67, and the pension plan should be adjusted to bring that about. This could be accomplished by offset provisions that already build some of those changes in or by direct changes in the pension accrual formula.

On the whole, this paper is one of the most successful empirical pieces that I have seen in the retirement area, and I hope that more work of its type will follow.

Reference

Lazear, Edward P. and Robert L. Moore. 1988. Pensions and turnover. In *Pensions in the U.S. economy*, ed. Zvi Bodie, John B. Shoven, and David A. Wise, 163–88. Chicago: University of Chicago Press.

8 The Joint Retirement Decision of Husbands and Wives

Michael D. Hurd

Whereas the retirement behavior of males has been rather intensively studied, very little attention has been paid to the retirement behavior of couples, most likely because in a self-weighting sample there are not many observations on working women of retirement age (for the retirement behavior of males, see Boskin and Hurd 1978; Burkhauser 1980; Mitchell and Fields 1983, 1984; Diamond and Hausman 1984; Hurd and Boskin 1984; Burtless and Moffitt 1985; Hausman and Wise 1985; Honig and Hanoch 1985; Gustman and Steinmeier 1986; and Sickles and Taubman 1986). For example, Pozzebon and Mitchell (1989) use just 139 observations from the Retirement History Survey (RHS) to study the retirement behavior of married women. Because the labor force participation rate of women has grown substantially over the last thirty years, the retirement behavior of women will become increasingly important in understanding many issues such as the future size of the labor force, the number of retirees, and the aggregate cost of Social Security benefits. Of particular interest is the joint retirement behavior of husband and wife, both because numerically couples of retirement age are more important than single people of retirement age and because the joint retirement decision is much more complex than the decision of an individual.

Most research on the retirement of males finds that the date of retirement is affected by the level of Social Security benefits, health, mandatory retirement, and, to a lesser extent, other aspects of the economic environment such as the wage rate and assets. For example, Hurd and Boskin (1984) find that the increase in Social Security benefits during the early 1970s provided a good

Michael D. Hurd is professor of economics at the State University of New York, Stony Brook, and a research associate of the National Bureau of Economic Research.

Support from the Social Security Administration under grant 10–P–98298–1–01 to the NBER is gratefully acknowledged. Many thanks to Tai Hsin Huang for excellent research assistance.

explanation for the decline in elderly male labor force participation during that period. They further find that bad health has a strong effect toward early retirement and that mandatory retirement at age 65 approximately doubles the probability of complete retirement at age 65. (The individual retires rather than finding another job.) Hausman and Wise (1985) obtain similar findings. This line of research generally considers only husbands whose wives are not working, so the issue of the joint choice of retirement dates does not arise. Studies of family labor supply, however, typically find that the wife's labor supply is influenced by the husband's wage rate or by the husband's income. It would not be surprising, therefore, to find that the wife's retirement date is influenced by the variables that help determine the husband's retirement date. Whether the husband's retirement date is similarly influenced by the wife's variables is more of an open question.

Although a correlation between husbands' and wives' retirement dates has yet to be firmly established, there are several kinds of reasons why one might expect to find such a correlation.[1] If men who have a particularly strong taste for goods marry women with similar tastes, one would find a positive correlation between retirement dates, even if retirement dates are not influenced by any economic variables. A correlation could also be caused by economic variables: for example, both the husbands and the wives in families with substantial assets may tend to retire early, which would induce a positive correlation in dates. A more interesting example is correlation caused by cross-wage effects. Cross-wage effects could be due to income effects on the retirement dates of both husband and wife and/or to compensated cross-wage effects. The compensated effects result from a utility function in which the own marginal rate of substitution of goods for leisure is affected by the leisure of the spouse. One might well imagine such an effect particularly with respect to years of retirement: own retirement years may be less pleasurable if the spouse is working because of constraints put on traveling and so forth. This kind of reasoning would suggest that husbands' and wives' years of retirement are compliments, so that, ceteris paribus, they would desire to retire at the same time.

This paper has two goals. The first is to give some empirical evidence on the correlation between retirement dates. Do husbands and wives in fact tend to retire at the same time, and how strong is the tendency? The results should provide a baseline for future research. The second goal is to find, within the constraints of the data, whether observable economic variables contribute to any correlation in retirement dates and to find evidence of compensated cross-equation effects.

The data set is the New Beneficiary Survey (NBS). It has the advantage of a substantial number of observations on working husbands and wives of retirement age. Its main disadvantage is that it is a choice-based cross section, which limits the complexity of the analysis that can be undertaken.

The main findings are that husbands and wives tend to retire at the same time. Some of the results can be interpreted to mean that their retirement years are compliments. There is weaker evidence that some of each spouse's economic variables influence the retirement age of the other, but the findings are not robust enough to attempt to find compensated effects.

8.1 Data

The NBS is a survey of individuals who first received social security benefits in the "window," June 1980–May 1981 (Maxfield 1983). The individuals and their spouses were interviewed in October–December 1982. Nine categories of recipients were defined. For this study, the important ones are retired male workers and retired female workers. A retired male worker received his first retirement benefits during the window and was entitled on his own earnings record, and similarly for retired female workers. A number of the female workers, in particular, were dually entitled. Within each category, sampling rates varied by the age of the recipient. The sample sizes and sampling rates are given in table 8.1.

Although the NBS is a choice-based sample, in a static population it can be used for analysis, provided the proper weighting is used. For example, suppose that one wanted to find the probability that an eligible 62-year-old would receive his first benefits at age 63. This is a conditional probability, conditioned on his not having previously received benefits. It is also called the hazard rate or risk of receiving initial benefits at 63. In a static population, the hazard would be the number of 63-year-olds in the NBS divided by the number greater than 62, all weighted by the inverse of the sampling rate. Even though one does not observe the actual population of 63-year-olds exposed to the risk of benefit receipt, that population can be estimated from the fractions of older vintages that reached 63 without having received benefits. However, in a dynamic

Table 8.1

	Sample Size	Sampling Rate
Male workers:		
62	1,442	1/213
63–64	1,466	1/115
65	1,388	1/67
66+	1,011	1/53
Female workers:		
62	1,319	1/236
63–64	1,074	1/95
65	1,045	1/50
66+	774	1/24

population this calculation loses accuracy because the population of 63-year-olds at risk is not the sum of the older recipients. For example, if the population were growing, the population at risk would be underestimated, so the risk would be overestimated. Similar reasoning applies to the estimation of the response of retirement age to economic variables. For example, suppose one wants to find how the wage affects the probability of retirement at 63. In a static population, one observes the entire distribution of wages and retirement dates, so that, in principle, the desired parameter could be estimated. If wages are growing over time, however, the older recipients in the NBS come from cohorts that had lower wages when they were 63 than the current 63-year-old recipients. One would associate low wages with late retirement. Even if the wage had no effect on retirement, one would estimate that the retirement hazard at 63 increases with the wage.

In the NBS, the respondents and their spouses were asked extensive questions about their work histories, incomes, assets, wages, and health condition. From the answers, one can construct their economic environment at the time of the interview, but not in the years before the interview. This limits the complexity of the retirement model that can be estimated with the NBS because one does not know the alternatives that caused them to continue to work in earlier years. This is a weakness of the NBS compared with other data sets such as the RHS. The strength of the NBS is that it has a generous number of observations on recently retired husbands and wives.

8.2 Data Analysis

The goal of this section is to present evidence on whether husbands and wives tend to retire at the same time. No economic variables will be taken into account, so the results will simply establish the kinds of behavior that have to be explained by a model.

In these data, someone is said to be retired when he or she is not working. In that all respondents are at least 63 years old by the time of the survey and have received retired workers' Social Security benefits, there is probably little unretirement. For the results of this section, the sample is restricted to couples in which both the husband and the wife have a date of leaving the last job. This eliminates couples in which the wife worked only when she was young because only jobs held after 1950 are recorded. For most of the results, the sample will be further restricted to include only couples in which both retired after the age of 54, so that the behavior accords more with what is generally taken to be retirement.

In the male-worker sample, 1,536 couples satisfied these requirements and several other minor requirements concerning missing data. The median difference between the husband's and the wife's retirement dates is about 3.8 years. In that the average age difference is about 3.1 years, this implies that many husbands and wives retire at about the same age. Table 8.2 gives the

Table 8.2   **Distribution of the Difference in Retirement Dates**

Difference in Retirement Dates	Husband's Retirement Age[a]						
	55–59	60–61	62	63–64	65	66+	All
Same month	9.0	12.0	5.8	5.8	4.2	5.4	6.1
One month	9.0	14.8	6.3	10.5	7.1	8.5	9.4
Two months	9.0	15.5	9.5	12.1	9.9	10.1	11.0
Same year	19.2	32.4	23.6	26.7	25.3	20.5	24.6
More than one year	80.8	67.6	76.4	73.3	74.4	79.5	75.4
Observations	78	142	190	397	355	386	1,548

	Wife's Retirement Age[b]						
	55–59	60–61	62	63–64	65	66+	All
Same month	8.9	6.1	10.4	8.1	6.1	11.9	8.5
One month	11.5	10.6	14.0	11.0	8.5	14.5	11.5
Two months	12.7	12.9	14.8	13.3	10.9	16.4	13.8
Same year	28.0	27.2	33.0	28.3	25.4	27.7	28.1
More than one year	72.7	72.8	67.0	71.7	74.6	72.3	71.9
Observations	157	132	115	173	165	159	901

Source: Author's calculations from the NBS.
Note: Entries are percentage of each column.
[a]Based on male-workers sample.
[b]Based on female-workers sample.

distribution of the difference between the husband's and the wife's retirement dates. In the male-workers sample, 6.1 percent of couples retired in the same month; 9.4 percent within one month of each other; 11.0 percent within two months of each other; and 24.6 percent in the same year. In the female-workers sample, even greater coordination of retirement dates is found: 8.5 percent retired within the same month. Although it is not shown in the table, no other concentration of the difference in retirement dates appears. That is, the distribution is flat everywhere except at differences of a year or less, where there is substantial mass. The table certainly suggests joint determination of retirement dates.

To find if the coordination of retirement dates could be induced by the Social Security system, the distribution was calculated by the retirement age of the respondent. The idea is that Social Security has different effects at different ages, so the amount of coordination of retirement dates should vary by age. For example, if eligibility for benefits at age 62 causes both husband and wife to retire at the same time, one would expect a greater concentration of the distribution among respondents who retire at 62 than among respondents who retire at 63 or 64. The table has some suggestion of such an effect in the female-workers sample, but it is not verified in the male-workers sample. In fact, no pattern is apparent in both data sets. The table does not distinguish coordination of retirement due to economic variables from coordination caused by complimentarity in leisure; but the table would appear to rule out coordination caused by assortative mating because, while assortative mating would induce a correlation between retirement dates, it would not cause such high concentrations within a year.

The remainder of this section will be devoted to other ways of studying the correlation in retirement dates that is suggested by the findings in table 8.2. The idea that husbands and wives desire to retire at the same time will be called the joint retirement hypothesis.

Table 8.3 shows the probability in the male-workers sample that the wife retires in a particular age interval as a function of the husband's age at retirement and of the difference in their ages. For example, among husbands who retire at age 62 and who are the same age as their wives, 30 percent have wives who retire between 55 and 59. This number is calculated from the relevant subsample of the male-workers sample by taking the ratio of the number of wives who retire at $55-59$ divided by the total number of husbands who retire at 62. The average is unweighted because the conditioning event means that approximately all the observations in a column receive the same weight. Many of the entries in the table are missing because of sample selection: having selected on husband's retirement age and age difference, one cannot observe the fraction of wives that retire at certain ages. Consider, for example, husbands who retired at 62 and are three years older than their wives. At the time of the survey, most of the husbands were 63; their wives were 60, and some of the wives were still working. One does not know how many will retire at 62. The table does not extend beyond age differences of four and minus one because the number of observations becomes small.

If the joint retirement hypothesis is correct, the wife's retirement probability will vary with the age difference: the wife's retirement probability should be greatest at the age difference when both husband and wife can retire at the same time. An example is when the husband's retirement age is 62 and the wife's retirement age is $55-59$. When the age difference is two, the wife is 60 at the husband's retirement; when the difference is three, she is 59. One would expect, therefore, the probability the wife retires at 59 to be greater when the age difference is three than when the age difference is two, and the table shows that to be the case. A counterexample is when the husband's retirement is 65, the wife's retirement is $63-64$, and the age differences are zero and one. One would expect a higher retirement probability to be associated with the greater age difference, but that is not the case. Only a few similar comparisons can reliably be made because of missing data or small samples. If one restricts comparisons to cells in which the husband and wife retire at the same time and cells adjacent to those, just five comparisons in which the probabilities are based on more than fifteen observations can be made. Table 8.4 is an extract of table 8.3; it has comparisons that are based on ten or more observations. The

Table 8.3   **Probability Wife Retires**

Wife's Retirement Age	Age Difference	Husband's Retirement Age					
		55–59	60–61	62	63–64	65	66+
55–59	4	-	-	-	.31	.04	.19
	3	b	.30	.41	.27	.14	.21
	2	.33	.37	.35	.26	.14	.19
	1	b	.17[a]	.15	.29	.25	.11
	0	b	.14[a]	.30[a]	.36	.20	.22
	−1	b	.20[a]	.13[a]	.09	.23[a]	.33[a]
60–61	4	-	-	-	-	.17	.13
	3	-	-	-	-	.10	.15
	2	-	-	-	-	.12	.06
	1	b	.50[a]	.26	.10	.19	.14
	0	b	.36[a]	.30[a]	.12	.07	.09
	−1	b	.30[a]	.33[a]	.18	.08[a]	.08[a]
62	4	-	-	-	-	-	.16
	3	-	-	-	-	.14	.17
	2	-	-	-	-	.12	.04
	1	-	-	-	-	.16	.11
	0	b	.14[a]	.10[a]	.06	.07	.09
	−1	b	.20[a]	.20[a]	.00	.08[a]	.08[a]
63–64	4	-	-	-	-	-	-
	3	-	-	-	-	-	-
	2	-	-	-	-	-	-
	1	-	-	-	-	.22	.17
	0	-	-	-	-	.27	.30
	−1	-	-	-	-	.23[a]	.25[a]
65	4	-	-	-	-	-	-
	3	-	-	-	-	-	-
	2	-	-	-	-	-	-
	1	-	-	-	-	-	.11
	0	-	-	-	-	.23	.04
	−1	-	-	-	-	.00[a]	.17[a]
66+	4	-	-	-	-	-	-
	3	-	-	-	-	-	-
	2	-	-	-	-	-	-
	1	-	-	-	-	-	.34
	0	-	-	-	-	.17	.26
	−1	-	-	-	-	.15[a]	.00[a]

Source: Author's calculations from the NBS.

Note: Based on male-workers sample. Age difference is husband's age minus wife's age. "-" means the probability is not reliably observed.

[a]Based on ten to fifteen observations.

[b]Based on fewer than ten observations.

Table 8.4   Comparison of Retirement Probabilities

Husband's Retirement Age	Wife's Retirement Age	Age Difference	Retirement Probability	Supports
60–61	55–59	1	.17[a]	Yes
		0	.14[a]	
62	55–59	3	.41	Yes
		2	.35	
62	60–61	1	.26	No
		0	.30[a]	
62	62	0	.10[a]	No
		−1	.20[a]	
65	60–61	4	.17	Yes
		3	.10	
65	62	3	.14	Yes
		2	.12	
65	63–64	1	.22	No
		0	.27	
65	65	0	.23	Yes
		−1	.00[a]	
66+	65	1	.11	Yes
		0	.04	

Source: Table 8.3.
[a]Based on ten to fifteen observations.

last column indicates whether the comparison supports the joint retirement hypothesis: six of the nine entries show support.

Table 8.5 has the probability the husband retires classified by the age at which the wife retires and by the age difference; the probabilities are based on the female-workers data. Seven comparisons of retirement probabilities similar to those in table 8.4 can be made; six support the joint retirement hypothesis. In total, then, twelve of sixteen comparisons support the hypothesis. The fraction of successful comparisons is different from ½ at about the .05 significance level.

These kinds of comparisons are not very systematic, and some subjective judgment is exercised in choosing the cases. Furthermore, one would think that age differences would shift the entire distribution of retirement ages, which would change the retirement probabilities at every age. For example husbands who are four years older than their wives should be less likely to retire at younger ages than husbands who are the same age as their wives.

Because husbands tend to be older than their wives, many of the retirement probabilities are not reliable in the male-worker data. The rest of the data analysis, therefore, uses only the female-workers sample. The object of analysis is the distribution of the husband's retirement age conditional on the retirement age of the wife. The joint retirement hypothesis implies that as the age difference increases the probability that the husband retires at an early age

Table 8.5   **Probability Husband Retires**

Husband's Retirement Age	Age Difference	Wife's Retirement Age					
		55–59	60–61	62	63–64	65	66+
55–59	4	.09	.00	.15[a]	.00[a]	.06	.16
	3	.25	.15[a]	.06	.07	.09	.09[a]
	2	.20[a]	.06	.06	.19	.12	.00[a]
	1	.22	.20	.21[a]	.06	.14[a]	.08
	0	.29	.09[a]	.11	.10	.00	.06
	−1	.00[a]	.30[a]	.00[b]	.08[a]	.13[a]	.13[a]
60–61	4	.09	.15	.23[a]	.00[a]	.06	.05
	3	.10	.15[a]	.06	.15	.05	.00[a]
	2	.00[a]	.13	.06	.07	.04	.13[a]
	1	.11	.10	.00[a]	.03	.29[a]	.08
	0	.12	.27[a]	.22	.00	.17	.00
	−1	.23[a]	.20[a]	.20[b]	.15[a]	.07[a]	.00[a]
62	4	.18	.10	.08[a]	.00[a]	.00	.00
	3	.15	.08[a]	.00	.07	.14	.27[a]
	2	.13[a]	.19	.17	.00	.12	.13[a]
	1	.11	.25	.07[a]	.13	.00[a]	.00
	0	.00	.09[a]	.33	.00	.06	.11
	−1	-	-	-	.15[a]	.00[a]	.13[a]
63–64	4	.14	.35	.08[a]	.09[a]	.18	.11
	3	.05	.15[a]	.29	.15	.09	.18[a]
	2	.13[a]	.25	.44	.11	.04	.13[a]
	1	-	-	-	.13	.00[a]	.00
	0	-	-	-	-	.39	.17
	−1	-	-	-	-	.40[a]	.07[a]
65	4	.14	.15	.08[a]	.00[a]	.35	.16
	3	.15	.23[a]	.29	.15	.14	.09[a]
	2	-	-	-	.15	.12	.07[a]
	1	-	-	-	-	.43[a]	.04
	0	-	-	-	-	.22	.06
	−1	-	-	-	-	-	.27[a]
66+	4	.36	.25	.38[a]	.91[a]	.35	.53
	3	.30	.23[a]	.29	.41	.50	.36[a]
	2	-	-	-	.48	.56	.53[a]
	1	-	-	-	-	.07[a]	.64
	0	-	-	-	-	.17	.61
	−1	-	-	-	-	-	.40[a]

Source: Author's calculations from the NBS.

Note: Based on female-workers sample. Age difference is husband's age minus wife's age. "-" means the probability is not reliably observed.

[a]Based on ten to fifteen observations.

[b]Based on fewer than ten observations.

decreases; that is, the entire distribution of retirement ages shifts toward greater ages.

The retirement distributions, conditional on the wife's retirement age, are given in table 8.6. They are found by summing the retirement probabilities in table 8.5. An example where the joint retirement hypothesis is generally supported is found in the column headed 60–61 and the rows labeled 55–62. If the husband is one year younger than the wife, he would have been 59 or 60 when the wife retired; 60 percent of such husbands retired before the age

Table 8.6   **Distribution of the Retirement Age of Husband**

Husband's Retirement Age	Age Difference	Wife's Retirement Age					
		55–59	60–61	62	63–64	65	66+
55–59	4	.09	.00	.15[a]	.00[a]	.06	.16
	3	.25	.15[a]	.06	.07	.09	.09[a]
	2	.20[a]	.06	.06	.19	.12[a]	.00[a]
	1	.22	.20	.21[a]	.06	.14	.08
	0	.29	.09[a]	.11	.10	.00	.06
	−1	.00[a]	.30	.00[b]	.08[a]	.13[a]	.13[a]
55–61	4	.18	.15	.38[a]	.00[a]	.12	.21
	3	.35	.31[a]	.12	.22	.14	.09[a]
	2	.20[a]	.19	.11	.26	.16[a]	.13[a]
	1	.33	.30	.21[a]	.10	.43	.16
	0	.41	.36[a]	.33	.10	.11	.06
	−1	.23[a]	.50	.20[b]	.23[a]	.20[a]	.13[a]
55–62	4	.36	.25	.46[a]	.00[a]	.12	.21
	3	.50	.38[a]	.12	.30	.27	.36[a]
	2	.33[a]	.37	.28	.26	.28[a]	.27[a]
	1	.44	.55	.29[a]	.22	.43	.16
	0	.41	.45[a]	.67	.10	.22	.17
	−1	.54[a]	.60	.60[b]	.38[a]	.20[a]	.27[a]
55–64	4	.50	.60	.54[a]	.09[a]	.30	.32
	3	.55	.54[a]	.41	.44	.36	.55[a]
	2	.47[a]	.62	.72	.37	.32[a]	.40[a]
	1	-	-	-	.45	.50	.32
	0	-	-	-	-	.61	.33
	−1	-	-	-	-	.60[a]	.37[a]
55–65	4	.64	.75	.62[a]	.09[a]	.65	.48
	3	.70	.77[a]	.71	.59	.50	.64[a]
	2	-	-	-	.52	.44[a]	.47[a]
	1	-	-	-	-	.93	.36
	0	-	-	-	-	.83	.39
	−1	-	-	-	-	.73[a]	.60[a]

Source: Author's calculations from the NBS.

Note: Based on female-workers sample. Age difference is husband's age minus wife's age. "-" means the probability is not reliably observed.

[a]Based on ten to fifteen observations.

[b]Based on fewer than ten observations.

of 63. If the husband is four years older than the wife, he would have been 64 or 65 when the wife retired. The joint retirement hypothesis implies that many of these husbands would retire at 64 or 65, so that few would retire before 63. The data show that to be the case: just 25 percent of such husbands retired before the age of 63. Generally, the probability the husband retires should increase in each block as one moves down each column. Similar reasoning implies that, holding constant the difference in age, the retirement probabilities should decrease as the retirement age of the wife increases. An example is the retirement probability at 61 or less of husbands who are the same age as their wives: when the wife retires at 55–59, 41 percent of the husbands retire before 62; when the wife retires at 66 or over, just six percent of the husbands retire before 62.

The entries generally seem to decrease both as the age difference increases and as the wife's retirement age increases. It is desirable, however, to verify this in a systematic way. One method is to calculate the trends in the table. Table 8.7 has the least squares estimates of the trends in the columns. The interpretation of the entries is the change in the husband's retirement probability for a change in the age difference. In the example mentioned before, in which the wife retires at 60–61, the probability that the husband retires before 63 decreases by .067 for each year of age difference. The average of all the entries in the table is −.033. This is a simple measure of the shift in the retirement distributions for an increase in the age difference. Twenty-one of the thirty entries are negative, which gives additional support to the joint retirement hypothesis. A rough idea of the change in husband's retirement age for a change in age difference can be calculated from the entries in table 8.7. Taking the retirement ages to be the midpoints of each interval (with 67 for the upper interval), one finds that a change of a year in the age difference is associated with an increase in the husband's retirement age of .44 year.

Table 8.8 has the change in the husband's retirement probability for a change in the wife's retirement age, holding constant the age difference. For example, when the age difference is zero, the probability that the husband retires before

Table 8.7   **Change in Husband's Retirement Probability for a Change in Age Difference**

Husband's Retirement Age	Wife's Retirement Age					
	55–59	60–61	62	63–64	65	66+
55–59	.009	−.042	.012	−.010	−.003	.005
55–61	−.016	−.057	.005	−.018	−.017	.013
55–62	−.021	−.061	−.067	−.036	−.011	.011
55–64	.015	−.010	−.090	−.101	−.069	.014
55–65	−.060	−.020	−.090	−.215	−.054	.007

Source: Calculated from table 8.6.

Note: Based on female-workers sample.

63 decreases by about .033 for each year the wife delays retirement. The average of the table is − .043. Twenty-eight of the thirty entries are negative. The increase in husband's retirement age for an increase in wife's retirement age is roughly .47. Again, these results are consistent with the joint retirement hypothesis.

A simplified summary of what the data reveal about the joint retirement hypothesis is given in table 8.9.[2] The entries are classified by age difference. They give the percentage distribution of the difference in retirement age. The table aims to show that the difference in age at retirement is systematically

Table 8.8   **Change in Husband's Retirement Probability for a Change in Wife's Retirement Age**

| Age Difference | Husband's Retirement Age | | | | |
	55–59	55–61	55–62	55–64	55–65
4	.005	− .004	− .024	− .031	− .023
3	− .016	− .026	− .016	− .008	− .017
2	− .012	− .005	− .008	− .020	− .013
1	− .015	− .010	− .027	− .040	− .285
0	− .024	− .040	− .033	− .140	− .220
− 1	.006	− .017	− .038	− .115	− .065

Source: Calculated from table 8.6.
Note: Based on female-workers sample.

Table 8.9   **Distribution of the Difference in Retirement Age**

| Difference in Retirement Age | Difference in Age | | | | | | | | | |
	− 4 to − 2	− 1	0	1	2	3	4	5	6–10	All
− 6 to − 2	43.1	17.3	15.3	10.6	12.0	10.8	5.8	14.7	10.2	14.8
− 1	9.3	24.0	9.8	5.8	1.4	2.6	6.6	6.4	6.9	7.1
0	10.6	15.4	25.8	14.0	7.7	6.2	7.3	2.8	5.7	10.4
1	6.6	10.6	11.7	28.0	18.7	5.7	5.1	5.5	6.5	11.7
2	4.0	4.8	9.8	10.1	23.0	14.4	9.5	6.4	5.3	10.3
3	11.3	5.8	6.8	6.8	12.0	23.2	14.6	10.1	5.7	10.7
4	5.3	1.9	4.9	5.3	6.7	10.3	29.9	14.7	6.5	9.0
5–6	4.6	11.5	9.2	9.7	10.1	12.4	11.7	26.6	22.5	13.1
7–9	5.3	8.7	6.8	9.7	8.6	14.4	9.5	12.8	30.6	12.9
Total Percent	100.0	100.0	100.0	100.0	100.0	100.0	100.0	100.0	100.0	100.0
Number of Observations	151	104	163	207	209	194	137	109	245	1,519

Source: Author's calculations from the NBS.

Note: Entries are percentage of each column. Difference in age is husband's age minus wife's age. Difference in retirement age is husband's retirement age minus wife's retirement age. Based on combined male- and female-workers samples.

related to the difference in age. For example, if the joint retirement hypothesis is correct, then husbands and wives who are the same age will tend to retire at the same age; thus, one ought to find that, if the age difference is zero, a high fraction will have the same retirement age. In table 8.9, 25.8 percent of husbands and wives of the same age retired at the same age. Similar reasoning suggests that the largest entries in the table should be along the diagonal: couples with the same difference in age will tend to have the same difference in retirement age. That is exactly what is found in the table: the greatest entry in every column is on the diagonal.

8.3   Models of Retirement Age

The results above certainly support the view that retirement dates are correlated, but they give no indication of the source of correlation: joint retirement could be induced by the economic environment, by taste variation, or by complementarity in leisure. For example, it may be that wives and husbands tend to retire at the same time because the wife's Social Security benefit, based on the husband's earnings record, cannot be drawn until the husband retires. One would then find correlation between retirement dates. Further cross-classification by levels of economic resources would allow one roughly to hold constant economic resources, but the counts in the cells would become too small to allow interpretation. A useful way to proceed is to introduce a model of retirement behavior. It will control for economic variables in a way dictated by the functional form. The reader can interpret the results as an extension of the cross-tabulations or as indicative of behavior.

The vehicle for exploring the influence of economic variables on retirement age will be the Stone-Geary utility function. It can quite naturally be parameterized to include both systematic and random taste variations that are econometrically identified. The thought experiment that will lie behind the estimation is as follows: given at age 55 a fixed wage and a stock of assets, workers choose the number of additional years to work. From this point of view, the age of retirement is an object of demand, and an equation that explains the retirement age is a demand equation. Because of the economic environment, however, there are some important differences from the usual kinds of demand estimation; these differences will be discussed below.

Suppose that the husband and wife maximize lifetime utility given by

$$(1 - B_1 - B_2)\ln(x - a) + B_1 \ln(b_1 - A_1) + B_2 \ln(b_2 - A_2),$$

in which x measure lifetime goods consumption; a is a parameter, necessary goods consumption; A_1 is the husband's years of work (retirement age); b_1 is the husband's taste parameter; and A_2 and b_2 are the wife's years of work and taste parameter. As suggested by the cross-tabulations in section 8.2, b_1 and b_2 will depend on the difference in ages and on random components that are correlated. In addition, they will vary with health status. For the moment, assume that the lifetime budget constraint is given by

$$px = w_1A_1 + w_2A_2 + Y,$$

in which p is the price of x, w_1 and w_2 are the wage rates, and Y is assets.[3] The retirement equations are

(1) $A_1 = (1 - B_1)b_1 - B_1(b_2w_2/w_1 + Y/w_1 - ap/w_1),$

       $A_2 = (1 - B_2)b_2 - B_2(b_1w_1/w_2 + Y/w_2 - ap/w_2).$

The taste index of each person enters his own equation and his spouse's equation. Let b_1 and b_2 have both systematic parts and random parts as

$$b_1 = X_1'\beta_1 + u_1,$$

$$b_2 = X_2'\beta_2 + u_2.$$

On substituting the specifications of b_1 and b_2 in the demand equations, the demand equations will have a systematic part that depends on $X_1'\beta_1$ and $X_2'\beta_2$ and error terms (derived from a_1 and a_2) that have a complicated variance-covariance matrix. From the specification, the structure of the variance-covariance matrix is known, and it offers cross-equation restrictions. With static wages and prices and realizations on A_1 and A_2, one could contemplate estimating the parameters, including the taste parameters and variance-covariance matrix.

In the NBS data, a number of obstacles stand in the way of estimation. One observes assets at about the time of retirement, so that the realizations on Y will depend on the realizations on A. Neither pensions nor Social Security has been mentioned, yet they surely affect the retirement decision. They have a wealth affect: couples with higher levels of pensions and Social Security will tend to retire earlier. They have price effects: the reward from working another year depends in a complicated way on age, the structure of the pension, the Social Security law, and the contribution history. The price effects act through actuarial reductions in benefits, recalculation of benefits to reflect an extra year's earnings, and within-period effects through the earnings test. Full-scale modeling of the influence of pensions and Social Security on the retirement of a single person is far beyond what can be supported by the NBS because the data give little information on these variables in the years before retirement. For example, even at retirement one does not know the increase in the pension or Social Security that would result from another year of work.

The approach to these problems is to assume that realizations on assets and on annuities (the sum of pensions and Social Security) are representations of the opportunities available to a worker who is contemplating retirement but that the realizations differ from the opportunities by a random component that depends partly on the actual retirement age chosen. This implies that assets and annuities should enter equations (1) as endogenous variables. Annuities should have a different coefficient from assets as they are a flow, not a stock.

Weighted averages of the data are shown in table 8.10. The weights account for the stratified sampling procedure. It is evident that there are systematic differences between the two samples. As would be expected, the wives in the female-workers sample have a greater attachment to the labor force than the wives in the male-workers sample: they retire later; they have higher wages and higher Social Security benefits and pensions. They are in better health as a smaller fraction say they have health problems that affect their jobs. The husbands in the female-workers sample are different from the husbands in the male-workers sample: they retire earlier; they have lower wages, fewer assets, smaller Social Security benefits and pensions, and worse health. The health of the husband is a possible reason for the differences between the two samples: the wives of husbands with bad health spent more time in the labor force; the husbands had lower earnings and greater health expenditures, resulting in lower assets at retirement.

The results from estimating the retirement-age equations (1) over the two samples can be found in table 8.11. The estimates certainly differ across the two samples. This is due at least partly to large standard errors. According to the Stone-Geary utility function, the error terms have heteroscedasticity as well as cross-equation correlation. This was not corrected in the estimation as later results suggest that the Stone-Geary framework may not be appropriate. The emphasis here will be on the average of the two estimates.

Reference to (1) shows that in the husband's retirement equation the vector that explains husband's tastes appears directly, whereas in the wife's equation the vector is multiplied by a factor of proportionality, $-B_2$. In the husband's equation, increases in the age difference increase b_1, which increases the

Table 8.10   **Weighted Average Values**

	Male-Workers Sample		Female-Workers Sample	
	Husband	Wife	Wife	Husband
Retirement age	63.1	58.4	61.2	62.7
Wage ($)	10.91	6.65	7.68	10.42
Assets ($)	96,190	96,190	76,452	76,452
Health limitations:				
None	.63	.55	.66	.44
Job	.14	.14	.10	.13
Home	.01	.01	.02	.01
Both	.22	.30	.22	.42
Social Security benefit (annual) ($)	6,368	2,656	4,384	5,540
Pension (annual) ($)	5,384	1,060	1,436	3,920

Source: Author's calculations from the NBS.

Note: Dollar entries in 1982 dollars.

Table 8.11   Stone-Geary Model of Retirement Age

	Male-Workers Sample		Female-Workers Sample	
	Husband Ret. Age	Wife Ret. Age	Wife Ret. Age	Husband Ret. Age
A. Husband's tastes:				
Age diff. ≥ 6	1.10[a]	−.02	.09	4.10[a]
6 > age diff. > −4	.16[a]	−.00	−.02	.35[a]
−4 $\geq$ age diff.	.51	−.47	−.17	−2.35[a]
Health:				
Work	−.48	.01	−.08	−.23
Home	.19	.09	.77	1.03
Both	−.60[a]	−.23	.04	−1.10[a]
B. Wife's tastes:				
Age diff. ≥ 6	.52	−3.90[a]	−.25	−.76
6 > age diff. > −4	.05	−.46[a]	−.07	−.05
−4 $\geq$ age diff.	−.68	3.02[a]	1.15	−1.20
Health:				
Work	.17	.04	−.49	.03
Home	2.73[a]	1.55	−.61	.84
Both	.50[a]	−1.19[a]	−.64	.34
C. Economic variables				
(all divided by own wage):				
Constant	−2.08	−.1.18	−.56	−1.29
Spouse wage	−.15	.22	.01	−.21
Own annuity (thous. annual ([b]))	.43	5.58[a]	.45[a]	.92[a]
Spouse annuity (thous. annual)	.56[a]	−.14	.11	1.39[a]
Assets (thous.) ([b])	−.014	−.067[a]	−.023[a]	.013
R^2	.06	.24	.09	.27
Observations	983	983	702	702

Source: Author's calculations from the NBS.
Note: Age diff. = husband age − wife age.
[a] = $|t| > 1.96$.
[b]Endogenous variable.

marginal utility of work and hence increases the retirement age.[4] The average of the effects in the two samples is about .26 per year of age difference: increasing the age difference by a year would increase the husband's retirement age by .26 year, holding constant the wife's taste parameter. If the factor of proportionality in the wife's equation is negative, which it should be, one finds the same pattern of signs on the age difference variables as in the husband's equations.

The husband's own health affects his retirement age in the expected way. It is interesting that the few husbands who say that health limits their work at home tend to retire later. In the wife's retirement equation, the same negative factor of proportionality that multiplies husband's health should multiply the age difference, yet there is little consistency of sign.

In the wife's retirement-age equation, the wife's taste index decreases in the age difference, which is symmetric with the husband's taste index. Thus, if the age difference decreases (the wife becomes older), the marginal utility of work of the wife increases, and she retires later, just as does the husband if his age increases. On average, a decrease of a year in the age difference increases the wife's retirement age by .27 year, holding constant the husband's taste index. The responses of the husband and wife are for practical purposes exactly the same. The effect of age difference on the wife's taste index in the husband's retirement equation should, at least, have the same sign over the two samples, but there is no such consistency.

In the wife's retirement equation, the wife's health indicators affect retirement in the usual way: if health affects work on the job, b_2 decreases, and the wife retires earlier. In the husband's equation, bad health increases the husband's retirement age. The effect is through b_2, which, if the factor of proportionality is negative, decreases with bad health. This reduces the wife's retirement age and increases the husband's.

The total effects of the economic variables cannot be read directly from the table because of interactions. As far as the own wage is concerned, it has a positive effect if all the other economic variables with which it is interacted are put to zero. However, if they are evaluated at their sample means, the wage effect takes the opposite sign: evaluating own wage, spouse wage, own annuity, spouse annuity, and assets at the sample means produces these estimates of the wage effects in years per dollar (see table 8.12). Thus, increasing the own wage tends to cause earlier retirement, although the change is not large.

The spouse's wage is interacted with the spouse's taste vector and with the own wage. Evaluated at no health limitation and no age difference, the average effect (over both samples) of the wife's wage on the husband's retirement is about $-.02$ year per dollar; the effect of the husband's wage on the wife's retirement is about .02 year per dollar. These effects are practically zero.

The effect of own annuity (the sum of Social Security and pensions) on retirement age averages about .04 year per thousand for husbands and .43 for wives. Both suggest that the price effect dominates income effects: apparently, the annuity gain from delaying retirement is substantial.

The effect of the husband's annuity on the wife's retirement age is practically zero. An increase in the wife's annuity on the husband's retirement age is positive and of moderate magnitude. An explanation for this is found

Table 8.12   **Effect of Own Wage on Own Retirement Age**

	Husband's Retirement	Wife's Retirement
Male Data	$-.02$	$-.31$
Female Data	$-.14$	$-.02$

in the wife's response to her own annuity: her retirement age increases, so the husband's retirement age also increases.

The average effect of assets on the husband's retirement age is practically zero. The average change in the wife's retirement age is about $-.006$ year per thousand dollars of assets. Because these data have considerable variation in assets across households, asset variation can reduce the wife's retirement age by several years.

Table 8.13 summarizes the effects of the economic variables. Part A gives the estimated change in retirement age associated with changing the economic variables from the twenty-fifth percentile point in the distribution of the variable to the seventy-fifth percentile point. Part B gives the changes in the variables that underlie the calculations. For example, a change of $5.2 thousand in the wife's annuity is estimated to increase the wife's retirement age by 2.24 years.

One might well ask whether the Stone-Geary utility function produces a reasonable representation of the data. The response of retirement age to the economic variables certainly seems reasonable, but this is not really a test of the functional form. The utility function implies a number of cross-equation restrictions that were not imposed in the estimation. They result from the appearance of both taste parameters in both retirement equations. The factor of proportionality is $-B_2/(1 - B_1)$ for the husband's index and $-B_1/(1 - B_2)$ for the wife's index, and $-B_1$ and $-B_2$ are the coefficients on assets. But it would be taking the model beyond reasonable bounds to estimate B_1 and B_2 from the coefficients on assets for the purpose of checking the equivalence of the index parameters because of other implicit factors. For example, wage rates are in dollars per hour, whereas the utility function refers to lifetime utility. A more generous test of the proportionality hypothesis rests on whether the 12×4 matrix

$$\hat{B} = (\hat{\beta}_1 \, \hat{\beta}_2 \, \hat{\beta}_3 \, \hat{\beta}_4)$$

has rank one. Each of the $\hat{\beta}$ is a twelve-vector of the estimated coefficients that give the husband's and wife's taste parameters. Each retirement equation produces two estimates of the $\hat{\beta}$, one from each data set. The form of the test comes from noting that one should be able to write each vector as

Table 8.13

	Own Wage	Spouse Wage	Own Annuity	Spouse Annuity	Assets
A. Changes in retirement age:					
Husband	$-.52$	$-.08$	.32	.47	.00
Wife	$-.61$	.10	2.24	.00	$-.40$
B. Changes in variables:					
Husband	6.5	3.8	8.0	5.2	67
Wife	3.8	6.5	5.2	8.0	67

$$\beta_i = k_i\beta,$$

where k_i is a scalar. This implies that B has rank one. The normalized characteristic roots of $\hat{B}'\hat{B}$ are

$$.45, .32, .17, .06.$$

The second and third are far enough from zero that a formal test was not conducted, and $\hat{B}$ was concluded to have rank greater than one.

The retirement equations derived from the Stone-Geary utility function are complicated and difficult to interpret because of the interactions. In that the cross-equation restrictions do not seem to hold, a simplified retirement equation was estimated. Retirement was made linear in all the variables. The results of that estimation are in table 8.14. As before, the estimation method is instrumental variables taking own annuity and assets to be endogenous variables.

As far as the effects of own taste variables on own retirement age are concerned, they are about the same as the average effects from the Stone-Geary formulation. Both formulations produce an increase in retirement age of husbands of about .25 per year of age difference and .27 for wives. The effects

Table 8.14   **Simplified Model of Retirement Age**

	Male-Workers Sample		Female-Workers Sample	
	Husband Ret. Age	Wife Ret. Age	Wife Ret. Age	Husband Ret. Age
Age diff. ≥ 6	1.46[a]	−3.88[a]	−.08	3.65[a]
$6 >$ age diff. > -4	.19[a]	−.47[a]	−.08	.31[a]
$-4 \geq$ age diff.	.04	2.37[a]	1.13	−3.16[a]
Own health:				
Work	−.42	.10	−.36	−.16
Home	.42	1.15	−.60	.69
Both	−.37	−1.52[a]	−.68[a]	−1.14[a]
Spouse health:				
Work	.80[a]	−.18	.50	−.01
Home	.81	.75	.28	.49
Both	.38	−.28	.20	.31
Own wage	−.00	−.04	−.01	−.04
Spouse wage	−.01	.03	−.00	−.01
Own annuity (thous. annual) ([b])	−.056	.615[a]	.415[a]	−.047
Spouse annuity (thous. annual)	.064[a]	−.037	.006	.106[a]
Assets (thousands) ([b])	.006	−.011	−.021[a]	.007
Observations	983	983	702	702
R^2	.06	.21	.09	.23

Source: Author's calculations from the NBS.
Note: Age diff. = husband age − wife age.
[a] = $|t| > 1.96$.
[b]Endogenous Variable.

of the own health variables on own retirement age are given in table 8.15. The effects are remarkably consistent across estimation methods, and they are very similar for husbands and wives. There is, of course, some question about the interpretation of these effects: they are based on the reported health status after retirement. They will be the result of a mixture of people who become seriously ill so that they cannot work, people who may have a chronic minor illness so that they choose not to work, and a range of people in between. Although only 1–2 percent of the individuals report their health affects work at home, they work about a half a year longer than people with no such health limitation.

The effects of the economic variables can be most easily summarized by giving the change in retirement age that would result from changing a variable from the twenty-fifth percentile to the seventy-fifth. The changes in retirement age are given in table 8.16. The own wage response is practically zero here, whereas in the Stone-Geary formulation it was about − .5 year. Other differences are that in these results an increase in own annuities causes the husband to retire earlier, whereas in the Stone-Geary results he retired later. The wife's response to assets is almost three times as great as before.

The correlation between the residuals from the husband's and wife's retirement equation is .29 in the male data and .32 in the female data. Thus, even taking into account the age differences and the spouse's economic variables, there still remains unexplained positive correlation between the retirement ages.

If someone desires to work beyond the normal retirement age associated with his primary job, often he must change jobs, and often the new job has a lower wage rate than the primary job (Burtless and Moffitt 1985; Gustman and Steinmeier 1986). One would, therefore, tend to find a negative association between the wage and the retirement age. Put differently, the wage on the last job depends on the retirement age, so that, according to this reasoning, it is endogenous in a retirement equation. To check the empirical importance of this observation, the simplified retirement equation of table 8.14 was reestimated taking the own wage as well as assets and own annuity to be endogenous. The

Table 8.15   Effect of Own Health on Own Retirement

	Husbands		Wives	
	Stone-Geary	Simple	Stone-Geary	Simple
Job	− .35	− .29	− .22	− .13
Home	.60	.56	.47	.28
Both	− .85	− .76	− .92	− 1.10

Table 8.16

	Own Wage	Spouse Wage	Own Annuity	Spouse Annuity	Assets
Husband	− .13	− .04	− .41	.44	.40
Wife	− .10	.10	2.68	− .12	− 1.07

results are very similar to those in table 8.14, so they are not reported. Of particular interest is that the own wage response remains small.

A further method to find the interaction between retirement ages is to estimate a conditional retirement equation. It specifies that the retirement age of, say, the husband depends on the retirement age of the wife. From such an equation one can directly read the magnitude of the dependence. The theoretical justification is based on the conditional distribution of bivariate normal random variables. If X and Y are bivariate normal random variables, then

$$E(Y|X) = \mu_y + \rho \frac{\sigma_y}{\sigma_x}(X - \mu_x),$$

in which μ_y is $E(Y)$; μ_x is $E(X)$; ρ is the correlation coefficient between Y and X; and σ_y and σ_x are the standard errors of Y and X. Let Y be the retirement age of the husband and X be the retirement age of the wife. Then the coefficient on the retirement age of the wife in the husband's retirement equation should be $\rho\sigma_y/\sigma_x$.

Table 8.17 has the estimated conditional retirement equations. The functional form is the simplified retirement equation of table 8.14 with the addition that the spouse's retirement age enters as a right-hand variable. The estimated coefficients are qualitatively similar to those reported in table 8.14, so they will not be discussed further. Of greater interest is that the spouse's retirement age is an important explanatory variable. Increasing the wife's retirement age by a year increases the husband's retirement age by about .25 year (average over both data sets); increasing the husband's retirement age by a year increases the wife's retirement age by about .37 year. As discussed earlier, a rough estimate of the effect of the wife's retirement age on the husband's retirement age can be found from the results in table 8.8. That effect is .47. Given the great difference in methods, this compares rather well with the estimate in table 8.17. These relations between retirement ages are in addition to any induced by the age difference, which by itself would tend to cause retirement dates to be correlated.

The conditional retirement results may be compared with unconditional results by using the theory of normal random variables. As discussed above, the coefficient on X in the relation $E(Y|X)$ should be $\rho\sigma_y/\sigma_x$. ρ was estimated to be .24, σ_y to be 2.71, and σ_x to be 4.15 over the male workers data in unconditional estimation of the retirement ages in the simplified model with endogenous assets, own annuity and own wage.[5] Thus, the coefficient on X, the wife's retirement age in the conditional equation for the husband's retirement age, should be .24 × 2.71/4.15 = .16. The actual value from table 8.17 is .18. Table 8.18 summarizes the comparisons.

The comparisons are quite close and support further the joint retirement hypothesis. The general impression is that the husband's retirement age has a greater effect on the wife's retirement age than the wife's on the husband's. This accords with the generally accepted view in the labor supply literature.

Table 8.17   **Determinants of Conditional Retirement Age**

	Male-Workers Sample		Female-Workers Sample	
	Husband Ret. Age	Wife Ret. Age	Wife Ret. Age	Husband Ret. Age
Age diff. ≥ 6	1.98[a]	−2.13[a]	−1.36[a]	3.68[a]
$6 >$ age diff. > -4	.26[a]	−.30[a]	−.09	.31[a]
$-4 \geq$ age diff.	−.41	2.27[a]	1.65[a]	−3.39[a]
Own health:				
Work	−.45	−.11	−.19	−.22
Home	.17	1.02	−1.24	.75
Both	−.43	−1.57[a]	−.85[a]	−1.10[a]
Spouse health:				
Work	.69[a]	−.09	.47	−.29
Home	1.07	.76	−.24	.37
Both	.57[a]	−.08	.37	.47
Own wage ([b])	−.02	−.05	−.01	−.01
Spouse wage	.00	.03	−.02	−.01
Own annuity (thous. annual) ([b])	.007	.801[a]	.546[a]	.038
Spouse annuity (thous. annual)	−.001	−.049	.017	−.004
Assets (thousands) ([b])	.003	−.012	−.033[a]	.007
Spouse retirement age	.18[a]	.38[a]	.36[a]	.33[a]
Observations	983	983	702	702
R^2	.12	.26	.14	.30

Source: Author's calculations from the NBS.
Note: Age diff. = husband age − wife age.
[a] = $|t| > 1.96$.
[b]Endogenous variable.

Table 8.18

	Effect of Wife's Retirement Age on Husband's Retirement Age	
Data Set	Directly Estimated (table 8.17)	From Normal Theory
Male workers	.18	.16
Female workers	.33	.19
	Effect of Husband's Retirement Age on Wife's Retirement Age	
	Directly Estimated (table 8.17)	From Normal Theory
Male workers	.38	.37
Female workers	.36	.27

8.4   Conclusion

The results support the idea that the retirement of husbands and wives is a joint process. Often both spouses retire within a short period. The difference in age seems to cause substantial variation in retirement age. The rough estimate from the retirement probabilities is about .45 year per year of age difference. From either the Stone-Geary or the simple model, it is about .25. Given the wide differences in estimation methods, these estimates are in good agreement and certainly support the joint retirement hypothesis.

Generally, the cross-economic variables do not have a strong effect on retirement ages, so they do not provide a good explanation for the correlation of retirement dates. But it would be surprising to have strong cross-effects given that the own effects are not strong. Surely, this is at least partly due to weaknesses in the data and to the simplified estimation methods required by the data. In particular, one cannot construct the economic environment in the years before retirement.

The residual correlation between the retirement ages of husbands and wives also supports the joint retirement hypothesis. Of course, one does not know the cause of the correlation: it could be due to neglected economic variables, assortative mating, or true complementarity in the utility function.

Much more research on the joint retirement decision is needed. In particular, a close modeling of Social Security and pensions should be able to separate the wealth effects from the price effects. Nothing was done here about adjustment of hours within a year, which is often accompanied by a reduction in the wage rate. One would hope that future research would be able to account for these problems and to find the extent of true complementarity in retirement.

Notes

1. Henretta and O'Rand (1983) find in the RHS that increasing the age of the wife decreases the probability that she will retire after the husband, which seems to imply a correlation. But this result cannot be interpreted as a joint retirement decision: one would get the same result if individuals in the sample were randomly attached to other individuals simply because increasing age is associated with decreased labor force participation.

2. This table was suggested by David Ellwood.

3. The model does not have a role for the adjustment of annual hours of work. In this formulation, the wage is implicitly the annual wage (earnings); but in the estimation the hourly wage is used as it is surely a better measure of the cost of leisure.

4. The dependence of tastes on the age difference was, in estimation not reported here, represented by ten dummy variables; the relation was close enough to linear that tastes were made linear in age differences between minus four and six.

5. This correlation is slightly different from what was reported earlier because it comes from an equation in which the own wage is endogenous.

References

Boskin, M., and M. Hurd. 1978. The effect of Social Security on early retirement. *Journal of Public Economics* 10 (December):361–77.

Burkhauser, R. 1980. The early acceptance of Social Security—an asset maximization approach. *Industrial and Labor Relations Review* 33 (4):484–92.

Burtless, G., and R. Moffitt. 1985. The joint choice of retirement age and postretirement hours of work. *Journal of Labor Economics* 3:209–36.

Diamond, P., and J. Hausman. 1984. Individual retirement and savings behavior. *Journal of Public Economics* 23:81–114.

Gustman, A., and T. Steinmeier. 1986. A structural retirement model. *Econometrica* 54 (3):555–84.

Hausman, J., and D. Wise. 1985. Social Security, health status and retirement. In *Pensions, labor, and individual choice,* ed. D. Wise. Chicago: University of Chicago Press for the NBER.

Henretta, J., and A. O'Rand. 1983. Joint retirement in the dual worker family. *Social Forces* 62 (December):504–20.

Honig, M., and G. Hanoch. 1985. Partial retirement as a separate mode of retirement behavior. *Journal of Human Resources* 20 (Winter):21–46.

Hurd, M., and M. Boskin. 1984. The effect of Social Security on retirement in the early 1970's. *Quarterly Journal of Economics* (November):767–90.

Maxfield, L. 1983. The 1982 new beneficiary survey: An introduction. *Social Security Bulletin* 46 (11).

Mitchell, O., and G. Fields. 1983. Economic incentives to retire: A qualitative choice approach. NBER Working Paper no. 1128. Cambridge, Mass.: National Bureau of Economic Research.

———. 1984. The economics of retirement behavior. *Journal of Labor Economics* 2 (January):84–105.

Pozzebon, S., and O. Mitchell. 1989. Married women's retirement behavior. *Journal of Population Economics* 2(1): 39–53.

Sickles, R., and R. Taubman. 1986. An analysis of the health and retirement status of the elderly. *Econometrica* 54 (November):1339–56.

Comment   Gary Burtless

Michael Hurd's paper has two main goals. The author would like to provide good baseline information about the presence and magnitude of correlated retirement *dates* among working spouses. Do working spouses tend to retire on or around the same day? How large is the correlation? The second goal is to determine whether and how much economic variables contribute to the correlation in retirement dates. Is the correlation in retirement more or less than would be expected given the correlation in other variables that affect each spouse's retirement age? When describing his latter goal, Hurd prudently adds

Gary Burtless is a senior fellow in economic studies at the Brookings Institution, Washington, D.C.

that he will try to establish the facts "within the constraints of the data." As we shall see below, the constraints imposed by the data are severe.

The author mentions three reasons to expect some correlation in retirement dates: (a) sorting of marital partners by tastes, so that men and women who like to work or shirk seek out and wed a similarly inclined spouse; (b) effects of economic variables, such as asset income, that are shared by both spouses and affect the behavior of each; and (c) simultaneous determination of the utility each spouse derives from retirement. A retired worker who has a working spouse may enjoy less utility—at the same income level—than the same worker would obtain if his or her spouse were retired.

The first two reasons for correlation in retirement do not cause serious problems for the separate estimation of the retirement equations of husbands and wives. If there is a correlation in taste for work among marriage partners, for example, no special problems arise in estimation. In estimating an equation that explains husbands' retirement age, it is interesting and useful to learn that a correlation exists in the retirement ages of the two spouses. We could improve the efficiency of the unknown parameters in the retirement equation if the correlation in the error terms were taken into account. But, if the correlation in errors is ignored, there seems no reason to believe that the parameter estimates would be biased.

Similarly, in a static retirement model it would sometimes be useful to know that retirement ages of husbands and wives are correlated because both spouses face similar environmental factors. But, when the analyst has no particular interest in this correlation, nothing is lost if it is ignored.[1] The simplest estimation strategy is to include the wage of both spouses, the health status of both spouses, and the pension incentives facing each spouse in the separate equations for each spouse.

The third issue seems to me much more difficult to handle. Suppose we were given a data set with good information on retirement ages and the economic, health, and demographic determinants of retirement. If husbands and wives tend to retire on the same calendar date, irrespective of the other determinants of their individual retirement ages, this fact may have to be explicitly taken into account if the analyst wants to obtain unbiased estimates of the other coefficients in the system. The retirement age of the wife may be influenced, not only by the exogenous determinants of her husband's retirement age, but also by the actual realization of that age. How important is the bias that follows from ignoring this correlation? Before reading this paper, I would have thought that the potential bias is small.

This set of issues is examined using the New Beneficiary Survey (NBS), a survey of workers who began collecting Social Security old age insurance (OAI) benefits between June 1980 and May 1981. The sample is explicitly selected on the basis of the retirement or benefit acceptance choice of respondents.

The choice-based nature of the selection process introduces serious problems in estimation, as Hurd clearly demonstrates in the paper. For example, if we consider the subsample of 62-year-old men, we note two types of sample exclusions that affect the representativeness of the remaining sample. First, the survey excludes those workers who have already retired and accepted Social Security disability insurance (DI) benefits. And it excludes 62-year-old men who will accept their OAI pension at a later age. If we are interested only in the retirement behavior of nondisabled men, the first exclusion is not very troubling. But the second exclusion—of nonretired 62-year-olds—is extremely serious. The NBS sample systematically excludes information on 62-year-olds who have greater taste for work and who have independent variables associated with above-average retirement ages. This exclusion will clearly bias any inference we want to draw about the retirement behavior of all nondisabled 62-year-old men.

As Hurd points out, the effects of the sample exclusion can be overcome under certain assumptions, in particular, under the assumption that the economic and demographic determinants of retirement are constant across time and across age cohorts. Although we are missing data on 62-year-olds who wish to retire later than average, we possess data on 65- and 70-year-olds who *do* retire later than average. If the population is static, the data set contains information on a good cross section of individual tastes and economic and demographic determinants of retirement.

In a sample as aged as this one, however, it may not be plausible to assume that population conditions are static. Mortality rates, especially among men, are quite high between ages 62 and 72. Some 62-year-old workaholics will never survive long enough to accept a Social Security pension. These are the hard drivers who work until they drop—or at least they drop sometime before age 72 when they would be mailed a check even without retiring. You always resented these characters in high school and college—unless you were one yourself. They messed up the grading curve in school, and now they screw up our econometric models by denying us deathbed information on critical X-variables.

In addition, Hurd points out that it would be dangerous to assume that the population is static, anyway. Economic variables—such as the wage—are not constant across successive cohorts. To take a simple example, if the wage is higher in each cohort, workers retiring at age 70 could have a worse earnings record than workers retiring at age 62. Even if the wage has *no* effect on retirement, the analyst using this data set might incorrectly conclude that low wages lead to later retirements.

Hurd might also have mentioned a further economic factor, one that seems especially significant in light of his views on the effects of Social Security on early retirement. The younger retirees in the NSB sample were affected by the most dramatic benefit *cut* in social security history. Those of you who read Dear Abby will know what I am talking about: the notorious Social Security "notch babies." They are not exactly spring chickens today, of course, since they turned 65 between 1982 and 1986. But these folks were hit by major benefit cuts as a result of the Social Security amendments passed in 1977, which became effective in 1979. About half Hurd's sample was born just before the notch took effect, while the remaining half had the bad luck to be born just after.

You might think this issue is relevant only to cranks who write Dear Abby or who badger hapless congressmen in Washington. To allay these suspicions, let me report a couple of numbers.

- If you were an average-wage worker, had worked steadily throughout your career, and turned 65 on 31 December 1981, you would have received a Social Security check on 1 January 1982 equal to 51 percent of your last month's earnings in December.
- If you had an identical earnings record but the great misfortune to turn 65 on 2 January 1982, your 1 February 1982 Social Security check would have been just 41 percent of your December wage earnings.

In other words, the benefit replacement rate dropped from 51 to 41 percent at midnight, 1 January 1982. For you who are a little slow at arithmetic, that is a 20 percent drop in real benefits for the identical earnings record.

Not only did notch babies receive sharply lower benefits if they retired at age 65, but they also obtained much smaller benefit increments if they delayed retirement for additional years.

Boskin and Hurd (1978) found that the benefit increase in 1972–73 had a major effect on retirement patterns after 1972. (That conclusion is repeated near the beginning of this paper.) I would expect equally dramatic effects of the benefit cut passed in 1977. Do we see any delay in retirement among "notch babies"?

Interesting though this question is, Hurd does not directly address it in this paper. Rather, he wants to know whether there is a correlation between the retirement dates chosen by husbands and wives. How important is this correlation? The evidence in the paper suggests that the issue merits some attention.

In his first set of tabulations, Hurd finds that there is some tendency for husbands and wives to retire near the same calendar date. Partly, this is because the husbands and wives he looks at tend to have similar calendar ages and because he excludes from his comparisons those couples who retire at widely different ages. Within the sample of couples he looks at, however, there appears to be some clustering of retirement dates.

The cross-tabulations used to draw this inference are based on a relatively small proportion of the observations in the NBS. One of the reasons is that families are excluded if either husband or wife stopped working by age 54. Another reason is that retirement ages were required for both husbands and wives—so, if the spouse of the new beneficiary had not yet retired by the interview date, the observation was excluded. Both these criteria will tend to exclude couples with wide differences in retirement ages and, presumably, in retirement dates.

Nonetheless, Hurd's conclusion appears to be borne out using a variety of different analytic techniques and number of cross-classification schemes. In the concluding section of the paper, Hurd presents estimates of a reduced-form joint retirement equation, one that links information about both husbands and wives in estimating the separate retirement behavior of the two spouses. Given the limitations of his data set, the exact coefficient estimates should probably be viewed with some skepticism.

Even taking account of all the statistical problems with the estimation procedures, however, it is still reasonable to conclude, as Hurd does, that the correlations in the data support his basic inference: for many couples in the sample, retirement is a jointly determined process. Only a fraction of the correlation in retirement dates is explained by the observable economic variables that affect both members of a married couple.

Having satisfied ourselves that Hurd's inference is a reasonable one, how should we alter the statistical methods typically used to estimate retirement models? In certain kinds of models, it is feasible to account explicitly for the correlation of husband and wife retirement dates. Where this is feasible, it certainly should be done. For many models, however, it would be extremely difficult, if not impossible, to control statistically for the correlation between retirement dates of husbands and wives. The results in this paper, while suggestive, do not seem strong enough to require us to toss out the findings obtained from the latter type of model.

Note

1. For example, most analysts have been interested in the effects of Social Security, private pensions, or health on retirement ages. If the specification of these factors in the individual retirement equations is correct, no explicit account need be taken of the correlation in spouses' retirement ages arising from the correlation in their environmental factors.

Reference

Boskin, M., and M. Hurd. 1978. The effect of Social Security on early retirement. *Journal of Public Economics* 10 (December):361–77.

9 How Do the Elderly Form Expectations? An Analysis of Responses to New Information

B. Douglas Bernheim

A large fraction of the existing work on the economics of aging and the retirement period procedes on the basis of life-cycle assumptions, which hold that individuals form very rational and deliberate long-range plans. Implicit in these assumptions is the notion that individuals develop well-informed opinions about the economic factors that will affect their well-being in the future. Despite the existence of a small body of work on the accuracy of expectations concerning Social Security benefits (Bernheim 1988), the timing of retirement (Hall and Johnson 1980; Parnes and Nestel 1981; Anderson, Burkhauser, and Quinn 1986; Wolpin and Gönül 1987; and Bernheim 1989) and inflation (see Zarnowitz 1984 and the references contained therein), very little is actually known about the manner in which individuals incorporate new information into expectations.

The purpose of this paper is to examine the evolution of self-reported expectations about Social Security benefits during the preretirement period and to examine the responses of these expectations to the arrival of new information. The central questions are as follows. Do expectations evolve in the manner predicted by theory? What kind of information leads individuals to revise their expectations, and what is the nature of the responses? Are revisions "rational," in the sense that they closely resemble the effects of new information on objective measures of expected benefits? Since models of consumer decision making inevitably invoke a host of assumptions concerning expectations, these questions logically precede any analysis of behavior. I plan to study the relation between self-reported expectations and behavior in subsequent work.

B. Douglas Bernheim is the Harold Hines Jr. Distinguished Professor of Risk Management of the J. L. Kellogg Graduate School of Management, Northwestern University, and a research associate at the National Bureau of Economic Research.

Funding from the National Institute on Aging through its grant to the NBER is gratefully acknowledged.

The current investigation employs a data sample drawn from the Retirement History Survey (RHS). The longitudinal nature of this survey makes it possible to observe and compare expectations reported by the same households at different points in time and to relate observed changes to intervening events. My central conclusions are as follows.

First, a variety of simple tests appear to reject the most basic implications of the theory that forms the basis for this analysis. As in Bernheim (1988), I attribute these apparent failures to the fact that reported expectations are extremely noisy. When one corrects for the presence of reporting error through the appropriate use of instrumental variables, the resulting estimates are generally consistent with the theory. In particular, one cannot reject the hypotheses that expectations evolve as a random walk and that innovations in this process are unrelated to prior information.

Having concluded that the data support these basic implications, I use the theory to formulate an empirical specification that relates changes in expectations to the arrival of new information. Using this specification, I estimate responses of expectations to informational events and test for the rationality of these responses. The results are striking. Responses to new information during the period immediately preceding retirement appear to be highly rational. The bulk of information affects the evolution of expectations only through its effect on actual benefit levels computed from contemporaneous benefit formulas and earnings histories. Furthermore, the data support the view that individuals form accurate assessments of the ultimate effect of new information on actual benefits.

These results contrast sharply with findings based on analyses of expected benefit *levels* rather than *changes* in expected benefits. In Bernheim (1988), I found that certain variables—especially current statutory Social Security benefit entitlements—were highly correlated with subsequent forecast errors. This implies that individuals do not make complete use of all the information contained in these variables. Nevertheless, these same individuals are very good at processing information that arrives just prior to retirement. Specifically, while they are apparently incompletely informed about the level of benefits associated with contemporaneous benefit formulas, they revise expectations as if they understand how new information affects the benefits prescribed by these formulas *on the margin*. This result suggests that individuals formulate expectations about the retirement period much more carefully as retirement approaches and therefore corroborates some speculative conclusions based on more sketchy evidence that appeared in Bernheim (1988). At the same time, this finding supports the hypothesis that, because individuals appreciate the links between behavior and benefits at the margin, benefit formulas may have incentive effects. This hypothesis has formed the basis for many previous studies of the retirement decision (see Hurd 1983).

The remainder of this paper is organized as follows. Section 9.1 presents the basic model of expectations. I discuss the data in section 9.2. Section 9.3

contains tests of the model's central implications, and section 9.4 examines responses of expectations to new information. The paper closes with a brief conclusion.

9.1   A Model of Expectations

Suppose that, at each point in time t, an individual forms an expectation, X_t^e, about the value of a variable X that is realized at some point in the future. During period t, he has access to certain information, which I denote Ω_t. Throughout, I assume that the individual's memory is perfect, so that all information available at time t is also available in period $t + 1$. Formally, $\Omega_{t+1} = (\Omega_t, \omega_{t+1})$, where ω_{t+1} represents information that becomes available between periods t and $t + 1$.

In subsequent sections, I interpret X as Social Security benefits. When an individual reports expected Social Security benefits, there is, of course, some ambiguity as to what this means. While he may have in mind something like a mathematical expectation, it is also possible that his report reflects his view of the most likely outcome (i.e., the mode). As long as the distribution of X is approximately symmetric and single peaked, this ambiguity is probably of very little consequence. However, it is important to bear in mind that the mathematical interpretation that one places on a reported expectation becomes a joint hypothesis with any other proposition that one wishes to test. In particular, failure of tests for "rationality" (discussed below) could simply reflect misinterpretation of the reported data. With this qualification in mind, I henceforth focus on the hypothesis that individuals report expected values, that is,

$$(1) \qquad\qquad X_t^e = E(X|\Omega_t),$$

where E is the expectations operator.

From equation (1), it follows that

$$(2) \qquad E(X_{t+1}^e|\Omega_t) = E\left[E(X|\Omega_t, \omega_{t+1})|\Omega_t\right] = E(X|\Omega_t) = X_t^e.$$

This expression describes the stochastic evolution of expectations through time and is the basis for the conclusion that expectations should follow a random walk. In particular, (2) implies that

$$(3) \qquad\qquad X_{t+1}^e = X_t^e + \eta_{t+1},$$

where

$$(4) \qquad\qquad E(\eta_{t+1}|\Omega_t) = 0.$$

Furthermore, η_{t+1} should be a function of new information received since period t, ω_{t+1}.

The analysis of this paper is based on the simple model described in equations (3) and (4). Using these as the basis for an empirical specification, I investigate the manner in which expectations respond to new information. The validity of my empirical results depends critically on the appropriateness of this underlying framework. It is therefore essential to test the framework as thoroughly as possible.

Fortunately, the model lends itself to a number of direct tests. Note that we can write

$$(5) \qquad \text{var}(X_{t+1}^e) = \text{var}(X_t^e) + \text{var}(\eta_{t+1})$$
$$= \text{var}(X_t^e) + \text{var}(X_{t+1}^e - X_t^e) > \text{var}(X_t^e).$$

Two implications follow directly from equation (5). First, the population variance of expectations reported at a particular point in time should be greater than the population variance of expectations reported at earlier points in time. Second, the difference between these population variances should be *exactly* the variance of their differences. In Bernheim (1987), I studied the first of these implications and found the data somewhat supportive. However, since the focus of that study was a comparison of expectations and realizations (rather than a comparison of expectations at different points in time), I did not consider the second implication.

Equations (3) and (4) also suggest a regression format that facilitates further testing of the underlying model. Suppose in particular that we use ordinary least squares to estimate an equation of the form

$$(6) \qquad X_{t+1,i}^e = \alpha + \beta X_{t,i}^e + \Omega_{t,i}\gamma + \epsilon_{t,i},$$

where i indexes individuals. Theory implies that we should obtain $\alpha = \gamma = 0$ and $\beta = 1$. Furthermore, our estimate of σ_ϵ^2 measures σ_η^2. This test is quite demanding, in that the underlying hypothesis includes the assertion that, in forming his expectation, the individual actually uses—and uses efficiently—all information observed by the econometrician. I therefore refer to it as a test of "strong" rationality. One can also conduct a weaker, less demanding test by omitting the informational variables and simply regressing X_{t+1}^e on X_t^e. Theory implies that the intercept and slope coefficients should be zero and one, respectively. This test allows for the possibility that individuals do not form expectations on the basis of all available information. However, the underlying hypothesis retains the key feature that expectations evolve as a random walk, responding only to new information.

If the tests of the underlying model prove favorable, then one can use the model of expectations embodied in equations (3) and (4) to measure responses of expectations to new information. Since η_{t+1} is related exclusively to *new* information, I write it as a function of *surprises:*

$$\eta_{t+1} = \psi[\omega_{t+1} - E(\omega_{t+1}|\Omega_t)].$$

Substitution into (3) yields an expression for adjustments in expectations:

(7) $$X^e_{t+1} - X^e_t = \psi[\omega_{t+1} - E(\omega_{t+1}|\Omega_t)].$$

This in turn suggests a regression of changes in expectations on variables that contain new information received after period t. The coefficients in this regression will reflect the magnitude of responses to particular types of information. Implementing this strategy is somewhat problematic, in that all variables have both expected and unexpected components and therefore measure blends new and old information. I take up specific estimation issues in section 9.4.

9.2 Data

The data for this study are drawn from the Social Security Administration's Retirement History Survey (RHS), which followed a sample of retirement-aged households (58–63 years old in 1969) for a period of ten years, beginning in 1969. Each household was surveyed once every two years (1969, 1971, 1973, 1975, 1977, and 1979). Although the initial wave included more than 11,000 households, there was substantial attrition over successive waves.

In 1969, 1971, and 1973, respondents reported the level of Social Security benefits that they expected to receive on retirement. In subsequent sections, the variables ESS71 and ESS73 (expected Social Security in 1971 and 1973, respectively) reflect answers to these questions, adjusted to an annual basis. Inspection of the data for 1969 revealed a low response rate (due in part to survey skip patterns) as well as a high frequency of nonsensical values. I have therefore confined attention to responses given in 1971 and 1973. In what follows, the variable CESS measures the *change* in expectations between these two years (i.e., CESS = ESS73 − ESS71).

Unfortunately, interpretation of expected benefits is somewhat problematic, in that the treatment of inflation is ambiguous. Certainly, the survey instrument does not specify whether the individual is to report a real or a nominal figure. Throughout, I simply assume that respondents report expected benefits in current (i.e., survey year) dollars. This seems the most natural choice since respondents would otherwise have had to forecast future inflation rates before formulating an answer to the question. To the extent that my assumption is incorrect, the scale of expectations may vary somewhat between 1971 and 1973.

Tests of the strong rationality hypothesis, as well as some of the other exercises conducted in section 9.4 of this paper, require the collection of informational variables that are candidates for inclusion in Ω_t. In this paper, I employ essentially the same informational variables as in Bernheim (1988). I group these into three distinct categories.

The first category contains variables that measure other reported expectations. These are natural candidates for inclusion in Ω_t since they necessarily reflect information that the individual has used to generate forecasts. If any of these variables appear with significant coefficients in estimates of equation (6), it would indicate that, at a minimum, individuals use different kinds of information to form different expectations. Definitions of specific variables follow:

ERET71:   Expected date of retirement reported in 1971.
ERET69:   Expected date of retirement reported in 1969.
EOI71:   Expected retirement income other than Social Security, reported in 1971.
EOI69:   Expected retirement income other than Social Security, reported in 1969.

Data on expectations are, of course, incomplete—many individuals who report expected Social Security benefits do not, for example, report an expected date of retirement. Accordingly, I also use dummy variables, DRET71 and DRET69, which equal one if the individual reports the associated expectation and zero otherwise. In the final sample (described below), all individuals responded to questions about retirement income other than Social Security, so no companion dummies for the EOI71 and EOI69 variables were required.

The second category includes various demographic variables and other household characteristics that might be useful in predicting future Social Security benefits. The list of variables includes:

AGE: The respondent's age.
SAGE: The respondent's wife's age.
ED: The respondent's education (measured in number of years).
SED: The respondent's wife's education.
W: The household's net wealth (including financial assets, businesses, and real property).
HGOOD: A dummy variable, indicating whether the respondent reports his health as being better than average for his age (1 = better, 0 = other).
HBAD: A dummy variable, indicating whether the respondent reports his health as being worse than average for his age (1 = worse, 0 = other).
KIDS: Number of living children.
COMPRET: A dummy variable, indicating whether the respondent's employer maintains a compulsory retirement age (1 = yes, 0 = no).
MOVE: A dummy variable, indicating whether the respondent has moved within the past two years (1 = has moved, 0 = has not moved).

The third and final category consists of a single variable, which is the individual's current Social Security entitlement, CSS71, defined as the level of benefits he would receive under current law if he retired immediately. CSS71 is, theoretically, part of each individual's information set in 1971, in that it depends only on his own past earnings history and on current law (which is public information). Special treatment of CSS71 is warranted in light of my earlier findings (Bernheim 1988), which indicated that individuals fail to use much of the information contained in this variable and furthermore that, quantitatively, this is by far the most important source of unused information.

Since this study focuses on the responses of expectations to new information, it is also essential to compile a list of variables that are candidates for inclusion in ω_{t+1}. Each of the following variables describes some aspect of a change in an individual's status between 1971 and 1973 and could conceivably be related to the ultimate realization of Social Security benefits:

HBET: A dummy variable, indicating whether the self-reported index of health status improved (1 = improvement, 0 = other).

HWOR: A dummy variable, indicating whether the self-reported index of health status deteriorated (1 = deterioration, 0 = other).

WIDM: A dummy variable, indicating whether the wife died between 1971 and 1973 (1 = wife died, 0 = other).

WIDW: A dummy variable, indicating whether the husband died between 1971 and 1973 (1 = husband died, 0 = other).

LJOB: A dummy variable, indicating whether the respondent was employed in 1971 but not in 1973 (1 = lost job, 0 = other).

GJOB: A dummy variable, indicating whether the respondent was employed in 1973 but not in 1971 (1 = obtained job, 0 = other).

CJOB: A dummy variable, indicating that the respondent was employed in different jobs in 1971 and 1973 (1 = different jobs, 0 = other).

NMOVE: A dummy variable, indicated whether the respondent moved between 1971 and 1973 (1 = moved, 0 = other).

CW: The change in the respondent's wealth between 1971 and 1973.

CCSS: The change in the respondent's statutory Social Security entitlement between 1971 and 1973.

Finally, while the focus of this analysis is on changes in expectations (rather than on the accuracy of expectations *per se*), some of the exercises in section 9.4 require measures of ultimate realizations. I calculate each realization by applying the benefit formula in effect at the individual's date of retirement to earnings histories from matching administrative records provided by the Social Security Administration. For details, I refer the reader to Bernheim (1988).

The basic sample population for this analysis consisted of RHS respondents who in 1971 were married and not yet receiving Social Security benefits. Individuals who failed to report expectations about Social Security benefits in 1971, as well as a few who reported nonsensical values (in excess of $20,000 per year), were dropped. In order to compare expectations across years, I restricted attention to respondents who still had not begun to receive Social Security benefits in 1973 and who reported an expectation in that year as well. I dropped a small number of observations for which key variables (marital status in 1973, health status in 1973, spouse's age, number of children, and compulsory retirement) were either missing or nonsensical. The resulting sample contained one individual who failed to report an expectation about retirement income other than Social Security in either 1969 or 1971—rather than create a dummy variable like DRET71, I simply dropped this observation. This left a total of 370 observations.

Since the sample used here is a rather small fraction of the total survey population, one naturally wonders whether it is very representative. In particular, the majority of individuals fail to report expectations. Nonreporting might itself reflect a failure to think seriously about the retirement process. If so, statistical analysis based on the fraction of the sample that reports expectations may be very misleading.

Fortunately, nonreporting appears to be fairly random and is perhaps more commonly attributable to fatigue resulting from the length of the survey instrument or to the styles of different interviewers. If nonreporting reflected a failure to think seriously about and plan for the retirement period, then one would expect nonreporting of expected benefits and nonreporting of expected retirement dates to be highly correlated. In fact, this is not the case. Of those married men who reported expected Social Security benefits in 1971, 42 percent also reported an expected retirement date. For those who did not report expected benefits in 1971, the figure was only slightly lower (40 percent). Of those who reported expected benefits in 1973, 34 percent also reported an expected retirement date. For those who did not report expected benefits in 1973, the figure was slightly higher (36 percent). In addition, there is only a mild correlation between reporting of expected benefits in 1971 and reporting of expected benefits in 1973. Forty-five percent of married males reported expected benefits in 1971, as did 39 percent in 1973. Of those who reported expected benefits in 1971, only 49 percent also reported this expectation in 1973.

One might also argue that those who reported expected benefits in both 1971 and 1973 could be atypical. Some insight into this issue can be gained from considering a few summary statistics. Table 9.1 contains means and standard deviations for the variables that measure expectations about Social Security benefit levels (ESS71 and ESS73), the change in expectations (CESS), and the actual realization (SS). Note that the average expected benefit rose just over 2 percent between 1971 and 1973. In 1971, expectations were about 10 percent

Table 9.1   **Summary Statistics on Expectations**

Variable	Mean	Standard deviation
ESS71	2,307	881
ESS73	2,362	1,164
CESS	55	1,229
SS	2,550	1,003

lower than realizations, while in 1973 they were about 8 percent lower. All these numbers (including the standard deviations) coincide very closely to summary statistics presented in Bernheim (1988). Those earlier calculations were based on much larger samples owing to the fact that it was not necessary to restrict attention to respondents who reported expected benefits *both* in 1971 *and* in 1973 (in that paper, the object was to compare expectations to realizations rather than to subsequent expectations). The similarity of these summary statistics suggests that the smaller sample is representative.

Before passing on to analysis of the data, it is important to discuss two potential problems. The first concerns sample selection biases. Many of the criteria for dropping observations are based on characteristics that were observed in 1971. In principle, such factors are part of Ω_{71}, the respondent's information set in 1971, and, according to theory, are therefore unrelated to η_{73}. Sample selection of this sort is therefore not likely to produce systematic biases. Other selection criteria are based on characteristics that are observed after 1971. In principle, these could be systematically related to new information and hence to η_{73}. In Bernheim (1988), I argued that some of these (e.g., attrition due to death) are not likely to create significant problems. Unfortunately, owing to the nature of the current excercise, I have had to impose more demanding requirements on data availability during the period after an expectation is reported (most important, the individual must report an expectation in 1973 as well as in 1971). This enhances significantly the probability that one or more of the selection criteria are in fact problematic. I have therefore given some explicit attention to these issues in the econometric implementation.

The second and perhaps more serious problem concerns nonindependence of realizations. Tests such as those described in section 9.1 are most commonly conducted with time-series data on the same individual or set of individuals, so that, under the null hypothesis, independence of the error terms is guaranteed. When one instead relies primarily on cross-sectional data from a short panel such as the RHS, theory does not rule out systematic correlation of error terms across observations. Correlation could arise for a variety of reasons.

The most important potential source of correlation is a macro event that affects a significant fraction (perhaps all) of the sample simultaneously. Suppose, for example, that subsequent to the date at which X_i^e is recorded,

Congress unexpectedly raises benefits by 20 percent. Assuming that individuals process this information, one would presumably discover that on average η_{t+1} is significantly positive. Such an event did in fact occur in September 1972. However, this was for the most part an across-the-board increase in benefit levels. As a result, it probably affected little more than the scale of expectations. To put it another way, one would not be surprised to find $\beta > 1$ in estimates of equation (6), and one should not construe this as contrary to theory. Indeed, through estimates of β, one can hope to discern the extent to which this change was either anticipated *ex ante* or ignored *ex post*. Finally, one would still expect to find $\alpha = \gamma = 0$ if the theory is accurate. The data would fail to satisfy these restrictions only if elements of Ω_{71} were related to the probability of processing information about the new law (or processing it correctly) or to the nature of behavioral responses to the law. I tend to discount both possibilities. In particular, the results in Bernheim (1988) suggest that the 1972 legislation was largely anticipated, and the summary statistics in table 9.1 show little evidence of an upward surge in expectations after 1972. Furthermore, the analyses of Burtless (1986) and Bernheim (1989) suggest that the effect of the 1972 legislation on the timing of retirement was small.

9.3   Tests of the Model

In this section, I test various implications of the model presented in section 9.1 using the data described in section 9.2. This nature of these tests is very similar to those in Bernheim (1988), except that in my earlier work I focused on the relation between realizations and expectations rather than that between expectations at different points in time. Many findings from my earlier study are relevant to, and corroborated by the results of, this section. Most important, the previous study found that survey responses to questions about expected benefits are quite noisy and that failure to deal with this problem leads to apparent rejection of the theory. However, when the noise is treated through an appropriate instrumental variables technique, the results are highly favorable to the hypothesis of weak rationality and indeed indicate that individuals are quite good at forming expectations based on the subset of information that they do use. These issues reappear in the current context and must be dealt with explicitly.

9.3.1   Tests of Weak Rationality

Section 9.1 describes a theory of information processing. That theory does not necessarily assume or imply that individuals use all the information that is in principle available to them. Fortunately, even in the absence of any prior knowledge about what kinds of information individuals do and do not use to form expectations, the theory still has some testable implications. As I have already discussed, there are several natural tests based on equation (5), and these certainly do not require knowledge of Ω_t. In addition, since X_t^e is (trivially) part of the information set used in forming expectations at time t, expectations always evolve according to equation (3), where in place of (4) we substitute

$$E(\eta_{t+1}|X_t^e) = 0,$$

(i.e., they always follow a random walk). Thus, another minimalistic test would be based on ordinary least squares estimation of the equation

(8) $$X_{t+1}^e = \alpha + \beta X_t^e + \eta_{t+1}.$$

Regardless of what Ω_t contains, theory implies that $\alpha = 0$ and $\beta = 1$. This section is devoted to the implementation of these tests.

I begin with tests based on equation (5). The summary statistics in table 9.1 are certainly consistent with the prediction that $\text{var}(X_{t+1}^e) > \text{var}(X_t^e)$, and indeed this corroborates the finding of Bernheim (1988). However, on the basis of these statistics, it is also evident that support for the theory is superficial at best. In particular, the difference between the variances *cannot* equal the variance of the differences (i.e., var[CESS]) since the latter by itself exceeds var(ESS73). Indeed, the standard deviation of ESS73 would have to be about 30 percent larger than its actual value in order to satisfy the equality in (5).

One can make this same point through estimation of equation (8). Results for ordinary least squares are contained in column 1 of table 9.2. Note that the intercept is quantitatively large and statistically significant, while the slope is less than one-half and estimated with great precision. On the basis of these estimates, one would be inclined to conclude that the data resoundingly reject even the simplest implications of our central hypothesis.

Fortunately, this negative conclusion is premature. As emphasized in Bernheim (1988), much evidence indicates that expectations about Social Security benefits are reported with a great deal of noise. This may at first seem peculiar. With a variable like wealth or income, noise may arise from imprecise measurement on the part of respondents. In contrast, an individual creates his own expectations and therefore cannot have any problem measuring

Table 9.2   **Tests of Weak Rationality**

Variable	Equation				
	1	2	3	4	5
Technique	OLS	IV	IV	IV-Heckit	IV-Heckit
Intercept	1,429	−559	−307	−93.1	−213
	(176)	(1,287)	(661)	(879)	(685)
ESS71	.400	1.27	1.16	1.37	1.22
	(.0791)	(.557)	(.285)	(.400)	(.373)
MILLS				−897	−314
				(757)	(546)

them. There are, however, other sources of noise. Some individuals may tend to exaggerate, reporting a higher number than they believe, while others may be prone to understate their assets. Alternatively, individuals may use relatively precise figures when formulating financial plans but provide only "ballpark" figures to interviewers. Respondents might also think in terms of replacement rates (i.e., the percentage of preretirement income provided by Social Security) rather than absolute levels and may err in the process of converting one to the other. Finally, some noise is undoubtably attributable to recording and coding errors.

The analysis of my previous paper established that a standard errors-in-variables specification, combined with the basic theory of expectations outlined above, explained the relation between expectations and realizations rather well. It is therefore quite possible that reporting error also accounts for the apparent failure of the theory in the current context.

Unfortunately, one cannot in the absence of additional information adjust the tests based on equation (5) for the presence of reporting error. Nevertheless, one can "back out" the variance of the measurement error that would make the observed variances consistent with theory. This is accomplished as follows.

Suppose that for each τ we observe $\tilde{X}_\tau^e$, which is related to X_τ^e as follows:

$$\tilde{X}_\tau^e = X_\tau^e + \mu_\tau ,$$

where μ_τ is uncorrelated with X_τ^e. Suppose further that the μ_τ are independently and identically distributed, with variance σ_μ^2. Then equation (5) implies that

$$\text{var}(\tilde{X}_{t+1}^e) - \sigma_\mu^2 = \text{var}(\tilde{X}_t^e) + \text{var}(\tilde{X}_{t+1}^e - \tilde{X}_t^e) - 3\sigma_\mu^2 .$$

From this expression, it follows that

$$\sigma_\mu^2 = \frac{\text{var}(\tilde{X}_t^e) + \text{var}(\tilde{X}_{t+1}^e - \tilde{X}_t^e) - \text{var}(\tilde{X}_{t+1}^e)}{2} .$$

Substitution of the summary statistics from table 9.1 into this formula reveals that $\sigma_\mu = 682$, so that approximately 60 percent of the variance in ESS71 and 35 percent of the variance in ESS73 is attributable to measurement error.

While the preceding calculation assumes the existence of reporting error, one can actually test this hypothesis through estimation of equation (8). The standard prescription for reporting error is to employ instrumental variables. One requires that the instrument is uncorrelated with both η_{t+1} and μ_t but correlated with X_t^e. Accordingly, valid instruments must be related to information that the individual actually uses to construct X_t^e. Thus, one necessarily tests the basic theory and the measurement error hypothesis jointly with the assumption that individuals actually use certain information (i.e., that contained in the instruments) in a manner consistent with theory.

The second column in table 9.2 contains estimates of (8) for which I have instrumented ESS71 with measures of other expectations (i.e., the first group of variables discussed in sec. 9.2 as candidates for inclusion in Ω_t). The use of these variables as instruments is based on the plausible assumption that individuals' expectations are internally consistent, in the sense that all expectations are based on the same information. The results in Bernheim (1988) lend strong support to this assumption. Note that the estimated coefficients change dramatically. The intercept is now negative and statistically insignificant, while the slope coefficient rises to 1.27 and is statistically indistinguishable from unity.

The third column in table 9.2 contains estimates of (8) for which I have instrumented ESS71 with various socioeconomic and demographic variables (i.e., the second group of variables discussed in sec. 9.2 as candidates for inclusion in Ω_t). The use of these variables as instruments is supported by the findings in Bernheim (1988)—while individuals do not appear to use all this information efficiently, the extent of the departure from theory is not of much quantitative importance. Once again, the estimated coefficients change dramatically. The intercept becomes negative and statistically insignificant, while the slope coefficient rises to 1.16 and is statistically indistinguishable from unity.

For both sets of estimates, one cannot reject the hypothesis that $\alpha = 0$ and $\beta = 1$ at reasonable levels of confidence. Of course, this is in large part due to the fact that standard errors are enormous. By itself, this evidence is only weakly supportive of the underlying hypotheses. It becomes far more persuasive in the context of my earlier results. In regressions of realizations on expectations (see Bernheim 1988), precisely the same pattern emerged— simple regressions produced large positive intercepts and slope coefficients of roughly .5, while instrumental variables techniques drove the intercepts toward zero and generated slope coefficients of about 1.1. Furthermore, since the earlier study made use of much larger samples, the precision of these estimates was substantially greater. The fact that the predicted pattern arises in two different estimation contexts lends strong support to the underlying joint hypotheses.

It is also possible to "back out" estimates of σ_μ from the IV results. Standard calculations reveal that the bias in the OLS estimate of the slope parameter is proportional to the noise-to-signal ratio. Furthermore, the IV estimates are consistent. Using these facts, it is easy to show that

$$\hat{\sigma}_\mu^2 = \hat{\sigma}_{\bar{x}}^2 (1 - \beta_{ols}/\beta_{iv})$$

yields a consistent estimate of σ_μ^2, where $\hat{\sigma}_{\bar{x}}^2$ is the population variance of $\bar{X}_t^e$, and β_{ols} and β_{iv} are, respectively, the OLS and IV estimates of β. The preceding paragraphs describe two sets of IV results. For the first set, the implied value of $\hat{\sigma}_\mu$ is 728, while for the second it is 712. Since the estimated β's are quite close to unity, these values are not far from the figure derived from equation (5) (i.e., 682). Moreover, one can undertake a similar exercise for the regressions of realizations on expectations contained in Bernheim (1988). The implied variance for measurement error for 1971 is 660, which is in the same ballpark. The striking similarity of estimates obtained from two distinct empirical exercises again lends support to the joint hypotheses outlined above.

In section 9.2, I mentioned that this analysis suffers from potential sample selection problems. To assess the importance of these factors, I introduced a statistical correction based on the procedure outlined by Heckman (1976). First, I created a larger data sample containing the original sample plus all the observations that were excluded on the basis of characteristics observed after 1971. Next, I estimated a probit relation that explained inclusion in the original sample as a function of the instrument list and used these estimates to form inverse Mill's ratios. I then augmented equation (8) with the inverse Mill's ratio term and estimated it with two-stage least squares, using both the original instrument list and the inverse Mill's ratio as instruments. This procedure treats both the endogeneity of ESS71 and the sample selection problem simultaneously and yields consistent estimates.

Results for the two instrument lists discussed above appear in columns 4 and 5 of table 9.2. While the slope coefficients rise slightly, this change is dwarfed by the original standard errors. In addition, the Mill's ratios do not appear to enter significantly (note, however, that I have not adjusted the standard errors for the fact that these terms are estimated rather than observed). Overall, the sample selection correction appears to make very little quantitative or qualitative difference. Indeed, none of the estimates in this paper were significantly affected by the introduction of similar corrections. In subsequent sections, I have conserved space by presenting only uncorrected OLS and IV estimates. Results based on sample selection corrections are available on request.

In summary, the data are consistent with the hypothesis of weak rationality. This fact is obscured by the presence of significant reporting error, which biases simple regression estimates and leads to apparent rejections of the theory. Unfortunately, estimates that correct for the presence of measurement error are imprecise, so that the associated tests have little power. However, taken in conjunction with previous work, this analysis validates the use of weak rationality as a maintained hypothesis in subsequent sections.

9.3.2   Tests of Strong Rationality

In my previous study of expectations and realizations (Bernheim 1988), I found that, while the data were consistent with the hypothesis of weak rationality, they were highly inconsistent with strong rationality. In particular, individuals appeared to ignore much of the information contained in current statutory entitlements and to a lesser extent failed to make complete use of several socioeconomic variables.

In the current context, tests of strong rationality have a much different flavor. To understand these differences, consider equation (6). If we replace X^e_{t+1} with X (so that the equation explains realizations rather than later expectations), then any failure to process information contained in Ω_t should show up as nonzero components in the coefficient vector γ. However, as the equation stands, elements of γ will be nonzero only if either (i) individuals are slow to adjust expectations, and incorporate certain aspects of Ω_t into their forecasts sometime after period t and before period $t + 1$, or (ii) individuals ignore elements of Ω_t that are useful in predicting events that these individuals *will* subsequently incorporate into their forecasts. Failure to reject the hypothesis that $\gamma = 0$ does not, in the current context, imply that individuals process all information correctly. Most obviously, if individuals *never* adjust their expectations, then we will certainly estimate $\gamma = 0$, despite the fact that expectations are not informationally efficient. Thus, the tests of strong rationality have power against a much narrower range of alternatives in the current context than in my earlier paper.

I implement these tests through estimation of equation (6). In light of my conclusions concerning the presence of reporting error, it is hardly surprising that OLS estimates of (6) are highly at variance with the theory. I therefore omit these results and turn directly to procedures that correct for this problem.

There are two alternative methods of dealing with measurement error. First, one can impose the constraint that $\beta = 1$, thereby moving $\tilde{X}^e_t$ to the left-hand side of the equation. The term μ_t then becomes part of the standard regression error; while it renders the estimates less precise, it does not affect consistency. One can then test the hypotheses that $\alpha = \gamma = 0$. Second, one can estimate (6) with instrumental variables. It is then possible to test all the relevant constraints (including $\beta = 1$). The drawback of this approach is that, as in the previous section, in order to identify instruments one must maintain the hypothesis that individuals actually use certain information.

Table 9.3 contains the results of the procedures outlined in the preceding paragraph. Estimates in the first column are generated by regressing the change in expectations (CESS) on the full list of informational variables. Note that none of the corresponding coefficients is significant at the 95 percent level of confidence. Even CSS71, which played such a large role in my earlier analysis of expectations and realizations, appears to explain very little of the change in expectations. In fact, the F-statistic for the hypothesis that $\gamma = 0$ is .834, and the F-statistic for the joint hypotheses that $\alpha = \gamma = 0$ is .829, so that it is impossible to reject strong rationality at any standard level of confidence.

Failure to reject might, of course, be attributable to imprecision. It is therefore appropriate to consider the magnitudes of point estimates. Certain

Table 9.3   **Tests of Strong Rationality**

	Equation		
Variable	1	2	3
Dependent variable	CESS	ESS73	ESS73
Technique	OLS	IV	IV
Intercept	−3,593	−4,427	10.2
	(2,913)	(6,352)	(554)
ESS71		1.24	.966
		(.688)	(.286)
ERET71	40.1		51.4
	(46.8)		(50.3)
DRET71	−2,801		−3,519
	(3,446)		(3,708)
EOI71/100	−.184		−.230
	(.173)		(.335)
ERET69	8.89		1.51
	(39.9)		(39.0)
DRET69	−649		−130
	(2,920)		(2,848)
EOI69/100	−1.92		−1.68
	(2.89)		(3.10)
CSS71	−.102	−.162	−.0284
	(.0744)	(.202)	(.0892)
AGE	49.5	63.0	
	(50.8)	(108)	
SAGE	13.8	9.74	
	(14.3)	(27.1)	
ED	−3.99	−5.15	
	(12.1)	(12.7)	
SED	1.14	−2.84	
	(11.5)	(16.4)	
$W/10^4$	.481	−1.05	
	(8.41)	(10.2)	
HGOOD	−156	−175	
	(141)	(157)	
HBAD	−122	−158	
	(223)	(251)	
KIDS	5.18	3.16	
	(39.0)	(38.2)	
COMPRET	329	408	
	(179)	(200)	
MOVE	−203	−219	
	(223)	(259)	

coefficients stand out as very large relative to the mean value of expected benefits. The most notable among these are DRET71 and DRET69. The reason for this is simply that the variables ERET71 and ERET69 have also been included in the regression. Since the mean value of ERET71 is around 74, the product of this variable with its coefficient is typically around 2,900. The corresponding dummy variable simply takes out the mean of this product so that the fitted value of CESS is not substantially different for those who do and do not report ERET71. Since the *t*-statistic for the coefficient of ERET71 is small, the standard error for the coefficient of DRET71 must be enormous.

Other variables with quantitatively significant coefficients are HGOOD, HBAD, COMPRET, and MOVE. Of these, only the coefficient of COMPRET approaches statistical significance. Nevertheless, it is somewhat disturbing that the standard deviations of these coefficients are so large. For example, although the point estimates indicate that a recent move is associated with roughly an 8 percent decline in expected benefits during the subsequent period, we are unable to determine with any reasonable confidence whether this association is the result of chance.

The second column of table 9.2 contains IV estimates, where the instrument list consists of other reported expectations (i.e., the first set of variables listed in sec. 9.2 as candidates for inclusion in Ω_t). The coefficient of ESS71 is only slightly changed from the corresponding regression in table 9.2. Of the various informational variables, only COMPRET appears with a significant coefficient. Of course, with a large number of informational variables, it is hardly surprising that one should appear with a coefficient that is significant at the 95 percent level of confidence. A formal test of the hypothesis that none of the informational variables matters ($\gamma = 0$) reveals that this hypothesis cannot be rejected. Similarly, the data fail to reject the full implications of strong rationality—$\alpha = \gamma = 0$ and $\beta = 0$—at the 95 percent level of confidence.

These conclusions follow with even greater force from estimates based on the use of socioeconomic and demographic variables (i.e., the second set of variables listed in sec. 9.2 as candidates for inclusion in Ω_t) as instruments. The associated results appear in the third column of table 9.3. Note that the intercept is nearly zero, that the estimate of β differs only slightly from unity, and that none of the informational variables appears with either a statistically significant or a quantitatively important coefficient (recall my earlier comments concerning the interpretation of the coefficient for DRET71). Not surprisingly, one cannot reject the hypothesis of strong rationality on the basis of these estimates.

Taken together, these results bear out the strongest implications of the theory outlined in section 9.1. One should, however, be cautious in interpreting these results. In this regard, it is worth reiterating some of the opening remarks for this subsection. This evidence suggests that we can rule out the possibilities that (i) individuals incorporate certain information into their expectations only after a lag and (ii) information that individuals fail to use is highly correlated with subsequent events that they do incorporate into their expectations. The evidence does not allow us to conclude that individuals make efficient use of all available information, and indeed the results of Bernheim (1988) suggest the contrary.

9.4   Responses to New Information

The analysis of section 9.3 lends support to the theoretical model of expectations outlined in section 9.1. Unfortunately, it does not tell us very much about the manner in which individuals process new information. For example, this evidence does not rule out the possibility that individuals form expectations at some early date and thereafter cling stubbornly to their original forecasts, ignoring all new information. The current section is therefore devoted to an analysis of the manner in which new information affects the evolution of expectations.

On the basis of the simple summary statistics in table 9.2, it seems apparent that some adjustment of expectations occurs. For one thing, the variance of CESS is very large. Of course, this could be partly attributable to the fact that both ESS71 and ESS73 contain measurement error—indeed, the observed variance of CESS could in principle be entirely spurious. If the variance of measurement error remains constant over time, then the variance of CESS simply equals the variance of the true change in expectations plus two times the variance of the measurement error, σ_μ^2. In section 9.3.1, I presented several different estimates of σ_μ, all of which clustered around 700. Combining this figure with the observed standard error of CESS, it is possible to recover the variance of the true change in expectations. Specifically, I calculate the standard error of the true change to be 728. Thus, individuals appear to have adjusted their expectations significantly between 1971 and 1973. One can illustrate this same point simply by comparing the variances of ESS71 and ESS73—unless measurement error increased dramatically between these years, the rise in variance must reflect the processing of new information.

The observations raise two important questions. First, what kind of information leads individuals to revise their expectations, and what is the nature of the response? Second, do individuals process new information "rationally," in the sense that the adjustment of observed expectations closely resembles an adjustment to some objective expectation of the realized value? The next two subsections are devoted to analyses of these questions.

9.4.1   Measurement of Responses

The starting point for this analysis is equation (7), which relates changes in expectations to unanticipated events. To the extent that such events determine subsequent earnings, applicable statutes, or the timing of retirement, they may also have large effects on eventual benefits. Estimation of equation (7) requires some notion of what the function ψ looks like as well as some technique for distinguishing between anticipated and unanticipated events. Lacking any prior information about the form of ψ, I simply estimate a linear approximation. In addition, I try out three different procedures for measuring unanticipated events.

It is natural to begin with the simple assumption that expectations are largely myopic, so that any change in status is unanticipated. This motivates a regression of CESS on the set of variables listed in section 9.1 as candidates for inclusion in ω_{t+1}. Since my earlier study (Bernheim 1988) suggested that individuals ignore much of the information contained in current statutory entitlements, I begin with a regression that omits CCSS (the change in current entitlement) from this list. The results appear in column 1 of table 9.4.

Only one of the variables in this regression—WIDW—appears with a coefficient that is significant at the conventional 95 percent confidence level. However, many of the other coefficients have t-statistics in the neighborhood of 1.5. It is therefore not surprising that the F-statistic for the hypothesis that all these coefficients equal zero is 2.09, which is significant at the 95 percent level of confidence. This joint hypothesis test indicates that some of the change in expectations observed between 1971 and 1973 is a response to the information contained in these variables.

It is also clear that the lack of statistical significance for a number of individual coefficients reflects imprecision rather than small point estimates. Several of the dummy variables have coefficients in the neighborhood of 600, which indicates that the event changes expectations by about 25 percent of its

Table 9.4   **Estimates of Responses to New Information**

Variable	Equation			
	1	2	3	4
Intercept	52.7	−163	55.1	55.1
	(81.4)	(116)	(60.2)	(61.0)
HBET	−633	−639	−38.2	−280
	(379)	(352)	(275)	(384)
HWOR	−604	−692	−322	−316
	(693)	(697)	(646)	(686)
WIDM	−659	−591	−313	−234
	(414)	(408)	(384)	(412)
WIDW	−804	−531	−181	−11.7
	(306)	(304)	(379)	(372)
LJOB	190	199	−46.7	−47.2
	(145)	(143)	(141)	(147)
GJOB	−602	−480	−444	−298
	(388)	(402)	(439)	(491)
CJOB	636	605	581	363
	(377)	(354)	(387)	(415)
NMOVE	239	264	191	253
	(170)	(169)	(166)	(183)
CW/100	−.442	−.450	−.307	−.307
	(.345)	(.337)	(.416)	(.383)
CCSS		.177	.441	.546
		(.0694)	(.0844)	(.114)

mean value. Nevertheless, standard errors are simply too large to say with confidence that the specific event (as opposed to events collectively) has an effect on expectations. Unfortunately, several coefficients also have counter-intuitive signs. Specifically, finding a job depresses expected benefits, while losing a job raises them.

It is particularly interesting to compare these results with the second column of table 9.4, which differs from the first only in that I have added CCSS (the change in statutory entitlement). Note first that the coefficient of this variable is statistically significant, which indicates that individuals do to some extent process information that affects their benefit levels through the benefit formulas. Furthermore, the addition of CCSS renders all other coefficients individually insignificant. Indeed, the F-statistic for the hypothesis that all these other coefficients equal zero is 1.71, which is significant at the 90 percent confidence level, but *not* at the 95 percent level. Closer inspection reveals that the introduction of CCSS renders the other coefficients jointly insignificant by reducing the estimated effects of several key variables (especially GJOB and WIDW) rather than by reducing the precision of these coefficients.

These results raise the interesting possibility that events affect expectations only through their effects on actual benefit calculations. This would entail a very high degree of rationality with respect to the processing of information received on the margin—certainly a much greater degree of rationality than was apparent in my analysis of the levels of expectations (see Bernheim 1988). Much of the following analysis is designed to investigate this possibility in greater detail.

The problem with the preceding set of estimates is, of course, that much of the observed changes in status may have been anticipated. This is especially important for the CCSS variable, in that statutory entitlements (what an individual would obtain on immediate retirement) rise steeply during the period immediately prior to retirement. Thus, much of the change in CCSS may have been anticipated. This would tend to bias the coefficient of CCSS toward zero, thereby overstating the extent to which other events affected expectations through channels other than the benefit formulas.

The next logical step is therefore to reestimate this specification using a more elaborate model for distinguishing between anticipated and unanticipated events. The object is to measure the component of an event that is unantici-pated, given whatever method individuals actually use to forecast these events. Since we do know that individuals use information contained in ESS71, one possibility is to forecast (through regressions) the informational events on the basis of ESS71 and to use the residuals as measures of the unanticipated components.

Results based on this procedure appear in the third column of table 9.4. The list of independent variables should now be interpreted as measures of unanticipated changes, constructed as described above. Note that the coeffi-cient of CCSS rises dramatically to .441 and its t-statistic now exceeds 5. In addition, the absolute value of *every other coefficient* declines, in some cases very significantly, and none of these other coefficients is even close to being statistically significant. Jointly, the significance of these other coefficients is no longer even marginal—the F-statistic for the hypothesis that they all equal zero is .65, which does not permit rejection at any meaningful level of confidence.

Even with this second procedure, measures of unanticipated events may still contain anticipated components. I therefore implement a third procedure in which the informational events are regressed on the full array of variables listed in section 9.2 as candidates for inclusion in Ω_i, as well as on ESS71. I then use the residuals from these variables as measures of the unanticipated changes. The justification for this procedure is that it is better to overexplain rather than underexplain the changes in status between 1971 and 1973. If one uses more information than do the respondents, then one's prediction will better than theirs, and the residual will then certainly reflect only unanticipated changes in status. Since the respondents' forecasts are presumed to be inferior, part of the predicted change will also be unanticipated. Fortunately, the nature of regression analysis is such that these other unanticipated components must be orthogonal to the residuals, and consequently the omission of these components will not bias the coefficients in a regression of CCSS on the residuals.

The results of this procedure appear in column 4 of table 9.4. The coefficient of CCSS again increases significantly to .546, and it remains highly significant. The absolute values of the coefficient estimates continue to decline significantly for WIDM, WIDW, GJOB, and CJOB. In fact, for WIDW, the coefficient is reduced practically to zero. In contrast, the coefficients for HBET and NMOVE rise somewhat. The statistical significance of these other individual coefficients continues to be low, and one cannot reject the joint hypothesis that they are all zero at any reasonable level of confidence.

Note that the second and third procedures described above implicitly treat the increase in average benefits between 1971 and 1973 as anticipated. Thus, the relative importance of CCSS does not simply reflect the fact that most individuals were aware of the benefit increase and adjusted their expectations accordingly. Rather, these results suggest that cross-sectional variation in unanticipated changes in statutory entitlements is the most important factor explaining cross-sectional variation in changes of expected benefits.

Two qualifications are in order. First, for the second and third procedures I have not adjusted the standard errors for the fact that the residuals are estimated rather than observed. It is in principle possible to obtain correct standard errors, as well as more efficient estimates, by estimating the entire system simultaneously through the use of seemingly-unrelated-regression (SUR) techniques. Unfortunately, computational requirements for SUR estimation of the full system exceeded the capacity of the available computer facilities. Second, the power of the tests discussed above is questionable in light of the fact that the standard errors of many coefficients are, from an economic point of view, extremely large.

Nevertheless, the general pattern of results, and especially the progression of coefficients through the second, third, and fourth columns in table 9.4, lends significant support to a remarkable conclusion: despite the fact that individuals do not appear to use all information contained in their statutory entitlements, the bulk of new, marginal information is incorporated into expectations through its effect on statutory entitlements. Although individuals do not appear to be well informed about the level of benefits, they appear to have a very good sense for how the benefit formulas operate on the margin.

The remaining question is whether these responses to new information are rational, in the sense that they closely resemble adjustments to an objective measure of expected benefits. Even if individuals incorporate new information as if they evaluate its effect on statutory entitlements, it is still possible that they do not fully exploit this information or that they misperceive the relation between entitlements and ultimate benefits. These issues are the subjects of the next subsection.

9.4.2   Evaluation of Response Quality

In order to test the rationality of responses to new information, it is necessary to add some additional structure to the basic model. I will suppose that the objective expectation concerning the realization of X is given by a linear function of information:

$$E(X|\Omega_t) = \Omega_t\zeta_1 .$$

When new information arrives, the objective expectation adjusts in response to unanticipated shocks. In particular, I suppose that

$$(9) \qquad E(X|\Omega_{t+1}) = \Omega_t\zeta_1 + [\omega_{t+1} - E(\omega_{t+1}|\Omega_t)]\zeta_2 .$$

I now allow for the possibility that reported expectations differ from objective expectations. Suppose in particular that subjective expectations are given not by equation (9) but rather by

$$(10) \qquad X^e_{t+1} = \Omega_t\theta_1 + [\omega_{t+1} - E(\omega_{t+1}|\Omega_t)]\theta_2 .$$

Then, combining (9) and (10), and using the fact that

$$X = E(X|\Omega_{t+1}) + v,$$

where v is uncorrelated with Ω_{t+1}, we have

$$(11) \qquad X - X^e_{t+1} = \Omega_t(\zeta_1 - \theta_1)$$
$$+ [\omega_{t+1} - E(\omega_{t+1}|\Omega_t)](\zeta_2 - \theta_2) + v.$$

The empirical analysis in Bernheim (1988) established that individuals do not process all available information in a fully rational manner (i.e., $\zeta_1 - \theta_1 \neq 0$). In this paper, I focus on the processing of new information (i.e., on the value of $\zeta_2 - \theta_2$).

To estimate the value of $\zeta_2 - \theta_2$, I regress the forecast error from expectations reported in 1973 on the 1971 information set as well as on measures of unanticipated events that occurred in the intervening period. I present estimates of equation (11) based on the three distinct methods of measuring unanticipated events discussed in the preceding subsection. It should be noted that the use of the first two procedures does not conform strictly to the theory outlined above.

Results appear in table 9.5. In order to conserve space, I have omitted coefficients for all the Ω_t variables and concentrate exclusively on the effects of new information. It is worth mentioning that the pattern of coefficients for the Ω_t variables was very similar to that obtained in my previous study. Most important, CSS71 entered with a positive, economically significant, and statistically significant coefficient, indicating that individuals fail to process all the information contained in statutory entitlements.

The first thing to notice about table 9.5 is that the results differ very little across the three procedures. There is a particularly striking similarity between the second and the third set of estimates. This should not be surprising—were

Table 9.5   **Estimates of Response Quality**

Variable	Equation		
	1	2	3
HBET	−28.0	33.5	34.1
	(688)	(643)	(655)
HWOR	473	493	496
	(334)	(347)	(342)
WIDM	9.95	54.8	50.5
	(232)	(246)	(243)
WIDW	−174	−101	−121
	(250)	(270)	(264)
LJOB	−205	−229	−228
	(139)	(137)	(137)
GJOB	325	357	348
	(373)	(378)	(376)
CJOB	−346	−352	−356
	(442)	(442)	(442)
NMOVE	−178	−186	−186
	(191)	(191)	(191)
CW/1000	6.68	6.91	6.87
	(3.64)	(3.62)	(3.63)
CCSS	.0141	.0654	.0532
	(.103)	(.122)	(.118)

it not for the presence of ESS71 in the first stage regressions, the independent variables would be related by a linear transformation, and the estimated coefficients for the new information variables would in fact be identical across procedures. The second and third sets of estimates differ only because the first-stage estimates for the coefficients of ESS71 differ.

Note that none of the variables in table 9.5 appears with a statistically significant coefficient in any regression (although the change in wealth variable, CW, does have t-statistics ranging from 1.8 to 1.9). In each case, one cannot reject the hypothesis that $\zeta_2 - \theta_2 = 0$ at any reasonable level of confidence. The data therefore support the view that individuals rationally process new information.

It is worth emphasizing that the CCSS variable has a statistically insignificant coefficient in each of these equations and that the point estimates of this coefficient are small in economic terms. Although individuals do not appear to use all information contained in statutory entitlements, they do seem to act rationally toward new information that changes statutory entitlements on the margin.

9.5   Conclusions

In this paper, I have outlined and tested a simple theory that describes the evolution of expectations concerning Social Security benefits during the preretirement period. While the raw data do not appear to support the empirically testable implications of this theory, the evidence indicates that this failure is attributable to the presence of measurement error. After correcting for the presence of this error, I find that expectations do appear to evolve as a random walk and that the innovations in this process are unrelated to previously available information.

After concluding that the data support the theory, I estimate responses of expectations to the arrival of new information and test for the rationality of these responses. The results here are striking. Although individuals do not form expectations on the basis of all available information, and in particular ignore much of the information contained in concurrent statutory entitlements to Social Security benefits, responses to new information during the period immediately preceding retirement appear to be highly rational. The bulk of information affects the evolution of expectations only through its effect on actual benefit calculations. Furthermore, the data support the view that individuals form accurate assessments of the ultimate effect of new information on actual benefits. These findings corroborate more speculative results from Bernheim (1988), which suggested that individuals formulate expectations about the retirement period much more carefully as retirement approaches.

References

Anderson, Kathryn H., Richard V. Burkhauser, and Joseph F. Quinn. 1986. Do retirement dreams come true? The effect of unanticipated events on retirement plans. *Industrial and Labor Relations Review* 39:518–26.

Bernheim, B. Douglas. 1988. Social Security benefits: An empirical study of expectations and realizations. In *Issues in contemporary retirement*, ed. E. Lazear and R. Ricardo-Campbell, 312–45. Palo Alto: Hoover Institution.

Bernheim, B. Douglas. 1989. The timing of retirement: A comparison of expectations and realizations. In *The economics of aging,* ed. D. Wise. Chicago: University of Chicago Press.

Burtless, Gary. 1986. Social Security, unanticipated benefit increases, and the timing of retirement. *Review of Economic Studies* 53:781–806.

Hall, Arden, and Terry Johnson. 1980. The determinants of planned retirement age. *Industrial and Labor Relations Review* 33:240–55.

Heckman, James J. 1976. The common structure of statistical models of truncation, sample selection, and limited dependent variables and a sample estimator for such models. *Annals of Economic and Social Measurement* 5:475–92.

Hurd, Michael. 1983. The effects of Social Security on retirement: Results and issues. State University of New York at Stony Brook. Mimeo.

Parnes, H. S., and G. Nestel. 1981. The retirement experience. In *Work and retirement,* ed. H. S. Parnes. Cambridge, Mass.: MIT Press.

Wolpin, Kenneth I., and Fürsun Gönül. 1987. On the use of expectations data in micro surveys: The case of retirement. Ohio State University. Mimeo.

Zarnowitz, Victor. 1984. Business cycle analysis and expectational survey data. NBER Working Paper no. 1378. Cambridge, Mass.: National Bureau of Economic Research.

Comment   Sherwin Rosen

This paper continues Bernheim's imaginative use of rational modeling and modern conditional expectations apparatus to analyze Social Security benefit expectations of persons close to retirement. The orthogonality and related restrictions on the survey expectation data studied here are of interest, but forging the linkages between survey expectation responses (or lack thereof) and actual behavior will make the work even more important. Expectations of agents are important insofar as they affect savings, labor force participation, and other economic decisions of the elderly, but we do not yet know if there is any relation of that kind in these data.

The orthogonality restrictions that are sought here in some sense celebrate what old-fashioned empirical investigators would have called "poor" results.

Sherwin Rosen is the Edwin A. and Betty L. Bergman Professor of Economics at the University of Chicago and a research associate of the National Bureau of Economic Research.

Indeed, lack of correlation among variables in the retirement history sample is not exactly unknown, as some of the few surviving readers of my own work with these data can attest. The extent of measurement error that Bernheim finds in his own data gives one pause about the quality of the entire data set, so it remains to be seen whether Bernheim's results are found because the implicit behavioral restrictions of the theory really apply or because the data are not very good. Barring replication in a new survey, examining the behavioral linkages with real behavior is the only way that the research can most meaningfully be assessed. Perhaps the next paper in this sequence will be devoted to that important task.

Let me turn now to a few remarks about the work on its own terms. The data are incomplete because many people do not take the trouble to report expectational data at all. Bernheim's checks on the biases caused by this go about as far as possible given the data available to him. Nonetheless, in extrapolating these results to the population at large, it is well to keep in mind that people who are hooked up to a retirement information network such as AARP or a private pension system administered by a large company or who are just more interested in retiring in the near future would have had easy access to much of the information requested in the survey questions, but others would not. These are after all very specific questions about a legal entitlement that was changing very often over the survey period, and in very confusing ways as well, such as double indexing. Social Security does not send out financial statements unless specifically requested to do so, and most people must make substantial efforts to get the necessary information. Perhaps it is not too surprising that many people do not report an expectation given the costs of it.

One of Bernheim's most remarkable results is that the rational expectations work better for changes in benefits than for levels of benefits. The meaning of this is not entirely clear. Given the many legislated changes in the Social Security law during the sample period, it is not surprising that most people would be confused and uncertain about their benefit amounts at retirement. Benefits are calculated from a complicated table mapping earnings histories into a monthly benefit amount, and the table changed many times in these years. Saying that people have expectations of benefits means that they implicitly have expectations concerning the table parameters that take earnings histories to retirement payments.

If the expectations process is thought of in these terms, the only thing that could make much difference to the benefit calculation over time is changes in these parameters. After all, covered earnings histories do not change very much in a one- or two-year period. Most of the action in changes in monthly benefit amounts is year-to-year changes in the statutes, but virtually none of the information variables used in the statistical work relate directly to the benefit calculation or even indirectly in terms of congressional actions concerning it. This might account for why that kind of information shows no effects in the regression, and to that extent the result may not be so remarkable. Whatever that may be, it is difficult to see how these individuals could be confused about benefit levels but at the same time be much more rational in reacting to new information given the political environment of that time. Surely knowledge of benefit levels is as important to the behavioral effects of Social Security as are changes in benefits.

10   Adjusting to an Aging Labor Force

Edward P. Lazear

The next few decades will witness some major changes in the composition of the labor force. Some trends that have already become apparent are the increased labor force participation of women and the declining ages of retirement among elderly men.[1] A number of observers view earlier retirement with alarm. As the baby boom generation ages, a larger proportion of the work force will be in its 60s and a relatively smaller proportion in its 30s and 40s. The implications of this change for the Social Security system have already been discussed in detail. But there are effects on private firms as well. Since older workers earn more than young, firms will become top-heavy and will be paying a higher average wage. Of course, to the extent that age-earnings profiles mirror age-productivity profiles, an older work force is also a more productive one, so the rising wage may be of no consequence. Still, life-cycle theories of wages, either human capital (as in Becker 1962) or incentive based (as in Lazear 1979), imply that the relation of earnings to productivity is a loose one. Promotion possibilities and the hierarchical structure of the firm may change as the age distribution of workers changes. Firms may react by altering age-earnings profiles, pension plans, explicit buyouts, and the shape of the promotion pyramid. The purpose of this paper is to consider those reactions. Before that can be done, however, it is necessary to have a clearer view of what the future holds. In particular, it is important first to describe the next century's labor force.

   Like most economists, I am reluctant to predict the future since I am certain to be proven wrong. Unfortunately, the task is unavoidable if one is to discuss

Edward P. Lazear is the Isidore Brown and Gladys J. Brown Professor of Urban and Labor Economics at the University of Chicago and senior fellow at the Hoover Institution.

   This work was supported in part by the National Science Foundation. The author thanks Finis Welch for helpful comments.

the way that institutions are likely to evolve. Thus, I defend what follows with the disclaimer that prediction is a dirty job, but someone has to do it.

10.1   Labor Force, Wages, and Productivity in the Decades Ahead

The first step is to project the labor force into succeeding decades. There are two basic ingredients. First, population by age and sex must be estimated for each year in the future. Second, labor force participation rates must be determined.

The Bureau of Census not only provides data on population by age for past years but also estimates age-specific population rates for the United States up through 2083. Those numbers are summarized in table 10.1. If the census predictions are to be believed, two trends can be noted. First, the proportion of the population between 60 and 70 will be 4 percentage points higher for both males and females in 2020 than it is today. Second, the proportion between 30 and 40 will be 3 percentage points lower in 2020 than it is today.

To get a sense of how large an effect changing population might have on the labor force, assume that age- and sex-specific labor force participation rates remain what they are currently (in 1987).[2] Using the various population weights predicted in table 10.1, an estimate of the age-specific labor force participation rate for each year can be estimated. This is done in table 10.2.

No standard errors are presented in table 10.2 primarily because standard errors for population estimates on which these numbers are based are unavailable. There are two main findings. First, the proportion of the male labor force between 55 and 69 years old will rise from 12 percent in 1990 to 18 percent in 2020. The proportion of the female labor force between 55 and 69 years old will rise even more dramatically, from 9 percent in 1990 to 17 percent in 2020. Second, the proportion of the male labor force between 25 and 44 years old will shrink from 55 to 45 percent over the same period. Again, the same basic effect applies to women. Additionally, the total male labor force will grow at an average rate of about ½ percent per year until 2020 and then will decline. For women, ½ percent annual growth occurs until 2010, and then labor force levels decline.

Of course, some key assumptions go into estimating the numbers in table 10.2. Population predictions are crucial, but so is the assumption that labor force participation rates will remain the same over time. The latter cannot be true, especially for women, and one might hope to do better. Since data on age-specific labor force participation rates are available over time, one can estimate age and year effects (cohort effects are redundant) and predict age-specific labor force participation rates for the future. This was done by estimating labor force participation rate trend equations (linear, quadratic, and logistic) for each age group. Labor force participation rates can be predicted as the out-of-period extrapolation of the estimates. Unfortunately, as one might expect, such extrapolations are likely to be almost uninformative. In fact,

Table 10.1   **Population Projections, U.S. Bureau of Census, 1983**

					Age					
Year	0–9	10–19	20–29	30–39	40–49	50–59	60–69	70–79	80–100	Total
Males:										
1983	17.3	19.0	21.6	17.6	11.9	10.8	9.1	5.1	1.8	114.4
1990	19.3	17.3	20.3	20.9	15.6	10.5	9.4	5.8	2.3	121.5
2000	18.6	19.7	17.5	20.5	20.7	14.8	9.0	6.5	3.1	130.5
2010	18.2	19.0	19.9	17.8	20.3	19.7	13.0	6.5	3.8	138.0
2020	18.9	18.5	19.2	20.1	17.6	19.3	17.2	9.5	4.0	144.5
2030	18.3	19.2	18.8	19.5	20.0	16.8	16.9	12.6	5.8	147.9
2040	18.3	18.7	19.5	19.1	19.3	19.1	14.8	12.4	8.0	149.1
Male proportion of total population accounted for by cell:										
1983	.15	.17	.19	.15	.10	.09	.08	.04	.02	1.00
1990	.16	.14	.17	.17	.13	.09	.08	.05	.02	1.00
2000	.14	.15	.13	.16	.16	.11	.07	.05	.02	1.00
2010	.13	.14	.14	.13	.15	.14	.09	.05	.03	1.00
2020	.13	.13	.13	.14	.12	.13	.12	.07	.03	1.00
2030	.12	.13	.13	.13	.13	.11	.11	.09	.04	1.00
2040	.12	.13	.13	.13	.13	.13	.10	.08	.05	1.00
Females:										
1983	16.5	18.2	21.4	17.9	12.5	11.9	10.8	7.4	3.9	120.4
1990	18.5	16.5	19.8	21.1	16.2	11.4	11.2	8.5	5.1	128.1
2000	17.8	18.8	17.0	20.3	21.1	15.8	10.6	9.3	6.8	137.5
2010	17.4	18.1	19.3	17.5	20.3	20.6	14.8	8.9	8.3	145.2
2020	18.0	17.7	18.6	19.8	17.6	19.8	19.2	12.6	8.7	152.1
2030	17.5	18.4	18.2	19.1	19.9	17.3	18.5	16.4	11.6	156.9
2040	17.5	17.8	18.9	18.7	19.2	19.5	16.2	15.8	15.8	159.4
Female proportion of total population accounted for by cell:										
1983	.14	.15	.18	.15	.10	.10	.09	.06	.03	1.00
1990	.14	.13	.15	.16	.13	.09	.09	.07	.04	1.00
2000	.13	.14	.12	.15	.15	.12	.08	.07	.05	1.00
2010	.12	.12	.13	.12	.14	.14	.10	.06	.06	1.00
2020	.12	.12	.12	.13	.12	.13	.13	.08	.06	1.00
2030	.11	.12	.12	.12	.13	.11	.12	.10	.07	1.00
2040	.11	.11	.12	.12	.12	.12	.10	.10	.10	1.00

Source: U.S. Bureau of the Census (1986).

eyeballing the estimates strains even the author's imagination for a large number of the age groups. An alternative is proposed. The estimation reveals that, for all male age groups, the trend has been toward lower labor force participation rates over time, although the change has become somewhat less dramatic recently. For females, labor force participation rates have risen for all age groups with the exception of women over 65. Thus, for the purposes of comparison with table 10.2, let us conjecture that males' labor force participation rates will decline linearly between 1990 and 2040 to seven-eighths their current levels. Let us also conjecture that female labor force participation rates will rise to five-fourths their current level over the same

Table 10.2   **Labor Force Projections**

	16–19	20–24	25–34	35–44	45–54	55–59	60–64	65–69	70+	Total
Labor force males, by age group in thousands:										
1990	4,009	8,026	20,689	17,708	11,210	3,845	2,695	1,149	542	69,872
2000	4,340	7,397	17,377	20,663	16,499	4,960	2,716	1,057	584	75,593
2010	4,460	8,596	17,658	17,435	19,265	7,099	4,219	1,392	596	80,719
2020	4,144	7,930	19,044	17,737	16,276	7,800	5,232	2,000	925	81,088
2030	4,377	8,072	17,760	19,089	16,616	6,380	4,573	2,187	1,169	80,223
2040	4,285	8,244	18,396	17,831	17,847	7,129	4,307	1,798	1,041	80,878
Males as proportion of total work force:										
1990	.06	.11	.30	.25	.16	.06	.04	.02	.01	1.00
2000	.06	.10	.23	.27	.22	.07	.04	.01	.01	1.00
2010	.06	.11	.22	.22	.24	.09	.05	.02	.01	1.00
2020	.05	.10	.23	.22	.20	.10	.06	.02	.01	1.00
2030	.05	.10	.22	.24	.21	.08	.06	.03	.01	1.00
2040	.05	.10	.23	.22	.22	.09	.05	.02	.01	1.00
Labor force females, by age group in thousands:										
1990	3,629	6,651	15,685	14,236	8,794	2,782	1,881	779	327	54,765
2000	3,935	6,121	13,068	16,300	12,723	3,534	1,859	699	345	58,586
2010	4,038	7,095	13,262	13,652	14,512	4,947	2,813	898	343	61,560
2020	3,753	6,544	14,268	13,837	12,158	5,296	3,418	1,258	517	61,051
2030	3,964	6,662	13,314	14,876	12,407	4,319	2,950	1,340	635	60,467
2040	3,880	6,802	13,786	13,902	13,271	4,816	2,766	1,096	554	60,875
Females as proportion of total work force:										
1990	.07	.12	.29	.26	.16	.05	.03	.01	.01	1.00
2000	.07	.10	.22	.28	.22	.06	.03	.01	.01	1.00
2010	.07	.12	.22	.22	.24	.08	.05	.01	.01	1.00
2020	.06	.11	.23	.23	.20	.09	.06	.02	.01	1.00
2030	.07	.11	.22	.25	.21	.07	.05	.02	.01	1.00
2040	.06	.11	.23	.23	.22	.08	.05	.02	.01	1.00

Source: U.S. Bureau of Census (1986) and unpublished data from U.S. Bureau of Labor Statistics.

period but impose the additional constraint that female rates cannot exceed male rates in any given cohort. While obviously arbitrary, these assumptions serve to illustrate the sensitivity of the results in table 10.2 to assumptions about labor force participation rates. As before, the census population estimates are multiplied by estimated labor force participation rates to obtain estimated labor force sizes. Results are contained in table 10.3.

Table 10.3 looks like table 10.2 in almost all respects. The graying of the labor force that showed up in table 10.2 is found in table 10.3 as well. The aggregate labor force growth patterns are similar to those in table 10.2, although growth is lower for males and higher for females as a result of the assumptions built into table 10.3. The estimates in table 10.3 can be contrasted with those in table 10.2 by subtracting table 10.3 results from those of table 10.2. The proportion differences are contained in table 10.4. Proportion difference is defined as follows:

Table 10.3   **Labor Force Predictions: Altered Assumptions**

	16–19	20–24	25–34	35–44	45–54	55–59	60–64	65–69	70+	Total
Labor force males, by age group in thousands:										
1990	4,009	8,026	20,689	17,708	11,210	3,845	2,695	1,149	542	69,872
2000	4,340	7,397	17,377	20,663	16,499	4,960	2,716	1,057	584	75,593
2010	4,460	8,596	17,658	17,435	19,265	7,099	4,219	1,392	596	80,719
2020	4,144	7,930	19,044	17,737	16,276	7,800	5,232	2,000	925	81,088
2030	4,377	8,072	17,760	19,089	16,616	6,380	4,573	2,187	1,169	80,223
2040	4,285	8,244	18,396	17,831	17,847	7,129	4,307	1,798	1,041	80,878
Males as proportion of total work force:										
1990	.06	.11	.30	.25	.16	.06	.04	.02	.01	1.00
2000	.06	.10	.23	.27	.22	.07	.04	.01	.01	1.00
2010	.06	.11	.22	.22	.24	.09	.05	.02	.01	1.00
2020	.05	.10	.23	.22	.20	.10	.06	.02	.01	1.00
2030	.05	.10	.22	.24	.21	.08	.06	.03	.01	1.00
2040	.05	.10	.23	.22	.22	.09	.05	.02	.01	1.00
Labor force females, by age group in thousands:										
1990	3,629	6,651	15,685	14,236	8,794	2,782	1,881	779	327	54,765
2000	4,016	6,427	13,721	17,115	13,360	3,711	1,952	734	362	61,399
2010	4,053	7,760	14,588	15,017	15,963	5,442	3,094	987	377	67,282
2020	3,667	7,070	16,409	15,913	13,982	6,091	3,931	1,446	595	69,103
2030	3,768	7,000	15,621	16,980	14,742	5,183	3,540	1,608	762	69,203
2040	3,586	6,950	15,723	15,429	15,690	6,020	3,458	1,370	693	68,919
Females as proportion of total work force:										
1990	.07	.12	.29	.26	.16	.05	.03	.01	.01	1.00
2000	.07	.10	.22	.28	.22	.06	.03	.01	.01	1.00
2010	.06	.12	.22	.22	.24	.08	.05	.01	.01	1.00
2020	.05	.10	.24	.23	.20	.09	.06	.02	.01	1.00
2030	.05	.10	.23	.25	.21	.07	.05	.02	.01	1.00
2040	.05	.10	.23	.22	.23	.09	.05	.02	.01	1.00

(labor force in cell in table 10.3 − labor force in cell in table 10.2)/
(labor force in cell in table 10.2)

The differences reported in table 10.4 reflect the effects of changes in behavior on labor force participation as distinguished from pure population effects.[3] For example, allowing the female labor force participation rates to rise implies that the female labor force between 45 and 54 years old will be 15 percent higher in 2020 than it would be if rates were not permitted to increase. To the extent that assumptions are important, obviously they are more likely to affect estimates further out in time. Additionally, at least for women, estimates for the older groups are more sensitive to the particular assumptions made.

A major form of behavioral change is ignored in this analysis. In particular, age-specific wage changes brought about by changes in labor supply and complementarities in the production function are not analyzed here.[4]

Table 10.4   **Proportion Difference between Tables 10.3 and 10.4**

	16–19	20–24	25–34	35–44	45–54	55–59	60–64	65–69	70+	Total
Males:										
1990	.00	.00	.00	.00	.00	.00	.00	.00	.00	.00
2000	− .02	− .02	− .03	− .03	− .03	− .02	− .02	− .03	− .02	− .03
2010	− .05	− .05	− .05	− .05	− .05	− .05	− .05	− .05	− .05	− .05
2020	− .08	− .07	− .07	− .07	− .08	− .07	− .08	− .08	− .07	− .07
2030	− .10	− .10	− .10	− .10	− .10	− .10	− .10	− .10	− .10	− .10
2040	− .12	− .12	− .12	− .12	− .12	− .13	− .12	− .13	− .13	− .13
Females:										
1990	.00	.00	.00	.00	.00	.00	.00	.00	.00	.00
2000	.02	.05	.05	.05	.05	.05	.05	.05	.05	.05
2010	.00	.09	.10	.10	.10	.10	.10	.10	.10	.09
2020	− .02	.08	.15	.15	.15	.15	.15	.15	.15	.13
2030	− .05	.05	.17	.14	.19	.20	.20	.20	.20	.14
2040	− .08	.02	.14	.11	.18	.25	.25	.25	.25	.13

Both tables 10.3 and 10.4 reveal that, at least for males, the shift toward an older labor force is not as pronounced as the shift toward an older population as shown in table 10.1. The reason is that earlier retirement reduces the effect of an aging population on labor force composition. Thus, the worker behavior moderates the effect of pure demographics. Before turning away from the crystal ball, it is useful to document some changes in pension formulas that have occurred over the years. Table 10.5 summarizes some important changes.

There are two obvious changes. First, pension coverage has grown tremendously between 1975 and 1984. There has been an increase of about 72 percent in the number of workers covered, which is much greater than the increase in the size of the labor force over the same period (about 13 percent). Second, the proportion of plans that are of the defined benefit type has declined dramatically. Firms are switching to defined contribution plans, or firms that previously did not offer pension plans are disproportionately adopting defined contribution plans. For reasons discussed below, it is far from obvious that this trend will continue in the future.

Table 10.5   **Pensions Trends**

	1975	1976	1977	1978	1979	1980	1981	1982	1983	1984
Number of participants (in millions):										
Defined benefit	33	33.2	35	36.1	36.8	37.9	28.9	38.6	40.1	40.9
Defined contribution	11.5	13.4	15.2	16.2	18.2	19.9	21.7	24.6	30	32
Total	44.5	46.6	50.2	52.3	55	57.8	50.6	63.2	70.1	72.9
Defined Benefit (%)	74	71	70	69	67	66	57	61	57	56

Source: Ippolito and Kolodrubetz (1986).

To summarize this section, the major changes that firms can expect over the next few decades is an aging of the labor force. There will be a larger proportion of workers between ages 55 and 70 and a decline in the proportion between 25 and 44. Additionally, there will be growth in the absolute size of the labor force until around 2015 and then a decline. What are the effects of these demographic shifts?

10.2   Financial Viability of the Firm

A number of observers have already cautioned that the Social Security system, a pay-as-you-go operation, may become insolvent.[5] These pressures are equally important for firms. As long as firms do not pay each worker his marginal product at every point in time, unanticipated changes in the age/tenure distribution of the firm can have significant effects. There are a number of models of life-cycle wage determination that suggest that workers are not paid their marginal products in a spot market sense. The theory of specific human capital implies that young workers are overpaid and old workers are underpaid relative to their marginal products (the classic reference is Becker 1962). Incentive theories of wage determination imply the reverse (see Lazear 1979). Insurance theories imply that all young workers are paid less than their marginal products and that highly able old workers are paid marginal product, whereas less able ones are paid above their marginal products (see Harris and Holmstrom 1982). As I have argued elsewhere, only incentive theories are consistent with pervasive mandatory retirement among old workers. Specific human capital implies the reverse, while insurance stories are implausible across ability types because of moral hazard.[6] Thus, in this section, I will assume that firms underpay young workers relative to marginal products and overpay older ones.

Surprisingly, underpayment of young workers and overpayment of old ones implies that competitive firms have wage bills that exceed the value of current output. (Firms make zero profit because they enjoy the return on past investment.) An unanticipated aging of the labor force increases that wedge and, in a pay-as-you-go operation where high current dividends have been paid in the past, may create current cash-flow problems. This doomsday tale is made more likely by unfulfilled expectations, which may be induced by a demographic shift. To understand the problem, let us be somewhat more formal.

Consider an age-earnings profile, $w(a)$, where a is age and w is the (annual) amount paid to a given worker. Let the worker's age-productivity profile, measured in dollars, be $q(a)$. Normalize so that the youngest workers are age 0 and the oldest are age 1. Further, let the distribution of worker ages within the firm at time t be given by $f_t(a)$, and let the size of the work force be N. The wage bill of the firm at time t is then given by

$$(1) \qquad W_t = N \int_0^1 w(a) f_t(a) da,$$

and total output at time t is given by

$$(2) \qquad Q_t = N \int_0^1 q(a) f_t(a) da.$$

The difference between wage bill and output is then

$$(3) \qquad D_t = N \int_0^1 [W(a) - q(a)] f_t(a) da$$

or

$$D_t/N = \int_0^1 [w(a) - q(a)] f_t(a) da.$$

When a worker is hired into the firm, competitive markets ensure that lifetime wages paid to the worker equal lifetime output. This means that

$$\int_0^1 w(a) e^{-ra} da = \int_0^1 q(a) e^{-ra} da$$

or

$$(4) \qquad \int_0^1 [w(a) - q(a)] e^{-ra} da = 0.$$

If equation (4) holds, then it cannot be true generally that the wage bill equals output at each point in time. Only if $f_t(a) = e^{-ra}$ would the wage bill equal current period output.

Suppose, for example, that all workers join the firm at age 0 and do not leave until age 1. Suppose further that the firm hires the same number of individuals each period. Then $f_t(t) = 1$ for all t, and wages exceed output for any positive interest rate. How can this be? The firm pays back in each period what it gained during the first few periods of its operation. This is not unlike pay-as-you-go Social Security. There, the first generation receives more than it puts in. Here, the firm pays interest on the "advance" that it received in early periods, and the interest just covers the value of the advance. Workers are essentially holding their firm's bonds. By accepting less than they are worth when young, they buy bonds that are paid back as wages that exceed marginal product when they are old. The difference between current wages and current output reflects the average return on bonds held by the workers. This is true even though the average age of individuals in the firm is constant in steady state and even though the distribution of worker ages within the firm is uniform.

As interesting as this may be, it is far from obvious that the firm must have negative net revenues or cash flow. If anything, the presumption goes the other way. The reason is that current cash flow depends on what the firm did with the capital that it received in earlier periods when workers were receiving less than average output on net. If the firm took the surplus received each period on every worker and put it, say, in a bond paying r rate of interest or invested it in the firm where the rate of return is at least r, then in a deterministic world it would always have exactly enough to cover the difference between wages and output. If, on the other hand, the firm paid the surplus as dividends to current stockholders, then it would face the problem of not being able to meet payroll in steady state.[7] There are two ways that problems can arise. First, some myopia may be present. Required is an inability to smooth receipts and payments over time appropriately. In this respect, the current problem has much in common with the labor market insurance literature (see Rosen 1985). This line is pursued first, not because we hold that the world is deterministic, but because this proves useful for comparison with the stochastic environment.

A changing demographic structure may be a catalyst for myopia in the deterministic context. Suppose that the supply of young labor rises and there is a concomitant increase in demand for the average firm's product. Nothing has caused the firm to change the shape of the age-earnings profile, and the age-productivity profile is similarly unaltered. If the typical firm anticipates that the inflow of workers has changed permanently, then the pay-as-you-go mentality means that the firm is expecting next generation's workers to support (at least in part) this generation by accepting wages less than marginal product. A reversion to the previous levels of population growth will cause a current deficit for this firm, which has mistakenly assumed that the increase in young person labor supply is permanent. Again, what makes this go is that firms have already spent the windfall that they received when the size of the young work force increased above the expected levels. (Recall that young workers receive less than they produce so the firm accumulates a surplus.) Let us be somewhat more formal.

First, it is shown that an aging labor force implies an increase in the current deficit (ignoring return on other accumulated assets). An elderly baby-boom generation can be parameterized as

$$
\begin{aligned}
(5) \qquad f_t(a) &= k_0 \quad \text{for} \quad a < a^* \\
&= k_1 \quad \text{for} \quad a \geq a^*,
\end{aligned}
$$

where $k_0 < 1 < k_1$ and

$$
(6) \qquad a^* k_0 + (1 - a^*)k_1 = 1.
$$

To show that an aging baby boom generation increases the difference between wage bill and current output, it is sufficient to show that

(7)
$$N \int_0^1 [w(a) - q(a)]da < Nk_0 \int_0^{a*} [w(a) - q(0a)]da$$
$$+ Nk_1 \int_{a*}^1 [w(a) - q(a)]da$$

(still assuming, for simplicity, that all workers enter the firm at age 0 and leave at age 1). The left-hand side is the deficit in the firm with a uniform age distribution. The right-hand side is the deficit in a firm with a disproportionately older labor force.

Define

$$R \equiv \int_0^{a*} [w(a) - q(a)]da$$

and

$$S = \int_{a*}^1 [w(a) - q(a)]da.$$

Since $w(a) - q(a)$ is increasing in a,

(8)
$$\frac{R}{a*} < \frac{S}{(1 - a*)}.$$

Note further that (6) can be rewritten as

(9)
$$\frac{a*}{1 - a*} = \frac{k_1 - 1}{1 - k_0}.$$

To prove the result, assume the opposite of (7). Then

$$\int_0^1 [w(a) - q(a)]da > k_0R + k_1S,$$

or

$$R + S > k_0R + k_1S.$$

So

$$\frac{R}{S} > \frac{k_1 - 1}{1 - k_0}.$$

But, from (8),

$$\frac{R}{S} < \frac{a*}{1 - a*}.$$

Substitute into (9) to obtain

$$\frac{a^*}{1 - a^*} > \frac{k_1 - 1}{1 - k_0}.$$

But

$$\frac{a^*}{1 - a^*} = \frac{k_1 - 1}{1 - k_0},$$

by (6), which is a contradiction.

This proof means that an aging labor force increases the firm's current deficit when the boom generation reaches old age when population size is fixed at N.[8] Again, two ingredients are necessary to make this a concern in a deterministic environment. First, the firm must operate on a pay-as-you-go basis. Second, the firm must dissipate the excess that it receives as a result of having a larger than equilibrium young work force.[9]

At the heart of this problem is what firms are able to forecast and how they save for the future. Whether poor planning by firms will create difficulties in a pay-as-you-go world is an empirical question. The business community's concern over cash-flow and dividend policies has puzzled economists ever since Modigliani and Miller (1958) put forth their famous theorem. In this context, only the most naive and myopic firms should find the current deficit an important variable. A more plausible alternative is that the world is not deterministic.

The firm can only assure that receipts equal payments in a deterministic world. But returns on investments are stochastic so that receipts are unlikely to match payments ever. Even a dedicated bond portfolio will not do the job. The reason is that the liability to the worker is real, whereas the dedicated bond portfolio guarantees only a nominal payment. Indeed, the frequently suggested dedicated portfolio strategy is likely to cause a larger standard deviation between receipts and payments than other investment strategies, in particular, the strategy of investing in short-term securities, like six-month Treasury bills. The reason is that short-term nominal interest rates are more closely correlated with nominal wage growth than are long-term rates.

Although there may be no investment strategy that guarantees that nominal liability equals nominal receipts, this does not imply that a pay-as-you-go structure increases risk of bankruptcy. Pay-as-you-go would have the excess of receipts over payments paid out as dividends or reinvested. Shortfalls are made up by selling off capital (physical or securities).

Define the pay as you go strategy as taking the current generation's loan, that is, the difference between output and wage payment to young workers, and investing it in the firm. Then the firm uses its resulting output to pay off the generation of old workers. If the firm is trying to minimize the probability of bankruptcy or simply trying to minimize the variance of the deficit, then it may well be better to invest all money in the firm and use the pay-as-you-go strategy. Let us formalize this as follows.

Consider two periods. The firm collects X from the worker in period 1 and promises to pay real wage W in period 2. The real wage is set so that the worker earns the appropriate real return on his investment and so that the worker bears no real risk. (All risk is borne by the risk-neutral firm in this contract.) If W were nonstochastic, then a dedicated portfolio of X of bonds yielding nominal rate r would exactly cover the current deficit. So if Q is output in period 2,

$$W - Q = X(1 + r)$$

when W and Q equal their expectations. Put alternatively, the amount that the worker lends the firm is, in equilibrium,

$$X = \frac{\bar{W} - \bar{Q}}{1 + r} ,$$

where $\bar{W}$ and $\bar{Q}$ are expected values.

An alternative strategy is to take the proceeds collected from the worker in period 1 and to reinvest in the firm. This is equivalent to raising the scale of the firm to $\bar{W}/\bar{Q}$ so long as output from the new capital moves in proportion to the old capital. Then, when $W = \bar{W}$ and $Q = \bar{Q}$, the amount invested should increase Q proportionately, that is, by

$$\frac{\bar{W} - \bar{Q}}{\bar{Q}} .$$

The deficit, if the expectation is realized, is then

$$\bar{W} - \bar{Q}\left(1 + \frac{\bar{W} - \bar{Q}}{\bar{Q}}\right) = 0.$$

In general, however, W is not identically equal to $\bar{W}$, and Q is not equal to $\bar{Q}$. The seemingly low-variance dedicated portfolio strategy is likely to be worse than the "high-risk" strategy of reinvesting in output and paying as you go.

The deficit in period 2 is

$$\begin{aligned} D &= W - Q + X(1 + r) \\ &= W - Q - \bar{W} + \bar{Q} \end{aligned}$$

with the dedicated portfolio and

$$D^* = W - \frac{\bar{W}}{\bar{Q}} Q$$

with the strategy that invests in the firm itself. Now, W and Q are random variables such that

$$W = \bar{W}P$$

and

$$Q = \bar{Q}R,$$

where

$$E(P) = E(R) = 1.$$

This implies that

$$D = \bar{W}P - \bar{Q}R - \bar{W} + \bar{Q}$$

and

$$D^* = \bar{W}P - \frac{\bar{W}}{\bar{Q}}\bar{Q}R$$
$$= \bar{W}(P - R).$$

Thus,

$$s_D^2 = \bar{W}^2 s_P^2 + \bar{W}^2 s_R^2 - 2 \, \text{cov}(\bar{W}P, \bar{Q}R),$$

and

$$s_{D^*}^2 = \bar{W}^2[s_P^2 + s_R^2 - 2 \, \text{cov}(P, R)].$$

If P and R are uncorrelated so that $\text{cov}(P, R) = 0$, then the dedicated portfolio is the lower-risk strategy since $\bar{Q}^2 < \bar{W}^2$. But, in general, P and R are positively correlated. At the other extreme, let $P = R$. Then D^* is equal to zero always. But if $P = R$,

$$D = P(\bar{W} - \bar{Q}) - \bar{W} + \bar{Q}$$
$$= (\bar{W} - \bar{Q})(P - 1),$$

so

$$s_D^2 = (\bar{W} - \bar{Q})^2 s_P^2 > 0.$$

The dedicated portfolio has higher variance, and the pay-as-you-go strategy is better. The best hedge is an instrument that is highly correlated with $W - Q$, for example, short-term bonds or, perhaps better, the firm's stock, since it picks up firm idiosyncratic risk. Pension funds often hold a large proportion of their firms' stock, despite the adverse consequences on diversification.[10] The reason may be that reinvesting pension funds in the firm reduces the risk of bankruptcy, which affects the expected wage payment.

The policy that seems to work as a way to guarantee that the firm does not run a deficit in period 2 does not guarantee zero deficit at all. Indeed, it may be worse than a pay-as-you-go strategy that puts everything into and takes everything out of the firm. The reason is that the commitment to the worker is a real liability, whereas the dedicated portfolio is a guaranteed nominal asset.

This discussion has direct bearing on pension liabilities. Even "funded" pensions have a portfolio that is attempting to cover a liability, the value of which is a random variable. If W is redefined to be pension liability and Q is defined as the realization of the pension portfolio set aside to cover that liability, then the analysis is identical. This implies that the dedicated portfolio strategy, where assets are purchased to match the payout structure or average duration of the estimated liability, may actually be the worst way to hedge. Because the value of the fund does not vary with the liability, the deficit increases when the net nominal liability increases to keep real value constant. This is surprising since some influential pension investment advisers recommend long bonds as a hedging strategy. Short-term Treasury bills, the value of which moves more with the rate of price and wage inflation, are likely to be a better hedge. Since the pension liability is a real one (almost all defined benefit plans are tied directly or indirectly to final salary), a certain nominal return is a poor hedge for that liability.[11]

The main point is that even forward-looking firms may find themselves in dire straits as a result of output that is too low to cover its wage bill. The pay-as-you-go strategy may be the best that one can do, but it still is not good enough to prevent bankruptcy when liabilities are random variables. Virtually all defined benefit pension plans and implicit wage commitments are, at least to some extent, real liabilities that are affected by unpredictable events.

Is this an important issue? Put alternatively, how large are the potential deficits relative to the wage bill? In order to know, it is necessary to have some idea about the difference between output and wages over the life cycle. The following example makes the point that small initial deviations of output and wage can result in large steady-state deficits.

Suppose that the work life is 45 years and that the worker's output in each of those years is $30,000. Suppose that a linear wage profile is used with wage at time zero equal to five-sixths of marginal product. It is easily verified that, if the discount rate is 2 percent real, the following wage function ensures that the worker receives the present value of lifetime marginal product ($820,660) over his career:

$$W(t) = 25,000 + 280t,$$

where t is year of employment and runs from 1 to 45. To convert to nominal dollars, let the inflation rate be 5 percent so that, by the end of the first year, nominal q is \$31,500 and nominal salary is \$26,544. The final nominal salary is \$254,848. Salary overtakes marginal product in the eighteenth year of work, or with 60 percent of the career remaining. If the distribution of work ages is uniform as before, then the average deficit per worker is \$7783 per year, which is slightly less than 8 percent of the worker's average (undiscounted) wage. That is, the firm's steady-state deficit equals about 8 percent of its wage bill. As compared with pension liability figures, the number is significant (see Ippolito 1986).

Incidentally, there is an irony in that the most productive firms may also run the largest deficit. If the difference between slope of the wage profile and slope of the productivity profile is positively related to output, as it might be for incentive reasons, then high-output firms will have the largest deficit. The current deficit reflects larger bond purchases by workers, which raise worker productivity over the life cycle.

Now suppose that a firm finds itself in a situation where it cannot meet its payroll. What can the firm do?

First, it can breach its contracts. The breach can take a number of forms. As already mentioned (Shleifer and Summers 1988), bankruptcy and reopening under new management may allow for an inexpensive way to breach a contract.[12] To the extent that bankruptcy or reorganization through mergers and acquisitions involve some social cost as a result of inefficient rent seeking, this alternative is not desirable. Whether transfers in ownership increase with the (unanticipated) aging of the firm's work force has not yet been documented.

Why not lower the wages of the generation of young that follows the baby boomers to cover the deficit? That strategy is not feasible in a competitive labor market. It implies that the current young workers are willing to subsidize older workers. Competing firms can offer each new worker his lifetime marginal product, as defined by (4). Bygones are bygones, and firms cannot make up for mistakes of the past by attempting to extract additional concessions from workers of the future. Promising even higher wages in the future to the new generation of young workers is not credible because that would imply further attacks on the next generation's young workers.

As Welch (1979) argued and MaCurdy and Mroz (1988) and Berger (1988) most recently corroborated, wage profiles depend on cohort size. In particular, age-earnings profiles for the peak baby boom cohort are flatter than those of other groups. Their age–real earnings profiles are actually negatively sloped during the 1970s, even though baby boomers were going through the part of life cycle when real wages are expected to grow most rapidly. Berger offers evidence of flatter profiles for baby boomers. The firm may be adjusting to the pay-as-you-go formula. The present value of lifetime earnings need not fall much since there are more baby boomers than current older workers so that the deficit is covered by withholding a smaller amount per worker for a larger number of workers. The converse holds when the baby boomers are older. But lifetime productivity would be expected to fall if the earlier profile provided incentives that are now reduced as a result of flatter profiles.

Perhaps the most likely solution to current deficits (and the one that comes closest to the topic at hand) involves changing the retirement behavior of the baby boomers. If older workers are paid more than they are worth, then lowering the average retirement age improves the firm's current cash-flow situation. There are a number of ways that this can be accomplished.

First are explicit buyouts. Let us assume that the firm wants to reduce the size of its older work force, either for the reasons discussed above or for any other reason. For example, older workers may possess obsolete human capital that has little value to the firm. If this reduces their marginal products below the alternative use of their time, a separation is efficient. The separation can be brought about by severance pay that takes the form of an explicit buyout.

Using the notation above, suppose a worker of age a_0 has $w(a_0) > q(a_0)$. Suppose further that the firm would "prefer" that he leave, either for reasons of cash flow or for efficient separation. How can this be accomplished while saving the firm money?

Let the worker's alternative use of time be given by $\bar{w}(a)$. To buy out a worker of age a_0 it is necessary to offer a buyout B such that

$$(10) \qquad B > \int_{a_0}^{1} [w(a) - \bar{w}(a)]e^{-ra}da.$$

In order for the firm to make money on the buyout, it is necessary that

$$(11) \qquad B < \int_{a_0}^{1} [w(a) - q(a)]e^{-ra}da.$$

Equations (10) and (11) imply that

$$(12) \qquad \int_{a_0}^{1} [\bar{w}(a) - q(a)]e^{-ra}da > 0.$$

Condition (12) is the efficiency condition for separation over the remainder of the worker's life. It says that a profitable buyout offer can be made only when a separation would be efficient, that is, only when the worker's alternative use of time exceeds his value to the firm. This is significant.

Suppose that the reason that the firm would like to rid itself of the worker is that his human capital has become obsolete. This implies that the $q(a)$ profile has shifted downward or has tilted to become less positively or more negatively sloped. If internal productivity falls more than external productivity, which is likely, especially when the alternative use of time reflects the value of leisure, then condition (12) is more likely to be met. Thus, profitable explicit buyouts are a feasible strategy in some cases where worker skills have become obsolete.

Now suppose that the $q(a)$ profile has not fallen over time but that the firm would like to become less "top-heavy" for cash-flow reasons. Buyouts offer no relief here. In order to buy the worker out, it must be true that (12) holds. But the retirement date a^* (in this case $a^* = 1$) must have been chosen in any ex ante efficient contract to solve

$$(13) \qquad \bar{w}(a^*) = q(a^*).$$

For all $a < a^*$, $q(a) > \bar{w}(a)$ so that condition (12) must be violated unless something else has changed. A changing demographic structure does not necessarily imply that $q(a)$ falls relative to $\bar{w}(a)$ for high values of a. The change in the shape of the productivity profile depends on imperfect substitution across age categories and the nature of their interaction in the production function (see Murphy and Welch 1988). As a result, it is unlikely that a current deficit caused by a demographic shift can be alleviated by an explicit buyout of older workers.

10.2.1   Pensions and Implicit Buyouts

As I have argued earlier (see Lazear 1983), worker turnover can be affected by using a defined benefit pension plan. These plans have the feature that expected present value of the pension stream declines, once workers remain with the firm beyond some date. Thus, the pension acts as severance pay since remaining for an additional year costs the worker benefits. Specifically, what the worker receives at time a_0 is

$$(14) \qquad \text{compensation } (a_0) = w(a_0) + \Delta \text{ pension } (a_0).$$

By selecting the appropriate defined benefit pension formula, any desired buyout structure can be achieved. For example, suppose that the interest rate is zero and a given individual is going to live to age 80. He began working for the firm at age 30. Suppose further that the firm would like to offer him a buyout of $11,000 at age 60. Let the firm offer the following (standard) pension formula:

> The worker receives ($1,000)(years of service at retirement) per year during every year that he lives after retirement.

If the worker retires at age 60, he has thirty years of service and receives $30,000 per year times twenty years, or $600,000 in pension. If he retires at 61, he has thirty-one years of service and receives $31,000 per year times nineteen years, or $589,000 in pension. The difference in pension is $11,000, so it costs the worker $11,000 to stay on one more year. The pension formula has produced the desired buyout at age 60.

While both common types of defined benefit pension formulas (pattern and conventional) can achieve any desired buyout structure, a defined contribution pension plan offers no potential for a buyout. Since defined contribution plans become the assets of the workers, and since contributions to the fund cannot be negative,[13] there is no possibility of structuring a contribution schedule such that the expected present value of the pension assets decline with years of work.[14]

The advantage of explicit buyouts over implicit ones is that the amount can be tailored to each case. But there are two problems with explicit buyouts. Explicit buyouts may create a moral hazard problem as workers try to make themselves undesirable so that the firm will increase the buyout offer. Additionally, they may be illegal. Explicit buyout programs are offered to workers in some age window, say, 55–59 years old. The firm may not want to offer as large a buyout to workers who are, say, 65 because the older workers have a higher probability of voluntary retirement in a given year (see *Karlen v. City College of Chicago,* U.S. 7th Circuit, R. Posner). But at least one court has ruled that this discriminates on the basis of age. Since 65-year-olds are not entitled to a benefit that 56-year-olds receive, they are adversely affected in a way that is related to age and not necessarily productivity. While the move makes good economic sense and may be efficient, courts have not always viewed economic efficiency as the relevant criterion.

Explicit buyouts create moral hazard. A worker who can depress his output, $q(a)$, by reducing effort can make it ex post profitable for a firm to buy him out. The worker who knows that behaves opportunistically, which can be prevented only by making buyout offers unanticipated. Each offer must be a once-and-for-all offer, and workers must not infer from it that similar offers will be available to them in the future. This is a difficult lie to tell continuously, especially since the worker knows that, ex post, it pays for the firm to buckle under and buy the worker out.

Implicit buyouts that operate through defined benefit pension plans may be equally ''illegal,'' but they are more subtle. As such, firms are likely to be able to use them with relative impunity. (There are obvious exceptions. Courts have already ruled that explicit service credit may not cease when a worker reaches some age, say, 65.) Thus, a switch from a defined contribution to defined benefit plan may be the right approach in occupations where retirement can occur on the job.

Table 10.5 now becomes particularly relevant. The trend reflects a shift from defined benefit plans toward defined contribution plans over time. There are a number of advantages of using defined contribution plans. They are easy to administer and cheap to subcontract out to third parties. More important, they usually offer workers more choice over the instruments used as investment vehicles in the pension fund. The major disadvantage is that they cannot be used as effectively to influence the retirement decision. Of course, if wages can be reduced, there is no need to use subtle pension buyout schemes to bring about retirement. But not only might wage reductions be viewed as breaches of implicit contracts; they are almost certainly a violation of ADEA. The same statute makes obsolete the use of mandatory retirement as a tool for adjusting the labor force, which means that implicit buyouts through defined benefit pension plans are even more important. Yet firms seem to be switching voluntarily to defined contribution plans, or at least new plans are disproportionately of this type. How can this be reconciled with the previous argument?

First, it is well known that the average age of retirement has fallen over time, at least for men. Table 10.6 presents some labor force participation rates.

For men, the decline in labor force participation rates among the older work force is quite pronounced. No similar pattern exists for females because two trends operate in opposite directions. Career women may be retiring earlier than in the past, but younger cohorts have higher average participation rates, which drives up the average, even for the 55–64 age group.

There is some evidence (for a review, see Morrison 1988) that the elimination of mandatory retirement will have a small effect on reducing that trend, but this may be a short-run phenomenon that pertains only to those workers whose wage offers were altered significantly by the unanticipated elimination of mandatory retirement. There are some occupations where elimination of mandatory retirement is likely to present significant problems. The most obvious of these is academics. Here, the working conditions are not well defined, so a worker may remain with the firm, doing relatively little, and still draw his normal salary. Because the pension is defined contribution and is owned by the worker (he may even borrow against it), there is no way that the pension can be used to induce him to retire. Universities have become quite concerned that this will create a major problem, and evidence has already accumulated that suggests reason for concern. At the University of Chicago, for example, since the retirement age was raised from 65 to 70, only one individual (an economist) opted to retire before 70.[15] Is this an issue, and how can firms in this situation deal with it?

Explicit and implicit buyout strategies are available. But the social and even private cost associated with a failure to induce individuals to retire may not be that great. When a tenure decision is made at 30, the firm must consider that the worker has an expected retirement age of, say, 73 rather than 65. The present value of the extra salary cannot be that large at the time the tenure

Table 10.6   Labor Force Participation Rates over Time

	Men		Women	
	55–64	65+	55–64	65+
1970	76	22	41	8
1980	72	19	41	8
1985	68	16	42	7

decision is made, even more so if the shape of the age-earnings profile can be altered to recapture some of the additional lifetime earnings. The true social cost is that retirement does not occur at the right age because workers are paid more than they are worth and the wage may exceed the reservation wage. But the difference between the value of true leisure and academic productivity plus leisure taken in one's final years as an academic may not be that large.

10.3   Too Much or Too Little Early Retirement?

Observers have been somewhat schizophrenic about retirement patterns. Some worry that there will be too many older workers and that there will be a need to induce them to leave the labor market. Others fear that early retirement patterns will continue and that aggregate output, ignoring leisure, will be too low. I believe that the issue will be one of having a top-heavy labor market for the following reasons.

First, the size of the labor force will be increasing steadily between 1990 and 2020, for both males and females. Despite a trend toward declining partici- pation rates among elderly males, which is in a rough way built into the male panel of table 10.3, the male labor force 60 and older will increase from 4.4 million in 1990 to 7.5 million in 2020. This is an increase of 72 percent over a thirty-year period.

Second, even the labor force participation rate for the group as a whole is estimated to rise between 1990 and 2020. To the extent that workers across age categories are imperfect substitutes for one another, it is unlikely that such large increases in the elderly labor force will not depress older worker productivity so that earlier retirement becomes efficient. If old and middle- aged workers were good substitutes for one another, then a stronger case could be made that the firms will want to retain, rather than discard, older workers. Welch's (1979) and subsequent authors' evidence suggests that imperfect substitution is important since an increase in the size of a cohort does not have age-neutral effects on wages. This is significant because the male aggregate labor force participation rate is projected to decline from about 77 percent to about 70 percent by 2020. The decline occurs as the age distribution of males shifts toward older and lower participation rate cells. It is perhaps this decline in labor force participation rates that has caused some to view with alarm the labor market of the future.

Third, the trend for women goes the other way, with the participation rate rising by the same amount as the male decline, to about 63 percent by 2020. Female rates rise because the effect of younger cohorts having higher labor force participation rates outstrips the adverse consequence of a shifting age distribution.[16] Additionally, the imperfect substitutability implies that induc- ing older males to work may not be much help even if there is a real "short- age" of labor.

Working in the opposite direction, however, are projected changes in the Social Security system. Most obvious are changes in age of entitlement, earnings test, and pension payments associated with the Social Security system. Those effects cannot be captured by past data because many of the changes are not scheduled for years to come. Reduced benefits and increased age of entitlement work toward increasing labor force participation among the elderly, so table 10.3 probably understates the aging of the labor force by ignoring these changes.

Exogenous shifts in the Social Security system, say, by changing age of entitlement, imply that the privately optimal retirement date must rise.[17] It is privately inefficient to attempt to offset the effects of this change by encouraging older workers to retire. Thus, exogenous shifts in the Social Security system offer an example of a situation where firms will not use changes in pension formulas or age-earnings profiles to induce early retirement. This is the opposite case of the one considered in the previous section. There, it was assumed that older workers had obsolete human capital, which meant a fall in productivity relative to alternative use of time and therefore an earlier optimal retirement date. Here, the alternative use of time falls between 65 and 68 as a result of a higher age of entitlement. This raises productivity relative to alternative use of time and therefore implies a later retirement date.

10.4   Other Institutional Factors

10.4.1   Pensions

A major consideration when demographics change is the effect of the change on the pension liability. Much of the gloom over the Social Security system relates to projections that the baby boom generation will imply too much in benefits to be supported by the younger generation. This is because the Social Security system has unfunded liability. Pensions plans with unfunded liability may be in serious trouble if the young generation declines relative to the old.

The earlier discussion has already debunked the notion that a dedicated portfolio of long-term bonds is a perfect or even good hedge. This means that a changing demographic structure has important implications for the solvency of pension funds, even if those funds are fully "funded." To the extent that a shift toward an aging work force and a shrinking younger population increases the variance of the difference between current output and current payments (which include pension payments), bankruptcy will become more common. To reduce the probability of bankruptcy, a strategy of holding short-term assets, the nominal value of which is highly correlated with nominal liabilities, can be followed. Whether firms will actually adopt such a strategy is a real question.[18]

10.4.2   Promotions and the Shape of the Pyramid

Tables 10.3 and 10.4 reveal an aging labor force. The typical firm will have a larger proportion of its work force in the 55–69 age category. This implies either that the probability of promotion will fall at the top of the hierarchy and rise at the lower levels or that the shape of the typical firm's pyramid will change. A pyramid with steeper sides will be necessary to keep all promotion probabilities the same. A proliferation of high-level jobs can be expected if wages must be tied to jobs, as Carmichael (1983) suggests. Otherwise, the shape of the age-earnings profile must change. Does changing the shape of the pyramid have any real consequence? Normally, economists do not worry about jobs, per se, and the question, What is a job, is too deep to be addressed here.[19] If tasks are somehow aligned with jobs and are inseparable in the production function, then a cost of having a changing work force is that the task structure of the firm will be altered somewhat. Carmichael suggests an incentive compatibility reason for having wages tied to jobs, but not for having the tasks assigned specifically to job titles. There seems little reason why the duties that are currently assigned to vice director of management information systems cannot be those that were previously under the direction of assistant vice director. The task breakdown in the firm would then be identical, except that many tasks were previously performed by younger workers with lesser job titles.

10.4.3   Teaching

The last point suggests some potential for real effects of a changing age distribution. Since tasks are not necessarily performed equally well by all age groups, it is unlikely that the new age distribution of tasks and the old one result in the same productivity. But there is no presumption that average productivity will fall. For example, older workers may be better teachers, and previous productivity may have been lower because of fewer qualified teachers. One possibility is that older workers have a larger amount of obsolete skills. Another is that they are the creators of skills in younger workers. A changing age distribution can have real effects on productivity, but changing the hierarchical structure of the firm should not necessarily have any effect on productivity.

10.4.4   Women in the Labor Market

Women are becoming more like men in their labor force participation patterns. Female participation rates not only have risen but also have smoothed out over the life cycle, no longer exhibiting the bi-humped pattern of the 1950s in the aggregate data. The smoothness in the aggregate data probably overstates the extent to which women have ceased to interrupt their careers, at least temporarily, on child bearing.[20] The growing importance of women in the market may help explain the move from defined benefit to defined contribution plan.

Women have a relatively greater demand for not merely vested pension plans but portable ones. Consider a defined benefit pension plan that vests immediately but is not portable. A split career, where a worker works at two different firms for twenty years each, results in lower pension than a unified career, where a worker works at one firm for forty years. This is because pension benefits are tied to final salary and salary at age 45 is likely to be lower than that at age 65. (Even pattern plans have ad hoc adjustments that are generally not awarded to vested, separated employees.) This is a greater concern to women than to men since women are more likely to have a split career than men. A portable pension is one that credits summed work experience and ignores movements across employers. Most professors have portable plans. TIAA/CREF is widespread, and most universities are subscribers. But that is unnecessary. Even if a professor were to move from a TIAA/CREF institution to a non-TIAA/CREF defined contribution institution, the pension would be portable in that no penalty is suffered for a job change. Contributions are made on a monthly basis, and only the value of assets determines the pension. It is independent of the identity of the employer, as is Social Security.[21] In fact, portability is a general characteristic of defined contribution plans, which suggests that women have a relative preference for them. The growth in defined contribution plans may well be a response to increased average turnover in the labor market that accompanies the larger proportion of the labor force composed of females. As already discussed above, what is sacrificed by moving to defined contribution plans is the ability to influence retirement decisions by adjusting pension formulas.

10.5 Conclusion

Some adjustments will be necessary as firms adapt to the effects of demographic changes on the composition and size of the labor force. The first task is to predict the ways in which the labor force is likely to change. The major predictions for labor force changes are as follows. First, the labor force will get older. The proportion of workers between 60 and 70 years old will increase 4 percentage points between 1990 and 2020, and there will be a corresponding decline in the proportion between ages 30 and 40. Second, the aging of the labor force will not be as pronounced for males as for females because the trend toward earlier retirement will offset demographic changes. This is true despite the elimination of mandatory retirement. Third, the size of the labor force will grow until about 2015 and then will decline. Given these trends, the following points are relevant.

1. In steady state, a firm does not cover its wage bill by current output. The deficit must be made up by returns on previous investments. The size of the firm's current deficit grows when the labor force ages.

2. Hedging the pension liability by using a dedicated portfolio of long-term bonds is trying to cover the promised real wage bill with assets that guarantee

nominal returns. The strategy is unlikely to be successful. A superior strategy, and one that may be adopted to a greater extent as labor force demographics change, is covering liabilities by investing in assets that are highly correlated with the value of the nominal liability. Short-term Treasury bills are a good candidate. Even better may be reinvestment in the firm, but changing demographics can have important effects when this strategy is used.

3. A firm that desires to reduce the size of its older work force may consider explicit buyouts. An explicit buyout is feasible only when productivity falls below the alternative use of time. The wage is irrelevant, and this implies that buyouts cannot be used to alleviate deficit problems.

4. Implicit buyouts, through strategically designed pension formulas, have the advantages over explicit ones that workers are less likely to reduce effort to increase the buyout offer and that they are less likely to be found in violation of ADEA. The disadvantage is that the buyout cannot be tailored to the individual as easily.

5. Defined benefit plans offer implicit buyout features that are absent in defined contribution plans. As a result, firms may shift back toward defined benefit plans in the future. This is particularly true for occupations where the elimination of mandatory retirement will have the largest effect. One explanation of the recent trend toward defined contribution plans is the growing importance of females in the labor force, who have a relative preference for portable plans.

6. While most evidence points toward declining age of retirement, the major exogenous factor working in the opposite direction is the change in the Social Security system. A decline in real benefits and an increase in age of entitlement work to raise the optimal retirement age.

7. There is may be a proliferation of high-level jobs, but the task distribution need not change.

8. Aging is likely to have effects on average productivity, but the direction of the change is not obvious. This depends on complementarities in the production function, among other things.

Notes

1. For a detailed examination of trends in retirement patterns, see Tuma and Sandefur (1988).

2. Labor force participation rates from Bureau of Labor Statistics data are available for ages 16–75. All other ages were assumed to have participation rates of zero.

3. Most entries for females in table 10.5 are positive since table 10.4 assumes that labor force participation rates are going to grow. There are exceptions, however, because the rates for females in table 10.4 are not permitted to exceed those for males in table 10.4. That constraint is not imposed on table 10.3.

4. Welch (1979) and more recently Murphy and Welch (1988) have analyzed these effects in detail.

5. "Insolvent" is not well defined, especially in the government context, where multiple budget items, as well as intertemporal considerations, are involved.

6. Highly able workers would shirk, passing themselves off as low-ability ones to collect the insurance premium. Additionally, empirical analyses have found that most wage variation is individual specific, which suggests that far from perfect insurance is found. See Lillard and Weiss (1979).

7. Shleifer and Summers (1988) have argued that an acquisition of one firm by another allows for less costly breach of the implicit promise made by old management to its work force. An omniscient stock market would see through this, and purchasers of the stock would take into account future liabilities of the firm that take the form of promises to workers.

8. The effect is reduced somewhat if generations that succeed the baby boom are of previous size rather than small enough to keep population constant. But the point still holds.

9. A permanent population increase from N to N^* causes an increase deficit without any need for an aging labor force. This follows directly from (3). But deficit per worker, which is independent of N, is not increased. In some sense, the normalized deficit increases only when the age distribution shifts.

10. As long as stock price is only minimally affected by factors other than current output, holding stock reduces the risk of bankruptcy and pension default. But stock price varies in ways unrelated to current output, which works against holding pension dollars in real assets of the firm.

11. All this begs the question of why a firm wants to hedge part or all of its liability to any one group.

12. Still, it can be argued that there is no obvious reason why new owners are better able to breach than old ones. This is especially true when there is separation of ownership and control.

13. This is true not only in practice but also as a result of recent court interpretations of the Age Discrimination in Employment Act (ADEA). In fact, contributions may not even fall off as a function of age according to the court ruling.

14. Clark, Gohmann, and McDermed (1988) find that defined benefit plans are more prevalent in large and unionized firms. They interpret this finding as consistent with a pensions-as-severance-pay interpretation.

15. Sherwin Rosen's committee on mandatory retirement (1988) provided the anecdotal evidence.

16. The census population projections are extrapolated from 1983. The weights that are used to obtain aggregate and age-group labor force participation rates are derived from these population estimates. There is reason to believe that they are already off by a reasonable amount since they predict somewhat higher than actual labor force participation rates for the current year.

17. Privately optimal means that the firm and worker perform joint maximization so as to induce the worker to leave when worker output falls below his alternative use of time, which includes the Social Security payment.

18. The macroeconomic implications of an economy-wide adoption of the short-term strategy are well beyond the scope of this paper and this author.

19. A less-than-satisfactory effort was made in Lazear and Rosen (1988). There, jobs were defined to be technologically determined investment opportunities.

20. Those data confound effects of cohort-specific labor force entry ages and cohort-specific mother's age at childbirth, so smoothing can result from averaging bi-humped patterns over different groups.

21. Exceptions include moving to government jobs, which are not part of the Social Security system.

References

Becker, Gary S. 1962. Investment in human capital: A theoretical analysis. *Journal of Political Economy* 70 (October):9–49.

Berger, Mark C. 1988. Demographic cycles, cohort size, and earnings. Working paper. University of Kentucky.

Carmichael, H. Lorne. 1983. The agent-agents problem: Payment by relative output. *Journal of Labor Economics* 1 (January):50–65.

Clark, Robert, R. S. Gohmann, and A. McDermed. 1988. Employment contracts, regulation and the choice of a pension. North Carolina State University. Typescript.

Harris, Milton, and Bengt Holmstrom. 1982. A theory of wage dynamics. *Review of Economic Studies* 49 (July):315–33.

Ippolito, Richard. 1986. The theory of underfunded pension plans. In *Pensions, economics, and public policy,* 167–86. Pension Research Council of the Wharton School.

Ippolito, Richard, and Walter W. Kolodrubetz. 1986. *The handbook of pension statistics.* Chicago: Commerce Clearing House.

Lazear, Edward P. 1979. Why is there manadatory retirement? *Journal of Political Economy* 87 (December):1261–64.

————. 1983. Pensions as severance pay. In *Financial aspects of the U.S. pension system*, ed. Zvi Bodie and John Shoven. Chicago: University of Chicago Press, for NBER.

Lazear, Edward P., and Sherwin Rosen. 1988. Male-female wage differentials in job ladders. Working paper. Hoover Institution, January.

Lillard, Lee A., and Yoram Weiss. 1979. Components of variation in real earnings data: American scientists, 1960–1970. *Econometrica* 47 (March):437–54.

MaCurdy, Thomas, and Thomas Mroz. 1988. Cohort wage patterns. Hoover Institution. Mimeo.

Modigliani, Franco, and Merton Miller. 1958. The cost of capital, corporation finance and the theory of investment. *American Economic Review* (June).

Morrison, Malcolm H. 1988. Changes in the legal mandatory retirement age: Labor force participation implications. In *Issues in contemporary retirement,* ed. Edward P. Lazear and Rita Ricardo-Campbell. Palo Alto, Calif.: Hoover Institution Press.

Murphy, Kevin M., and Finis Welch. 1988. The structure of wages. University of California, Los Angeles. Typescript.

Rosen, Sherwin. 1985. Implicit contracts: A survey. *Journal of Economic Literature* 23 (September): 1144–75.

————. 1988. Report to the Committee on Faculty Retirement. University of Chicago.

Shleifer, Andrei, and Lawrence H. Summers. 1988. Breach of trust in hostile takeovers. In *Corporate takeovers: Causes and consequences,* ed. Alan J. Auerbach. Chicago: University of Chicago Press.

Tuma, Nancy Brandon, and Gary D. Sandefur. 1988. Trends in the labor force activity of the elderly in the U.S., 1940–1980. In *Issues in contemporary retirement,* ed. Edward P. Lazear and Rita Ricardo-Campbell. Palo Alto, Calif.: Hoover Institution Press.

U.S. Bureau of the Census. 1986. *Projections of the population of the United States by age, sex and race: 1983 to 2080.* Current Population Reports, series P-25, no. 952. Washington, D.C.: U.S. Government Printing Office.

Welch, Finis. 1979. Effects of cohort size on earnings: The baby boom babies' financial bust. *Journal of Political Economy* 87 (October):565–597.

Comment   Finis Welch

Eddie Lazear is always provocative. You can't be intellectually alive and not be stimulated by this guy's work.

We all know that the U.S. population is aging, but in this paper Lazear provides a valuable service by taking the Census Bureau's population age distribution projections and superimposing current sex by age labor force participation rates on them, to forecast future age distribution of labor force participants. His calculations are that, although the working population will age less rapidly than the total population, the working population will age significantly for the next twenty years or so. After that, Lazear's forecasts show a reasonably stable age distribution of workers.

This, of course, is preliminary. It is a given that the work force will age, and Lazear's objective is to delineate the problems that he believes will result and then to describe alternative resolutions of them.

The basic idea is that the worker/firm labor contract is one where the worker's productivity exceeds compensation in the early career and compensation exceeds productivity in the late career. The two related justifications for this view are first that the worker's implicit posting of a bond (through early career compensation deficits) creates incentives not to shirk on the job. Shirking risks detection and being fired so that the late career compensation surpluses are at risk. The second justification is that the late career excess of compensation over productivity creates incentives for mandatory retirement. This may be a simplification of Lazear's interpretation of mandatory retirement, but I believe that it captures the essence of his argument.

He then notes that, if the compensation-productivity career profile is as he suggests, a worker's undiscounted lifetime compensation exceeds his or her undiscounted productivity. This is because net (of compensation) productivity is positive in the early career and competitive pressures with positive time discounts ensure full career equality of discounted productivity and compensation profiles. A firm with a uniform age distribution of workers will therefore have a wage bill on current account that exceeds labor's current product. Moreover, the wage bill-product deficit will increase as the age distribution shifts toward older workers.

None of this creates a problem when firms save or invest productivity surpluses that they retain in the early career to cover late career liabilities unless the returns earned on the funds that are set aside are less than the return assumptions that are embedded in the worker's calculations of alternatives. When firms are myopic or unlucky in their investments, the risks of breaching worker/firm contracts increase as the work force ages.

Finis Welch is professor of economics at the University of California, Los Angeles, and chairman of Unicon Research Corp.

The remainder of Lazear's paper is concerned with strategies that firms might adopt to reduce risks of breaching worker contracts. Since I have nothing to contribute on this front, I restrict my comments to describing an alternative view of the nature of lifetime contracts and then describe some of the problems that I expect to accompany an aging work force.

In introducing the argument for current account wage bill deficits, Lazear describes the human capital and incentive views as alternatives. According to the human capital view, the firm invests in the worker in the early career so that costs exceed productivity and the investment is recouped in the late career. The incentive view is described above, and Lazear sees the existence of mandatory retirement (until it was legislatively proscribed) as evidence for the incentive view.

It seems to me that the two views are alternatives only in a two-period world where investments in one period are recouped the next and when investments are not firm specific. Since Lazear's illustrative calculations assume a forty-five-year work life, it seems safe to assume that there are more than two periods. Now consider the human capital model presented by Becker (1962).

In the early career, the firm invests in the worker, and the worker invests in the firm. The sharing of firm-specific investments provides partial insurance against subsequent attempts to preempt rents, by either the firm or the worker. The firm invests if the product it receives is less than the worker's cost (compensation plus explicit training costs), and the worker invests if the compensation received is less than would be received in a (perhaps hypothetical) alternative job. There is nothing contradictory in joint investment because the worker's product to the firm bears no necessary relation to his or her alternative wage.

Similarly, there is no contradiction in an assumption that both investments are productive. It is only necessary that, subsequent to the firm's investment, the worker's product must exceed compensation by an amount that is sufficient to recoup investment costs. From the worker's perspective, it is necessary only that, subsequent to the investment, compensation from the firm must exceed the alternative wage. The specificity of the investment breaks the link between productivity within the firm and the alternative wage, and the existence of multiple periods suggests that the timing of returns on investments need not coincide with approaching retirement.

Notice that, if firms invest in workers in the early career, then undiscounted lifetime product exceeds undiscounted lifetime compensation. With a uniform age distribution of workers, the firm realizes a current account surplus, and the surplus increases as the age distribution shifts toward older workers. This implication is the opposite of the one Lazear analyzes.

The next question is whether the existence of mandatory retirement (or, under current law, the potential existence) can provide information regarding time profiles of compensation-productivity differentials or, from the worker's perspective, of compensation-alternative wage differentials. If there is a relation, I do not see it. Long careers simply offer too much room for flexibility in timing. For what it is worth, I think of mandatory retirement as follows.

In a world of independent worker productivities with costless recontracting, retirement or any other separation between worker and firm would occur only with mutual agreement. All that matters is the contrast between the worker's productivity to the firm and the alternative value of time (in retirement or working elsewhere). If the value of the worker's time with the firm exceeds the value elsewhere, there must be a compensation package that would keep the worker with the firm. Similarly, if the worker's perception of the value of the time spent elsewhere exceeds the firm's perception of the value of the worker's time with the firm, there should be no agreement that would keep the worker in place.

I believe we have mandatory retirement because productivities are interdependent and because recontracting is expensive. Interdependence includes the ability to work with colleagues as well as the expectations and aspirations of younger workers concerning opportunities for advancement, and it extends to personnel relations involving satisfaction when others are treated no better than I am treated or envy when others receive what I see as superior treatment. Mandatory retirement has the advantage of even-handedness, and it facilitates planning. Coupled with unvested pensions etc., mandatory retirement can be considered simply as variance reducing.

In closing, I will list but not develop problems that I see as coincident and perhaps caused by an aging work force. One is that aging is coincident with reduced population growth and, in closed economies, perhaps with reduced growth in product demand. A firm that is organized vis-à-vis promotion ladders etc. that incorporate continuing growth will have to reorganize internally. With reduced growth there may be reduced opportunities for internal advancement.

Worker careers are interdependent not only in the sense of promotion ladders but also in the sense of spot productivity enhancement. Current estimates are that the productivity of mid-aged workers, for example, is increased by increased numbers of younger workers—in part, perhaps, because the older workers are assisted by and in turn help train the younger workers. A reduced inflow of younger workers will probably reduce the productivity of mid-aged workers.

There are macro- as well as micro-effects of a changing age distribution. Consider as an example the stereotyped career of a physicist. The early phase is brash and fast; it is where the innovations are produced. Next, there is consolidation, where numbers of publications may be great but are tending toward reiteration, minor extension, and development of applications. During this phase, the emphasis shifts from doing to teaching. Then, in the late career, say age 40, there is nothing left but administration. Physicists represent an amazing proportion of graduate school deans at major universities. The micro implication of an aging work force may be only that the ratio of deans to research associates will increase. The macro implication may be that rates of discovery will fall as the first-phase entry resides.

Fortunately for economics (the other major source of graduate school deans), the most productive are either gray or bald.

Eddie Lazear is one of the outstanding labor economists who is interested in the human resource side of human capital research, and he has been able to extend his insight in these areas into some aspects of labor relations. In the present paper, he has drawn on earlier work on mandatory retirement. He ignored his work on tournaments, that is, on the incentive aspects of promotion ladders. The omission is unfortunate. If there are important consequences of an aging working population, one of them must be the implications for opportunities for advancement within firms. Promotional ladders that coincide with rapid population growth cannot resemble those that exist with falling populations.

Reference

Becker, Gary S. Investment in human capital: A theoretical analysis. *Journal of Political Economy* 70 (October):9–49.

11 Behavior of Male Workers at the End of the Life Cycle: An Empirical Analysis of States and Controls

John Rust

This is the second installment in a series of three papers studying the behavior of men at the end of the life cycle. The first paper (Rust 1989) constructed a theoretical model based on the hypothesis that workers maximize expected discounted lifetime utility. The model treats observed behavior as a realization of a *controlled stochastic process* $\{x_t, d_t\}$ derived from the solution to a stochastic dynamic programming problem (DP). Estimation of the DP model requires observations of the worker's *state* x_t and *control* d_t and a specification of the Markov transition probability density $\pi(x_{t+1}|x_t, d_t)$ representing a stochastic "law of motion" that embodies workers' beliefs of uncertain future events.

This paper uses the Retirement History Survey (RHS) to construct state and control variables $\{x_{ti}, d_{ti}\}$, $t = 1, \ldots, T_i$, $i = 1, \ldots, I$, for a sample of $I = 8,131$ male respondents interviewed biennially from 1969 to 1979. I discuss some of the conceptual problems involved in constructing measurements of $\{x_t, d_t\}$ so that the resulting discrete-time, discrete-state DP model makes the best possible approximation to the underlying continuous-time, continuous-state decision process. I present my solutions to the measurement problems and conduct an extensive comparative data analysis to assess the

John Rust is professor of economics and director of the Data and Computation Center and the Social Systems Research Institute at the University of Wisconsin and a research associate of the National Bureau of Economic Research.

The author is extremely grateful for financial support from the National Institute on Aging and the National Science Foundation, which provided a work station for preparing the data and supercomputer time for estimating the DP model. He is equally thankful to the Institute for Empirical Macroeconomics at the Federal Reserve Bank of Minneapolis, which financed six months of uninterrupted research time during which this research was completed. Finally, he would like to thank B. J. Lee for his able research assistance and Lawrence Christiano, Finn Kydland, Edward Prescott. David Runkle, Christopher Sims, and Dick Todd for helpful comments on his work during seminars presented at the Federal Reserve.

overall quality of the resulting variables. Finally, I present estimates of workers' beliefs, in the form of an estimated transition probability matrix $\hat{\pi}$.

All this work is building up to the third paper of the series, which will use the constructed state and control variables and the estimated transition probability matrix as inputs to a "nested fixed point" maximum likelihood algorithm (Rust 1988) to estimate the unknown parameters of workers' utility functions. The success of the final stage depends critically on accurate measurements of $\{x_t, d_t\}$ and correct specification of workers' beliefs π.

The paper is organized as follows. The key parts of the paper are sections 11.1 and 11.2, which summarize the principal findings. Section 11.1 describes the state and control variables constructed from the RHS data set and presents the main conclusions of the data analysis. Section 11.2 specifies the functional form of workers' beliefs and summarizes the conclusions about workers' beliefs π. The remaining sections present details on the construction of $\{x_t, d_t\}$ and the specification and estimation of $\hat{\pi}$ that compose the evidence for the conclusions drawn in sections 11.1 and 11.2; they can be skipped or skimmed by readers who are content to accept my view of the "stylized facts."

11.1 State and Control Variables: Main Findings

Following the notation of Rust (1989), the DP model requires a vector of state variables, $x_t \equiv (w_t, y_t, aw_t, sr_t, h_t, a_t, e_t, ms_t)$, defined by

w_t: accumulated net financial and tangible nonfinancial wealth,
y_t: total income from earnings and assets,
aw_t: Social Security "average monthly wage,"
sr_t: Social Security status (receiving OASDI/not receiving OASDI),
h_t: health status of worker (good health/poor health/disabled/dead),
a_t: age of worker,
e_t: employment status (full time/part time/not employed),
ms_t: marital status (married/single),

and control variables, $d_t \equiv (c_t, s_t, ss_t)$, defined by

c_t: planned consumption expenditures,
s_t: employment search decision (full time/part time/exit labor force),
ss_t: Social Security decision (apply for OASDI/do not apply for OASDI).

In the last twenty years, several panel data sets have accumulated sufficiently detailed data to permit construction of the required variables: the Panel Survey on Income Dynamics (PSID), the National Longitudinal Survey (NLS), and the Retirement History Survey (RHS). Of these, the RHS has the largest and most comprehensive coverage of older workers since it was explicitly designed by the Social Security Administration (SSA) to obtain a detailed picture of the transition from work into retirement. A special feature of the RHS is the availability of matching records from the Census Bureau and

SSA that permit direct validation of response error in several key variables. The Social Security Earnings Record (SSER) contains each covered worker's wage earnings (up to the statutory maximum taxable earnings) and quarters of coverage from 1939 to 1974. The Social Security Master Beneficiary Record (SSMBR) contains actual payments of Social Security old age, survivors, disability, and death benefits (OASDI) to each respondent, spouse, and dependent from 1969 to 1978. The combination of finely detailed data, large sample size, and long duration, plus the existence of linked Census and SSA records, makes the RHS the data set of choice for estimating the DP model.

Having said this is not to deny the sober truth that, even with the linked RHS records, there is a limit to how accurately one can measure the "true" states and decisions of individuals. Besides the obvious problems of missing data, response and coding error, estimation of the DP model presents three additional problems: choice of time discretization, choice of state discretization, and construction of observable indicators of latent state and control variables.

Although the individual's actual decision process is best modeled in continuous time, the data are collected and the DP model is formulated in discrete time. In theory, use of discrete-time models is not a limitation since it has been shown that under very general conditions one can formulate a discrete-time DP model that approximates an underlying continuous-time DP model arbitrarily closely as the time interval goes to zero (van Dijk 1984). One can account for absence of data on (x_t, d_t) between survey dates by forming a marginal likelihood function that "integrates out" the missing observations. In practice, however, computational and data limitations forced me to use fairly coarse two-year time intervals. The computational limitations arise from the numerical integrations required to form the marginal likelihood function and the "curse of dimemsionality" inherent in DP models with fine time grids. The data limitations stem from the lack of measures of income flows for intervals shorter than one year.

Even if a complete set of "instantaneous" state and control variables could be constructed, I would still prefer to use annual measures in the belief that they better capture the worker's retirement behavior than a series of "snapshots" at fairly widely spaced time intervals. Analytically, the disadvantage of the discretization is that it implicitly precommits workers to fixed consumption and labor supply values over two-year time intervals. I should point out, however, that, even with a two-year time interval, the worker is given thirty opportunities to revise his decisions between age 58 and the terminal age, 108. Such a model is quite a bit more flexible than the standard approach, which models retirement as a once and for all choice from a nonlinear budget set that describes alternative consumption/work levels that are assumed fixed for the duration of the worker's lifetime (see, e.g., Burtless and Moffitt 1984). These sorts of static perfect-certainty models do not allow for any *ex post* revision in consumption or labor supply in light of new information. Whether a model with thirty periods (sixty years) can provide sufficient flexibility to model workers' decision processes accurately is a deeper question. I leave the analysis of the consequences of time aggregation to the actual estimation of the DP model in the third paper of this series.

The state variables y_t, w_t, and aw_t, which are typically treated as continuous, must also be discretized in order to estimate the DP model. Similar to the discretization of time, there are theorems guaranteeing that one can approximate a continuous-state DP model arbitrarily closely by a discrete-state DP model (Bertsekas and Shreve 1978). In previous work, I have found that the DP solution is not very sensitive to the discretization of the state variables and that one can obtain a good approximation using fairly coarse grids (Rust 1987). In this study, I use a grid size of $1,000 (1968 dollars), which turned out to be more than adequate given the two-year time discretization that I ultimately adopted.

The most difficult problem, however, was construction of good measurements of latent variables such as health h_t, labor search s_t, and consumption c_t. My approach was to use all relevant survey responses to define observable indicators that might be regarded as "best approximations" of the underlying latent variables. Measurement of consumption proved to be particularly challenging, a fact that many economists may find disturbing. Even though the RHS asked respondents to list the amount spent on individual consumption items, in my opinion the list was too incomplete to construct reliable estimates of total consumption.[1] Since the RHS has much more complete, detailed data on income and wealth,[2] my approach was to infer c_t from the budget equation

$$(1) \qquad\qquad w_{t+1} = w_t + y_t - c_t .$$

Unfortunately, the RHS recorded income only in the even-numbered years immediately preceding each survey date. Thus, in order to construct c_t I needed to impute income in odd-numbered years. This in turn necessitated construction of complete labor force histories for each worker, including total annual hours worked in each year.[3] Using hours worked together with annual wage earnings data from the SSER (available up to 1974), I was able to impute income in odd-numbered years and construct estimates of c_t over the two-year sample interval. A limitation of the income data is absence of information on capital gains. I dealt with this problem by attributing 100 percent of the change in house value to capital gains (provided the respondent was a homeowner and had not moved within the interval) and by excluding workers who had substantial real estate or equity holdings. I faced equally difficult problems constructing h_t and s_t, but I will defer the details of their construction until later.

Good measurements of $\{x_t, d_t\}$ are absolutely critical to the success of the DP model since it is highly nonlinear in variables and there currently is no good theory of errors in variables for such models. Wherever possible, I have attempted to obtain independent measures of the variables to assess the magnitude of the measurement error. I have also constructed an array of associated "flag variables" to indicate the degree of confidence in each of the constructed state and control variables. By setting the appropriate flags, I can screen out questionable cases to obtain a core subsample for which confidence in the data is relatively high. To guard against the possibility that such screening could produce unpredictable sample selection biases, I have compared the distribution of each variable to its distribution in the full sample using all available observations. Because presentation of tabulations of the flag variables takes us too much into the "guts" of the computer programs that generate the state variables, I have decided against presenting them. Instead, I describe the nature of any special data or sample selection problems where appropriate.[4]

I can state the major conclusions of the data analysis as follows.

1. At the aggregate level, the data show workers making a smooth transition from work into retirement, gradually reducing consumption and labor supply but maintaining wealth levels intact. This is consistent with the behavior of a neoclassical, risk-averse consumer who attempts to smooth consumption and leisure streams and to provide bequests to his heirs. However, at the individual level, the data are anything but smooth: measured consumption shows erratic fluctuations, and labor supply has an abrupt discontinuity, with the typical worker staying at his full-time job up until retirement age (62–65), at which time he applies for Social Security, quits his job, and remains out of the labor force for the rest of his life.

2. Constructing consumption expenditures from the budget equation, $c_t = w_t - w_{t+1} + y_t$, is susceptible to frequent and often large measurement errors in wealth, possibly exacerbated by absence of good information on capital gains. The majority of the erratic variations in measured consumption appear to be attributable simply to response errors in wealth.

3. The distribution of real wealth changes is centered about zero, but with a large variance. On average, net worth is not very large, about four times annual income, and a substantial fraction of this wealth, 50–60 percent, is tied up in housing. These facts provide additional support for the view that the large swings in measured consumption are simply a result of response errors in wealth rather than erratic consumption/savings behavior. Although a simple test of the null hypothesis H_0: $c_t = y_t$ versus H_A: $c_t \neq y_t$ rejects at the 5 percent level (but not at the 1 percent level), the fact that the average change in wealth is $\$-658$ with a standard deviation of \$47,015 makes it very hard to distinguish between alternative theories of consumption/savings behavior. Because of the problems involved in accurately measuring wealth and therefore consumption, I have opted to start with a simpler DP model based on the hypothesis that $c_t = y_t$. In this model, workers choose labor force participation strategies to maximize the expected discounted value of the utility of income, abstracting from wealth and bequests.

4. Although respondent's total income is recorded only for even-numbered years, the existence of independent income measures in the SSER and SSMBR data sets allowed me to construct reliable income imputations in odd-numbered

years. Thus, if wealth changes are indeed an insignificant component of consumption, total imputed income will be a good measure of actual consumption.[5]

5. The distribution of total annual hours worked is highly bimodal, with most of its mass at either 0 or 2000. While some of this bimodality is likely an artifact of response error (with workers simply rounding their responses to forty hours/week, fifty weeks/year), it does indicate that the tripartite classification of labor force status e_t into 1 = full time, 2 = part time, or 3 = unemployed does not grossly misrepresent the data and that the measure is robust to fairly large variations in the hours cutoffs defining the three e_t states. Overall, the distributions provide little evidence to support the view that workers treat annual hours of work as a continuous decision variable.

6. A systematic response error problem known as the *seam problem* produces exaggerated estimates of labor state transitions across the survey dates, or seams, of the RHS. This leads to artificial cyclical variations in the transition probabilities for "across-seam" transitions as compared to "between-seam" transitions. The variation is apparently due to imperfect recall of labor force history in the earlier year of the two-year interview frame, leading to inconsistencies between recalled labor force status in the current interview and the labor force status reported in the last interview. One can ameliorate the seam problem by "skipping over the seams" and tracking transitions between the even-numbered years immediately preceding the odd-year survey dates in order to reduce the amount of recall on the part of respondents. This convinced me to formulate a DP model with a time period of two years rather than with a more fine-grained model with a one-year time period.

7. There are three possible measures of the "job search" control variable: SR, self-reported planned hours of work in the year following the survey; NE, actual hours worked in the year following the survey; and PC, actual hours worked in the year following the *subsequent* survey. The last measure corresponds to a "perfect control" model wherein an unemployed worker who decides to go back to work is successful with probability one. This analysis focuses on the other two measures, which correspond to "imperfect control" models where unemployed workers who decide to look for a full-time job have less than a 100 percent chance of being successful. Probably reflecting the fact that "talk is cheap," it appears that the first measure of s_t is a much more noisy measure of actual job search behavior than is the second measure. The data show that the second measure allows for a more intuitive and predictable relation between job search decisions and subsequent employment outcomes.

8. The four-way classification of health status h_t into 1 = good health, 2 = health limitation but not disabled, 3 = disabled, and 4 = dead seems to produce sensible results despite the inherently subjective nature of health status. Use of actual benefits paid from the SSMBR data was critical to the quality of h_t since self-reported measures of health significantly underestimate

the occurrence of health state 3 owing to systematic underreporting of Social Security disability receipts by respondents. The Social Security requirement of doctor examination for disability qualification seems to be a significant factor in identifying individuals with substantially greater health problems as indicated by their significantly higher ex post mortality. An unfortunate aspect of the disability classification is the fact that no workers become disabled after age 62. This is an artifact of Social Security rules that automatically convert disability payments into OASI payments after age 62.[6]

9. The SSMBR data allow me to identify when individuals actually apply for and receive OASI benefits. Thirty percent of eligible recipients apply for benefits as soon as they are able to receive them at the early retirement age 62, and another 30 percent apply for benefits at the normal retirement age 65. Overall, nearly all nondisabled workers apply for and receive Social Security retirement benefits between the ages of 62 and 65. The implied retirement hazard and frequency distributions computed using the SSMBR data and a definition of "retirement" as the age of first entitlement to OASDI differ significantly from the distributions computed by other researchers using the RHS data and other definitions of retirement. In order better to understand the phenomenon of early retirement and the pronounced bimodal distribution of retirement dates, I have incorporated a new control variable sr_t defined by

$$(2) \qquad sr_t = \begin{cases} 0 \text{ if worker has not applied for OASI,} \\ 1 \text{ if worker first applied for OASI} \\ \quad \text{ before age 65 (early retirement),} \\ 2 \text{ if worker first applied for OASI} \\ \quad \text{ after age 65 (normal retirement),} \end{cases}$$

and corresponding control variable ss_t defined by

$$(3) \quad ss_t = \begin{cases} 1 \text{ if worker applies for Social Security benefits,} \\ 0 \text{ if worker does not apply for Social Security benefits.[7]} \end{cases}$$

Including sr_t and ss_t allows me to avoid *ad hoc* definitions of "retirement," separating the analysis of retirement behavior (i.e., collection of OASI) from labor supply behavior.

11.2 Estimation of Worker's Beliefs: Main Findings

The DP model represents workers' beliefs about uncertain future events by a Markov transition probability density $\pi(x_{t+1}|x_t, d_t)$. Under the assumption of homogeneity and rational expectations, one can "uncover" these beliefs from data on the realizations of $\{x_t, d_t\}$. Given the discretization of time and state variables proposed in section 11.1, π is a matrix with approximately 130 million elements. Even with my comparatively large data set of over thirty thousand observations on $\{x_t, d_t\}$, the standard nonparametric estimate of π is out of the question since nearly all cells of $\hat{\pi}$ would be estimated as identically zero even though workers might believe that the corresponding transitions occur with positive probability. Nonparametric approaches such as kernel and nearest-neighbor regressions also have problems since their estimates of π depend critically on arbitrary choices of kernel, window-width, and other smoothing parameters whose proper values I have little intuition about.[8] My approach is to find a parametric specification $\pi(x_{t+1}|x_t, d_t, \theta)$ that depends on a much lower-dimensional vector of unknown parameters θ in such a way that all relevant cells of π are assigned nonzero probabilities. It is also important to choose a specification that is parsimonious yet sufficiently flexible so that the estimated model is consistent with the data. Above all, it is crucial that the estimated beliefs are "sensible" if we expected to get "sensible" estimates of workers' preferences.

Direct parameterization of a 130 million element matrix seems out of the question, so a more clever approach must be employed. The strategy I have followed is to decompose π into a product of conditional and marginal densities and estimate each of the components separately. To see this more clearly, note that without loss of generality one can decompose a bivariate transition density f as follows:

$$
(4) \qquad f(x_{t+1}, y_{t+1}|x_t, y_t) = f_1(y_{t+1}|x_{t+1}, x_t, y_t)f_2(x_{t+1}|x_t, y_t)
$$
$$
= f_3(x_{t+1}|y_{t+1}, x_t, y_t)f_4(y_{t+1}|x_t, y_t),
$$

where f_1, f_2, f_3, and f_4 are defined from f in an obvious way. Although (4) shows that the ordering of the decomposition of f is irrelevant, it does make a difference when the functional form of f must be estimated from the data, especially where data measurement problems can lead to decompositions which exhibit "spurious causality." Having tried various decompositions of π, the one I found most plausible is given below

$$
(5) \quad \pi(y_{t+1}, e_{t+1}, sr_{t+1}, ms_{t+1}, h_{t+1}|y_t, e_t, sr_t, ms_t, h_t, a_t, s_t, ss_t) =
$$
$$
\pi_y(y_{t+1}|e_{t+1}, ms_{t+1}, h_{t+1}, y_t, e_t, sr_t, ms_t, h_t, a_t, s_t, ss_t) \times
$$
$$
\pi_e(e_{t+1}|ms_{t+1}, h_{t+1}, y_t, e_t, sr_t, ms_t, h_t, a_t, s_t, ss_t) \times
$$
$$
\pi_{ms}(ms_{t+1}|h_{t+1}, y_t, e_t, sr_t, ms_t, h_t, a_t, s_t, ss_t) \times
$$
$$
\pi_h(h_{t+1}|y_t, e_t, sr_t, ms_t, h_t, a_t, s_t, ss_t).
$$

Note that the decomposition (5) excludes the state and control variables c_t, w_t, aw_t from the original list presented in section 11.1. Consumption c_t and wealth w_t were excluded because of the measurement problems discussed in conclusion 3 of section 11.1. The Social Security average monthly wage aw_t (a complex average of the worker's historical earnings) was excluded since it turned out to be sufficiently collinear with current income y_t that I could reduce the dimensionality of the model by making y_t do double duty as a proxy for

aw_t. Finally, future age a_{t+1} and Social Security status sr_{t+1} were excluded since with probability one they obey trivial nonstochastic transition rules:

$$a_{t+1} = a_t + 2,$$

$$sr_{t+1} = sr_t \quad \text{if } sr_t \; 0,$$

$$sr_{t+1} = 1 \quad \text{if } sr_t = 0, \; ss_t = 1, \; a_t < 65, \; a_t \geq 62,$$

$$sr_{t+1} = 2 \quad \text{if } sr_t = 0, \; ss_t = 1, \; a_t \geq 65.$$

The motivation for the decomposition of π given in (5) is that income y_t and employment status e_t are the most important state variables of the DP model, and therefore their evolution should be predicted as well as possible. If we view (5) as specifying π as a direct product of individual transition matrices, then π_y is the "innermost" component of the direct product, in the sense that income transitions are conditioned on the contemporaneously realized values of all the remaining state variables. From an empirical standpoint, including these contemporaneous values substantially improves the fit of the income regressions estimated in section 11.8.

The outermost component of the direct product, health status h_t, has additional structure resulting from the definition of health states $h_t = 3$ and $h_t = 4$. If I fix the values of the other variables $(y_t, e_t, ms_t, a_t, d_t)$, then π_h represented by the 4×4 transition probability matrix:

$$(6) \qquad \pi_h = \begin{bmatrix} \varphi_{11} & \varphi_{12} & \varphi_{13} & \varphi_{14} \\ \varphi_{21} & \varphi_{22} & \varphi_{23} & \varphi_{24} \\ 0 & 0 & \varphi_{33} & \varphi_{34} \\ 0 & 0 & 0 & 1 \end{bmatrix}.$$

According to (6), death is treated as an absorbing state. Note that disability is also treated as an absorbing state in the sense that, once a worker becomes disabled, he can only continue to stay disabled or die. This restriction was necessitated by data limitations. Although the Social Security SSMBR data set includes the variable "date of termination of disability benefits," there were only a handful of cases where actual termination was observed. Perhaps this indicates problems in Social Security record keeping, but it is more likely just an artifact of my Social Security–based definition of "disability." According to Social Security rules, disabled workers who receive SSDI benefits past age 62 are automatically reassigned OASI benefits after turning 62. Thus, there is no real incentive for Social Security to keep track of the date when the actual physical disability terminates once the worker is older than 62. One can try to partially rectify the problem the following way: reclassify workers who received disability benefits prior to age 62 and who are now older than 62 and reporting that they are in good health as being in state $h_t = 1$ rather than

$h_t = 3$. Unfortunately, this reclassification scheme has its own problems: although it allows transitions from disability to good health ($h_t = 3$ to $h_{t+1} = 1$), there is no way to record transitions from $h_t = 3$ to $h_{t+1} = 2$ since the RHS variables do not allow us to distinguish between the states "existence of a health problem that limits one's ability to work" and "disability."

The remaining sections of the paper discuss the construction of the state and control variables in more detail and present estimation results for each of the four components of the decomposition of π given in (5). Having conducted an extensive specification search to find an appropriate functional form for π, I can summarize the main findings below.

1. Age and income are relatively unimportant determinants of death rates after controlling for health, employment, and marital status. Death rates decrease slightly with income and actually decrease with age until age 67.[9] Not surprisingly, single workers are significantly more likely to die than married workers. However, even this variable has a small effect relative to health h_t and the labor supply/retirement decision (s_t, ss_t). Workers who are in poor health ($h_t = 2, 3$) are two to four times more likely to die than healthy workers. There is an equally strong association between the job search decision s_t and the probability of death, but the nature of the relation depends critically on the worker's health and retirement status. If the worker is retired or disabled ($h = 3 \ or \ ss \in \{1, 2\}$), any attempt to return to work on either a full- or a part-time basis is extremely hazardous, significantly increasing the risk of death. However, if the worker has not already retired and is in relatively good health ($h \in \{1, 2\} \ and \ ss = 0$), the decision to quit work is associated with significantly higher death rates. Although this latter finding may represent spurious causality because of failure completely to control for all dimensions of health status, from the standpoint of a worker behaving according to the DP model the association is necessarily interpreted as cause and effect.

2. The probability of becoming disabled is a sharply decreasing function of age, a result that is an artifact of the definition of disability discussed above. It is clear that disability is an endogenous state variable (i.e., the outcome of an unmodeled underlying decision process), as evidenced by the fact that the probability of becoming disabled decreases well before age 62. The explanation is that the process involved in applying and qualifying for SSDI imposes significant costs on the worker, including doctor examination at the worker's expense. Naturally, the closer one is to the early retirement age of 62, the less incentive one has to incur the costs of applying for SSDI, especially when the probability of qualification is significantly less than one. Given the difficulty of constructing a sensible "objective" measure of disability, and given the fact that by law disabled workers have essentially no further labor supply/retirement decisions,[10] I have decided to treat disability/death as a combined absorbing state since the certification standards appear successfully to identify a group of workers who have serious health problems, as confirmed by *ex post* mortality rates which are twice as high as for nondisabled workers. Another

finding of interest is the fact that both single and higher-income workers are significantly less likely to become disabled.[11]

3. The probability of being in good health is a declining function of age and an increasing function of income. All other things being equal, marital status has no significant effect on the probability of being in good health. By far the most important determinant of future health is current health. Currently healthy workers are three times more likely to be in good health than currently unhealthy workers ($h_t = 2$). There is weak evidence that continuing to work on a full- or part-time basis is associated with a higher probability of being in good health. Conversely, the decision to quit working is associated with a deterioration in health. This result is corroborated by the fact that retired workers, $sr \in \{1, 2\}$, are significantly less likely to be in good health. As with my comments in point 1, the association might indicate spurious causality due to imperfections in the measure of health status: healthier workers continue working, while unhealthy workers quit and retire.

4. By far the most important variable predicting future marital status is current marital status: an older single worker has less than a 7 percent chance of finding a new mate over the two-year survey period. Older workers are more likely to lose their spouse, while higher-income workers are less likely to become single, at least up to an income of $30,000. There is weak evidence that, among single workers, the worse one's health, the more likely one is to remain single, although unhealthy married workers have a higher chance of remaining married. Economic decisions such as the labor search decision s_t or the retirement decision ss_t appear to have little or no effect on future marital status.

5. As one would expect, future employment status e_{t+1} is most strongly affected by the employment search decision s_t.[12] In addition, the worker's previous employment state e_t has a significant effect on probability that the search decision s_t is realized. Thus, currently employed workers who decide to continue working full time have a higher probability of remaining fully employed than part-time or unemployed workers. Interestingly, unemployed workers appear to have a significantly higher chance of being successful in gaining a full-time job than part-time employed workers. If a worker decides not to work, he is more likely to "realize" his decision if he is currently unemployed than if he had a full- or part-time job. Full-time workers are more likely to realize their quit decisions than part-time workers. Health status also has a very strong effect on employment status. Workers who become disabled are two and a half times more likely to be out of the labor force, and their chances of staying in a full-time job are less than one-third that of nondisabled workers. There are clear aging effects on the ability to continue working full time; for example, the probability that a 67-year-old worker will be successful in keeping or finding a full-time job is only one-third as high as that of an equivalent worker under 60. Income appears to be a statistically significant proxy for employability, with high-income workers being 60 percent more likely to keep or obtain a full-time job than

low-income workers. Somewhat surprisingly, changes in marital status have no significant effect on employment status. Less surprising is the fact that workers who are receiving OASI are less likely to be fully employed and more likely to be unemployed, all other things equal.

6. In order to match the long-tailed cross-sectional income distributions, the stochastic process for income was assumed to have a transition density with a conditionally heteroscedastic lognormal distribution. Income is strongly autocorrelated with an autoregressive coefficient of .95, and there is evidence of nonlinearity in this relation in the sense that higher powers of current income y_t enter the model with highly significant coefficients. The higher powers of y_t were needed primarily to enable the model to fit the complicated patterns of conditional heteroscedasticity that exist in the data. The estimated model has a variance of future income y_{t+1} that is an increasing function of current income, but the relation is far from proportional: a worker earning $50,000 has a standard deviation in y_{t+1} of $12,000, whereas a worker earning $5,000 has a standard deviation in y_{t+1} of $2,000. Health status has a significant effect on income prospects: healthy workers expect a 3 percent increase in real income, and disabled workers expect a 5 percent increase in income. However, currently healthy workers who become disabled expect a 20 percent drop in income. Changes in marital status have large and statistically significant effects on income. A worker who loses his wife expects a 25 percent drop in income, and a bachelor who has no prospects of remarriage expects his income to fall by about 20 percent. However, by far the most important determinant of future income y_{t+1} is the worker's employment status/search decision (e_t, s_t). Workers who keep working at their full-time jobs expect a 20 percent increase in income, while workers who exit from the labor force expect a 20–30 percent decrease in income.[13] The estimated income process successfully captures the main features of OASDI benefit rules, including the regressive nature of the payoffs, the extra benefits to a spouse, the early retirement penalty, and the effect of the "earnings test" for workers under 70.

7. It is possible that there exist unmeasured differences or *heterogeneity* among workers that create systematic differences in workers' beliefs but that are not captured in the list of state and control variables set forth in this paper. In order to assess the potential magnitude of this problem, I included several demographic variables in the estimation of workers' beliefs π, including a variable classifying the respondent as a "work lover" or "leisure lover" as well as his education, race, and the industry and occupation of his longest held job. Surprisingly, except for the finding that blacks expect significantly lower incomes than whites, none of these variables had a major effect on the estimated transition probability $\hat{\pi}$. Thus, the available evidence indicates that the list of state and control variables set forth in this paper provides a reasonably complete set of "sufficient statistics" for the states and decisions of my sample of workers. In particular, there is no compelling evidence that the failure to account for unmeasured heterogeneity leads to a gross misrepresentation of workers' beliefs.[14]

The remaining sections of the paper present the numerical evidence supporting the conclusions drawn in sections 11.1 and 11.2 and can be skipped or skimmed by readers who are willing to accept them at face value.

11.3   Analysis of Age, Marital Status, and Demographic Variables

A set of variables that we ought to be able to measure accurately are the identity of the respondent, his or her age, and basic demographic variables such as race, education, and the occupation/industry of the respondents' longest job. By and large this is true of the RHS data, although cross-checks of self-reported values with Census and Social Security records do indicate discrepancies. For example, out of an initial 1969 sample of 8,131 males, reported and recorded Census date of birth differed by more than one year in fifty-three cases, in some cases by more than ten years. In order to estimate the DP model, I need to track each of the 8,131 original male respondents over the ten-year survey period. RHS respondent identifiers allowed me to distinguish the original male respondent from his surviving spouse (or other household members), and, in conjunction with comprehensive death records compiled by Paul Taubman, I was able to determine whether the original respondent died, even if he was no longer responding to the survey. Table 11.1 provides a response summary that shows that the basic sample of original male respondents decreased from 8,131 in 1969 to 4,298 in 1979. There was significant attrition of the original 1969 male respondents over the survey. Table 11.1 shows that the attrition was due to the respondent's death in 2,327 cases and nonresponse in 1,506 cases. A discrepancy exists between the individual subrecord identifier in the SSER tapes and the respondent identifiers on the original RHS tapes: the former showed 8,091 original respondents in 1971 versus 7,054 in the RHS. The former figure could not possibly be right given that 433 respondents had died by the 1971 interview. Indeed, a second cross-check using the Census nonresponse file[15] agreed with the RHS identifiers. This provided a sobering reminder that one cannot necessarily trust the SSA's internal accounting data more than the RHS interview data.

Relatively minor discrepancies exist in the data on marital status. For example, nine individuals reported being married with spouse not present in

Table 11.1   **RHS Response Summary**

	71	73	75	77	79
Original '69 male respondent responds	7,054	6,239	5,541	4,811	4,298
No response, '69 respondent still alive	534	889	1,104	1,315	1,426
No response, '69 respondent dead	152	361	610	917	1,245
Surviving spouse responds, '69 respondent dead	244	488	722	908	1,075
Other relation responds, '69 respondent dead	37	58	54	60	7
Other relation responds, '69 respondent alive	110	96	100	120	80
Total	8,131	8,131	8,131	8,131	8,131

1969 but reported having never been married in 1971; two cases reported having a deceased spouse in 1969 and never having been married in 1971. Thirty-five cases classified themselves as being a surviving spouse in 1971 but listed themselves as having a "spouse in '69 but not in '71" instead of the correct response, "'69 spouse deceased, no '71 spouse." Using the corrected marital status data, I defined the marital state variable ms_t as follows:

$$ms_t = \begin{cases} 1 \text{ if respondent is married,} \\ 2 \text{ if respondent is widowed, separated, divorced, or never married.} \end{cases}$$

Table 11.2 presents the computed two-state Markov transition matrices for marital status (where M denotes cases that are missing owing to death or nonresponse). The transition matrices change in the expected way over time: the probability of becoming a widower over the two-year survey frame increases from 6 percent in 1969 to 9 percent in 1977. The probability of remarriage decreases over time from 7 percent in 1969 to 2 percent in 1977.

Table 11.3 presents the estimation results for π_{ms}, the marital status component of the decomposition of π given in (5). The elements of π_{ms} were estimated by maximum likelihood, using a linear-in-parameters, binomial logit specification of the probability that $ms_{t+1} = 2$.[16] The estimation results

Table 11.2   Markov Transition Matrices for Marital Status

Year of Transition	Cell Counts					Transition Probabilities	
	1	2	M	Total	%	1	2
1969–71:							
1	6,180	386	512	7,078	87	94	6
2	65	814	174	1,053	13	7	93
				8,131	100		
1971–73:							
1	5,434	405	406	6,245	84	93	7
2	66	976	158	1,200	16	7	93
				7,445	100		
1973–75:							
1	4,760	410	330	5,500	80	92	8
2	63	1,140	178	1,381	20	5	94
				6,881	100		
1975–77:							
1	4,141	391	312	4,844	75	91	9
2	48	1,310	215	1,573	25	4	96
				6,417	100		
1977–79:							
1	3,602	372	220	4,194	72	91	9
2	32	1,434	239	1,705	28	2	98
				5,899	100		

Table 11.3   **Estimates of Marital Status Transition Probability**
                        (dependent variable: $I\{ms_{t+1} = 2\}$)

Variable	Estimate	t-statistic
$s_t = 1$	$-.05$	$-.3$
$s_t = 3$	$-.08$	$-.6$
$ms_t = 2, h_{t+1} = 1$	-1.87	-1.6
$ms_t = 2, h_{t+1} = 2$	-2.05	-1.8
$ms_t = 2, h_{t+1} = 3$	-2.68	-2.2
$ms_t = 1, h_{t+1} = 1$	4.06	3.6
$ms_t = 1, h_{t+1} = 2$	4.15	3.7
$ms_t = 1, h_{t+1} = 3$	4.67	4.2
a_t	$-.02$	-1.0
y_t	$.15$	8.5
$y_t \cdot y_t$	$.002$	-7.1
$ss_t \in \{1, 2\}$	$-.13$	$-.8$
$ss_t \in \{1, 2\}, ms_t = 2$	$.02$	$.1$
Log likelihood	$-2,347.8$	
Grad • direc	6 E-025	
Correctly predicted (%)	97	
Total observations	18,833	

in table 11.3 are based on a smaller subsample than table 11.2 (18,833 vs. 34,773 observations) as a result of conditioning on the availability of complete observations for the state and control variables entering π_{ms} and conditioning on a sample Boolean variable. The Boolean excludes respondents who are not the original 1969 male respondents and further excludes respondents who are farmers or farm owners, respondents with significant pension wealth, and respondents who made sufficiently erroneous or suspicious responses as determined from the flag variables described in section 11.1. Overall, the estimation results in table 11.3 support the conclusions drawn in point 4 of section 11.2.

11.4   Health Status

A key variable in the DP model is the worker's health status. This variable shifts the worker's mortality hazard and affects his ability to work and enjoy leisure. In order to construct the health status variable, I used mortality data from Paul Taubman's "death tape" and a battery of over seventy-five questions on health status in the RHS. It turned out, however, that two of the seventy-five RHS health variables were most relevant for classifying health status: HLIM, "Do you have any health condition, physical handicap, or disability that limits how well you get around?" and HWRK, "Does your health limit the kind or amount of work or housework you can do?" Originally, I used these variables, together with fifteen other health-related questions and the respondent's report as to whether he received SSDI benefits, to classify health status h_t into one of four states: 1 = respondent is in good health, 2 = respondent has a health problem that limits his ability to work or get around but is not severe enough for the worker to qualify for SSDI, 3 = respondent has a health problem severe enough for him to qualify for SSDI, and 4 = respondent is dead. My original construction of this variable yielded significantly lower estimates of the probability of being on SSDI than those of Bound (1986): 1.17 percent in 1969 versus Bound's estimate of 7.1 percent for men aged 55–64 in 1970. In addition, the data appeared to show an unexpected mass outbreak of poor health in 1975, with only 1,254 respondents classified as h_t = 1 and 3,958 classified as h_t = 2. By using the SSMBR OASDI payments data, I was able to directly verify whether a worker was classified as disabled by SSA by determining whether he qualified for SSDI payments. Furthermore, analysis of the health input variables revealed that the HWRK variable had 5,956 missing values in 1975 and that the remaining cases contained a disproportionate percentage of workers reporting a health limitation (1,476 out of 2,200). This turned out to be an artifact of a survey skip pattern introduced in 1975 that was different from skip patterns in other survey years: HWRK75 was asked only if respondent was in the labor force, whereas in other survey years the HWRK question was not conditioned on being in the labor force. I "fixed" the problem by using only the HLIM variable to classify workers into health state h = 1 or h = 2 and merging the disability data from the SSMBR to classify disabled workers h = 3.

Another problem arose from the fact that the RHS survey did not attempt to track workers who became institutionalized; it simply records them as missing. There is good reason to believe that the failure to track institutionalized workers induces a sample selection bias since single workers are less likely to have a family support network to rely on and are therefore more likely to become institutionalized and be lost from the sample. To correct this problem, I merged data from the Census nonresponse file, which records the reasons for nonresponse, including institutionalization. Analysis of health status of the institutionalized workers showed that among the sample of 113 institutionalized workers (36 percent of who were single in 1969 as compared to 13 percent for the sample as a whole), in only one case did the worker return to the RHS sample with improved health: the preponderant majority of institutionalized workers died within a few years after entering the institution. Based on this evidence, I decided to redefine health state 4 as an absorbing state for workers who are either dead, disabled, or institutionalized.

A final problem was more difficult to resolve. Although I have fairly complete data on the month and year that a worker died, in order to be included in the estimation of the health transition probability matrix, I must observe the worker's state and control vector (x_t, d_t) in the survey period immediately preceding his death. Unfortunately, there are many cases where the worker failed to respond to the survey for two or more survey periods preceding his death. Analysis of these cases shows that a disproportionate number consist of single men. One solution is to "remove" the intervening periods of missing data by treating the death as occuring just after the last survey to which the worker responded. Unfortunately, this approach has the effect of "accelerating" the deaths of a fairly large group of workers, distorting the estimates of age-death profiles. I decided, therefore, to leave the data as they were and simply acknowledge the possibility of sample selection bias that might lead to an underestimate of mortality rates for single workers.

Table 11.4 displays the transition probability matrices for my final definition of h_t. The data show a much more reasonable rate of disability receipt, 8.1 percent in 1969, which is much closer to Bound's estimate. The transition matrices generally appear to be quite reasonable, with workers in worse health states having significantly higher risk of death and disability. Mortality rates appear fairly stable over time and are in rough agreement with independent

Table 11.4   Health Transition Probabilities

Year	Cell Counts							Transition Probabilities			
	1	2	3	4	*M*	Total	%	1	2	3	4
1969–71:											
1	4,347	630	111	211	470	5,769	71	82	12	2	4
2	562	790	84	116	147	1,699	21	36	51	5	8
3	0	0	506	106	46	658	8	0	0	83	17
4	0	0	0	0	0	0	0	0	0	0	100
					8,126		100				
1971–73:											
1	3,629	730	76	181	296	4,912	70	79	16	1	4
2	449	688	51	126	107	1,421	20	34	52	4	10
3	0	0	533	113	56	702	10	0	0	83	17
4	0	0	0	0	0	0	0	0	0	0	100
					7,035		100				
1973–75:											
1	2,975	707	20	177	240	4,119	66	77	18	1	4
2	371	831	12	149	76	1,439	23	27	61	1	11
3	0	0	541	89	38	668	11	0	0	86	14
4	0	0	0	0	0	0	0	0	0	0	100
					6,226		100				
1975–77:											
1	2,495	510	0	164	217	3,386	61	79	16	0	5
2	422	877	2	171	87	1,559	28	29	59	1	11
3	0	0	454	92	43	589	11	0	0	83	17
4	0	0	0	0	0	0	0	0	0	0	100
					5,534		100				
1977–79:											
1	2,133	540	0	131	130	2,934	61	76	19	0	5
2	316	867	0	158	60	1,401	29	23	65	0	12
3	0	0	359	73	27	459	10	0	0	83	17
4	0	0	0	0	0	4	0	0	0	0	100
					4,798		100				

estimates calculated by Mott and Haurin (1985) using NLS data. Note that the transition probabilities in table 11.4 imply that disability is an absorbing state: once a worker becomes disabled, he either remains disabled, becomes institutionalized, or dies. This is simply a reflection of the data limitations discussed in section 11.2: the SSMBR data do not record the date of termination of disability. As a result, in each survey year there are approximately one hundred workers who report that they have no health problem that limited their ability to work or get around despite the fact that Social Security records indicate that they are disabled. Because the existing classification of disability confirms my a priori belief that disabled workers have significantly higher mortality rates, and, more important, because this classification matches the aggregate disability rates compiled by Bound, I decided not to reclassify these workers as $h_t = 1$.

Another apparent contradiction exists between Census/Social Security death records, the RHS death records, and the death records independently compiled by Paul Taubman. The RHS date of death differs from that in Taubman's data in thirty-six cases, which in turn differs from the Census and Social Security death date (from the SSMBR tape) in 302 cases. Case-by-case cross-checks resolved the discrepancies between Taubman's data and RHS, and cross-checks of Taubman's data with the Census data reveal that in 285 cases Taubman's data recorded the respondent as dead while Census and SSA had no record of death. Individual cross-checks reveal that Taubman's data are probably right in these cases. In fact, one can identify at least twenty-six cases of apparently fraudulent behavior involving a surviving spouse who continued to collect both her and her husband's OASI benefits even though the husband had been deceased for several years.[17] The final death data that I used to construct the health variable are Taubman's original data, edited in approximately sixty cases where case-by-case examinations revealed that either the RHS or the SSMBR death date was correct.

I conclude this section with tables 11.5–11.7, which present the estimates of the transition probabilities for health, disability, and death, respectively. Each of the transition probabilities was specified to have linear-in-parameters binomial logit functional forms. Products of the estimated probability functions can be multiplied out to compute the estimated health transition matrix, $\hat{\pi}_h$. The interpretation of the estimation results has been listed in points 1, 2, and 3 of section 11.2 and will not be repeated here. However, in order to get more intuition about how workers believe their health declines with age, I present figure 11.1, which shows $\text{pr}\{h_{t+1} = 1|a_t\}$, $\text{pr}\{h_{t+1} = 3|a_t\}$, and $\text{pr}\{h_{t+1} = 4|a_t\}$, respectively.

The age-health profile graph in figure 11.1 shows the probability of remaining in good health as a function of age for four configurations of the remaining state variables. All four curves show that health declines with age; however, changes in the other variables have a stronger effect on health than age alone. The top two curves (marked with circles and squares) represent the health expectations of workers who are already in good health and who retire

Table 11.5   **Estimates of Health Transition Probability**
(dependent variable $I\{h_{t+1} = 1\}$)

Variable	Estimate	t-statistic
$h_t = 1, s_t = 1$	-2.28	-4.7
$h_t = 1, s_t = 2$	-2.15	-4.3
$h_t = 1, s_t = 3$	-1.84	-3.7
$h_t = 2, s_t = 1$	$-.13$	$-.2$
$h_t = 2, s_t = 2$	$-.21$	$-.4$
$h_t = 2, s_t = 3$	$.20$	$.4$
a_t	$.01$	1.6
y_t	$-.05$	-7.2
$y_t \cdot y_t$	$.001$	5.2
$ms_t = 2$	$.02$	$.3$
$ss_t \in \{1, 2\}$	$.17$	2.9
Log likelihood	$-8,470.7$	
Grad • direc	2 E-028	
Correctly predicted (%)	79	
Total observations	17,536	

Table 11.6   **Estimates of Disability Hazard Function**
(dependent variable: $I\{h_{t+1} = 3\}$)

Variable	Estimate	t-statistic
Constant	-27.83	-12.7
$h_t = 1, s_t = 1$	$.68$	2.2
$h_t = 1, s_t = 3$	$-.39$	-1.0
$h_t = 2, s_t = 1$	$-.65$	-2.0
$h_t = 2, s_t = 2$	$-.73$	-1.7
$h_t = 2, s_t = 3$	$-.95$	-2.6
a_t	$.51$	14.9
y_t	$.41$	3.0
$a_t \cdot y_t$	$.00$	-3.0
$ms_t = 2$	$.73$	2.5
Log likelihood	$-1,048.4$	
Grad • direc	7 E-27	
Correctly predicted (%)	99	
Total observations	17,763	

at ages 62 and 65, respectively (the latter worker also has 10 percent higher income). The bottom curve represents the health expectations of a worker who is in poor health, $h_t = 2$, and who retires at age 62. The remaining curve, marked with x's, shows the health expectations of a healthy worker who continued to work until age 70, at which time he fell ill ($h_t = 2$), quit his job, and began collecting OASI. The combination of all these events at age 70 produced a dramatic downturn in the worker's health outlook.

Table 11.7   **Estimates of Mortality Hazard Function**
                    (dependent variable: $I\{h_{t+1} = 4\}$)

Variable	Estimate	t-statistic
$h_t = 1, s_t = 1$	3.02	14.0
$h_t = 1, s_t = 2$	1.67	3.6
$h_t = 2, s_t = 1$	2.47	7.0
$b_t = 2, s_t = 2$	2.35	2.3
$h_t = 2, s_t = 3$	.20	.5
$h_t = 3, s_t = 1$	−1.83	−7.4
$h_t = 3, s_t = 2$	−.93	−3.4
$h_t = 3, s_t = 3$	−.33	−2.6
y_t	.01	1.5
$a_t \in [0, 60)$	2.15	15.7
$a_t \in [60, 62)$	2.35	20.1
$a_t \in [62, 65)$	2.71	26.5
$a_t \in [65, 68)$	3.03	28.1
$a_t \in [68, 71)$	2.92	24.3
$a_t \geq 71$	2.79	15.2
$ms_t = 2$	−.31	−4.3
$h_t = 1, s_t = 1, ss_t \in \{1, 2\}$	−3.15	−15.0
$h_t = 1, s_t = 2, ss_t \in \{1, 2\}$	−1.82	−3.9
$h_t = 1, s_t = 3, ss_t \in \{1, 2\}$	−.27	−2.5
$h_t = 2, s_t = 1, ss_t \in \{1, 2\}$	−3.40	−9.6
$h_t = 2, s_t = 2, ss_t \in \{1, 2\}$	−3.14	−3.1
$h_t = 2, s_t = 3, ss_t \in \{1, 2\}$	−.84	−2.3
Log likelihood	−4,713.9	
Grad • direc	2 E-027	
Correctly predicted (%)	94	
Number of observations	24,233	

Figure 11.1 also shows the probability of becoming disabled as a function of age. In this case, age effects dominate, reflecting sharp declines in workers' incentives to incur the costs of applying for disability benefits as they approach the early retirement age, 62. The topmost curve corresponds to a low-income married worker who is currently in poor health ($h_t = 2$), while the lowest curve corresponds to a high-income single worker who is in good health.

Finally, figure 11.1 plots the estimated death hazard function. As discussed in section 11.2, it was difficult to identify the independent effect of age on death rates. Both linear and quadratic specifications of age effects produced ultimately falling death hazards, a result I found implausible. Using age dummies, I discovered the explanation: the age dummies reveal that workers' death rates decrease until age 67, after which they begin rising with age. However, because the RHS surveyed men between 58 and 63 in 1969, the oldest possible age reached during the survey is 73. This implies that there are relatively few observations beyond age 67, so that both the linear and the quadratic specifications attempted to fit the downward-sloping part of the death

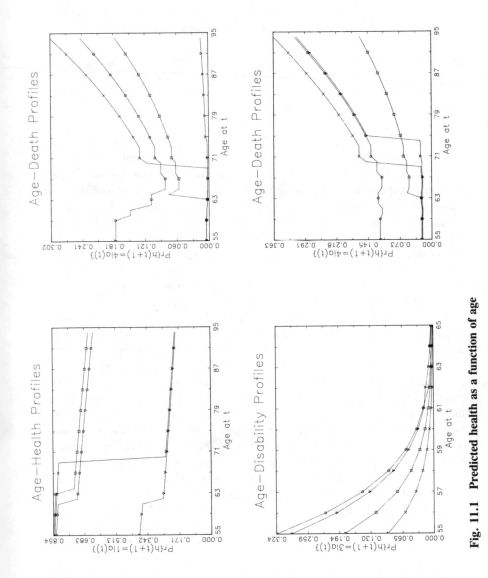

Fig. 11.1 Predicted health as a function of age

hazard function from age 58 to age 67, ignoring the upturn that occurred afterward owing to a lack of observations. Unfortunately, while the age dummies allow the model to fit the data well, it implies that the risk of death is constant after the worker reaches his early 70s. Aggregate mortality statistics show (unconditional on health and employment status) that death rates increase with age, which implies that a model containing only age dummies from 58 to 73 will ultimately underpredict death rates. To correct this, I added a pure age trend to the model in order to match the aggregate mortality statistics from age 74 to age 95.[18] Figure 11.1 (which incorporates the age trend after age 73) displays mortality expectations for four different workers. The V-shaped curve marked with circles corresponds to a single, low-income disabled worker. While his death rate is much higher than average, it shows significant improvement until age 67, after which it begins to worsen steadily. The bottom curve, marked with triangles, shows the mortality expectations of a high-income "workaholic" who is in good health and who continued working full time until his health deteriorated to $h_t = 2$ at age 75, after which he started working part time. In spite of his health problems, the workaholic never retired, in the sense of collecting OASI. The remaining two curves (marked with squares and x's, respectively) show the death rates of two average-income workers who retire at 65 and 70, respectively. The latter worker retired at 70 owing to the fact that his wife died and his health deteriorated from $h = 1$ to $h = 2$; this explains the dramatic increase in his death rate.

There are two features of figure 11.1 that seem implausible: the sharp V-shaped death hazard for the disabled worker and the significantly lower death rates for the high-income "workaholic" in comparison to the two average-income workers who retired at 65 and 70. Looking back to the estimation results in table 11.7, it appears that these predictions result from the fact that Social Security recipients ($sr_t \in \{1, 2\}$) have significantly higher death rates. As discussed in conclusion 1 of section 11.2, this is probably due to the fact that h_t does not capture all dimensions of health status. Workers who are in worse health are probably more likely to retire than healthy workers. However, from the standpoint of the DP model, the relation is necessarily treated as cause and effect: it implies that collection of OASI can be hazardous to your health. To avoid this problem, I reestimated the model without the sr_t interactions. While there was a significant drop in the log-likelihood (from $-4,714$ to $-5,045$), the graph in the lower-right-hand corner of figure 11.1 shows that the resulting model seems to produce more reasonable predictions. In particular, the age effects now show a slightly increasing rather than decreasing hazard rate, and the gross disparities between the workaholic (who never collected OASI) and his average-income colleagues have disappeared. Based on these results, I have decided to exclude the sr_t interactions in the specification of the mortality hazard, even though they clearly improve the fit of the model.

11.5   Employment Status

Accurate classification of employment status e_t is the key to the entire undertaking: employment status is the most important variable affecting income and utility levels in the DP model and is a crucial input into the income imputation routines that construct biennial income. They are also key inputs for the construction of biennial consumption expenditures in section 11.7. The RHS data set allowed me to construct three independent measures of labor force status: self-classification of employment status (SE), instantaneous employment status (IE), and historical employment status (E). Each of the measures assumes three values, 1 = full time, 2 = part time, and 3 = not employed. The SE variable was directly recorded in a trichotomous format from the survey question "Do you consider yourself partly retired, completely retired, or not retired at all?" The IE measure was determined from the survey question "How many hours per week do you usually work on your current job?" Using this response, I defined IE = 1 if the worker worked more than twenty-five hours per week, IE = 2 if the worker worked between five and twenty-five hours per week, and IE = 3 if the worker was not currently employed or worked less than five hours per week. The historical employment status measure E is an annual measure based on the total number of hours worked in the preceding year. I defined E = 1 if the respondent worked more than 1,300 hours in the past year, E = 2 if the respondent worked between 200 and 1,300 hours, and E = 3 otherwise. Because the worker might have had multiple jobs in the two years preceding the RHS interview, computation of total hours worked required direct reconstruction of the underlying continuous-time labor force histories from a battery of more than 130 questions in the "Work Experience" section of the RHS survey. Previous studies have used the IE and SE measures of employment status, probably because they were among the easiest variables to pull off the RHS tapes. Constructing retrospective labor force histories is a considerably more complicated undertaking owing to the existence of complicated skip patterns in the survey questionnaire and the need carefully to account for the beginning and ending dates of jobs when there are multiple transitions within the interview frame. To my knowledge, this is the first study to construct complete labor force histories using the RHS data.

Table 11.8 presents aggregate employment distributions using each of the definitions of employment status. Although there are significant differences between the measures, all three confirm conclusion 1 of section 11.1 that the aggregate data show workers making a smooth transition from work into retirement. The main differences are that SE appears to overestimate substantially the occurrence of part-time work relative to the E and IE measures, and E appears to overestimate part-time work relative to the IE measure. The latter effect is to be expected from the nature of the definition of E: a worker who worked at a full-time job until mid-year and then retired would be classi-

Table 11.8   **Cross-sectional Distributions of Measures of Employment Status**

	Historical Employment Status (%)										
	E68	E69	E70	E71	E72	E73	E74	E75	E76	E77	E78
1	71	72	61	54	40	34	23	19	14	13	10
2	9	9	12	13	15	15	16	15	14	14	14
3	20	19	27	33	45	51	61	66	72	73	76
N	8,117	7,379	7,379	6,837	6,837	6,392	6,392	5,871	5,871	5,415	5,415

	Instantaneous Employment Status (%)					
	IE69	IE71	IE73	IE75	IE77	IE79
1	74	61	40	24	16	12
2	4	5	7	9	10	10
3	22	34	53	67	74	78
N	8,117	7,434	6,897	6,392	5,871	5,415

	Self-reported Employment Search Decision (%)					
	SR69	SR71	SR73	SR75	SR77	SR79
1	72	56	36	22	13	10
2	5	12	13	15	13	12
3	23	32	51	63	74	78
N	7,894	7,434	6,897	6,392	5,871	5,415

	Self-Employment Status (%)					
	SE69	SE71	SE73	SE75	SE77	SE79
1	77	60	36	21	12	9
2	8	12	16	18	19	18
3	15	28	48	61	69	73
N	8,070	7,431	6,881	6,387	5,861	5,407

fied as being in state 2 by the E measure and in state 3 by the IE measure.

The SE variable seems like the poorest candidate for use as a measure of employment status owing to the ambiguity of the term "retired." Some people may interpret being "retired" as quitting their career job and will report being fully or partly retired even though they are working full time at a new job. Other people may interpret "retired" as meaning "are you working now?" and will report that they are not retired if they had quit their main career job but are currently working at a new full-time job. Still others may report being partly retired even though they are not working because they like to think that they have the virility to return to work at some unspecified future date. The latter problem seems to be reflected in table 11.8, which shows that the SE measure substantially overestimates the incidence of part-time work, some-times as much as 200 percent in comparison to the IE measure. I decided not to use the SE measure because of the problems of ambiguity and subjective interpretation and also, for reasons I elaborate below, because SE is an "instantaneous" measure that does not correspond well to the time intervals of the DP model.

The instantaneous employment status IE variable completely avoids the subjective definition of the concept "retired." Like SE, IE has a high response rate and is easy to pull from the tapes. However, it too has certain drawbacks from the standpoint of estimating the DP model. Since I am using a relatively coarse two-year time interval (for computational reasons discussed in sec. 11.1), the instantaneous IE measure would not provide a good measure of the worker's actual state over the whole time period. In principle, workers may have changed jobs many times in the two-year time interval or may have retired only recently, so there may be only a weak association between IE and the respondent's actual labor force status over the last two years.

From the standpoint of the discrete-time DP model, the most appropriate measure of labor force status is the historical employment status measure, E. The main drawbacks of this measure are that (1) it requires the worker to recall his employment history (which may be especially difficult in the cases where the worker had multiple job transitions) and (2), since E is a flow measure, it may overestimate the occurrence of part-time work by misclassifying full-time workers who retire in mid-year. Table 11.9 sheds some light on the last problem by summarizing the distribution of employment histories (using the E measure of e_t) over the eleven years of the RHS survey. To keep the table manageable, the 11^4 possible employment sequences have been "collapsed;" for example, the sequence $(1, 1, 1, 2, 2, 3, 3, 3, 3, M, M)$ (where M represents missing data) is classified as a "1–2–3" sequence.[19]

The first thing to notice is that, in contrast to the aggregate employment statistics, the individual employment sequences are far from smooth: only 18 percent of the sample is observed to phase out of work gradually in a "1–2–3" employment sequence. If I reclassify all "1–2–3" sequences with only one intervening year in state 2 as actually being a misclassified "1–3" sequence, then only 3 percent of the sample is observed to follow a smooth employment transition; a plurality of the sample, 33 percent, are observed to follow the discontinuous "1–3" sequence. Another 28 percent of the sample have complex "nonmonotonic" employment histories, with periods of un-employment followed by subsequent reemployment. Of course, many of the "1" and "1–2" sequences may actually be right-censored sections of an ultimate "1–2–3" sequence; however, since these sequences account for only 14 and 4 percent of the sample, respectively, accounting for censoring will not change the basic picture.

For comparison, table 11.9 presents the distribution of employment se-quences for the IE and SE measures of e_t and also for an annual measure of

Table 11.9   **Distribution of Employment Sequences**

Measure of Employment State	Sequence	Cases	
		N	%
E	1 . . .	1,174	14
	2 . . .	91	1
	3 . . .	1,033	13
	1–3 . . .	1,488 (2,700)	18 (33)
	2–3 . . .	255	3
	1–2 . . .	306	4
	1–2–3 . . .	1,450 (238)	18 (3)
	Others	2,334	29
	Total	8,131	100
IE	1 . . .	1,321	16
	2 . . .	28	1
	3 . . .	1,337	16
	1–3 . . .	3,269	40
	2–3 . . .	112	1
	1–2 . . .	276	4
	1–2–3 . . .	308	4
	Others	1,480	18
	Total	8,131	100
SE	1 . . .	1,239	15
	2 . . .	131	2
	3 . . .	897	11
	1–3 . . .	2,642	33
	2–3 . . .	298	4
	1–2 . . .	601	7
	1–2–3 . . .	748	9
	Others	1,575	19
	Total	8,131	100
NLS[b]	1 . . .	585	23
	2 . . .	13	1
	3 . . .	187	7
	1–3 . . .	1,052	42
	2–3 . . .	29	1
	1–2 . . .	90	4
	1–2–3 . . .	89	4
	Others	452	18
	Total	2,497	100

Note: Numbers in parentheses obtained by reclassifying all "1–2–3" sequences with only one intervening year in state $e_t = 2$ as a "1–3" sequence. See sec. 11.4 for further explanation.

[a]An annual measure of employment status similar to E. This measure was constructed by Berkovec and Stern (1989), who wrote more than 2,000 lines of Fortran code to accurately follow NLS skip patterns to reconstruct the employment histories.

e_t similar to the E measure but computed from the NLS data by Berkovec and Stern (1989). Notice that, in all the tables, only 3–4 percent of all workers are observed to follow a "1–2–3" sequence. The NLS data show a somewhat higher fraction of workers following a "1" sequence, but this is to be expected given that the NLS sample follows a younger group of men, who were initially aged 45–59 in the first year of the survey, 1966.[20] Based on the comparison of the employment measures presented in table 11.9, I decided to reclassify all "1–2–3" employment sequences with only one intervening year in state 2 as a "1–3" sequence by reassigning the state $e_t = 2$ as either $e_t = 1$ or $e_t = 3$, depending on whether hours worked in that year are greater than 1,000.

Overall, table 11.9 casts doubt on the notion that most workers gradually phase out of their full-time jobs through a spell of "partial retirement," a view promoted by Gustman and Steinmeier (1984) and suggested from casual interpretation of the macro data in table 11.8. Even if I counted all "1–2" and "1" sequences as forming part of an eventual "1–2–3" sequence, the number of "smooth" employment transitions would be at most 23 percent. In reality, most of the "1" sequences will form part of an eventual "1–3" sequence, and a large fraction of the "3" sequences are actually left-truncated "1–3" sequences. If I count all these sequences as "1–3" sequences, I obtain an estimate that approximately 75 percent of all retirement sequences involve discontinuous transitions from a full-time job into unemployment. Table 11.9 also shows that a significant fraction of the sample, over 18 percent, follow "nonmonotonic" sequences involving some form of "unretirement," that is, a return to full employment from a state of unemployment or partial employment. Table 11.10 provides more detail on the structure of the nonmontonic employment sequences for the E, IE, and SE measures of employment status. The structure of these transitions is extremely complex, as can be seen from table 11.10. The most common nonmonotonic sequences are "3–1–3," "1–3–2," "1–3–1," "1–3–2–3," and "1–3–1–3." Even though a majority of workers follow the "1–3" sequence, the traditional approach to modeling retirement behavior as an *ex ante* choice of a fixed retirement date after which the worker ceases to work is incapable of explaining the labor force history of at least 20 percent of the sample.

The discussion above suggests the possibility that the discretization of the labor force status variable into just three states could seriously misrepresent the labor force participation decision. Other researchers (e.g., MaCurdy 1983) have suggested that the labor force participation decision can be modeled as a continuous choice variable, say, as choice of annual hours of work. There are strong practical reasons for maintaining this viewpoint: an interior solution allows one to derive stochastic Euler orthogonality conditions that permit estimation of identified parameters by the method of moments (Hansen 1982). Figure 11.2, which displays the distribution of annual hours of work over the period 1968–78, provides convincing evidence against this view. The distribution

Table 11.10   Distribution of Nonmonotonic Employment Sequences

	IE			E			SE		
Sequence	N	% of 1,480	% of 8,131	N	% of 2,334	% of 8,131	N	% of 1,575	% of 8,131
1313	99	6.69	1.22	36	1.54	.44	39	2.48	.48
1312	28	1.89	.34	20	.86	.25	15	.95	.18
1213	47	3.18	.58	75	3.21	.92	46	2.92	.57
1212	33	2.23	.41	83	3.56	1.02	71	4.51	.87
1231	10	.68	.12	21	.90	.26	24	1.52	.30
1232	28	1.89	.34	101	4.33	1.24	85	5.40	1.05
1321	30	2.03	.37	30	1.29	.37	18	1.14	.22
1323	100	6.76	1.23	115	4.93	1.41	158	10.03	1.94
2131	1	.07	.01	2	.09	.02	0	.00	.00
2132	1	.07	.01	11	.47	.14	7	.44	.09
3131	12	.81	.15	6	.26	.07	0	.00	.00
3132	8	.54	.10	9	.39	.11	5	.32	.06
3231	2	.14	.02	3	.13	.04	0	.00	.00
3232	6	.41	.07	10	.43	.12	8	.51	.10
3121	5	.34	.06	5	.21	.06	2	.13	.02
3123	17	1.15	.21	90	3.86	1.11	8	.51	.10
3213	2	.14	.02	15	.64	.18	3	.19	.04
3212	0	.00	.00	7	.30	.09	3	.19	.04
2121	3	.20	.04	10	.43	.12	2	.13	.02
2123	15	1.01	.18	77	3.30	.95	26	1.65	.32
2321	2	.14	.02	3	.13	.04	1	.06	.01
2323	7	.47	.09	34	1.46	.42	34	2.16	.42
2312	1	.07	.01	0	.00	.00	1	.06	.01
2313	3	.20	.04	3	.13	.04	1	.06	.01
131	122	8.24	1.50	35	1.50	.43	78	4.95	.96
121	105	7.09	1.29	122	5.23	1.50	109	6.92	1.34
132	201	13.58	2.47	137	5.87	1.68	204	12.95	2.51
321	12	.81	.15	12	.51	.15	7	.44	.09
312	19	1.28	.23	25	1.07	.31	8	.51	.10
323	57	3.85	.70	80	3.43	.98	68	4.32	.84
313	176	11.89	2.16	102	4.37	1.25	35	2.22	.43
213	34	2.30	.42	75	3.21	.92	46	2.92	.57
231	2	.14	.02	5	.21	.06	4	.25	.05
232	5	.34	.06	22	.94	.27	24	1.52	.30
212	5	.34	.06	20	.86	.25	25	1.59	.31
31	77	5.20	.95	51	2.19	.63	60	3.81	.74
32	40	2.70	.49	45	1.93	.55	43	2.73	.53
21	9	.61	.11	30	1.29	.37	24	1.52	.30
Others	156	10.54	1.92	807	34.58	9.92	283	17.97	3.48
Total	1,480	100.00	18.20	2,334	100.00	28.70	1,575	100.00	19.37

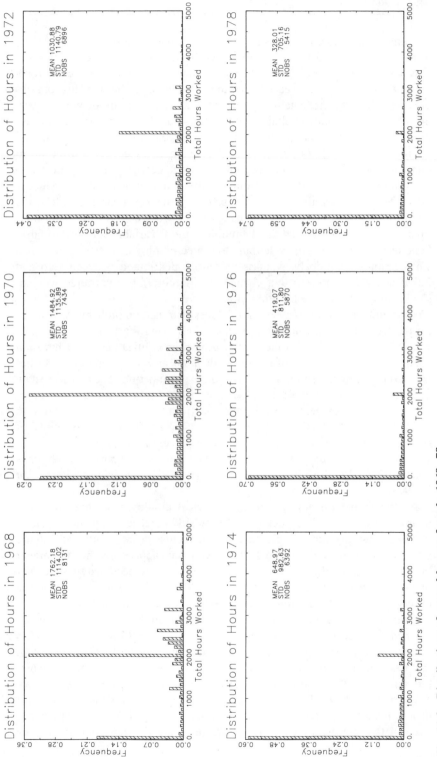

Fig. 11.2 Distributions of annual hours of work, 1968–78

has almost all its mass at two spikes, one at zero and the other at 2,000. The distributions are almost excessively concentrated at the two spikes, suggesting a systematic tendency of respondents to round their reponses (e.g., forty hours/week, fifty weeks/year). Nevertheless, I believe that the distributions provide solid evidence against the notion that annual hours of work is best modeled as a continuous choice variable that satisfies an interior first-order condition. This notion is also supported by the work of Gustman and Steinmeier (1983, 1984), who present convincing evidence of widespread minimum hours restrictions and significant wage cuts associated with transitions from full-time work to part-time. These constraints, combined with the Social Security "earnings test," are probably the key factors that lead the majority of workers to follow a "bang-bang" work/no work decision rule. Figure 11.2 also shows that the definition of the E variable is robust to fairly large changes in the cutoffs defining the three employment states: there is a small amount of probability mass uniformly distributed between zero and 2,000 hours of work, so that changes in the cutoff in this range will not significantly alter the distribution of e_t.

I conclude this section by presenting Markov transition probability matrices for the IE and SE measures of e_t in table 11.11 and the E measure in table 11.12. These are "uncontrolled" transition probabilities because I have not conditioned on a measure of the respondent's search decision, s_t. Nevertheless, the resulting transition matrices are quite illuminating. The matrices show a clear pattern of age effects: for example, table 11.11 shows that the probability of reemployment (i.e., a transition from $e_t = 3$ to $e_{t+1} = 1$) is 16 percent in 1969 but falls to 2 percent by 1977 and that the probability of remaining fully employed declines from 75 percent in 1969 to 55 percent in 1977. Interestingly, the probability of retiring from a full- or part-time job peaks at approximately 40 percent between 1971 and 1973, declining to 30 percent in 1977.

A strange pattern appears in the historical employment state transition matrices in table 11.12. Notice how the transition matrices appear to cycle in two-year intervals: for example, the (1, 1) elements appear significantly higher in even-numbered years, while the (3, 3) elements appear significantly higher in the odd-numbered years. For a long time, I was convinced that these regular fluctuations had to be an artifact of my FORTRAN code for processing the observations. I labored for many weeks to make sure that my program accurately followed the complicated skip patterns in the survey questionnaire but had no success in eliminating the strange fluctuations in the transition matrices. Only recently have I become aware of work by Daniel Hill (1988) that has convinced me that the fluctuations are not artifacts of my computer programs but rather symptoms of a systematic response error problem known as the *seam problem*. The seam problem arises from the way the RHS collects data on retrospective labor force history in successive two-year survey frames. Each of the odd-numbered survey years represents a seam, and the survey

Table 11.11   **Transition Matrices for IE and SE Measures of Employment Status**

IE69 to IE71 (N = 8,117)			SE69 to SE71 (N = 8,070)		
76	4	20	73	11	16
30	37	33	19	42	39
16	3	81	6	6	88
IE71 to IE73 (N = 7,434)			**SE71 to SE73 (N = 7,431)**		
59	6	35	55	15	30
19	39	42	12	45	43
6	3	91	4	7	89
IE73 to IE75 (N = 6,897)			**SE73 to SE75 (N = 6,881)**		
52	9	39	50	17	33
15	46	39	9	54	37
3	4	93	2	7	91
IE75 to IE77 (N = 6,392)			**SE75 to SE77 (N = 6,387)**		
53	11	35	45	23	32
15	51	34	7	54	39
3	4	93	2	6	92
IE77 to IE79 (N = 5,871)			**SE77 to SE79 (N = 5,861)**		
55	15	30	52	22	26
18	48	34	10	56	34
2	4	94	2	6	92

questionnaire required the respondent to recall his labor force history in the two-year survey frame prior to the interview. It appears that, while respondents offer an internally consistent view of the preceding two years, their view of history changes between survey dates in a way that generates inconsistent labor force transitions across seams. For example, to compute the across-seam transition probability matrix from 68 to 69, I needed data from two different surveys: the 1969 survey gave me retrospective data on labor force states in 68, and the 1971 survey gave me retrospective data on labor force states in 69. On the other hand, the between-seam transition probability matrix from 69 to 70 was computed entirely from retrospective data obtained at the 1971 interview. The pattern of fluctuations in the transition matrices indicates that men in state $e_t = 1$ are more likely to remain in state 1 for across-seam transitions than for between-seam transitions, whereas men in state $e_t = 3$ are less likely to remain in state 3 for across-seam transitions than for between-seam transitions.

I have recomputed table 11.12 using the flag variables to eliminate observations that showed any evidence of internally inconsistent responses.

Table 11.12   Markov Transition Matrices for Historical Employment Status

E68 to E69 (seam: $N = 8,117$)			E73 to E74		
91	3	6	65	14	21
30	43	27	9	61	30
23	8	69	0	2	98
E69 to E70			E74 to E75 (seam: $N = 6,392$)		
82	7	11	70	10	20
18	58	24	14	58	28
2	1	97	2	5	93
E70 to E71 (seam: $N = 7,379$)			E75 to E76		
82	5	13	63	16	22
29	51	20	9	65	27
5	7	88	1	2	97
E71 to E72			E76 to E77 (seam: $N = 5,871$)		
71	10	19	76	9	15
11	59	30	11	64	25
1	2	97	1	5	94
E72 to E73 (seam: $N = 6,837$)			E77 to E78		
74	8	18	66	22	12
21	57	22	11	67	22
3	7	90	0	3	97

While the sample sizes were significantly reduced, the seam problem persisted. Although an analysis of the perceptual/psychological factors underlying the seam problem is beyond the scope of this paper, it appears that, by using between-seam transitions based on data from a single survey frame, one is much more likely to obtain a consistent set of transition probabilities. Indeed, looking at the between-seam transition matrices in table 11.12 one can see that they change in a sensible way over time, with no suspicious patterns indicative of further inconsistencies. In particular, while the transition matrices do not closely match the IE or SE transition matrices (the latter two are two-year transition matrices, while the E transition matrix is for one-year intervals), the matrices follow the same general pattern as the IE and SE transition matrices, namely, a probability of reemployment and continued employment that gradually declines over time. I conclude that the seam problem is sufficiently severe to make it inadvisable to build a DP model based on annual data even though such a model is superior from a theoretical viewpoint since it has "finer grain" and thus suffers less from problems of time aggregation. Instead, I will focus on constructing a model of biennial transitions, using consistent data on employment transitions between seams rather than across seams.

11.6   Job Search Decision

The DP model requires a control variable s_t that represents the respondent's labor force search/participation decision. In a discrete-time model, the agent is in labor force state e_t at time t, and, conditional on e_t and his search decision s_t, he makes a transition to a new labor force state e_{t+1} at time $t + 1$. Thus, the DP model gives an employed worker the option of quitting ($e_t = 1$ or $e_t = 2$, and $s_t = 3$) and an unemployed worker the option of returning to work ($e_t = 3$, and $s_t = 1$ or $s_t = 2$). Unfortunately, while it is convenient to trichotomize s_t into three values ($1 =$ search for full-time job, $2 =$ search for part-time job, and $3 =$ quit the labor force), the "true" search decision is essentially a latent variable: a complicated, possibly multidimensional variable encompassing the variety and intensity of each of the worker's possible search activities over the period. In the RHS, there are three possible variables from which to construct a measure of s_t:

SR: self-reported planned hours of work in the year following the survey,
NE: actual hours worked in the year following the survey,
PC: actual hours worked in the year following the *subsequent* survey.

The latter measure corresponds to a perfect control DP model where workers' search decisions are successful with probability one. The PC measure may seem implausible given the well-known labor market problems of older workers, yet on the other hand it necessarily suffers much less from measurement error. In this paper, however, I focus on the other two measures of s_t.

Using the SR and NE measures, I constructed a trichotomous estimate of s_t using the same cutoffs that I used to construct the e_t variable described in section 11.5. Table 11.8 summarizes aggregate distribution of the self-reported measure of s_t. This measure follows very much the same trends as the E, SE, and IE measures of e_t: a gradual phase-out from full employment into unemployment. The NE measure of s_t is recorded in the odd-year columns of the E distribution at the top of table 11.8. At least on the aggregate level, the two measures appear to track each other fairly closely.

To get a better handle on the issue of which measure of s_t better approximates the underlying latent employment search decision, I computed the controlled transition probability matrices that predict the probability of e_{t+1} conditional on e_t and s_t. Table 11.13 presents the controlled transition matrices using the E measure for e_t and the SR measure for s_t. These matrices show a very weak relation between employment search decisions and *ex post* realized employment states. If control were perfect, the transition matrix should have ones in the column corresponding to the value s_t assumes. However, in table 11.13 we see that under the SR measure control is highly imperfect. For example, a full-time worker who reported an intention to quit working in 1969 still has a 25 percent chance of remaining at work in 1971. A worker who had a full-time job in 1968 and who reported an intention to start working part time

Table 11.13 Controlled Transition Probabilities, SR Measure of Job Search Variable, s_t

E68 to E70 Given SR69 = 1 (N = 5,707)			E72 to E74 Given SR73 = 1 (N = 2,508)		
81	7	12	60	14	26
58	20	22	40	34	26
50	17	33	27	28	45

E68 to E70 Given SR69 = 2 (N = 394)			E72 to E74 Given SR73 = 2 (N = 859)		
33	13	54	12	20	67
24	51	25	14	55	31
3	20	77	4	35	61

E68 to E70 Given SR69 = 3 (N = 1,793)			E72 to E74 Given SR73 = 3 (N = 3,470)		
26	12	62	3	6	91
14	20	66	5	20	75
15	5	80	2	4	94

E70 to E72 Given SR71 = 1 (N = 4,150)			E74 to E76 Given SR75 = 1 (N = 1,372)		
71	10	19	58	14	28
54	25	21	31	36	33
29	29	42	13	16	71

E70 to E72 Given SR71 = 2 (N = 884)			E74 to E76 Given SR75 = 2 (N = 981)		
4	20	76	7	20	73
14	54	32	11	55	34
5	34	61	6	22	72

E70 to E72 Given SR71 = 3 (N = 2,345)			E74 to E76 Given SR75 = 3 (N = 4,039)		
5	6	89	1	11	88
8	17	75	3	17	80
2	4	94	2	4	94

in 1969 has only a 20 percent chance of actually realizing his intentions by 1970. An unemployed worker in 1974 who reports the intention to return to work full time in 1975 has only a 13 percent chance of actually being employed in 1976. Thus, the SR measure of s_t leads to a DP where control is too *imperfect*, in the sense that there is an implausibly low correspondence between employment search decisions and subsequent labor market outcomes.

Table 11.14 presents controlled transition probabilities for the E measure of e_t and the NE measure of s_t. Comparing tables 11.13 and 11.14, we can see that, while the NE measure of s_t does reflect imperfect control, the relation between s_t and e_{t+1} is much stronger than for the SR measure of s_t. For example, consider the probability that a worker who intends to quit his full-time job is successful (i.e., the transition from $e_t = 1$ to $e_{t+1} = 3$ given

Table 11.14   **Controlled Markov Transition Probabilities, NE Measure of Employment Search Decision, s_t**

E68 to E70 Given E69 = 1 (N = 5,348)			E72 to E74 Given E73 = 1 (N = 2,183)		
83	6	11	67	12	21
76	15	9	48	36	16
78	11	11	61	21	18

E68 to E70 Given E69 = 2 (N = 554)			E72 to E74 Given E73 = 2 (N = 817)		
14	58	28	7	54	39
23	57	20	11	61	28
12	60	28	7	69	24

E68 to E70 Given E69 = 3 (N = 1,477)			E72 to E74 Given E73 = 3 (N = 3,335)		
3	2	95	1	1	98
1	4	95	1	10	89
1	1	98	0	2	98

E70 to E72 Given E71 = 1 (N = 3,767)			E74 to E76 Given E75 = 1 (N = 1,167)		
72	9	19	66	13	21
55	25	20	38	39	23
67	20	13	60	13	27

E70 to E72 Given E71 = 2 (N = 645)			E74 to E76 (Given E75 = 2 (N = 790)		
10	54	36	4	49	47
14	56	30	10	67	23
6	71	23	7	70	23

E70 to E72 Given E71 = 3 (N = 2,376)			E74 to E76 Given E75 = 3 (N = 3,914)		
1	3	96	1	5	94
4	13	83	2	9	89
0	1	99	0	2	98

$s_t = 3$). In 1968, the NE measure gives a 95 percent chance that the decision will be realized, compared to only 62 percent for the SR measure of s_t. In the case of an unemployed worker who intends to return to work, the data for 1974 show that, according to the NE measure of s_t, the worker will have a 60 percent chance of success, compared to only a 13 percent chance for the SR measure of s_t. It is perhaps not surprising that the NE measure of s_t should have a strong correspondence with e_{t+1} since s_t is simply a lagged value of e_{t+1} and the $\{e_t\}$ process is highly serially correlated. However, it is somewhat surprising that the SR measure of s_t has such a weak correspondence with subsequent employment outcomes. This may be an indication of the fact that "talk is cheap": it is one thing to say that you intend to remain employed or return to work but quite another thing actually to go out and do it. A model using the

NE measure is a compromise between the implausible perfect control model implied by the PC measure of s_t and the perhaps equally implausible imperfect control model implied by the SR measure.

Tables 11.15 and 11.16 present the maximum likelihood estimates of the controlled transition probabilities using the E measure of e_t and the NE measure of s_t. The estimates correspond to the component π_e in the decomposition of π given in (5). The probabilities were estimated using a

Table 11.15   **Estimates of Employment Status Transition Probability (dependent variable: $I\{e_{t+1} = 1\}$)**

Variable	Estimate	t-statistic
$e_t = 1, s_t = 1$	3.64	9.15
$e_t = 2, s_t = 1$	2.50	6.06
$e_t = 3, s_t = 1$	2.96	7.01
$e_t = 1, s_t = 2$	$-.92$	-2.06
$e_t = 2, s_t = 2$	$-.22$	$-.51$
$e_t = 3, s_t = 2$	-1.12	-2.38
$e_t = 1, s_t = 3$	1.66	2.18
$e_t = 2, s_t = 3$	.85	1.15
$e_t = 3, s_t = 3$	1.42	1.98
$h_t = 1, h_{t+1} = 1$	.04	.45
$h_t = 1, h_{t+1} = 2$	$-.09$	$-.79$
$h_t = 1, h_{t+1} = 3$	$-.86$	-2.60
$h_t = 2, h_{t+1} = 1$	$-.01$	$-.07$
$h_t = 2, h_{t+1} = 3$	$-.50$	-1.32
$h_t = 3, h_{t+1} = 3$	$-.82$	-2.43
$a_t \in [0, 60)$	.46	3.17
$a_t \in [60, 62)$	.37	3.01
$a_t \in [62, 65)$	.16	1.56
$a_t \in [65, 68)$	$-.05$	$-.50$
$y_t \in [0, 4)$	$-.52$	-2.60
$y_t \in [4, 7)$	$-.55$	-3.23
$y_t \in [7, 10)$	$-.45$	-2.69
$y_t \in [10, 13)$	$-.43$	-2.50
$y_t \in [13, 21)$	$-.34$	-1.92
$y_t \in [21, 31)$	$-.15$	$-.73$
$ms_t = 2, ms_{t+1} = 2$	$-.10$	$-.29$
$ms_t = 1, ms_{t+1} = 2$	$-.17$	$-.44$
$ms_t = 1, ms_{t+1} = 1$	$-.21$	$-.64$
$ss_t \in \{1, 2\}, s_t = 1$	-1.50	-15.96
$ss_t \in \{1, 2\}, s_t = 2$	$-.76$	-3.47
$ss_t \in \{1, 2\}, s_t = 3$	-2.09	-3.42
Log likelihood	$-9,154.9$	
Grad • direc	7 E-028	
correctly predicted (%)	82	
Number of observations	18,778	

Table 11.16   **Estimates of Employment Status Transition Probability (dependent variable: $I\{e_{t+1} = 3\}$)**

Variable	Estimate	t-statistic
$e_t = 1, s_t = 1$	$-.52$	-1.24
$e_t = 2, s_t = 1$	-1.19	-2.67
$e_t = 3, s_t = 1$	$-.81$	-1.77
$e_t = 1, s_t = 2$	-1.52	-2.97
$e_t = 2, s_t = 2$	-1.87	-3.66
$e_t = 3, s_t = 2$	-1.89	-3.65
$e_t = 1, s_t = 3$	2.75	4.09
$e_t = 2, s_t = 3$	1.70	2.58
$e_t = 3, s_t = 3$	3.49	5.35
$h_t = 1, h_{t+1} = 1$	$-.44$	-5.15
$h_t = 1, h_{t+1} = 2$	$-.02$	$-.25$
$h_t = 1, h_{t+1} = 3$	$.73$	2.48
$h_t = 2, h_{t+1} = 1$	$-.38$	-3.03
$h_t = 2, h_{t+1} = 3$	$.77$	2.20
$h_t = 3, h_{t+1} = 3$	$.48$	2.53
$a_t \in [0, 60)$	$-.12$	$-.77$
$a_t \in [60, 62)$	$.24$	1.98
$a_t \in [62, 65)$	$.41$	4.30
$a_t \in [65, 68)$	$.08$	$.86$
$y_t \in [0, 4)$	$.27$	1.28
$y_t \in [4, 7)$	$.20$	1.00
$y_t \in [7, 10)$	$.32$	1.62
$y_t \in [10, 13)$	$.44$	2.11
$y_t \in [13, 21)$	$.53$	2.51
$y_t \in [21, 31)$	$.32$	1.28
$ms_t = 2, ms_{t+1} = 2$	$-.27$	$-.81$
$ms_t = 1, ms_{t+1} = 2$	$-.42$	-1.10
$ms_t = 1, ms_{t+1} = 1$	$-.41$	-1.28
$ss_t \in \{1, 2\}, s_t = 1$	1.03	6.80
$ss_t \in \{1, 2\}, s_t = 2$	1.08	3.45
$ss_t \in \{1, 2\}, s_t = 3$	$.46$	$.87$
Log likelihood	$-9,154.9$	
Grad • direc	7 E-028	
Correctly predicted (%)	82	
Total observations	18,778	

linear-in-parameters specification of a trinomial logit model of the probability that e_{t+1} assumes the three values $\{1, 2, 3\}$. Table 11.15 presents the parameter estimates corresponding to the event $I\{e_{t+1} = 1\}$ (full-time work), while table 11.16 presents the parameter estimates corresponding to the event $I\{e_{t+1} = 3\}$ (unemployment).[21] The interpretation of the estimation results has already been summarized in conclusion 5 of section 11.2 and will not be repeated here.

11.7   Income, Wealth, and Consumption

Next to employment status, the most important state variables of the DP model are income y_t and wealth w_t. The RHS has detailed information on assets and debts in each of the odd-numbered survey years, 1969–79, as well as detailed information on the components of income in the preceding even-numbered years, 1968–78. Although consumption c_t is treated as an observable control variable, in reality it is essentially a time aggregration of thousands of individual unobserved buy/no buy decisions over the two-year period. My strategy was to use the budget equation $w_{t+1} = w_t + y_t - c_t$ to infer consumption expenditures from measurements of w_{t+1}, w_t, and y_t. There are two obstacles to this approach: the RHS has no data on capital gains income, and the RHS records income only in even-numbered years. Thus, capital gains and income in odd-numbered years must be imputed. A key to accurate income imputations is the use of the retrospective labor force histories to construct the e_t state variable.

I initially tried to impute the missing income values by regressing income in even-numbered years on variables available in both even- and odd-numbered years. Among the variables available in both even and odd years were the SSER earnings records (up until 1974) and the SSMBR OASDI benefit data (from 1969 to 1978). Despite the inclusion of these variables and retrospective data on total hours worked in odd-numbered years, the fits of the income regressions were not very impressive, with R^2 values of 60 percent at best. Using the estimated regressions to fill in the missing income values produced intuitively unreasonable results, generating wide swings in income that occasionally turned negative or exceeded reasonable values.

An approach that turned out to work much better was a simple *ad hoc* procedure I call "full information interpolation." One can divide income into four sources: (1) wage income, (2) OASDI income, (3) unemployment insurance, and (4) other income. Since I have OASDI income in all years, that variable does not need to be imputed.[22] In addition, since other income is predominantly asset and pension income, which is largely independent of labor force participation, I obtained an estimate for category 4 by simply averaging observed other income in adjacent even-numbered years. The problem thus reduced to computing wage income and unemployment compensation. Using the retrospective employment histories, I obtained an estimate of total hours worked in each year. Dividing hours worked into observed wage income, I obtained a wage rate that I used to compute total wage income in odd-numbered years.[23] If there was evidence that the worker had become involuntarily unemployed during the period, I imputed unemployment compensation as well. The resulting interpolation estimates appeared much more reasonable than the regression-based imputations. In particular, there were far fewer wild swings in income, very few excessively large values, and no negative income values. Figure 11.3 plots the imputed and reported income distributions for the six-year period 1973–78. There is evidently little difference between the imputed and the reported income distributions; both have the characteristic lognormal shape. There is a noticeable leftward shift in the distribution over time as more and more workers withdraw from the labor force. This shift is not as pronounced as it might be because of the replacement of wage income by OASDI and pension receipts. If I were to plot wage distributions only, the leftward shift would be much more pronounced.

The existence of the seam problem in the employment data discussed in section 11.4 led me to suspect the possibility that these inconsistencies might have contaminated the imputed income data. To see whether there was any evidence of this, I plotted the distributions of income changes in figure 11.4. These distributions show no evidence of the seam problem, perhaps because wage income became an increasingly less important source of income over the survey and because the SSER earnings records and the SSMBR OASDI benefit data allowed me to get relatively accurate measurements of the main components of income for the majority of the sample. In any event, I conclude that my income imputations appear to be fairly reliable measures of actual income.

Having said this is not to deny the existence of systematic response errors in reported wage and OASDI benefits. For example, section 11.3 discussed the widespread underreporting of Social Security disability benefits. To assess how accurately respondents reported their income, I used the SSER and SSMBR data sets to compare reported and actual earnings and OASDI benefits. Because of the Social Security maximum earnings limitation, OASDI recipients had a clear incentive to deny or underreport their wage earnings since the survey was conducted for SSA. On the other hand, OASDI benefits themselves do not enter into the ''earnings test,'' so there is no obvious incentive to underreport these receipts. Figure 11.5 presents the distribution of the percentage difference between reported wages and SSER earnings in 1970 and the distribution of percentage response error in total OASDI benefit in 1974.[24] The figure shows no obvious evidence of systematic underreporting, although each contains spikes at − 100 percent indicating a nonnegligible fraction of respondents falsely reporting that they had no wage or OASDI income. On the basis of these comparisons, I set flags indicating the degree of accuracy of the respondent's reports of his wage and OASDI benefits. I then used these flags in the construction of a sample boolean to screen out questionable respondents.

I used the Hurd wealth data (see n. 2 above) to compute respondents' net worth. Net worth consists of financial and real assets less total indebtedness, but excludes pensions, life insurance, and annuities (the latter two are fairly uncommon in the RHS anyway).[25] Wealth data are extremely hard to cross-check because major components of wealth, such as the market value of the respondent's house, are often subjective guesses. Figure 11.6 plots the distribution of wealth for the six survey years. Notice that there is a significant

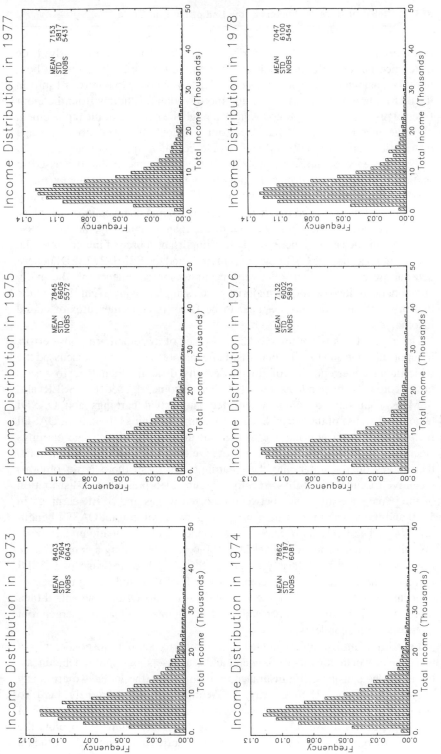

Fig. 11.3 Distributions of actual and imputed income, 1973–78

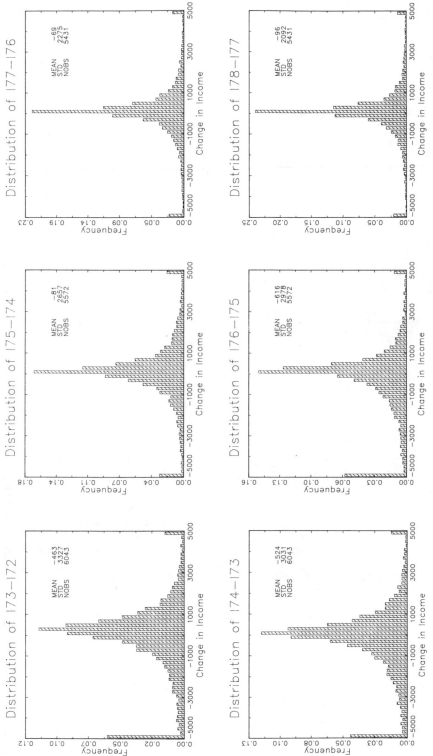

Fig. 11.4 Distributions of changes in income, 1973–78

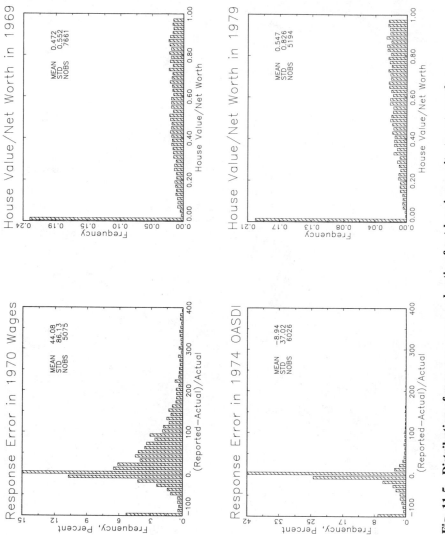

Fig. 11.5 Distribution of response error and ratio of net housing equity to net worth

fraction of respondents, about 10 percent, who report that they have essentially no tangible wealth. Mean wealth levels are about $28,000 1968 dollars, equal to approximately four years of income. These distributions provide little evidence that respondents consume their wealth as they age. Figure 11.5 plots the distribution of housing value to net worth in 1969 and 1979. It shows that a large fraction of workers' wealth is tied up in housing: homeowners have an average 56 percent of their wealth tied up in housing in 1969, increasing to 65 percent in 1979. The failure of wealth to decrease over time may be partly due to the appreciation of housing in the inflationary 1970s.

Using Hurd's wealth data and my imputed income series, I constructed an imputed biennial consumption series using the budget identity $c_t = w_t - w_{t+1} + y_t$. The resulting consumption distributions are plotted in figure 11.7. Overall, the distribution of consumption looks very similar to the distribution of income plotted in figure 11.8; both income and consumption show a noticeable tendency to shift leftward over time. This fact is not an accident since figure 11.9 shows that the distribution of wealth changes is centered about zero, suggesting that to a first approximation, $c_t = y_t$. Indeed, the mean wealth change (averaged over all periods and workers) is -658, with a *standard deviation* of $47,015. Given that average wealth is $28,000, it is difficult not to conclude that most of the variation is due to measurement error. The large standard deviation suggests that it would be difficult to reject the hypothesis that $c_t = y_t$. However, a simple hypothesis test of H_0: $c_t = y_t$ versus H_A: $c_t \neq y_t$ yields a χ^2 statistic of 6.2 with a marginal significance level of just over 1 percent: a rejection that is perhaps not surprising given that I have 31,348 observations on wealth changes.[26]

Whether the large variance in wealth reflects explainable differences in behavior or simple measurement error is an open question, but my initial investigations suggest the dominance of the latter. Like the employment data, aggregate consumption appears fairly smooth, slowly declining over time in apparent accord with the standard life-cycle hypothesis. However, at the individual level, measured consumption is anything but smooth, making violent, unpredictable swings over time. Overall, a total of 1,984 respondents have negative measured consumption in at least one of the five biennial survey periods, and in successive periods more than half the sample is recorded as having either a consumption increase of more than 200 percent or a consumption decrease of more than 50 percent. These large swings in consumption fly in the face of intuition and personal observation of the consumption behavior of the elderly, suggesting that most of the swings are due to measurement errors in wealth.

One possible reason for negative consumption is the failure to account for capital gains. Given the subjectivity of respondents' assessment of housing values and the fact that a majority of workers continue to live in the same house rather than "size down," it seemed reasonable to attribute all changes in net housing wealth to capital gains (provided the respondent did not move).

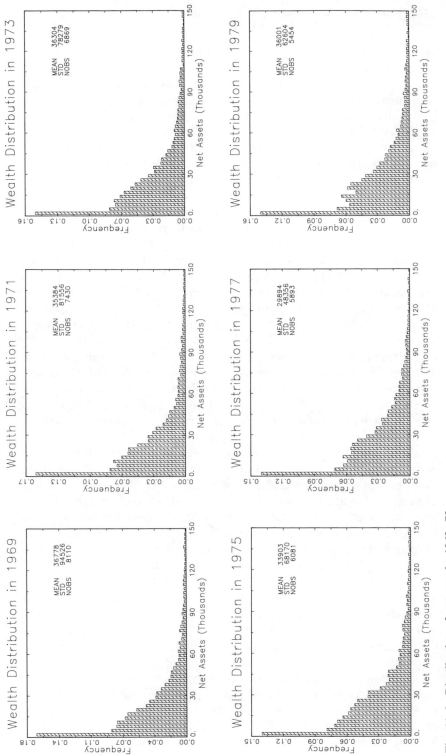

Fig. 11.6 Distribution of net worth, 1969–79

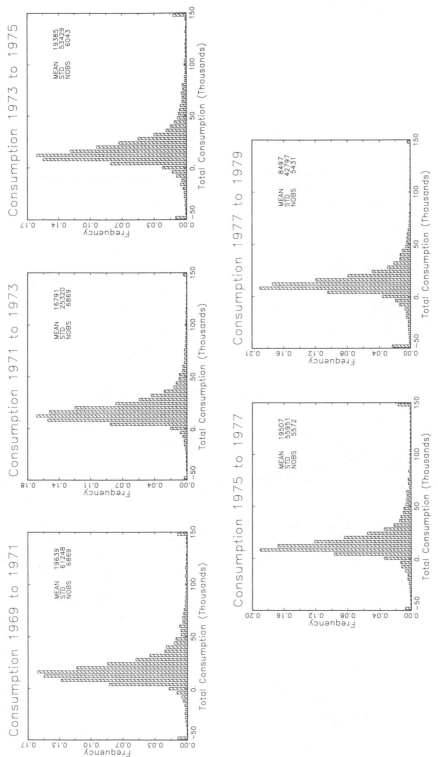

Fig. 11.7 Distribution of measured biennial consumption, 1969–79

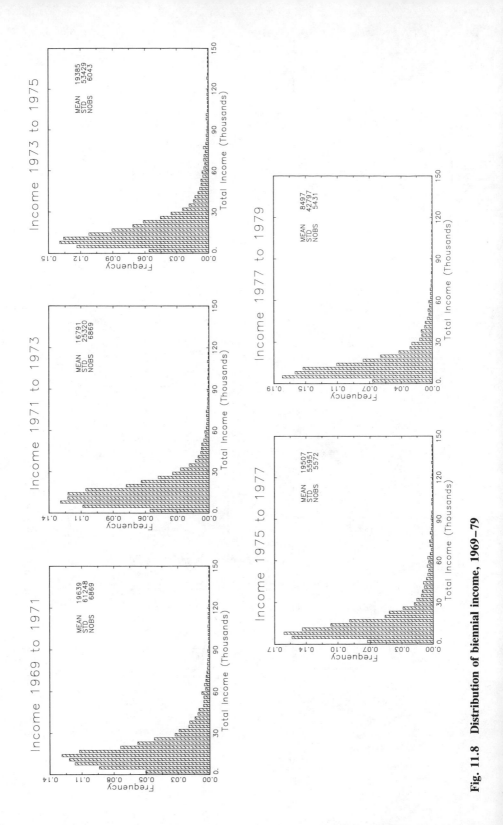

Fig. 11.8 Distribution of biennial income, 1969–79

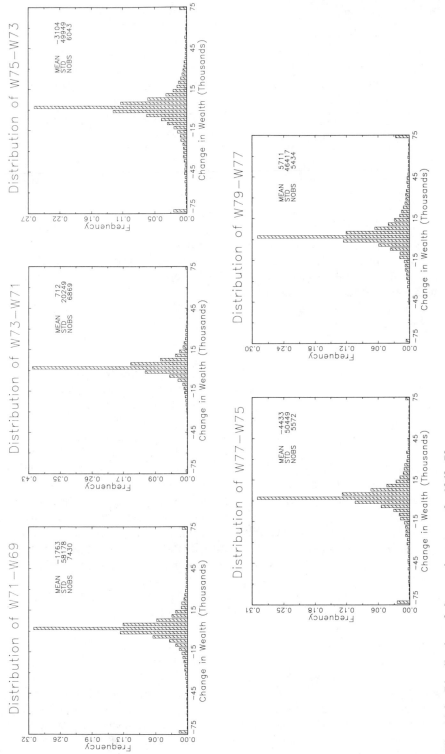

Fig. 11.9 Distribution of changes in net worth, 1969–79

Adding these housing capital gains (or losses) did reduce the number of negative consumption cases somewhat, to 1,522, but overall the distribution of consumption including capital gains looked very similar to the distribution of consumption without capital gains.

The notion that response errors in wealth are driving the violent swings in consumption is confirmed by examining individual data records. Having access to a complete data record over the survey period often provides enough contextual information to enable one intuitively to identify reporting and recording errors that are responsible for negative consumption values. Table 11.17 presents relevant data for a "typical" respondent (ID 6886) with negative measured consumption. This man—call him Bob—is coded as having the occupation of craftsman in the construction industry; most likely, Bob is a carpenter. Bob responded in all six of the survey waves and provided very complete answers; all the variable flags (with the exception of consumption) indicated very high confidence levels in his responses. Bob is married, living with spouse, and was working full time until 1975, when he turned 65, quit his job, and started collecting Social Security (Bob had no pensions). By all accounts, Bob is just the kind of guy I want in my sample: a typical blue-collar worker who seems to provide complete, reliable answers, who has slightly above average income, and who has most of his wealth in housing. However, we can see from table 11.17 that, while Bob's income declined slightly from $12,000 to $11,000 over the decade and his measured consumption was about equal to his income stream in four out the five two-year periods, for some reason his consumption over the period of 1976–77 is recorded as $ − 35,630. Analysis of his balance sheet reveals that, between the 1975 and the 1977 interviews, his house value increased from $14,000 to $100,000, increasing his overall net worth from $10,794 to $57,376.[27] This sudden increase in wealth is responsible for the recorded negative consumption in the 1976–77 biennium. A possible explanation for the increase is coding error: Bob may have reported his house value to be $10,000 in 1977, but it was mistakenly recorded as $100,000. However, this explanation becomes less plausible when we realize that his house value is recorded at $150,000 in 1979: it seems very unlikely that we would get the same kind of coding error in the same variable in two consecutive years.

If we look further into the data, we find that Bob moved between 1975 and 1977. This suggests several possibilities. Bob and his wife may have moved into the house of his wealthy son and mistakenly reported the value of his son's house as his own. Bob may have previously grossly underestimated the value of his old house and used the capital gains on the sale of the old house to finance the purchase of his new house. Bob may have won a lottery, which provided an unrecorded capital gain that he used to purchase his retirement dream home. Bob may have owned other real estate which he failed to report in previous interviews and has since used to buy his retirement home. Or, being a carpenter, Bob may have built his own retirement home and, blinded by the pride of creation, grossly overestimated its value. Given the wealth of possible

Table 11.17   **Selected Financial Data for "Bob," (RHS ID, 6886)**

	1969	1971	1973	1975	1977	1979
Personal data:						
a_t	59	61	63	65	67	69
ms_t	1	1	1	1	1	1
h_t	1	2	1	1	2	2
Employment data:						
IE	1	1	1	1	3	3
SR	1	1	1	2	3	3
SE	1	1	1	2	3	3
Financial data ($1968):						
w_t	10,698	12,523	13,950	10,794	57,376	71,555
y_t	M	12,033	11,951	10,199	10,952	11,429
c_t^a	M	10,196	10,524	13,354	−35,630	−2,750
c_t^b	M	11,154	12,047	12,272	−35,630	11,151
Capital gains	M	958	1,523	−1,082	0	13,901
Balance sheet (nominal):						
House value	8,000	10,000	13,000	14,000	100,000	150,000
Mortgage	0	0	0	0	0	0
Other house debt	0	0	0	0	0	0
Farm value	0	0	0	0	0	0
Farm mortgage	0	0	0	0	0	0
Business value	0	0	0	0	0	0
Business debt	0	0	0	0	0	0
Real-estate value	0	0	0	0	0	0
Real-estate debt	0	0	0	0	0	0
Auto value	2,490	2,490	2,495	2,500	3,237	4,980
Auto debt	0	0	0	0	0	0
Savings bonds	2,000	2,000	2,408	0	0	0
Stocks	0	0	0	0	0	0
Credit card debt	0	200	236	0	0	500
Checking account	190	900	900	900	900	1,080
Savings account	0	0	0	0	0	0
Face value life ins	1,000	1,000	913	2,000	2,000	2,000
Face value annuities	0	0	0	0	0	0
Medical debts	834	0	0	0	0	0
Store debts	100	0	0	0	0	0
Bank debts	0	0	0	0	0	0
Personal debts	0	0	0	0	0	0

[a]This measure of c_t does not include imputed capital gains.
[b]This measure includes imputed capital gains as described in the text.

explanations, it is not easy to know what to do. One can simply exclude cases with negative measured consumption, but that still leaves the problem of hundreds of cases with implausibly large or small measured consumption or cases where consumption changes vary erratically from year to year.

In conclusion, while one might attempt to identify reporting problems by examining observations on a case-by-case basis, it is unrealistic to think that one could screen out a sufficiently high fraction of "bad" cases to end up with a subsample for which consumption is measured accurately. Not only is case-by-case examination of 8,131 individuals impossibly time consuming, but the resulting data set would be susceptible to the criticism that the sample had been "hand picked" to support an *a priori* theory. If an error-identification strategy is to be successful, one should be able to write out a series of objective classification rules, say in the form of a computer program, that would allow other researchers to replicate the subsample. I have not been successful in constructing a computer program with sufficient "intelligence" to examine the wealth data on a case-by-case basis, recognize the existence of a data problem, and take appropriate corrective action. As I discussed above, it is not sufficient simply to screen out cases with negative consumption because the remaining cases still suffer from reporting problems that produce unrealistically large swings in consumption. Because of these problems, I have opted against using consumption data in my first attempts at estimating the DP model. Until I see convincing evidence that changes in wealth are not dominated by measurement error, or until I am successful in constructing an "artificial intelligence" program that reliably discriminates accurate survey responses from inaccurate responses, I will adopt the null hypothesis that $c_t = y_t$ and focus on "explaining" the joint dynamics of $x_t = (y_t, e_t, sr_t, a_t, ms_t, h_t)$ and $d_t = (s_t, ss_t)$, excluding w_t and c_t from the model.

11.8   Estimating the Stochastic Process of Income

All that remains is to specify and estimate the final component of workers' beliefs, the transition density for income π_y. The lognormal shapes of the income distributions plotted in section 11.7 suggest that the transition density π_y should have a lognormal distribution with parameters (μ, σ) that are parametric functions of the state and control variables listed in the decomposition (5). As is well known, if a random variable $\bar{y}$ has a lognormal distribution, then its mean and variance are given by

$$(7) \qquad E[\bar{y}] = \exp\{\mu + \sigma^2/2\},$$

$$\text{var}[\bar{y}] = \exp\{2\mu + 2\sigma^2\} - \exp\{2\mu + \sigma^2\}.$$

It is extremely important to allow both μ and σ to depend on the state variables since, if σ is fixed, then (7) and the autoregressive properties of the income process will imply that the variance of y_{t+1} is a quadratically increasing function of current income y_t. Thus, by failing to specify σ properly, one is making an implicit assumption about the form of heteroscedasticity that may grossly misrepresent workers' actual beliefs. Once we have decided on the appropriate functional forms for μ and σ, the lognormal model is fairly easy to estimate: one obtains initial estimates of (μ, σ) by a log-linear regression and uses these as starting values for computing the final parameter estimates by maximum likelihood.[28] There is a minor problem concerning the fact that the DP model requires y_t and its transition density π_y to be discretized. My approach was to discretize y_t as an independent variable entering (μ, σ) but to do the estimation treating the dependent variable y_{t+1} as a continuous variable. After estimating the relevant parameters, it is easy to generate a discrete transition probability matrix $\hat{\pi}_y$: simply compute the area under the lognormal density corresponding to each of the discrete income cells for y_{t+1}.

The hard part is to specify how the parameters (μ, σ) depend on the underlying state and control variables. The specification is crucial here because not only must π_y embody workers' expectations about how future income depends on their current employment, health, and marital status but it must also embody the relevant rules and actuarial structure of the Social Security OASDI system, including the regressive nature of the payout schedule, the extra payments to spouse, the penalty for early retirement, and the "earnings test" for workers under 70. As I discussed in my earlier paper, by estimating π_y using income data over the decade of the 1970s (during which Social Security benefits increased more than 50 percent in real terms), I have implicitly assumed that workers have "semirational" expectations: that is, they correctly anticipated the increase in benefits over the 1970s but did not expect any benefit changes thereafter.[29]

My initial attempts to estimate π_y yielded disappointing results. Although the coefficient estimates for the marital status, employment status, and search variables had reasonable signs and magnitudes, the variables representing the structure of OASDI benefits either had small, insignificant coefficients or else had the wrong sign. The estimated model looked as if workers were unaware of key features of the OASDI benefit plan, and the few provisions they did know about seemed to be regarded as taxes instead of benefits. Apparently, the Social Security benefit structure was "drowned out" by sample selection bias. A simple explanation of the problem goes as follows. High-income workers typically continue working beyond retirement age and delay collection of Social Security, whereas low-income workers stop working and begin collecting Social Security as soon as they can, typically at age 62. A regression model attempts to fit the data by flipping the sign of Social Security variables: collection of Social Security benefits is spuriously predicted to reduce total income. My solution to the problem was to augment the data set with "artificial" data on the incomes that retired workers would have received in the absence of OASDI payments. Thus, corresponding to each data record for a retired worker receiving OASDI ($ss_t \in \{1, 2\}$), I created a duplicate record deducting all OASDI benefits from the worker's income y_t and setting $ss_t = 0$. This procedure, which nearly doubled the number of observations, produced dramatically improved results. In particular, nearly all the Social Security variables had significant coefficients with correct signs and magnitudes. In effect, the augmented data "drowned out" the sample selection bias, allowing me to capture the true underlying OASDI benefit structure more accurately.

The existence of the SSMBR data set was absolutely crucial to the success of this procedure since, as I have shown, the magnitude of response error in the self-reported values of certain Social Security benefits such as SSDI is so large as to render them useless.

A final problem I encountered concerned the estimation of age-income effects. In my initial specifications, I included the polynomial terms in the age variable a_t to capture the independent effects of aging on income. Just looking at the estimated coefficients, the estimated model seemed quite reasonable, with age terms all entering with highly significant coefficients. However, when I plotted out the age-income profiles, the results were clearly far from reasonable. In models that included only a linear term in a_t, the age-income profile sloped upward, whereas in models with quadratic and cubic age terms the age-income profile was hump shaped: rising until age 70 and then falling sharply thereafter. The incomes predicted by the hump-shaped profiles were completely unreasonable: at the top of the hump a 70-year-old worker who was currently earning $10,000 could expect to earn nearly double that amount two years later if he continued working. On the other hand, on the downward sloping part of the profile, say at age 80, the worker would only expect to make half as much even if he continued working. The reason behind these strange results is lack of data on earnings for very old men. As I have discussed before in section 11.4, the RHS has no data on workers older than 73. Thus, estimation of age-income profiles beyond age 73 requires pure extrapolation over a region where there are no observations to guide us. Including polynomial age terms in the regression produced unreasonable forecasts because the estimation procedure chose the coefficients to get a good fit in the region where there are a lot of observations, namely, for ages 58–68. Since there are no observations beyond age 73, the regression does not "care" what its predictions are in that range, producing unreasonable results. In order to avoid the extrapolation problems inherent in the use of polynomial terms, I tried specifications using age dummies, which entail the implicit extrapolation that age-income profiles are constant after age 73. In spite of my hopes, the age dummies also yielded somewhat disappointing results: the estimated age-income profile fluctuated up and down with no clear pattern. Since I have little a priori knowledge of the correct shape of the age-income profile, I decided simply not to include a_t in the estimation of π_y.

Table 11.18 presents the specification for π_y that I finally settled on. The main implications of table 11.18 have already been discussed in conclusion 6 of section 11.2 and will not be repeated here. However, to convince the reader that the estimated model really does endow workers with sensible income expectations, I present a graphic summary of the predictions of the model in figure 11.10.

Figure 11.10 presents the estimated transition densities $\hat{\pi}_y$ for four configurations of the conditioning variables listed in (5) corresponding to the beliefs of four different workers about their future income, $\tilde{y}_{t+1}$. The sharply peaked density marked with triangles represents the expectations of a single man, aged

Table 11.18   **Estimates of Income Transition Probability (dependent variable: $\ln[y_{t+1}]$)**

Variable	σ Parameters	
	Parameter Estimates	Corrected t-Statistic
Constant	− .25	− 8.8
$\ln(y_t)$	− .51	− 31.9
	μ Parameters	
Constant	− .12	− 2.8
$\ln(y_t)$	.94	161.6
$h_t = 1, h_{t+1} = 1$	.02	3.8
$h_t = 1, h_{t+1} = 3$	− .27	− 4.1
$h_t = 2, h_{t+1} = 2$	.01	.6
$h_t = 2, h_{t+1} = 3$	− .24	− 3.5
$h_t = 3, h_{t+1} = 3$	.05	2.9
$s_t = 1, e_{t+1} = 1$	.22	14.2
$s_t = 1, e_{t+1} = 3$	− .24	− 11.7
$s_t = 2, e_{t+1} = 1$	.19	7.4
$s_t = 2, e_{t+1} = 2$	.00	.1
$s_t = 2, e_{t+1} = 3$	− .31	− 11.9
$s_t = 3, e_{t+1} = 1$	.02	.3
$s_t = 3, e_{t+1} = 2$	− .03	− 1.2
$s_t = 3, e_{t+1} = 3$	− .18	− 10.7
$s_t = 3, e_{t+1} = 3, y_t < 4$	− .08	− 7.1
$s_t = 3, e_{t+1} = 3, y_t > 15$	− .11	− 3.8
$ms_t = 2, ms_{t+1} = 2$	− .19	− 4.7
$ms_t = 1, ms_{t+1} = 2$	− .30	− 6.2
$ms_t = 1, ms_{t+1} = 1$	− .04	− 1.2
$ss_t \neq 0, ms_t = 2, ms_{t+1} = 2$[a]	− .04	− .9
$ss_t \neq 0, e_{t+1} = 1$[a]	.04	1.8
$ss_t \neq 0, e_{t+1} = 2$[a]	.47	10.7
$ss_t \neq 0, e_{t+1} = 3$[a]	.52	23.1
$ss_t = 2, e_{t+1} = 1$[a]	− .01	− .4
$ss_t = 2, e_{t+1} = 2$[a]	.01	.2
$ss_t = 2, e_{t+1} = 3$[a]	.19	7.9
$ss_t \neq 0, a_t \geq 70, e_{t+1} = 1$[a]	.36	2.3
$ss_t \neq 0, a_t \geq 70, e_{t+1} = 2$[a]	.33	3.8
Log likelihood	− 2.9 E + 5	
Grad • direc	2 E-026	
Number of observations	39,494	

[a]These variables are all multiplied by $1/\ln(y_t)$.

75, who is disabled, out of the labor force, and receiving a total income of $y_t = \$4{,}000$. The density marked with the circles corresponds to a 65-year-old retired man who is married, in health state $h_t = 2$, and receiving an income of $y_t = \$7{,}000$. The density marked with boxes corresponds to a married 58-year-old man who is in good health, working full time, with a total income

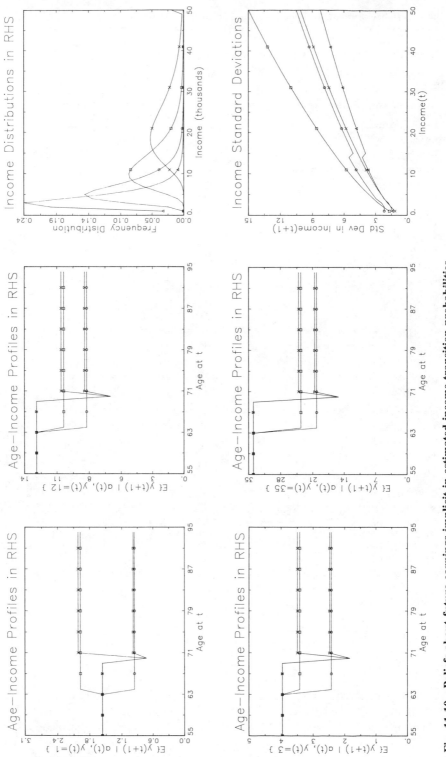

Fig. 11.10 Beliefs about future earnings implicit in estimated income transition probabilities

of $y_t = \$12,000$. Finally, the curve marked with x's corresponds to a wealthier 80-year-old man who is not retired, married, in good health, and continues to work full time, earning an income of $y_t = \$20,000$.

Figure 11.10 also presents estimates of workers' expected income, $E\{y_{t+1} | e_{t+1}, ms_{t+1}, h_{t+1}, x_t, d_t, a_t\}$, plotted as a function of their age. Although the profiles are flat by construction (the estimated model excluded a_t), the figures provide an indication of the dynamics of income as workers retire. Each of the figures contains four curves, corresponding to four different retirement paths. The curves marked with boxes correspond to working full time until age 65 and then collecting OASI. The curve marked with circles shows what the worker would expect if he quit working but did not start collecting OASI. The other two curves represent the expectations of a worker who works full-time until his early 70s but then becomes disabled and has to quit work. The lower curve represents what the worker would expect if there were no OASDI program to cover him; the higher curve represents what the worker would expect if he applied for OASDI. Note carefully that the curves in figure 11.10 represent conditional expectation functions: they are not the same as the sample paths of the income process. Given the strong autocorrelation in income, actual sample paths of income will look quite a bit different. The figure clearly shows the progressive nature of the Social Security system. Indeed, a very low-income worker actually expects to do better by retiring and collecting OASDI than continuing to work at his low-paying full-time job. However, figure 11.10 shows that, for a very high-income worker, the percentage replacement rate of OASDI benefits is much smaller: Social Security is not such a good deal for these workers.

Finally, figure 11.10 also includes a plot of the standard deviation of $\bar{y}_{t+1}$ as a function of current income, y_t. The four curves are all upward sloping, representing the fact that, the higher a worker's current income is, the more uncertain he is about his future income. Note that, while uncertainty does increase with y_t, the increase is far from proportional: this is a direct consequence of the fact that $\ln(y_t)$ enters the σ parameter with a large, significant negative coefficient, as you can see from table 11.16. The four curves in the figure correspond to four classes of workers. The curve marked with boxes corresponds to a 60-year-old worker who is married, in good health, and working full time. The curve marked with circles corresponds to a worker who is 88, disabled, and out of the labor force. The curve marked with triangles corresponds to a worker who is 68, single, in health state $h_t = 2$, and is retired and receiving Social Security. The final curve, marked with x's, corresponds to a 55-year-old man who is single, in health state $h_t = 2$, and working part time.

11.9   Modeling the Retirement Decision

The SSMBR data allow me to determine exactly when a worker applys for and receives OASI benefits. In my opinion, the only sensible and precise treatment of the concept of "retirement" is to define it in terms of collection of OASI benefits. I used the SSMBR data set to construct the control variable ss_t defined in (2). Figure 11.11 summarizes this variable in terms of the implied distribution of age of first entitlement to OASDI.[30] The distribution has a pronounced bimodal shape, with peaks at the early retirement age 62 and at the normal retirement age 65. Overall, nearly all the sample applies for benefits between the ages of 62 and 65.[31]

One can, however, define retirement in terms of withdrawal from the labor force. The discussion in section 11.5 indicates that this is an extremely tricky business since there is no clear-cut way to define "withdrawal from the labor force." Figure 11.11 presents a "retirement age" distribution tabulated by Burtless and Moffitt (1984), who used the RHS data, the instantaneous measure of labor participation IE, and a definition of "retirement" to be a sudden, discontinous drop in labor supply to under thirty hours per week. This distribution is significantly more spread out than the distribution of age of entitlement to OASDI. In particular, the peaks at ages 62 and 65 are much less pronounced, and there are much larger fractions of workers retiring before and after ages 62 and 65, respectively. Figure 11.11 also presents similar distributions tabulated from the RHS by Sueyoshi (1986), using instantaneous hours of work data and still another definition of retirement, and finally my own tabulation based on my classification of the workers' employment history (i.e., for workers' following the standard "1–2–3" and "1–3" employment sequences, retirement is defined as the age at which the worker first enters employment state 2 or 3; for those with nonmonotonic employment sequences, it is defined as the age at which the worker first begins collecting OASDI). Although each of the definitions yields a significantly different retirement age distribution, it is difficult to say which is the "right" one. However, it turns out that both the Burtless and Moffitt and the Sueyoshi distributions significantly understate the number of early age 62 retirements and overstate the number of age 65 retirements. While it is likely that their definitions of retirement have obscured some important features of the data, this analysis suggests that a debate about the "correct" definition of retirement age is simply ill posed in the context of a more realistic dynamic model of employment transitions.

What we can conclude from figure 11.11 is that there are a significant number of workers who apply for OASI in their mid-60s but continue working for several more years. One can see this most clearly by comparing the distribution of the age at which respondents were first entitled to OASDI versus the distribution of ages at which they first received six or more months of OASDI benefits (an indirect indicator of withdrawal from the labor force). The peak of early retirements at age 62 is nearly identical in both graphs: the primary differences are a shift in probability mass from retirements in the 63–65 age group to the age 66–72 age group and a near doubling of the number of respondents who never ended up collecting OASI benefits at all, from 687 to

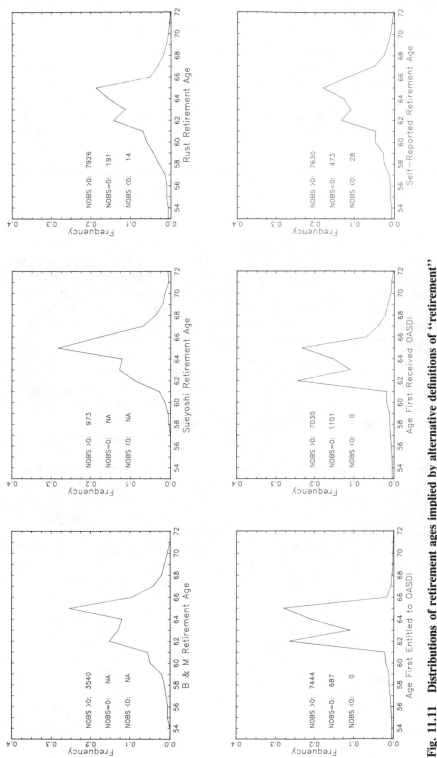

Fig. 11.11 Distributions of retirement ages implied by alternative definitions of "retirement"

1,101. There are four main reasons why the subsample of 1,100 workers never collected OASDI benefits: (1) the worker died before he had a chance to receive benefits (458 cases); (2) the worker was not eligible for OASDI, either due to the fact that he was not in a covered occupation or had not accumulated sufficient quarters of coverage to qualify for benefits (405 cases); (3) the worker applied and was entitled to OASI but lost 100 percent of his benefits owing to earnings well in excess of the Social Security earnings test (184 cases), and (4) the worker never applied for benefits even though he was eligible (fifty-four cases). Nearly all workers in the latter group had sufficiently high earnings that they would not have received benefits even if they had applied. Only four or five cases can be identified where an unemployed worker apparently "forgot" to apply for his Social Security benefits. Among the subsample of workers who ultimately collected OASI benefits, there is a two-year average delay between application and first receipt, from age 64 to 66, primarily due to that fact that benefits were taxed away due to earnings in excess of the earnings test levels. However, the predominant majority of this sample, 71 percent, first collected benefits in the same year that they became eligible. Approximately 18 percent began collecting one year after their entitlement, another 6 percent began collecting two years after entitlement, and the remaining 5 percent collected benefits three to nine years after first entitlement. This raises the question, Is it irrational to apply for benefits before age 65 yet continue working up until the normal retirement age and thereby lose nearly all benefits due to the earnings test? Close inspection of the Social Security regulations reveals that this is not irrational behavior. Section 729 of the 1974 *Social Security Handbook* provides for *ex post* adjustment of the early retirement benefit reduction factor to exclude months between ages 62 and 65 for which work deductions were imposed. Thus, even though a worker has applied for benefits before age 65, his ultimate reduction factor is based on his age when benefits are first paid. Early application simply provides an option for immediate collection of benefits in the event of unexpected unemployment but does not necessarily imply a permanent reduction in benefit levels.

Further insight into the issue is provided by the distribution of "self-reported" retirement age, defined as the age at which the worker first reports being "retired or partly retired." This distribution supports the view that, even though a large number of workers apply for OASI at age 62, many of them continue working for several years thereafter. Further analysis (beyond the scope of this paper) indicates that the majority of workers who apply for benefits at age 62 and continue working are either low-wage/income workers whose total annual earnings at ages after 62 are not significantly higher than the earnings test level or are a smaller group of workers who apparently initially intended to quit working at age 62 but experienced adverse financial problems or encountered a particularly attractive job opportunity that prompted them to return to work. But by far the biggest discrepancy between the entitlement and labor force withdrawal definitions of retirement is for a

10 percent subsample of wealthy professionals and self-employed workers who apply for Social Security benefits by age 65 but continue working well into their 70s. This type of behavior is evidently not irrational.

By in large, the analysis and estimation results in the previous sections of the paper suggest two main conclusions about the decision to retire and collect OASI: workers who retire and receive OASI appear to be less healthy than their counterparts who continue to work; and, once a worker starts collecting OASI, he is significantly less likely to return to work on either a full- or a part-time basis.

Finally, analysis of the RHS data provides clear evidence of the role of self-selection in the decision to collect OASDI; poorer, less healthy workers are more likely to quit their jobs and retire early, even given the permanent 20 percent penalty for early retirement. This may be rational behavior given the reduced life expectancy of unhealthy workers and the well-known fact that the OASI benefit structure is not actuarially fair. A more complete analysis of these issues must await the estimation of the DP model in the third part of this series.

Notes

1. For example, there is no attempt to measure consumption flows from durable goods such as housing, automobiles, furniture, etc. The questionnaire also requires estimates for expense categories that may be very hard to recall, e.g., amount spent in restaurants, amount spent for newspapers, amount spent for haircuts, etc. In fairness, I should mention that some authors, such as Hurd (1990), have attempted to use this data in an attempt directly to impute total consumption c_t. Other authors, such as Skinner (1987), propose using explanatory variables common to the more complete Consumer Expenditure Survey to compute regression-based imputations of consumption.

2. The wealth and income data used in this study were produced by the program IMPUTE, written by Beth van Zimmerman and Phil Farrell, research associates of Michael Hurd, State University of New York at Stony Brook. Besides imputing missing values, the program estimated the value of service flows for owned assets such as autos and housing at a presumed opportunity cost of 3 percent.

3. Constructing labor force histories turned out to be a major undertaking, requiring over eighty pages of FORTRAN code and over four months of full-time work to write and debug. The difficulties arose from the need carefully to track the survey skip patterns to extract the required variables from a battery of more than 130 questions in the "Work Experience" section of the RHS. Fine attention to detail was required to avoid misclassifying 20 percent of the sample of workers with "nonstandard" employment histories with multiple job transitions within the two-year survey period.

4. Of course, I will be happy to provide the reader with the data and documented versions of all computer programs used to generate the variables so that other researchers can verify any of my results, should they choose to do so.

5. Bienniel income was used only for purposes of constructing a measure of consumption. Based on conclusions 2 and 3 above, I have decided to exclude

consumption/savings decisions and formulate a DP model with biennial time intervals, measuring workers' states over the preceding even-numbered survey years. Thus, the DP model will actually use the annual income flows that were recorded in the surveys. For further justification of this approach, see conclusion 6.

6. A related problem with the disability classification, the fact that the probability of becoming disabled declines sharply to zero at age 62, is also an artifact of Social Security rules and is discussed further in conclusion 2 of sec. 11.2.

7. This decision is relevant only for workers who are over 62, have sufficient quarters of coverage to qualify for fully insured status, and have not previously applied for Social Security.

8. Cross-validation procedures can be used to fix values for some of the smoothing parameters, but ultimately many choices, such as the functional form of the kernel, are completely arbitrary.

9. The latter conclusion disappears if I exclude the variable sr_t distinguishing respondents who are receiving OASDI. Since men who collect OASDI have higher death rates, excluding sr_t produces a model where death rates increase slightly with age.

10. Social Security law prohibits a disabled worker from engaging in "substantial gainful activity" unless they are over age 62, at which time benefits convert to retirement benefits and are subject to the usual earnings test. Disabled workers are allowed to participate in a nine-month trial work program, after which continued work leads to termination of disability benefits. However, very few disabled workers ever return to work. Modeling the underlying decision process of whether to apply for disability benefits is hampered by lack of data on respondents who applied for and were denied disability benefits.

11. The finding for single workers might be partly a result of sample selection bias: single workers are presumably less likely to have a family support network to rely on, so they are more likely to become institutionalized if they have serious health problems. Such workers are lost from the sample since the RHS did not attempt to interview institutionalized individuals.

12. Here, s_t is proxied by the NE measure of the employment search decision defined in section 11.1.

13. Recall that my income measure includes net asset income (including imputed income from assets such as net housing equity), non–Social Security pension income (although the sample selected out individuals who had significant pension income), and income from relatives and other sources. My estimates of the reduction in income from retirement (defined here as quitting the labor force and applying for Social Security benefits) are somewhat higher than those of Fox (1984), who found that retirement leads to a 30 percent median percentage drop in total income for workers without private pensions.

14. In order to keep the length of this paper within bounds, I have chosen not to present the estimation results that lead to this conclusion. I defer the presentation of the results to the third paper of the series, which will examine the heterogeneity issue in more detail.

15. The nonresponse file was compiled by the Census in the process of conducting the RHS interviews and was used by SSA as part of an internal auditing system to remove cases in which the interviewer was unable to contact the original 1969 respondent or related household members. For some reason, the nonresponse data were not included on the RHS tapes and are available only separately as a subfile of the SSMBR tape. The nonresponse file will also be used in sec. 11.4 to identify men who were institutionalized after the 1969 interview.

16. Note that the parameter standard errors and t-statistics have been corrected using White's (1982) formula.

17. Although the total number of cases seems small, think of the millions of unnecessary tax dollars spent if this error rate exists in the population at large.

18. The aggregate mortality rates were obtained from the *Statistical Abstract of the United States* (U.S. Census 1979). In future work, I would like to formally incorporate auxiliary mortality data for very old men into a pooled maximum likelihood estimation of the death hazard model. A difficulty of this approach is the likely absence of associated health and employment status in any auxiliary data set. This will require me to "integrate out" these variables, which in turn requires further distributional assumptions on the cross-sectional distributions of health and employment status for very old men. Given these problems, I decided to use the short-cut described above.

19. I collapse those sequences for which M's occur only as trailing sequences. Cases where there are intervening occurences of M's (respondents who missed one survey but were subsequently interviewed) are classified in the "others" category in table 11.9.

20. The NLS contained an enriched sample of black respondents, who are presumably more likely to be unemployed. Apparently, the effect of a more youthful sample in the NLS dominated the effect of a larger proportion of blacks, leading to the discrepancies noted above.

21. Since probabilities sum to one, it is not necessary to present parameter estimates for the event $I\{e_{t+1} = 2\}$, which is equivalent to normalizing the parameters corresponding to the event $I\{e_{t+1} = 2\}$ to zero.

22. I substituted actual OASDI benefits from the SSMBR rather than reported OASDI benefits to calculate total income in even-numbered years.

23. Workers whose imputed wage appeared to be either unreasonably large or small or whose wage rate changed significantly were flagged and reexamined. Many of the unreasonable cases appear to be a consequence of reporting errors in income or employment status. The income distributions presented in figures 11.3, 11.4, and 11.8 do not screen out these questionable cases, however.

24. The "actual" wage income was taken as the value recorded by Social Security in the SSER data set. This income measure is right censored at the Social Security maximum earnings levels of $7,800 in effect over the period 1968–71. I have not attempted to use the quarters of coverage data to impute actual total wage earnings according to the method of Fox (1976).

25. While pensions are much more common than annuities in the RHS sample, exclusion of pension wealth is not a problem since the sample boolean already excludes workers with pensions.

26. The hypothesis actually tested was H_0: $w_t = w_{t+1}$ vs. H_A: $w_t \neq w_{t+1}$. It is easy to see that the budget identity implies that this is equivalent to the hypothesis test listed above. I assume that appropriate regularity conditions hold in order to justify the asymptotic χ^2 distribution for the test statistic, e.g., weak mixing conditions on the level of serial dependence in the observations.

27. Note that no capital gains are imputed since Bob moved during the period, making it impossible to determine how much of the value of the new house came from capital gains on the sale of the old house.

28. Although the likelihood function is concave, using the regression starting values (as opposed to zero starting values) substantially reduces the number of iterations needed to converge.

29. In fact, the large benefit increases in the 1970s put severe strain on the Social Security trust fund, necessitating substantial tax increases to fund the system. Fully rational workers might have plausibly expected real benefit *decreases* in the future.

30. A worker is entitled to OASDI if he (1) is at least age 62, (2) has filed a valid application for benefits, and (3) has sufficient quarters of coverage to qualify for retirement benefits. If the worker is under age 62, he is entitled to disability benefits

if he filed a valid application and was granted disability insured status by the Social Security Administration.

31. The fact that so few workers apply for benefits after age 65 might initially appear somewhat surprising in light of the fact that a significant number of higher-income workers continue working full time well into their 70s. It turns out that, under Social Security rules, there is no reason to delay application for benefits after age 65 since workers must first be entitled to OASI in order to be entitled to Medicare hospital insurance coverage (cf. sec. 104-A of the 1974 *Social Security Handbook*). Since Social Security benefits are automatically recomputed after initial entitlement, there is no benefit penalty (owing to the computation of average monthly wage) to delaying application beyond age 65. In addition, delayed retirement credits are determined on the basis of the worker's age when he is *first paid* benefits rather than on the worker's age when he applied. All these factors of the benefit structure explain why hardly anyone applies for benefits after age 65. I also take it as *prima facie* evidence that nearly all workers are cognizant of the Social Security benefit regulations.

References

Berkovec, J., and S. Stern. 1987. Job exit behavior of older men. University of Virginia. Typescript.

Bertsekas, D., and S. Shreve. 1978. *Stochastic optimal control: The discrete time case*. New York: Academic.

Bound, J. 1986. The disincentive effects of the Social Security disability program. University of Michigan. Typescript.

Burtless, G., and R. Moffitt. 1984. The effect of Social Security benefits on the labor supply of the aged. In *Retirement and economic behavior,* ed. H. J. Aaron and G. Burtless. Washington, D.C.: Brookings.

Fox, A. 1976. Alternative measures of earning replacement for Social Security benefits. Research Report no. 47. Office of Research and Statistics, Social Security Administration.

———. 1979. Earnings replacement rates for retired couples: Finding from the Retirement History Study. *Social Security Bulletin* 42:17–39.

———. 1982. Earnings replacement rates and total income: Findings from the Retirement History Study. *Social Security Bulletin* 45:3–24.

———. 1984. Income changes at and after Social Security benefit receipt: Evidence from the Retirement History Study. *Social Security Bulletin* 47:3–23.

Gustman, A. L., and T. L. Steinmeier. 1983. Minimum hours constraints and retirement behavior. *Economic Inquiry* 3:77–91.

———. 1984. Partial retirement and the analysis of retirement behavior. *Industrial and Labor Relations Review* 37:403–15.

———. 1986. A structural retirement model. *Econometrica* 54(3):555–84.

Hansen, L. P. 1982. Large sample properties of generalized method of moments estimators. *Econometrica* 50:1029–54.

Hill, D. 1988. Response error around the seam: An analysis of change in a panel with overlapping reference periods. In *Individuals and families in transition: Understanding change through longitudinal data*, 277–88. U.S. Bureau of Census compilation of papers presented at the 1988 Social Science Research Council, Annapolis, Maryland.

Hurd, M. 1990. Consumption, wealth, and bequests. Typescript. State Univ. of New York, Stony Brook.

MaCurdy, T. E. 1983. A simple scheme for estimating an intertemporal model of labor supply and consumption in the presence of taxes and uncertainty. *International Economic Review* 24(2): 265–89.

Mott, F. L., and R. J. Haurin. 1985. Factors affecting mortality in the years surrounding retirement. In *Retirement among American men,* ed. H. Parnes. Lexington, Mass.: Lexington.

Parnes, H. S., ed. 1981. *Work and retirement.* Cambridge, Mass.: MIT Press.

Parnes, H. S., et al. 1985. *Retirement among American men.* Lexington, Mass.: Lexington.

Rust, J. 1987. Optimal replacement of GMC bus engines: An empirical model of Harold Zurcher. *Econometrica* 55 (5):999–1033.

———. 1989. A dynamic programming model of retirement behavior. In *The economics of aging,* ed. D. Wise, 359–98. Chicago: University of Chicago Press.

———. 1988. Maximum likelihood estimation of discrete control processes. *SIAM Journal on Control and Optimization* 26(5):1–19.

Skinner, J. 1987. A superior measure of consumption from the Panel Study of Income Dynamics. *Economics Letters* 23:213–16.

Stock, J. H., and D. A. Wise. 1989. Pensions, the option value of work, and retirement. Kennedy School of Government, Harvard University. Typescript.

Sueyoshi, G. 1986. Social Security and the determinants of full and partial retirement: A competing risks analysis. University of California, San Diego. Typescript.

U.S. Census. 1979. *Statistical abstract of the United States.* Washington, D.C.: U.S. Government Printing Office.

van Dijk, N. M. 1984. *Controlled Markov processes: Time discretization.* CWI Tract II. Amsterdam: Mathematische Centrum.

White, H. 1982. Maximum likelihood estimation of misspecified models. *Econometrica* 50:1–26.

Comment   Angus Deaton

This paper is a remarkable member of a remarkable sequence. Following the example of Trollope and Dickens, Rust is telling us his story in installments, each of which ends suspensefully; the next in the series will surely reveal all and resolve the tension. The mystery here is whether the trick can be done at all. Will the Retirement History Survey (RHS) yield to the calculus of stochastic dynamic programming and reveal the true story of aging and retirement? Or has structural estimation in econometrics at last attempted too much, even structural estimation in the hands of John Rust and the super-computer? We shall have to wait another year to find out, but the latest installment, as it should, certainly serves to complicate the plot. It also

Angus Deaton is professor of economics and international affairs at the Woodrow Wilson School, Princeton University, and a research associate of the National Bureau of Economic Research.

provides a peculiarly inappropriate position from which to review the research; anything said now is likely to look foolish at the next round.

The most difficult task in applied econometrics is to make a clean transition from theory to implementation. I am referring not to the estimation or the interpretation of results but to the intermediate stage where sharply delineated theoretical notions have to be matched up to imperfect and error-ridden data. In the face of complex reality, theoretical concepts quickly lose their sharpness (what is retirement?), and even the best surveys turn out to have omitted the simplest and most important questions. This paper, which is the second in the sequence, is concerned with cleaning data and matching it to the demands of the theory. Rust's model is one of *discrete* choice, where controls are set at a limited number of positions so as to affect outcome states, each of which must also be discretely defined. The constraints facing optimizing consumers are the laws of motion of the system, the transition probabilities that govern the evolution of the state variables, conditional on their own past values and on the values of the controls. Apart from the data exercises, the specification and estimation of these probabilities is the main task of the paper.

One of the benefits of a series of papers is that it is possible to detail much of the important material that would typically be suppressed in journals. Rust has done an extraordinarily good job of laying out exactly what he has done; honesty and care shine out from every page. This paper and its predecessor are the best counterexamples I know to the accusation that high-tech econometricians care little about their data (or that those who care about numbers know nothing else!). The amount of work that has gone into data preparation is astonishing; the RHS tapes have been matched to the census, to the SSA records, and to the results of earlier researchers' work. Each observation has been multiply "flagged" to indicate assessments of data reliability and every detail of the process encoded and preserved to enable replication by other scholars. When the next installment comes and we find out whether a DP model can fit the RHS, it will be impossible to ascribe failure to inadequate data preparation or to suspect data "cleaning" for results that look too good.

But commentators are not supposed to express unbounded admiration, or at least not *only* unbounded admiration. So I should like to identify a few points in the paper where I was left feeling uneasy, where the compromises that had to be made seemed to be beginning to threaten the structure. There are two issues that I should like to draw out, both concerning methodological questions about this sort of structural modeling, as opposed to the more ad hoc or reduced-form analyses that has been adopted by most other researchers. The first concerns data quality. There are many points at which an important theoretical variable has to be replaced by a *very* imperfect substitute. There are also many magnitudes that appear to contain egregious errors of measurement, errors that are more than usually exposed through Rust's tireless analysis of the data. As Rust notes, the model that will eventually be estimated is (to say the least) nonlinear, and there is no good way of handling measurement errors in such a model. So it is going to take some extraordinarily sensitive testing of the final model to try to separate those parts of the results that are due to measurement error and those that are credible and robust.

The second issue concerns Rust's modeling of the "laws of motion of the system," the transition probabilities that govern the consumer's progress from state to state. Ideally, these laws of motion would be given, like the laws of physics, they could be set up as constraints, and the calculation and estimation of the DP could begin. But, of course, the transition probabilities are not known and have to be estimated. Rust summarizes his findings in section 11.2. Given the discretization of the states, the transition probability matrix contains some 130,000,000 elements, all of which have to be estimated from the data. Since most of the transitions are never actually observed in the sample, nonparametric estimation is not possible. Instead, Rust imposes structure on the probabilities, equation (5), and then estimates a system of logits. The structure used is a recursive one; health status is influenced only by lagged variables, current health status and lagged variables influence marital status, health and marital status jointly condition employment, while health, marital status, and employment condition the evolution of income. All this is perfectly reasonable, but of course it may not be correct. Rust tells us that, having tried various decompositions of the transition probabilities, the one that he found most plausible was the one discussed above. It is hard not to be reminded of the analogies with structural and reduced-form debate in macroeconomic modeling. It was exactly this use of "reasonable" (but arbitrary) exclusion restrictions that had much to do with the retreat toward less structured approaches, and I felt uncomfortable finding the same sort of issues in the current context. The next stage of the research, the calculation of a maximizing strategy in the face of the constraints, will ruthlessly expose any flaws in the modeling at this stage. If there is some cheap but absurd method of generating utility, the algorithm will find it. Again, there is analogy with macro, where the first wave of enthusiasm for optimal control of Keynesian econometric models quickly foundered on those models' lack of a supply side; optimal plans clearly involved eating the capital stock. Rust is too good an economist to fall into any of these obvious traps, but my feeling of discomfort remains. Are the estimates of the transition probabilities really soundly enough grounded to support the very great strain that is about to be placed on them?

There are some specific points in the paper where concern about the two general issues comes to a head. First, the consumption data, imputed from income and wealth changes, are too dreadful to use, so that it is going to be necessary, at least at first, to estimate a model that maximizes, not the expected utility of consumption, but the expected utility of income. This may not do too much harm, but it is a pity that so many of the important issues (life-cycle saving, wealth accumulation or decumulation, saving and retirement dates) are thereby lost from the analysis. Rust discounts the possibility of using the partial consumption data in the survey, but the decision might be worth some further consideration.

My second point concerns the definition of one of the two control variables, search effort in the labor market. Rust considers three possible measures: a self-reported intended hours next year; the actual hours two years hence, that is, in the next actual sample period; and the actual hours in the intermediate year. The first is rejected because "talk is cheap" and because the quantity bears little relation to outcomes. The second is rejected because it implies complete control. Fine, but I find it hard to see why the last measure is likely to be a good proxy either. While it is true that it predicts employment quite well, there are any number of reasons why it should, not all of which are consistent with it being a good proxy for search effort. Indeed, a worker might record a large number of hours, though fully intending to be unemployed next period, and a partially or totally "retired" worker could easily be searching very actively. Some workers may even take early retirement in order to search more actively for a suitable subsequent occupation.

My third, and final, point is again on the estimation of the transition probabilities, and again it is an issue of which Rust is fully aware. Heterogeneity of workers, or equivalently incomplete accounting of states, is quite likely to lead to inconsistent estimates or to spurious identification of causality. There are obvious examples throughout the paper, many of which are dealt with, such as the fact that "collecting OASI can be hazardous to your health." I was also amused to discover that, once single, a worker has less than a 7 percent chance of finding a new mate and that bachelors, who have no prospect of remarriage, can expect their income to fall at 20 percent a year. But, more seriously, I would expect heterogeneity to be a serious problem, and, although Rust evidently worries about it less, I should have been happier had some of the supporting evidence been included in the paper. Perhaps in the next installment.

Contributors

Chunrong Ai
Department of Economics
Massachusetts Institute of Technology
50 Memorial Drive
Cambridge, MA 02139

Alan J. Auerbach
Department of Economics
Room 160, McNeil Building
3718 Locust Walk
University of Pennsylvania
Philadelphia, PA 19104

B. Douglas Bernheim
Kellogg Graduate School of Management
Northwestern University
Leverone Hall
2001 Sheridan Road
Evanston, IL 60208

Axel H. Börsch-Supan
Department of Economics
Universität Mannheim
Postfach 10 34 62
Gebäude A5, 6
6800 Mannheim 1
Federal Republic of Germany

Gary Burtless
Brookings Institution
1775 Massachusetts Avenue, N.W.
Washington, DC 20036

Angus Deaton
Woodrow Wilson School
Princeton University
Princeton, NJ 08544

David T. Ellwood
Kennedy School of Government
Harvard University
79 Kennedy Street
Cambridge, MA 02138

Jonathan Feinstein
Graduate School of Business
Stanford University
Stanford, CA 94305

Alan M. Garber
National Bureau of Economic Research
204 Junipero Serra Boulevard
Stanford, CA 94305

Michael D. Hurd
Department of Economics
SUNY Stony Brook
Stony Brook, NY 11794

Thomas J. Kane
Kennedy School of Government
Harvard University
79 Kennedy Street
Cambridge, MA 02138

383

Laurence J. Kotlikoff
National Bureau of Economic Research
1050 Massachusetts Avenue
Cambridge, MA 02138

Edward P. Lazear
Graduate School of Business
University of Chicago
1101 East 58th Street
Chicago, IL 60637

Herman B. Leonard
Kennedy School of Government
Harvard University
79 Kennedy Street
Cambridge, MA 02138

Thomas MaCurdy
Department of Economics
Stanford University
Stanford, CA 94305

Daniel McFadden
Department of Economics
Massachusetts Institute of Technology
50 Memorial Drive
Cambridge, MA 02139

John N. Morris
Hebrew Rehabilitation Center for the
    Aged
1200 Center Street
Roslindale, MA 02131

Joseph P. Newhouse
Division of Health Policy Research and
    Education
Harvard University
25 Shattuck Street, Parcel B
Boston, MA 02115

Henry Pollakowski
Research Fellow
Joint Center of Urban Studies
53 Church Street
Cambridge, MA 02138

Sherwin Rosen
Department of Economics
University of Chicago
1126 East 59th Street
Chicago, IL 60637

John Rust
Department of Economics
University of Wisconsin
1180 Observatory Drive
Madison, Wisconsin 53706

James H. Schultz
Director
Policy Center on Aging
Heller Graduate School
Brandeis University
Waltham, MA 02254

James H. Stock
Kennedy School of Government
Harvard University
79 Kennedy Street
Cambridge, MA 02138

Steven F. Venti
Department of Economics
Dartmouth College
301 Rockefeller Center
Hanover, NH 03755

Finis Welch
Unicon Research Corporation
10801 National Boulevard
3rd Floor
Los Angeles, CA 90064

David A. Wise
National Bureau of Economic Research
1050 Massachusetts Avenue
Cambridge, MA 02138

Author Index

Subject Index